TEXAS GOVERNMENT
POLITICS AND ECONOMICS

2ND EDITION

TEXAS GOVERNMENT
POLITICS AND ECONOMICS

Kenneth R. Mladenka

Texas A & M University

Kim Quaile Hill

University of Houston, Clear Lake

Texas A & M University

BROOKS/COLE PUBLISHING COMPANY

PACIFIC GROVE, CALIFORNIA

Brooks/Cole Publishing Company
A Division of Wadsworth, Inc.

Printed in the United States of America

10 9 8 7 6 5 4 3 2 1

Library of Congress Cataloging-in-Publication Data

Mladenka, Kenneth R., 1943–
     Texas government: politics and economics. Kenneth R. Mladenka,
     Kim Quaile Hill. —2nd ed.
          p.   cm.
     Includes bibliographies and index.
     ISBN 0-534-09948-3 : $13.50
     1. Texas—Politics and government. 2. Local government—Texas.
     I. Hill, Kim Quaile, 1946–   . II. Title.
     JK4816.M53   1989   88-39046
     320.9764—dc19   CIP

ISBN 0-534-09948-3

Texas Marketing Representative: Maureen Allaire, Dean Allsman, Sherril
     Briggs, Bill Hoffman, Ragu Raghavan, Julie Wade

Sponsoring Editor: Cynthia C. Stormer
Editorial Assistant: Mary Ann Zuzow
Project Coordinator: Joan Marsh
Production Service: Sara Hunsaker EX LIBRIS
Manuscript Editor: Sara Hunsaker
Permissions Editor: Carline Haga
Interior Design: Sara Hunsaker
Cover Design: Roy Neuhaus
Cover Photo or Illustration: Texas capitol dome courtesy of Lorenzo de
     Zavala Archives, Texas State University
Interior Illustration: Ayxa Art
Photo Researcher: Bill Hoffman
Typesetting: Omegatype Typography, Inc.
Cover Printing: Philips Offset Company
Printing and Binding: Maple-Vail Book Manufactoring Group

To Linda and Patricia

PREFACE

I n *Texas Government, Second Edition,* we consider the changing politics of Texas in detail. Considerable emphasis is given to the political economy of the state and the ways in which the new economy has profound consequences for the distribution of power and resources. A high-tech economy may well contribute to the erosion of the middle class and the polarization of political conflict between a high-tech professional elite on the one hand and a larger group of underemployed service and menial workers on the other.

The population and culture of Texas also come under our scrutiny. The changing demography of the state has created a more diverse and cosmopolitan set of political attitudes. Industrialization has produced a variety of new groups that have begun to challenge the dominant elites for a larger share of political and economic rewards. Both developments merit our attention.

We also examine the historical development of the state. The struggle for independence, the Indian Wars, the settling of the frontier, the Civil War, Reconstruction, and major political movements such as populism have all shaped the political culture, processes, and institutions of state government. The frontier ideology emphasized rugged individualism, self-reliance, and inventiveness. These traits continue to play an important role in the political ideology of the state. Increasingly, however, they are coming into conflict with the demands and expectations of a highly complex industrial society that is more likely to emphasize teamwork and the group and the community rather than the "rugged" individual.

Attention also is given to the great growth in government and the significant increase in the level and types of public services. The role of the bureaucracy in distributing these services is studied. The increasing prominence of the bureaucracy at all levels in Texas represents a major development in the government and politics of the state.

The politics and policies of urban areas deserve special emphasis. The rapid urbanization of the state has fundamentally transformed the ways in which Texans live and work. In several chapters we analyze the ways in which urban Texans participate politically, the types of public services they use, and the various governments (city, suburban, special district) under which they

vii

live. A separate chapter examines the organization, functions, and policies of county government. The massive urbanization of the state has forced the county to assume an increasingly complex array of responsibilities and functions. As a result, the county may well become a major form of government in those areas where urbanization has spread across several different governmental jurisdictions.

Special attention is given to the process of change in Texas government and politics. The state today is fundamentally different from the Texas of thirty years ago. It is a land of great cities and big government, and its economy is both industrialized and diversified. These changes will produce a variety of political consequences. For example, the Republican party will become stronger at the same time that government grows larger. Political conflict in the state will be dominated by the clash between, on the one hand, a traditional conservative ideology that emphasizes limited government and low taxes, and, on the other, the requirements of a modern industrial society that demands extensive services and an active partnership between government and business.

We appreciate the contributions from our reviewers: Thomas Clay Arnold, University of Texas, Arlington; Jeremy Curtoys, Tarleton State University; E. Larry Dickens, Sam Houston University; Jim Dukes, Richland College; Patricia Caperton Parent, Southwest Texas State University; Larry Pool, Mountain View College.

Kenneth R. Mladenka
Kim Quaile Hill

CONTENTS

INTRODUCTION

Old images die hard. There are many who believe that Texas is still rural and agrarian, that government plays a small role in the affairs of the state, that oil continues to dominate, and that the economy is neither industrialized nor diversified. They would be wrong on all counts. Most Texans live in urban areas and great numbers live in huge cities. Texas has three of the ten largest cities in the country. The Dallas-Fort Worth metropolitian area alone has well over 3 million people, and the Houston metroplex contains another 3 million. Texas has become a land of city dwellers and suburbanites. Few Texans remain to farm the land and raise cattle. The great wide-open spaces are still there, but the people have moved to the city.

And while oil and agriculture are vital to the state's economy, other economic activities have assumed major significance. In fact, construction and services such as finance, insurance, and transportation account for a majority of the economic activity in the state. Texas is now one of the most industrialized states in the country. It ranks fifth in manufacturing employment and is one of only five states with more than a million manufacturing jobs.

The computer has emerged to challenge the cow and the oil well as one of the state's dominant economic symbols. The silicon chip, invented by an engineer employed by Texas Instruments, promises to revolutionize the economy of the nation as well as the state. There are more than four thousand high-tech firms in Texas. The state ranks only behind California and Massachusetts in the number of high-tech jobs, and it is first in the number of *new* high-tech jobs available.

These economic changes have fundamentally transformed the state. The great cities demand a vast array of public services ranging from police and fire protection, water, garbage collection, and education to transportation, flood control, and parks and recreation. The size and scope of government have increased dramatically to meet these demands. Local governments in Texas employ well over half a million workers, and state government employs 160,000 more.

Another major change has been the great growth in the population. There are not only many more Texans but they are better educated and wealthier than ever before. The state ranks third in the nation in terms of personal income. Moreover, the population is now more diverse. The great influx of residents from other states and countries has had an impact on attitudes and values. Economic development has created a large middle and upper class of urban dwellers who work in white-collar, service, professional, and managerial occupations. The diversity of this urban population has produced a more cosmopolitan and tolerant set of attitudes. According to one sardonic observer, Texans "can now drink, fornicate, abort, dress, dope, and loaf with a freedom unprecedented in Texas."

It would be a mistake, however, to assume that Texas is identical to any other highly industrialized and urbanized state. From the beginning, Texas was a land of incredible harshness. Its unending vastness both dwarfed its human explorers and inspired them to great feats of courage and vision. Texans have always planned and executed their mighty enterprises on a grand scale. Their great bursts of energy secured independence, defeated the Indian, fought the Yankee, settled the frontier, and created vast empires based on cattle, commerce, and oil.

The frontier gave no quarter and the early Texans expected none, and out of their great failures and triumphs emerged the Texan of legend. Texans have always delighted in cultivating an image of themselves and their exploits as larger than life. But within every myth is a core of reality, and the Texas Myth has become indelibly stamped on the present reality of the state. The frontier demanded self-reliance, rugged individualism, and inventiveness. Frontier and agrarian societies are deeply conservative, and survival depends on hard work, one's own wits, and a powerful dose of good luck. There is little sympathy for the shiftless, the disadvantaged, or the simply unfortunate.

Government was not to be trusted, nor was it looked to by the early Texans as a substitute for their own wits in improving their lot in life. And so Texans wrote constitutions that would keep the public sector small and government power fragmented. The bitterness of the Reconstruction era that followed the Civil War merely strengthened the Texan's deep-seated suspicion of government, and the effects of that period have continued to the present.

Conservative thinking emphasized private solutions to problems and disdained government as a drain on the energies, creativity, and resources of the free market. But a closer look at the history of the state reveals that powerful economic groups have always used government to achieve their goals. Government power was enlisted to eliminate the Indians and tame the frontier. Later, the Populists would use government to regulate the railroads and punish the insurance companies, and oil and agriculture too relied upon government to provide essential if minimal services.

The conservative ideology presents a major paradox for Texas politics. On the one hand, the conservatives advocate a limited role for government. On the other, they recognize that the power of government can be used to protect and advance their economic interests. In reality, then, government is perceived as a threat only if groups other than the dominant economic elite control it. From business's point of view, as long as government is allied with the business community it can prove to be very useful indeed.

In fact, recent developments in Texas politics reveal that the success or failure of various policy initiatives hinges on whether the policy is perceived as crucial to the economic growth of the state. Proposals that will strengthen basic services and enhance the state's business image generate widespread support. Policies that promote the social well-being of racial minorities and other disadvantaged groups are resisted as handouts to the undeserving.

The ideology of Texas politics draws a powerful distinction between government that benefits the dominant economic interests of the state and government that seeks to promote the welfare of the weak and the powerless. Therefore, policies that promote economic development such as an improved transportation system, better schools, and an adequate water supply will enjoy strong support. Policies in the areas of prison reform, public housing, health, and welfare for the poor and elderly, however, will evoke charges of "big government," "high taxes," "waste and inefficiency," and "public handouts."

In fact, the intense scramble to attract high-tech firms has strengthened the partnership between government and business. Both business and political leaders frequently mention the need to improve the quality of education and transportation services if Texas is to remain competitive with California, Massachusetts, and North Carolina in the battle for high-tech industries.

The business and political community has courted the federal government long and effectively. Federal aid has contributed enormously to the economic development of the state by financing the construction and operation of airports, freeways, medical centers, schools, water systems, flood control and drainage, wastewater treatment plants, space centers, and ports and ship channels.

The conservative ideology does not reject *all* government. Instead it opposes those government policies that are not designed to promote economic growth and development. The business of Texas government, therefore, is business. These attitudes about the appropriate role of government are deeply rooted in a frontier mentality that could not afford to develop much sympathy for the weak and unfortunate. The harshness of life in Texas forced people in their struggle against nature and other people to use every tool at their disposal. And government was one of those tools. It is important to note, however, that it was simply a tool in the fight for survival—not a positive force that would substitute for the individual's own wits, hard work, self-reliance, and luck.

Thus attitudes toward government in Texas remain different from those found in other industrialized states. Texans are more likely to emphasize private solutions to problems. The great inequalities produced by the play of free-market forces are a small price to pay for great rewards, the argument goes, and government is seen as a force that can assist in the private sector's struggle. Yet the Texan's frequent criticism of "big government" are not simply a demonstration of basic hypocrisy with respect to the role of government. Many Texans genuinely fear an expanded role for government, for if government can assist powerful economic groups in their pursuit of larger economic rewards, it can also assist the poor, the aged, the disadvantaged, and racial minorities in carving out a larger slice of the economic pie. If government can be used as a tool to improve one's position in the free-market competition, it can also be used to regulate and control the free market itself. If government could be structured in such a way that its only function would be to maintain security and stimulate economic development, then the proper relationship between government and the private sector would have been discovered.

The government that is directed to foster economic growth can also be enlisted to improve the lot of the old, the poor, and the otherwise disadvantaged. It is this possibility that will define political conflict in Texas for the rest of the century. For it is a certainty that government will grow in terms of both size and function. There are three reasons why this is so. First, the period of dramatic increases in federal aid appears to have ended. In fact, some aid programs have been eliminated and others sharply curtailed. Political leaders are already bemoaning the absence of federal aid dollars as a solution to the state's water problems. The Reagan administration is forcing the state to practice more self-reliance than it has been accustomed to for the past thirty years. Consequently, state government will have to assume more responsibility in the face of federal retrenchment.

Also contributing to a growth in government is the industrialization and urbanization of the state. Complex industrial economies are characterized by great cities. These cities require much more in the way of expensive public services than small towns and rural areas. An industrial society requires high levels of police and fire protection, transportation, education, recreation, refuse collection and disposal, water, sewerage, flood control, and land use and planning. An industrial, urban-based economy cannot survive without essential services. Consequently, government will have to provide them.

Government in Texas will also continue to grow because of the increasingly important partnership between politics and business that has developed to attract commerce and industry. Many believe that failure to improve essential services will damage the state's business image and diminish its attractiveness as a mecca for high-tech firms. Consequently, expenditures for services such as education and transportation will no doubt continue to increase.

This greatly increased size of government is crucial to the future of politics in Texas because a government that controls high amounts of revenue and performs a variety of complex functions is much more powerful than a government with few resources and few functions. Further, higher expenditures eventually mean higher taxes. At some point, the various sales taxes that Texas relies on will no longer provide sufficient revenue to fund public services. The revenue crunch will be made more severe by the decline in federal aid and the drop in oil revenues.

Therefore, it can be expected that one major series of political battles will be fought over the adoption of a state income tax. Ironically, conservatives have done much to contribute to the growth of government. Their support of high service levels to maintain a favorable climate for business has produced higher expenditures. Moreover, competition between the political parties is likely to become more intense, and the Republican party will probably grow in strength. It will represent one of the great ironies of Texas politics that the likely triumph of the Republican party in state government will bear witness to the probable adoption of an income tax and a greatly expanded role for government.

The convergence of three great forces—industrialization, urbanization, and big government—presents the citizens of Texas with the rare opportunity to alter their government and political system in fundamental ways. The state will experience immense change during the next few decades. The economy will be transformed, the minority population will dramatically increase, the tax structure will be altered, and government, at all levels, will grow more powerful. The old Texas is dying. The one that takes its place will be more open, diverse, and democratic. For many Texans, these changes will be for the better.

THE POLITICAL
ECONOMY OF TEXAS

S ome of the most fundamental influences on the government of a state arise from the economy. The character of the economy—its principal industries and occupations, the amount and distribution of wealth, and the changes it is undergoing—shapes the political life of the state. These forces determine the level of resources available for the governmental sector and the nature of many policy problems faced by the government. The distribution of economic resources profoundly affects the political status of individuals and groups in the state, as well. The importance of these matters for politics has long been recognized, and the study of such relations is often called the study of *political economy.*

The present character of the Texas economy, and the changes it is currently experiencing, are closely linked to a number of topics to be raised in subsequent chapters. Thus the political economy is an underlying theme of many discussions in this book. Many Texans are at least somewhat aware of the connections between politics and the economy of their state. Yet many of those same people may often base their opinions on outdated stereotypes about the character of the Texas economy. Those stereotypes, in other words, arise out of what the economy used to be, rather than what it is today.

At the turn of the present century Texas had an economy based overwhelmingly on agriculture. Some 70 percent of the work force was employed in that sector. Employment in manufacturing, in trade, and in anything comparable to today's technical and professional fields was quite modest. Relatively early in the century, however, the oil and natural gas industries began to boom, leading to the development of the manufacturing sector. Many Texans probably assume that agriculture and the oil and gas industries are still the backbone of the state's economy. The traditional symbols of that economy have been cattle, cotton, and oil wells. Yet there has already been considerable movement toward a more diversified economic system. Such movement is, as well, still proceeding at a relatively rapid pace.

THE CURRENT CHARACTER OF THE TEXAS ECONOMY

The Texas economy is today one of the leaders in the nation. That position is itself based on strength in several quite different areas. As some indication of its status, in 1981 Texas ranked first among the states in crude oil production and refining capacity, first in marketed natural gas production, first in receipts from cattle sales, first in cash receipts from total cotton production, and third in cash receipts from all farm commodities. Yet the state also ranked second in total construction, second in retail sales, third in commercial bank deposits, and fifth in total manufacturing employment. Thus both traditional activities and new sectors are today quite prominent in the Texas economy.

The economy of the state has shown particularly strong growth in recent years, and table 1–1 illustrates some of the achievements since 1970. Between 1970 and 1982, Texas moved from sixth to third place in personal income, from fifth to third in total employment, from fourth to third in nonmanufacturing employment, and from third to first in housing starts. The state also rose from eighth to fifth place in manufacturing employment. Only California, New York, Pennsylvania, and Ohio had more manufacturing jobs in 1982 than did Texas.

Based on its recent past, the Texas economy is clearly more diversified than many might assume (Arnold, 1983). Although the oil and gas and the agricultural sectors continue to be important, they are no longer as dominant as earlier in this century. Table 1–2 provides further evidence on this point with information on the shift in the character of the work force since 1940. In 1940, agriculture was by far the largest employment sector. Today it is only a tiny part of the picture. Since 1940, employment in manufacturing, in finance, insurance, real estate, and in government has virtually doubled. Employment in professional services (such as health care, education, and social and legal services) has more than doubled. Within the manufacturing sector itself in 1980, chemical and petroleum workers accounted for only about 12 percent of that category. While employment is not the only way to index the importance of different economic sectors, the information in table 1–2 provides ample testimony to the present diversification of the Texas economy.

The Economic Regions of Texas

Although data on the Texas economy are usually statewide figures, there are distinguishable regions within Texas that have different economic characteristics. The State Comptroller's Office has identified six such regions (figure 1–1): East Texas, Metroplex, Plains, Border, Central Corridor, and Gulf Coast (State Comptroller, 1983a). A brief review of the economic base of each of these regions will suggest how they differ.

East Texas   East Texas has an economy that is heavily dependent on timber, oil, and coal. In 1980, this region accounted for 80 percent of the total timber production in the state. Moreover, it produced 68 percent of the coal, 12 percent of the oil, and 9 percent of the natural gas in the state. Fifty thousand East Texans, or about 15 percent of the region's nonagricultural work force, worked in oil and oil-related industries.

TABLE 1–1 Top Ten States in Overall Economic Activity: 1982

Rank	Population	Personal Income	Total Employment	Manufacturing Employment	Nonmanufacturing Employment	Housing Starts
1	California	California	California	California	New York	Texas
2	New York	New York	New York	New York	California	Florida
3	Texas	Texas	Texas	Pennsylvania	Texas	California
4	Pennsylvania	Illinois	Illinois	Ohio	Illinois	N. Carolina
5	Illinois	Pennsylvania	Pennsylvania	Texas	Pennsylvania	Georgia
6	Ohio	Ohio	Ohio	Illinois	Florida	Arizona
7	Florida	Florida	Florida	Michigan	Ohio	Virginia
8	Michigan	Michigan	Michigan	N. Carolina	Michigan	Oklahoma
9	New Jersey	New Jersey	New Jersey	New Jersey	New Jersey	Colorado
10	N. Carolina	Massachusetts	Massachusetts	Massachusetts	Massachusetts	New York

Top Ten States in Overall Economic Activity: 1970

Rank	Population	Personal Income	Total Employment	Manufacturing Employment	Nonmanufacturing Employment	Housing Starts
1	California	California	California	New York	New York	California
2	New York	New York	New York	California	California	Florida
3	Pennsylvania	Illinois	Pennsylvania	Pennsylvania	Illinois	Texas
4	Texas	Pennsylvania	Illinois	Ohio	Texas	Georgia
5	Illinois	Ohio	Texas	Illinois	Pennsylvania	Michigan
6	Ohio	Texas	Ohio	Michigan	Ohio	Ohio
7	Michigan	Michigan	Michigan	New Jersey	Michigan	New York
8	New Jersey	New Jersey	New Jersey	Texas	Florida	Illinois
9	Florida	Florida	Florida	N. Carolina	New Jersey	N. Carolina
10	Massachusetts	Massachusetts	Massachusetts	Indiana	Massachusetts	Pennsylvania

Source: U.S. Department of Commerce and U.S. Department of Labor.

3

**TABLE 1–2   Composition of Texas Employment by Industry:
1940 and 1980**

Industry	1940 (%)	1980 (%)
Agriculture, forestry, fishing	30.4	2.9
Mining	2.9	3.3
Construction	5.3	8.6
Manufacturing	9.9	17.9
Transportation, communications, public utilities	6.6	7.5
Wholesale and retail trade	18.1	21.9
Finance, insurance, real estate	2.7	6.0
Domestic and related services	14.1	8.8
Professional services	6.5	18.6
Government	2.4	4.5
Not reported	1.3	—

Sources: Texas Past and Future: A Survey (1982:24) and *General Social and Economic Characteristics: Texas,
1980 Census of Population* (1983:116).

Agriculture is another significant economic sector in East Texas. Important crops include rice, peanuts, cotton, and soybeans. Poultry and cattle also contribute to this sector. Thus the entire economy of this region is dependent on natural resources, whether in oil, coal, timber, or the soil.

The Metroplex   The Metroplex has the most diversified economy in the state. Dominated by the Dallas–Fort Worth area, the Metroplex economy relies principally upon services, trade, and manufacturing. More people are employed in durable goods manufacturing (16 percent of the work force) in this region than in any of the others. High-tech industries are also assuming greater significance in this economy. Defense spending—which fuels much of the high-tech industry—totaled more than $4 billion here in 1982, which represents 40 percent of the state's total.

More people in the Metroplex work force are employed in services and wholesale trade than in any other part of the state. The region ranks second in the country as an insurance center, third in the concentration of corporate headquarters (36 major corporations located in the Metroplex from 1979–1985), and fifth as a banking center. Tourism and the convention business are also significant. This economy is quite diversified, therefore, with manufacturing, service, and high-tech industry as major parts of the diverse mix. Agriculture and oil, on the other hand, are relatively unimportant here.

The Plains   The Plains region is heavily dependent on oil and agriculture. The area from Lubbock north to Amarillo is an important agricultural and cattle region. In fact, the Plains region accounts for a majority of farm production in Texas. At the same time, 66 percent of all the oil and 40 percent of

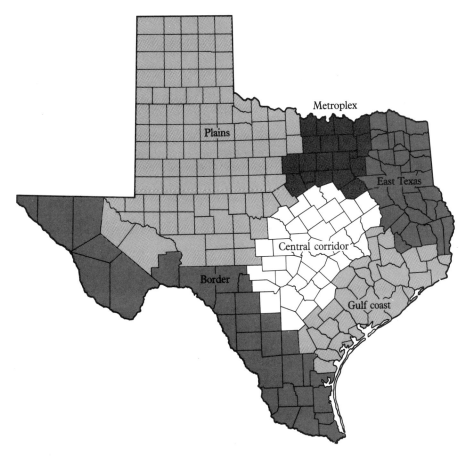

FIGURE 1–1   Economic Regions of Texas
Source: Texas Comptroller of Public Accounts

the natural gas produced in the state come from the Plains. The latter industries are centered in the Midland–Odessa area.

The Border   The Border region's economy is closely tied to that of Mexico, indicating one of the important international ties to the overall Texas economy. In fact, the condition of the Mexican economy has considerable impact on this region, as recent devaluations of the peso have shown. When the peso is devalued, trade from Mexican citizens and businesses across the border falls because of the peso's decline in purchasing power. When the devaluation is drastic, it can produce a business recession in the Border region. Because of major devaluations recently, unemployment has been quite high in this region.

Government and agriculture are also key sectors of the Border economy. Twenty-two percent of all workers are employed by government, and 14 percent are employed by local government alone. Oil and gas production are also of modest importance to the economy of this region. The largest city is El Paso, known for the five C's—cattle, copper, cotton, clothing, and climate. El Paso continues to play an important economic role. It is the site of Fort Bliss, which is a major military installation.

The Central Corridor   The Central Corridor includes the Waco, Austin, and San Antonio area along Interstate 35 plus Bryan–College Station. Like the Metroplex, this region has a diversified economy. Forty percent of the work force is employed in service industries, and 20 percent are government employees. Health and education are the most prominent of the service industries. This region also receives about a third of the federal government's defense contracts in Texas. This economy, then, is a mix of health and education services, government employment, and military installations and defense spending.

The Gulf Coast   The Gulf Coast is heavily dependent on oil and gas and the petrochemical industry. This region produced 27 percent of the state's output of oil and gas in 1981. More than three-fourths of the state's employment in the refining and petrochemical industries is also in this region, and about a third of the total work force of the region is employed in either production, refining, or service industries associated with oil and gas—industries particularly affected by the international market and international politics. Hence the economy of the Gulf Coast, like that of the Border region, is especially sensitive to international influences. The same international oil market forces affect the petroleum portion of the Plains economy.

   Although oil and petrochemicals dominate the Gulf Coast economy, other sectors are also significant. These include steel production, shipbuilding, fishing, and agriculture. Moreover, Houston is a center for banking, finance, and international and domestic trade.

The Special Place of the Oil and Gas Industries

Despite the diversification of the overall economy and the existence of distinctive economic regions in Texas, the oil and gas industries continue to be vitally important to the state as a whole. The magnitude of that importance is suggested by the prominence of the Texas oil and gas industries in the entire United States. One-third of all the oil produced in the United States is from Texas. By way of example, in 1983, it produced 46 percent more oil than Alaska, the next leading producer. That same year Texas also outproduced Louisiana, its closest competitor in natural gas production, by 12 percent. In fact, the state's oil industry accounts for 5 percent of the *world's* crude oil production. If Texas were a separate country, it would be tied with Iran for fifth place among world producers. Only the USSR, the rest of the United States, Saudi Arabia, and Mexico outrank Texas in terms of oil production.

Industries of this size would be important in the economy of any state. As the State Comptroller's Office (1984) has indicated:

The oil and gas business is a $37 billion enterprise employing more than 400,000 Texans in getting oil and gas out of the ground and in numerous companies which support and supply the industry. Twenty-seven percent of the nation's oil-related jobs are in Texas. . . . In 1983, oil and gas companies spent an estimated $8.5 billion drilling for energy resources. Because much of this was spent buying materials and supplies from Texas businesses, the ripple effects through the Texas economy were great.

Figure 1–2 suggests how those ripple effects might operate. Research on the economic impact of the industry, for example, has shown that every dollar spent drilling for oil in the state generates an additional $1.75 in economic activity. Further, every job in the oil drilling industry creates four jobs in other sectors of the state's economy. Thus expansion—or contraction—of the oil and gas industries stimulates—or depresses—activity in all the other sectors indicated in the figure. Similarly, the explicitly political importance of these industries is indicated by the fact that 28 percent of the state government's tax revenues comes from the oil and gas industries (Fletcher, 1985).

The boom in the oil and gas industries that lasted from 1974 to 1981 and the recession that began in 1982 illustrate both the good and the unfortunate effects of heavy dependence on a single industry. Employment, business expansion, and tax revenues rose substantially in the first of those periods, and they all fell in the second phase. Because most observers have predicted that these industries will remain relatively depressed throughout the 1980s, oil and gas have imposed a continuing drag on the state's economy. Recognition of this fact, however, has led many of the state's political and business leaders to work even harder to promote economic diversification—precisely to minimize such effects in the future.

THE DEPRESSED OIL ECONOMY

The oil economy began its swift decline in December 1985 when the Organization of Petroleum Exporting Countries (OPEC) abandoned production and price controls in an ill-fated effort to get non-OPEC nations to decrease their production. The price of oil quickly fell from $31.72 a barrel, in November 1985, to $14.17, in February 1986. And by August it had fallen to $11 a barrel. Although it slowly recovered to $15 a barrel by the end of 1986 and to $19.63 a barrel by September of 1987, it suffered another drop to only $15 a barrel by the end of 1987. The shocks were profound in both economic and psychological terms.

An examination of the employment statistics for the period reveals that the state had an unemployment rate of 6.9 percent in January 1986. By June, that rate increased to 11.1 percent. Some areas of the state were hit much harder

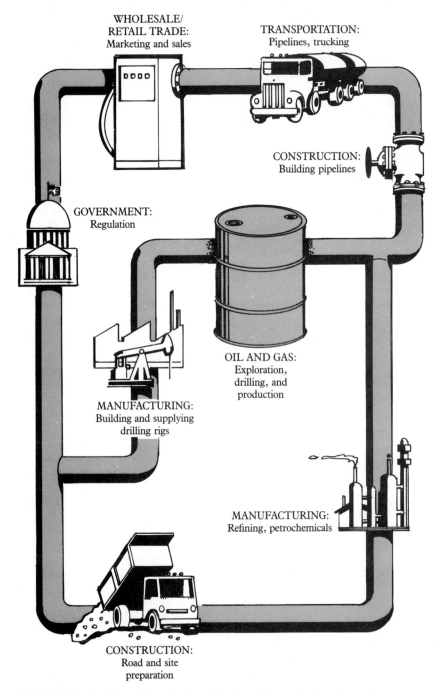

FIGURE 1–2   The Oil and Gas Pipeline Through the Texas Economy

than others. In June 1986, Austin had an unemployment rate of 6.9 percent (the lowest in the state). The rate in Houston was 12.6 percent and in McAllen 21 percent. Ironically, while the employment picture nationally experienced significant improvement, the number of unemployed workers in the state reached record levels. Of the eleven most populated states in the country in May 1986, only Michigan had a higher unemployment rate.

The Texas economy lost nearly 300,000 jobs in natural resources and manufacturing between 1981 and 1987, with most of this loss occurring in the oil and gas industry. In 1986 alone, 80,000 nonagricultural jobs were lost. The devastation of the oil economy is demonstrated by the fact that production from oil fields in the state in 1987 dropped below 2 million barrels a day for the first time since 1944. In 1981, 28 percent of the state's economic activity was bound up with the oil and gas industry. In 1987, that share had declined to 17 percent.

Some economic regions of the state were hit much harder than others. The dependence of the Plains region upon an economy dominated by agriculture and oil made it particularly vulnerable to the deterioration of these sectors. The close ties between the Border region and Mexico ensured that the economy of the former would be particularly hard hit by the rampant inflation in the Mexican economy.

The experience of the Gulf Coast region is illustrative. This region prospered during the oil boom of 1970–1981. During that period, employment grew from 1.1 million to 2.1 million jobs. The Gulf Coast, in fact, accounted for 34 percent of all jobs in the state in 1981. However, the price of oil reached its zenith at $37.29 a barrel in February 1981. As a result of the recent plunge in oil prices, the Gulf Coast economy has lost 128,000 nonfarm jobs. Total oil industry employment (drilling, refining, production, marketing) currently accounts for 290,000 jobs, a decline of 31 percent from a high of 421,000 in 1981. In 1982, the oil industry provided one in five of all jobs in the Gulf Coast. In 1987, it accounted for only one in seven. The evidence indicates that this ratio is falling.

The agricultural sector of the state's economy also suffered severe blows. Since 1981, 49,000 Texas farms have gone out of business, and the farm debt statewide has surpassed $14 billion. Although the diversification of Texas agriculture (it produces more than 60 commodities and is evenly divided between livestock and crops) has traditionally provided some measure of stability against market fluctuations, recent developments have combined to drive down net income in this sector from $2 billion in 1979 to $1.3 billion in 1985. When inflation is taken into account, real income in 1985 was only one-third of what it was in 1979. The decline can be traced to several factors.

1. Other countries have increased their agricultural production. Self sufficiency has been achieved by countries that in the past purchased agricultural commodities from the United States.

2. Higher interest rates and lower inflation strengthened the dollar and increased the cost of American exports. Although the dollar has weak-

ened recently against other currencies, any improvement for the Texas farm economy will be slow in coming.

3. Higher interest rates also drove up operating expenses. Since agriculture is capital intensive, farmers are forced to borrow large sums. Interest costs accounted for only 7 percent of the typical farmer's operating budget in 1970. That amount had increased to 16 percent by 1984.

It should be emphasized, however, that most sectors of the state's economy remain quite strong. In fact, the nonoil economy is growing at an average annual rate of 8 percent compared to 7 percent for the nation as a whole and has added several hundred thousand new jobs in the past few years.

THE ECONOMIC BOOM: BUSINESS EXPANSION IN TEXAS

The recent growth of the Texas economy is part of what has been called an economic boom. Like several other Sunbelt states, Texas has benefited since the early 1960s from three corporate strategies:

1. The first strategy has been the relocation of corporations or corporate headquarters to the state. This occurs, for example, when an oil, chemical, insurance, or other company closes its headquarters office in another state and moves it to Texas.

2. A second strategy that has operated to the benefit of Texas has been plant expansion. This occurs when a corporation, perhaps in Boston or Chicago or New York City, decides to expand its operations and selects Texas as the location for its new plant or division. Increasingly in the last two decades, Texas has been a favorite choice for expanded corporate operations.

3. A third strategy that has produced enormous economic benefits for the state has been the selection of Texas as the site for *new* industry. Many of today's industries either did not exist twenty or so years ago or were in their infancy. Such industries include many of those in the broad fields of computer developments and applications, electronics, telecommunications, and fiber optics. These are, of course, leading examples of what have come to be called the high-tech industries.

Texas Instruments provides an excellent illustration of this business trend. This giant computer and electronics firm got its start in the oil equipment and instrument business but quickly capitalized on the electronics revolution. One of its engineers even invented the silicon chip that has been so central in that revolution. Thus this company did not transfer or expand its operations into the state from outside; instead it represents a part of what is essentially a new industry.

Texas has been particularly successful in attracting both new high-tech companies and also some that have transferred into the state from elsewhere. In fact, many of the state's government and business leaders have worked diligently to attract more growth of this kind. Many believe this set of industries will have great significance for the future of the state just as the oil and gas industries have been important in the past and present. Because of these hopes for Texas's high-tech future, we will discuss that portion of the economy in detail shortly. First, however, we want to offer some general comments about the likely future of the economic boom—and about the forces that have sustained it.

THE FUTURE OF THE TEXAS ECONOMY

All of the economic changes discussed so far—the economic boom in general, the ongoing diversification of the economy, the rise of high-tech industries— indicate that Texas clearly has an economy in transition. These changes suggest, as well, that the traditional bedrock industries of the Texas economy— agriculture and mineral extraction and refining—are either declining or at least losing their prominence to "postindustrial" or high-tech activities.

The precise character of the state's economic future is, however, a topic of considerable debate. One prominent forecast of that future, for example, concludes:

> *Texas is on the eve of a great transformation. The state's economy, which today is relatively underindustrialized and strongly oriented toward energy producing, consuming, and servicing activities, will become highly industrialized and diversified by the end of the century. [Plaut, 1983:1]*

The same study argues that "manufacturing investment has been, and will continue to be, the major driver of Texas economic growth. And manufacturing investment in Texas outside of petroleum and chemicals will increase throughout the forecast period." Significant growth is expected, as well, in the service sector, while a substantial decline is projected for agriculture and mining. While the latter two areas accounted for 18.4 percent of the gross economic product of the state in 1981, they are expected to drop to only 5.7 percent by the year 2006. Similarly, the growth of the government sector is expected to be modest during this period, rising from 9.5 to only 11.8 percent of the gross product.

For manufacturing, the greatest growth over the next twenty or so years is expected to be in the computer industry, in oil drilling equipment and other industrial machinery, in paper and pulp products, printing, rubber, and plastics. Petroleum refining and the chemical industry will continue to grow, but at a slower pace. Overall, however, the manufacturing sector is expected to show the highest growth rate. Following that sector, transportation, communications, public utilities, personal services, and wholesale and retail trade are expected to lead the state's economic development. Moderate growth is also anticipated for the construction, finance, insurance, and real estate fields.

EXPLANATIONS FOR THE ECONOMIC BOOM

A number of separate yet presumably related explanations have been advanced to account for the economic boom experienced to date. Among those explanations are the following:

Low Taxes   Texas does not have a state or local tax on personal income or corporate profits as many states do. In fact, the overall tax load Texans bear is among the very lowest in the nation. It has frequently been argued, in consequence, that these low taxes have played a major role in attracting business to the state.

Weak Labor Unions   The weakness of the organized labor movement in Texas is often mentioned as a factor that contributes to the favorable business climate in the state. Only 11.4 percent of Texas workers are unionized, compared to a national average of 25 percent. State law also includes an "open shop" provision that forbids requiring workers to join a union as a condition of employment (Glover and King, 1978). The limited scope of the union movement is also believed to explain the relatively low wages in the state (when compared to those in highly unionized states). Lower wages and the absence of possible union strikes are viewed favorably by corporate managers contemplating a relocation.

Good Transportation System   Trucking and airline service both play major roles in today's economy. Because of the excellent interstate freeway system in the Sunbelt, Texas and its neighboring states are well positioned to take advantage of the heavy reliance on this mode of transportation. Moreover, the central location of the state in the nation and its relatively good air service, particularly in the major cities, give Texas a good rating in that category, as well.

Improved Public Services   Texas is today more attractive to corporate managers and their employees because the state and local governments provide better public services than was the case several years ago. Although the quality of schools, parks and recreation facilities, police and fire protection, and libraries is not as high as in many other states, it is certainly higher than it was in Texas a decade or two ago.

Competent Work Force   Texans are perceived by business executives as eager and willing workers. The work ethic is strong in the state, and these attitudes about work contribute to a favorable image. Furthermore, rising levels of worker education and training also strengthen the state's claim to being a place where business can count on a competent and dependable work force.

Federal Aid   Texas has reaped enormous benefits from federal money over the last thirty to forty years. Federal dollars have greatly stimulated economic development in the state by paying for airports, roads, bridges, freeways, flood and drainage control, sewer and wastewater treatment systems, and even recreational facilities associated with water management projects. These improved services make the state more attractive to business.

Low Energy Costs   Because of the local importance of the oil and gas industries and because of the state's Sunbelt location, energy costs are generally lower in Texas than in much of the nation, especially the Northeast and Midwest. The prices of oil and gas have traditionally been low in Texas, in part because of low transportation costs from producer to consumer. The relatively mild and short winters experienced by the state also tend to lower energy costs.

Pro-Business Bias   Texas actively seeks to attract new business to the state through the efforts of local chambers of commerce as well as state government agencies. Although virtually every state now attempts to attract business through advertising campaigns and various economic incentives (ranging from tax relief to the provision of direct services at public expense), Texas and other Sunbelt states have worked especially hard at this task in recent years. This concerted effort to portray Texas as a "business state," coupled with very modest state regulation of business, has allegedly returned handsome economic dividends.

Economic Transformations

While all these factors apparently have contributed to Texas's economic development, they do not really explain the state's explosive business growth. Instead, that growth must be explained in considerable part by profound changes at work in both the Texas and the American economies. In other words, the rapid expansion of the Texas economy is largely a product of the long-term evolution of the national economy.

That evolution is highly influenced by the existing transportation and communication systems. Bryan D. Jones (1983) has argued, for example, that cities have always been hostages to transportation systems. Since cities are the centers of commercial and industrial economies, the economy, too, is dependent on transportation. The great industrial cities of the late nineteenth and early twentieth centuries, for instance, depended heavily on rail and water transport.

The prevailing modes of transportation and communications had other effects on the early industrial city. Such cities had to be compact, with all their major elements and residents located in close proximity to one another. In the absence of mass transit and the automobile, workers had to live close to the factory rather than far away in the suburbs. Managers, too, had to remain physically close because of the need to supervise and control lower-level workers. Moreover, the need to make continuous decisions about production, scheduling, and marketing required that management be close at hand. The primitive nature of communications prevented the coordination and direction of manufacturing and distribution from a distance.

Capital and financial support also had to be located nearby. There developed, in consequence, in the industrial city an extensive network of support services ranging from banking and insurance to accounting and retail services. The industrial city was an interdependent city that emphasized physical proximity.

Although raw materials and markets did not have to be as close to the factory as workers and managers, even these components were generally located in the region. The limited nature of transportation and communication systems ensured that supplies of raw materials, as well as markets, had to be closer to manufacturing and production centers than they must be today.

Great advances in the last several decades in transportation and communications have rendered the physical compactness and closeness of the industrial city unnecessary. There is no longer a need for the major elements in the economy to be close to one another. Jet travel, the trucking industry, and the automobile have greatly expanded transportation options and opportunities. Telecommunications and the computer have similarly wrought a revolution in business communications.

Because of these advances, the economic system can be decentralized. A corporation no longer needs to be tied to the central business district of a large city, itself located only in a region with close access to raw materials and markets. In today's economy, workers can be in one state or even another part of the world; management in yet another state; raw materials elsewhere; and capital, research, and markets in still other locations.

Control and coordination of the various components in the early industrial economy could be accomplished only by concentrating those components in one location. Today the manager can exert control over widely dispersed operations. This dispersion operates, as well, to the advantage of states like Texas. New businesses that once would have had to locate in the Midwest or Northeast to be close to raw materials or markets are now free to consider any part of the country for their site. Corporate planners can now, in effect, take account of the other advantages and disadvantages of a wide variety of alternative locations. In some sense, it has been the evolution of transportation and communications that has allowed businesses to consider the various factors described earlier: the tax load, the degree of unionization, and the work force of different states.

This new freedom of location, coupled with Texas's image as a state that works hard to create a good environment for business, has resulted in enormous economic benefit for the state. There is no guarantee, however, that this freedom will continue to work to Texas's advantage. If business is no longer tied to old industrial regions, why should it be permanently tied to Texas? If business is free to locate in virtually any part of the nation or even the world, what is to prevent it from moving to other locations in a constant search for more profitable circumstances?

The entire national economy is undergoing a profound transformation as it shifts from a manufacturing, industrial base to one increasingly dominated by high-tech, information processing, and service industries. In such a transition only continuing change can be predicted with any confidence. Texas has profited by these changes so far; yet the state's business and government leaders may have to work long and hard to ensure that it will continue to do so. It is clear, as well, that the leaders of most states will be working hard to reap the benefits of this economic transformation. Thus the competition for new business development will surely be keen.

Locating New Businesses in Texas

In recent years Texas has certainly been successful in its efforts to attract new industry. Between 1972 and 1977, for example, there were 3,513 decisions to build new plants or expand existing ones in the state. Moreover, a survey of the thousand largest corporations in the country found that 11 percent picked Texas as their most likely location for a new plant. This figure placed Texas first among all the states, with California ranking second as the choice of 8 percent of the companies (Pollard and Monti, 1980).

When corporate planners are asked what influences their choice of new sites for expansion, the following factors are listed as the most influential (Pluta, 1980):

1. Availability of raw materials
2. Access to markets
3. Labor supply
4. Adequacy and cost of transportation
5. Availability of water and utility services

According to one report, "Texas ranks high in locational studies because it offers central location, good transportation facilities, a large work force, a growing population, a good climate, a healthy economy, and a general image that favors economic growth. It does not appear that minor changes in the business tax base or tax rates would offset or greatly enhance these advantages" (Pluta, 1980:51–52).

The omission of taxes as one of the major considerations might be especially surprising to some. There has long been a widespread belief that the tax level is the major factor in such decisions. Research on actual corporate decision making, however, does not support such an influential role for taxes. In fact, low taxes can even work to the disadvantage of a state. As Pluta (1980:48) argues:

> *Even a low-tax image may work to a state's disadvantage, since very low taxes may also imply a low level of public services as well. One location criterion often cited by businesses is the availability of adequate or exceptional public services, particularly at the local level. If services like police and fire protection are inadequate, firms may have to provide costly private security and fire protection. Further, businesses must consider the needs of their employees in selecting a location. The adequacy of public education, recreational facilities, and similar services may be as important as low taxes.*

Jones (1987) also found that neither corporate taxes nor personal income taxes exerted an impact upon economic growth. He concluded that state and local taxes have little effect upon a corporation's business costs. In fact, after a careful review of the research literature, Jones found that:

> Economic growth in states is not related to specific incentives designed to attract business. State and local governments have designed a whole host of specific incentives to attract business and jobs to their states, including tax abatements, subsidized loans, tax increment financing, job training programs, special business parks, etc. While these incentives may help in attracting a particular business, none of these promote overall economic growth. . . . They are basically taxpayer subsidies to business, yielding no public benefits. They do, of course, give state and local economic development officials something to offer prospective clients, and each state feels compelled to up the ante when trying to lure businesses in today's competitive environment.

THE SPECIAL PROMINENCE OF HIGH-TECH INDUSTRIES

Many business and government leaders in Texas have wished particularly to lure high-tech industries to the state. Electronics, alone, is a $230 billion industry in the United States and provides 2.5 million jobs. Such businesses are thought to be especially attractive for a variety of reasons, and they are believed by many to be the wave of the future. Because of this prominence, it is important to consider the character of high-tech development in some detail.

One might ask, initially, just what is meant by the term *high tech*. A particularly useful explanation is offered by Harry Hurt (1984:134–135):

> The term usually refers to the vast array of businesses that all rely upon the same essential element: the silicon chip. Makers of semiconductors, microprocessors, and most forms of computer hardware and software obviously fall into this category. Other businesses termed high tech include producers of telecommunications devices, automatic bank tellers, fiber optics and character-recognition equipment, aerospace guidance systems, and certain types of medical instruments and industrial robots.

But the term *high tech* also refers to various industries that are just beginning to emerge into prominence. Biotechnology, for example, holds extraordinary promise. Examples would include the development of "biochips" that might be used to create computers with living organisms, the use of microscopic germs to clean up oil spills and detect toxic wastes, and the production of grains that are capable of fighting drought, insects, and disease as well as creating their own fertilizer. San Antonio is already advertising itself as a major center for biotechnology research and development.

The commercial use of space is another emerging industry. Many of the conditions on earth that enormously complicate manufacturing processes—gravity, atmospheric pressure, vibration, convection currents—are absent in space. Consequently, traditional production techniques might derive enormous benefit from a space location. In addition, biotechnology firms anticipate that space might well provide an ideal environment for the development and testing of biochips, biosensing devices, and agricultural organisms. Houston hopes to capitalize on the Manned Spacecraft Center and emerge as a leader in the field of space business. Already, the Houston Economic Development Council has spent several hundred thousand dollars in an effort to attract firms interested in space ventures.

In 1978 there were 1,638 high-tech firms in Texas. By 1982, this number had grown to 4,071, an increase of 26 percent a year (State Comptroller, 1983c). These firms had $8 billion in gross sales in 1982 and employed almost 3 percent of the state's work force. The latter figure translates into 205,000 jobs. In 1980, Texas also accounted for 4.6 percent of the entire nation's high-tech work force. Yet Texas was first in terms of the number of *new* jobs available in this field. The state has been creating new openings at a rate 60 percent greater than California's (Hurt, 1984).

Table 1–3 indicates that the state's high-tech industry is concentrated in only a few urban areas. Dallas–Fort Worth accounted for 38 percent of all taxable high-tech sales in 1982, while Houston accounted for 34 percent. Dallas had 33 percent of all communication equipment business in the state, 41 percent of the electronics components industry, and 51 percent of the aircraft parts business. Of the 205,000 high-tech jobs in Texas, 118,767 were in the Dallas–Fort Worth area.

By 1987, high-tech employment in the Metroplex had increased to 158,000, while 41,000 workers in the Central Corridor and 33,000 in the Gulf Coast owed their jobs to the high-tech sector. Although Houston is the home of the Manned Spacecraft Center, it has not successfully competed for high-tech firms. The region has only 6.9 high-tech employees per thousand population compared to 26.3 in the Central Corridor and 42.4 in the Metroplex.

Table 1–4 shows the composition of the state's high-tech industries. The leading divisions of the sector, in terms of taxable business, were electronic components, computer and data processing services, electronic computing equipment, and aircraft parts.

Defense Spending and High Tech

The federal government spent $12 billion on defense in Texas in 1982, and the state ranked third in the nation in number of defense dollars received (behind California and Virginia) and second (behind California) in the number of

TABLE 1–3   Percentage of High-Tech Taxable Sales by SMSA: 1982

Standard Metropolitan Statistical Area (SMSA)	Sales (%)	Total Employed
Bryan–College Station	0.1	781
San Antonio	2.4	11,014
Austin	1.5	14,966
Dallas–Fort Worth	37.5	118,767
Houston	33.8	26,995
Rest of state	24.7	32,210

Source: State Comptroller (1983c).

Department of Defense employees. Texas had 255,716 Department of Defense civilian and military employees in 1982. By comparison, there were fewer than 200,000 state government employees and 301,400 workers in the oil and gas industry. Those oil and gas employees were paid $7 billion in wages while Department of Defense workers received salaries and retirement benefits of $5 billion.

By any standard, therefore, defense spending plays a major role in the Texas economy. Although the largest portion of defense contracts (37 percent) in the state goes for the purchase of petroleum, military spending also stimulates high-tech industries. Aircraft frames, electronics and communications, aircraft equipment, and missile and space systems accounted for a combined total of 46 percent of all prime military contracts in Texas. Currently, military spending provides the greatest stimulus to the growth and development of high tech in Texas. A considerable portion of the future of high tech in Texas appears, therefore, to be closely linked to the federal government's future defense priorities. This fact indicates another way in which the state's economy is linked to the international arena. The level of international political tension and the desire for increased security through weapons development—because of such tensions—both operate to boost defense spending.

The Future of High Tech in Texas

Although high-tech industries accounted for only 3 percent of all jobs in Texas in 1983, many people expect far bigger things for this industry in the future. John Naisbitt, in his book *Megatrends* (1982:72), argued that "ten years from now the electronics industry will be bigger than the auto and steel industries today." Texas public officials hope, of course, that the state will enjoy more than its fair share of this field.

TABLE 1-4   **Percentage of High-Tech Sales by Industry: 1982**

Industry	Sales (%)	Total Employed
Guided missiles and space vehicles	1.7	10,716
Computer equipment stores	3.5	NA
Computer and data processing service	11.8	30,059
Electronic computing equipment	8.8	21,997
Optical instruments	0.2	550
Research and development laboratories	1.4	7,054
Scientific and research equipment	1.6	4,452
Measuring and controlling instruments	6.2	9,756
Electronic components	13.0	52,345
Aircraft parts	8.0	42,827
Communication equipment	3.8	24,977

Source: State Comptroller (1983c).

One major development that bodes well for the high-tech future of the state was the decision of the Microelectronics and Computer Technology Corporation (MCC) to locate in Austin. MCC is a joint research firm controlled by eighteen microelectronics and computer companies, including Honeywell, Motorola, Control Data, Rockwell International, Lockheed, Eastman Kodak, and Martin-Marietta. The intent of MCC is to pool private resources in order to undertake major research programs in areas ranging from a new generation of computers to computer-assisted design and manufacturing. The corporation anticipates that it will eventually employ four hundred scientists and engineers and spend $100 million per year. It is widely hoped, as well, that the selection of Texas as the site for this highly ambitious research venture will attract a large number of other high-tech firms to the state.

In part, these optimistic expectations have already been realized. In January 1988, Sematech, a consortium of fifteen of the country's major semiconductor firms, decided to locate in Austin. Semiconductors are essential components of most electronic products and systems. Sematech will undertake advanced semiconductor research and development projects and make the findings and results available to its member firms. It is anticipated that the operation will create about 11,000 new jobs in the area and will further enhance the Central Corridor's reputation as an emerging center for high-tech research and development.

The predictions for high tech in Texas are, however, not all rosy. The state government spends only $9.2 million per year for research in the field, although the current budget provides for doubling that amount. An advisory committee to the State Senate Special Committee on Business, Technology, and Education recently observed that "we are playing amateur hour against people who are far more professional." These "professionals" are the states of California and Massachusetts, whose universities have long held the lead in research related to high tech. Some have recommended, therefore, that Texas spend a great deal more per year on high-tech research. The state's universities and businesses will have to compete more energetically, as well, for federal research funds in this area. Recently Texas has been garnering about 4 percent of such research support yearly—in contrast to the 23 percent won annually by California.

Beyond funded research, a number of observers have argued that one of Texas's critical weaknesses in the high-tech race lies in its educational system. At the highest level, Texas's best universities have not been able to match the success of such institutions as the Massachusetts Institute of Technology, Johns Hopkins, Stanford, and other major East and West Coast universities. And at the lower levels, Texas's elementary and secondary schools are believed by many to be seriously underfunded and considerably deficient in preparing their students for the challenges of high-tech professions.

High Tech—Famine or Fortune?

Despite these concerns, it is still possible to imagine a glowing high-tech future for Texas. Some observers predict that the state will be a mecca for such industries. Yet two things could upset this prediction. First, it is possible to overestimate the rapidity and extent to which high tech will revolutionize the economy of the state. There is no guarantee that computers and robots will replace cattle and oil wells as the prime economic symbols of Texas. In light of the competition with other states for such business, high tech may grow slowly and constitute only a small fraction of the Texas economy for many years to come.

The second problem with many forecasts for a high-tech future is that they may misapprehend the actual character of the high-tech age and its social and political implications. Some of the more careful forecasters have pointed out, for example, that the number of jobs for true high-tech professionals may always be a rather small portion of total employment. These forecasters suggest that the future demand for service-industry workers will be far higher. As Bob Kuttner (1983:60) has observed:

> As the economy shifts away from its traditional manufacturing base to high tech-
> nology and service industries, the share of jobs providing a middle-class standard
> of living is shrinking. An industrial economy employs a large number of relatively
> well-paid production workers. A service economy, however, employs legions of key
> punchers, salesclerks, waiters, secretaries, and cashiers, and the wages for these
> jobs tend to be comparatively low.

A high-tech economy, in other words, may produce one very small group of highly paid professionals and managers and one very large group of marginally rewarded clerks, secretaries, fast food workers, and janitors. The former group will reap enormous benefits from the system; the latter group will suffer underemployment, low wages, and little opportunity for advancement. As Kuttner implies, such a system might literally result in the shrinking of the middle class. Former U.S. Secretary of Labor Ray Marshall (1984:11) has added:

> While nobody knows for sure what kinds of jobs will be created and how much
> unemployment will result, my guess is that, in the absence of a comprehensive
> economic policy, the pessimists will be right: There will be widespread unemploy-
> ment and a continued polarization of society between a few haves and many and
> growing numbers of have nots.

It is possible, therefore, to project several negative trends in an economy dominated by high-tech industries. Such class distinctions and differences in economic fortunes, should they arise, will surely have political consequences, as well. On the one hand, those with disproportionate economic power and status will also have disproportionate political power, just as the leaders of the agriculture and oil and gas industries have had such power to date. The polarization of social classes that some see in the future could also lead to considerable discontent and even political conflict arising from those at the bottom of the high-tech society. The people at the bottom, if their circumstances prove to be as poor as Marshall's "pessimists" suggest, may rise to challenge the political power of the high-tech elite.

While none of these unfortunate social and political consequences are inevitable, one must expect that the current transformation of the American economy will lead to considerable stress and strain. The transition from an agricultural to an industrial economy in the late nineteenth and early twentieth centuries serves as an excellent example of what one generally might expect in the near future. That earlier transformation brought extraordinary changes in living patterns—shifting the bulk of the society from a dispersed rural background to a concentrated urban one. It fundamentally altered people's work lives and work settings. It led to broad movements of social and political protest, beginning with the Populists and the Progressives. It brought a transformation in government policy as, over a number of decades, government assumed responsibility through various regulatory activities of moderating the most hazardous aspects of industrial and urban life and maintaining the health of the national economy. While it may not be possible to anticipate precisely the character of the economic transformation currently before the nation, one must expect that its long-term consequences will be equally far-reaching.

But before too much is made of a high-tech future for the state, it will be recalled that only a relative handful of Texans work for high-tech firms. Further, the state is adding relatively few high-tech jobs each year. In fact, if defense expenditures decline even the already unimpressive high-tech growth rate will slow. Even though it is probable that high tech will emerge as a major sector of the state's economy in the future, it is likely that that future will be somewhat distant. By 1987, there were still fewer than 275,000 high-tech jobs in the state. At that rate, the high-tech industry is adding 10,000–15,000 jobs a year to the state's work force. By way of comparison, 278,000 Texans work in travel industry jobs.

It should also be noted that high tech may not be able to deliver the number of jobs that many are counting on. A U.S. Labor Department study found that high tech accounted for only 10 percent of the new jobs nationally from 1975–1982. In addition, the report projected that only 6 percent of the new jobs added to the economy from 1982–1995 would be in the high-tech sector (Moore, 1986).

CONCLUSION

Texas is no longer economically backward. In fact, it ranks in the top five states on a variety of economic indicators. The economy has also become increasingly diversified. While Texas remains a national and even world leader in oil and gas and agricultural production, several other sectors of the economy are growing rapidly to challenge the primacy of these fields. Large numbers of Texans are employed in manufacturing, in services, in wholesale and retail trade, and in a variety of other areas. The state even ranks third in the nation in high-tech employment.

Most observers argue that the trend toward diversification should continue and that it should do so at an even faster pace. Manufacturing and services should grow particularly fast, while agriculture and mining should decline in importance in the overall economy. The dominant economic symbols of Texas—

cows, cotton, and oil wells—are slowly but surely declining in importance. Yet while new and different industries are rising to challenge the older ones, the health of Texas's traditional economic sectors remains critical to the overall economy in the near term. The recession in the oil and gas industries beginning in 1982 clearly demonstrated that fact. The recognition of this circumstance, however, by the state's political leaders has simply provided one more impetus for diversification. Thus in the future other economic activities will surely come to rival and even surpass these old sectors.

And what impact will these changes in the economy have on the political life of the state? Their consequences will be considered in detail in later chapters, but a brief sketch here will indicate their variety and importance. One of these effects is simply that economic growth has become a prominent concern of state and local government officials in recent years. Texas has begun an especially vigorous campaign to attract new industry—in part to build its high-tech base, in part to counter the overreliance on the oil and gas industries, and in part because so many other states are doing the same thing. Texas must pursue such policies to compete effectively with other states and to ensure its share of the future growth of the nation.

The effort to attract new industry to the state illustrates the impact of the economy upon politics. The major problem facing the legislature in the last session was the revenue shortfall caused by the depression in the oil industry. One logical solution to the revenue crisis would have been the adoption of a state income tax. However, this option was never seriously considered. Why? Opponents of the income tax were extremely vocal and effective in pointing out that the adoption of such a tax would frighten away prospective new businesses. However, there is no valid evidence to support the argument that the adoption of an income tax would damage the state's economy. In fact, it might even help it if the additional revenues were used to improve public services in areas such as education, transportation, health, and police protection. In any event, economic concerns were seized upon to prevent political change. Instead of adopting an income tax, which would have provided for a more equitable distribution of the tax burden, the legislature decided to increase the rate of existing regressive taxes (sales tax).

Education policy has also been significantly influenced by the state's economy. The revenue crisis initially raised fears in higher education circles that funding for the state university system would be severely cut. As it turned out, the higher education budget fared much better than expected. Why? The legislature decided that increased expenditures for education will contribute to economic growth. This expectation is based upon the assumption that high-tech industries are attracted to states with a well-funded university system. In turn, these universities will attract top-notch faculties and develop into major research centers. The universities are seen as the panacea to the state's economic woes. They will help diversify the economy and lead the state into a glowing high-tech future. In the short run, therefore, higher education has escaped the severe budget cuts initially projected. In the long run, however, it will be interesting to see what happens when these unrealistic expectations of the higher education system are only partially realized.

The long-term economic transformation the state is facing will have a number of social consequences of direct political relevance, too. The decline of agriculture, mining, and parts of the oil and gas industry will weaken the political power of rural areas in the state, which traditionally have dominated state government. The rise of manufacturing, services, and high-tech fields will strengthen the power of urban and suburban areas, traditionally politically weak ones in Texas. New economic elites and new interest groups will arise out of this same process to challenge established ones centered in the old industries. There may even be a sharp decline in the size and economic power—and hence the political power—of the middle class in the state. These are all substantial social changes that will fundamentally reshape political power in Texas.

Some of these changes will also affect the political party system of the state. The long-dominant Democratic party has traditionally been tied to elites in agriculture, in oil and gas, and in the cattle industry. The rise of new elites and interest groups will mean more conflict within the Democratic party and the prospect, as well, for an increasingly stronger Republican party.

Many of these economic and social changes will undoubtedly lead to demands for more and better public services. Growing urban areas—the locales of most of the state's economic expansion—require increasing expenditures both for capital improvements and for routine services like police, fire, and public health protection. New industries often have new service needs, as well. And the leaders of high tech and other new industries are often powerful advocates of increased service levels. Indeed, some new firms may choose to locate in Texas only if there are guarantees of certain public services or amenities. Thus economic transformation may well reshape the public policies of the state of Texas.

Inevitably, demands for more and better services will result in higher taxes. Some of the most difficult, and perhaps bitterly fought, decisions in the state in the next decades will revolve around the issues of whether to increase public services, which ones should be increased, and what taxes—and hence which taxpayers—should bear the burdens of those increases. These decisions will be made, moreover, during a time when the distribution of political power in the state will be undergoing a transformation itself.

There are, then, a variety of intimate connections between the Texas economy and the political life of the state. While the outlines of the economy, the directions in which it is changing, and the character of some of those connections have been discussed here, the same issues constitute important themes that will appear in later chapters.

REFERENCES

Arnold, Victor. 1983. *Texas: Trends and Forecasts*. Austin: Bureau of Business Research, University of Texas.

Fletcher, Sam. 1985. "Official Paints Gloomy Picture Based on Declining Oil Prices." *Houston Post* (April 5):H3.

General Social and Economic Characteristics: Texas, 1980 Census of Population. 1983. Washington, D.C.: Bureau of the Census, U.S. Department of Commerce.

Glover, Robert W., and King, Allan G. 1978. "Organized Labor in Texas." In Louis J. Rodriguez (ed.), *Dynamics of Growth: An Economic Profile of Texas*. Austin: Madrona Press.

Hurt, Harry. 1984. "Birth of a New Frontier." *Texas Monthly* (April):130–135.

Jones, Bryan D. 1986. "Stimulating Economic Growth in a Changing Texas: The Role of State and Local Government." (unpublished paper).

Jones, Bryan D. 1983. *Governing Urban America*. Boston: Little, Brown.

Kuttner, Bob. 1983. "The Declining Middle." *Atlantic Monthly* (July):60–72.

Marshall, Ray. 1984. "High Tech and the Job Crunch." *Texas Observer* (April 6):7–11.

Moore, W. John. 1986. *National Journal*. (November 15).

Naisbitt, John. 1982. *Megatrends*. New York: Warner Books.

Plaut, Thomas. 1983. *A Supply Side Model of the Texas Economy and Economic and Population Forecasts to the Year 2000*. Austin: Bureau of Economic Research, University of Texas.

Pluta, Joseph E. 1980. "Taxes and Industrial Location." In Joseph E. Pluta (ed.), *Economic and Business Issues of the 1980s*. Austin: Bureau of Business Research, University of Texas.

Pollard, Robert F., and Monti, Lorna A. 1980. "Industrial Location Decisions in Texas." In Joseph E. Pluta (ed.), *Economic and Business Issues of the 1980s*. Austin: Bureau of Business Research, University of Texas.

State Comptroller. 1983a. "The Economic Regions of Texas." *Fiscal Notes* (March):10–16. Austin: Office of the State Comptroller.

State Comptroller. 1983b. "The 1970s: A Milestone for Growth in the Texas Economy." *Fiscal Notes* (July):1–5. Austin: Office of the State Comptroller.

State Comptroller. 1983c. "Texas Maintains Its Share of High Technology." *Fiscal Notes* (December):8–24. Austin: Office of the State Comptroller.

State Comptroller. 1983d. "Texas Rakes in Defense Dollars." *Fiscal Notes* (December):1–7. Austin: Office of the State Comptroller.

State Comptroller. 1984. "Texas Energy Production Leads the Nation." *Fiscal Notes* (June):16–18. Austin: Office of the State Comptroller.

Texas Past and Future: A Survey. 1982. Austin: Texas 2000 Project, Office of the Governor.

THE POPULATION
OF TEXAS

J ust as a state's political life is closely tied to its economic opportunities and problems, it is influenced by such population characteristics as its citizens' cultural roots, their distribution through the state, and their ethnicity, education, and wealth. This chapter will show how these features of the Texas population affect Texans' evaluation of, demands on, and participation in their government. Moreover, these population characteristics reveal many of the most important policy problems facing the state of Texas.

THE HISTORY OF POPULATION GROWTH IN TEXAS

By 1987 Texas was estimated to have about 16.8 million citizens, ranking the state as the nation's third largest. The most notable division of those 16.8 million people is probably along ethnic lines. About 58 percent of Texans are Anglo-American, 21 percent are Mexican-American or "Spanish surnamed," and 12 percent are black Americans. The remaining 9 percent of the population is a mixture of mostly Asian, American Indian, and Middle Eastern ethnics with no other single ethnic group constituting as much as 1 percent of the total population.

Many of the social and cultural traits dealt with in this chapter could simply be elicited from the percentages just cited—as could many of the state's major political problems. The relationships among the state's ethnic groups and the particular political interests and needs of those groups have shaped much of Texas political life. Yet we cannot fully understand the influence of ethnic variations on Texas politics unless we consider at least briefly the history of population growth in the state. Of particular importance in that history are the migration and settlement patterns of the major ethnic groups noted above.

Table 2–1 presents historical population data for Texas's major ethnic groups since 1850, the date of the first complete census after Texas became a state. Because of incomplete and changing census methods, however, some of these figures must be taken only as reasonable estimates. The figures on the Mexican-American population of the state, for example, have always been rough approximations—in part because the U.S. Census Bureau has used several different definitions for counting the "Spanish surname" population and in part because of the difficulty of accurately counting illegal Mexican aliens. Nonetheless, table 2–1 gives fair estimates of population trends with one qualification: The 1980 figures on Spanish-surname residents of the state probably underestimate the actual number of such people, perhaps by as much as a third.

Table 2–1 indicates a relatively continuous trend of growth not only in the total population but also in each of the three ethnic subgroups. Yet some qualifications to that overall trend are noteworthy. First, the relative positions of the state's two ethnic minorities have been reversed in the time period covered in the table. In 1850 blacks accounted for almost 30 percent of the total population, while the Spanish surnamed were only 5 percent of the total. By 1980 blacks were only 12 percent of the population, and the Mexican-American minority—which had burgeoned in the twentieth century—constituted over 20 percent of the population in official U.S. census data. If an accurate estimate of the number of illegal Mexican aliens were available, the percentage of Texas residents who are Spanish surnamed would be even higher. A second qualification concerns the impression of continuous growth. Behind these figures are, in fact, some notable patterns of a much less continuous character. To understand these patterns, we must look into the history of migration of the state's major ethnic and national groups.

Anglo-American Migration

Anglo-American migrants have always constituted the largest source of the state's eventual citizens. Even as early as 1850 almost 60 percent of the state's residents were of Anglo-American birth, and 54 percent of the population had migrated from the southern United States (Jordan, 1969). Thus it was not only

TABLE 2–1 Population Growth in Texas

Year	Total Population	White	Black	Spanish Surname
1850	213,000	154,000	59,000	11,000
1880	1,592,000	1,197,000	393,000	N/A
1900	3,049,000	2,427,000	621,000	165,000
1920	4,663,000	3,918,000	742,000	510,000
1940	6,415,000	5,488,000	924,000	N/A
1960	9,580,000	8,375,000	1,187,000	1,418,000
1980	14,228,000	11,198,000	1,710,000	2,986,000

Note: All the numbers are rounded to thousands. Spanish-surname individuals have been included among those identified as "white" in Census Bureau tabulations, as well as detailed in the Spanish-surname column.

Sources: Principally U.S. Census Bureau data supplemented—for the Spanish-surname estimates—by Barrera (1979:75).

American migrants but those from a particular region and culture who formed the backbone of early Texas society. Of these southern American migrants alone, about half were from the "Lower South" states of Alabama, Georgia, Louisiana, and Mississippi where the economy was heavily reliant on the plantation system served by slave labor. The remaining half of the southern Americans were from the "Upper South" and border states of Arkansas, Kentucky, Missouri, and Tennessee where small farms had been more the rule (Jordan, 1967).

The vast bulk of the Anglo-American migrants who arrived before the Civil War settled in the eastern half of Texas in patterns somewhat regionalized in terms of their original states of origin. In other words, Upper South and Lower South migrants generally settled in different areas of Texas as indicated in figure 2–1. These immigrants also replicated as much as possible the agricultural systems of their original home states. Thus migrants from the Lower South brought substantial numbers of black slaves and established a slave-labor system based primarily on cotton production. Upper South migrants were predominately reliant on the production of wheat and small grains with relatively modest use of slave labor (Jordan, 1967).

Migration to Texas by all groups was interrupted by the Civil War and Reconstruction. But in the 1870s migration on a large scale began again. The major source of that migration was the southern United States. In this period,

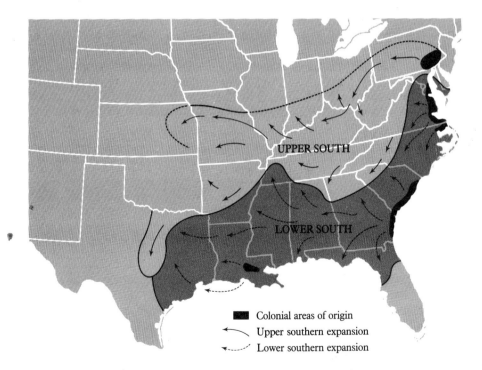

■ Colonial areas of origin
←\ Upper southern expansion
←------' Lower southern expansion

FIGURE 2–1   Anglo-American Migration to Texas: 1860
Source: Jordan (1967:668)

therefore, the cultural patterns of earlier migrants were largely reinforced by those of the newly arrived residents. And the numbers of new Texans were quite large. As D. W. Meinig (1969:64) notes of the last third of the nineteenth century: "In any one of those years well over half the population of Texas had been born outside the state."

Migrants from the southern United States have continued to be important through most of the twentieth century, as well. Yet two shifts in Anglo migration in this century are notable. First, around 1900 the contribution of the Old South to new migrants to Texas began to decline. In the place of this group, the states bordering Texas furnished the largest number of migrants until around 1950. Second, and more important for the different cultural values they carried, a notable if smaller stream of American Northeasterners and Midwesterners began to flow to Texas after 1900. These two regions provided a steady number of new Texans through the first six decades of this century. Then, because of the dramatically shifting economic fortunes of certain regions of the United States in the 1970s, the number of such migrants swelled.

These "Yankees," as "native" Texans like to label them, have also been termed "Sunbelt" migrants. The 1970s and early 1980s witnessed a substantial in-migration of such people, joined by a large number of Californians and a modest continued flow of Southerners. The number of such migrants declined after about 1982, when the state's economy went into recession. Yet research on the *kinds* of people who came to Texas mostly in this period suggests they may have an influence on the state greater than their numbers might suggest. The migrants of this period—and even those coming as recently as 1987—were predominately young, relatively well-educated, white-collared professionals (Schwaller, 1983; Yuen, 1987). Additionally, many of these people brought social and political values to Texas that were quite different from those of the state's traditional Southern and Southwestern culture. Thus, because of both their economic and professional positions and their cultural values, these people may be a significant force for change in the social and political life of the state.

The Migration of Blacks

The vast majority of blacks in Texas in 1850 had been brought to the state as the slaves of Anglo-American migrants from the Lower South. Thus most black Texans at the time came from the same cultural and social background as did those Anglo-Americans. But the blacks, of course, suffered a very different position in that original setting, just as they did in Texas. Another result of this dual migration was that black Texans in 1850 were regionalized in their areas of residence along with their Anglo masters.

The importation of slaves continued up until the Civil War, and the black population continued to increase faster than the total population until about 1870. After 1870, however, the numbers of black Texans continued to grow, but at a much slower rate than the numbers of the other major ethnic groups. Like most of the Old South, Texas never attracted particularly large numbers of new black residents after Reconstruction. The state actually witnessed substantial out-migration of blacks in the decades 1900–1910, 1940–1950, and 1950–1960.

The Migration of Mexicans

Although Texas was part of Mexico until 1836, the area had not been heavily settled by Mexican nationals in the nineteenth century. Cary McWilliams (1949:52) estimates that as late as 1848 there were only about 5,000 Mexicans in what is now Texas. In the 1850 census the Spanish-surnamed population of the state constituted only 11,212 or just over 5 percent of the total population. Of this group, about 40 percent had been born in Mexico.

The Mexican-American population of Texas grew rapidly, however, during the latter half of the 1800s. Estimates of the number of Mexican-origin Texans in any year are subject to some error but, as table 2–1 shows, their numbers had grown substantially by the turn of the century. The bulk of these people worked as cowboys and herders on the cattle and sheep ranches of South Texas or as agricultural workers, particularly in cotton. Most of the original Mexican landowners had, by one means or another, been driven from their land by Anglos after the Texas Revolution. While there were modest middle-class Mexican-American contingents in some of the towns of Central and South Texas, these people suffered the same discrimination as all the others of their background. They typically worked only within Mexican-American communities or were hired by Anglo business establishments to serve their Mexican-American customers.

Around the turn of the century there began the first of three cycles of Mexican immigration to Texas that are not revealed by the aggregate figures in table 2–1 (Fogel, 1979:9–18). These cycles were closely related to the shifting fortunes of the Texas economy; hence they constitute historical examples of political economy forces. From around 1900 to the beginning of the Great Depression in 1929, there was growing demand for cheap Mexican labor to work in the cattle, cotton, railroad, and fruit and vegetable industries—all of which were expanding across Texas.

Moreover, throughout much of this period there was considerable social and political strife in Mexico—leading up to and following the revolution of 1910 in that country. To make the prospects for immigration even more attractive, there was virtually no effort by the United States government to control Mexican immigration—legal or illegal—during this period. Thus both immigration and the Spanish-surname population of Texas swelled during these years.

The Great Depression beginning in 1929, however, brought an entirely different set of circumstances that actually reversed the flow of migrants from Mexico. The demand for foreign laborers fell sharply. Domestic workers replaced foreign nationals in most of the available jobs. And a wave of antiforeign sentiment and vigorous government efforts to "repatriate" Mexican nationals ensued (Kiser and Silverman, 1979). As a result, the number of Mexican nationals in Texas fell by around 30 to 40 percent in the 1930s. Even some American citizens of Mexican descent (many of them children of Mexican nationals born in the United States and thus dual nationals) were "repatriated" to Mexico. Many others, both American and Mexican citizens, left voluntarily for Mexico because of the antiforeign sentiment of the time. This period of a significant return flow of people back to Mexico thus completed the first cycle of twentieth-century Mexican migration in Texas.

A second cycle of massive immigration from Mexico—also beginning with large numbers of immigrants and ending with a sharp outflow reinforced by U.S. government action—occurred in the period 1945–1965. Once again the major stimulus for this immigration came from the labor demands of agricultural and other industries in Texas and the relative attractiveness of employment in the United States as opposed to Mexico. A good portion of this second wave of immigration came under the auspices of the contract labor (or popularly termed *bracero*) programs agreed to between the United States and Mexican governments. But much of the migration in this period was illegal, as well.

In the mid-1950s the United States government began a massive effort to stem the flow of illegal immigration. And most observers agree that, through aggressive Border Patrol and Immigration Service activities, the policy was a success for a time. The flow of illegals apparently fell off sharply between 1956 and 1965 and was, in part, replaced by greater numbers of contract laborers allowed into the United States each year. Yet the contract program, which had always been controversial, was terminated in 1965, a victim of the reformist mood of the U.S. Congress at the time (Hawley, 1979).

In the middle and late 1960s there began what looks like the third cycle of Mexican immigration to Texas. This is, of course, the period of heavy illegal immigration that has continued to the present. The relative attractiveness of even low-paying jobs in America, especially in light of the difficulties suffered by the Mexican economy during this period, is once again the major stimulus for this flow. The tide of immigration has run high despite relatively vigorous U.S. government efforts to slow it.

In 1986 the U.S. government passed the Immigration Reform and Control Act in an attempt to solve the problem of illegal immigration. Under the act, illegals who have lived continuously in the United States since January 1, 1982 are offered temporary legal residency and the chance to gain permanent residency and U.S. citizenship. Further, employers who hire illegal aliens in the future could face stiff fines. Experts are divided on how successful this effort will be in stopping the flow of illegal immigration. Yet in 1987 the number of new illegal migrants to Texas dropped dramatically. Arrests of illegals by the U.S. Border Patrol dropped 45 percent from the prior year, and the decline was attributed to knowledge by Mexican nationals that jobs for undocumented workers are far more difficult to find because of the new law.

One major difference between the present cycle and the former ones—and a change that can be explained in terms of the shifting Texas economy—is the much greater prevalence of illegal immigrants in unskilled, semiskilled, and service jobs in urban areas (Barrera, 1979:125–126). Several of Texas's major cities, particularly San Antonio, Houston, and Dallas, today harbor large numbers of such illegal aliens. Recent estimates place the number of illegal Mexican aliens in the entire state around 1 million.

Before leaving the subject of Mexican immigration, a few words are necessary about the pattern of the "illegal" portion of that flow. Through most of the twentieth century the typical Mexican illegal immigrant has been a young male, usually between the ages of seventeen and thirty, who comes to the United States for seasonal employment and then returns home to Mexico within a year (King and Rizo-Patron, 1978; Fogel, 1979:75–81). Most of these men also save the bulk of their earnings in the United States to send home to the families in Mexico they help support. While these men might make their round-trip journey many times, the pattern of immigration they follow is clearly distinct from the so-called European pattern of people seeking permanent residence in the United States. Obviously, as well, while this pattern of Mexican immigration creates social strains and public problems, these problems are somewhat different from those that would arise if all these people were seeking permanent residence in the United States. Thus, as long as the traditional pattern holds, the vast majority of these million or so illegal aliens in Texas are not here permanently but are seeking temporary employment of a seasonal or short-term character. Furthermore, if the dynamics of past cycles of immigration hold true, they are here subject to the shifting labor market demands of the American and Mexican economies.

There are no firm estimates of how many illegals stay in the United States permanently, but certainly over the period of the entire twentieth century the cumulative numbers, even if small at any single time, have been crucial in the growth of the Mexican-American population of Texas. Thus 80 percent or so of all the Spanish-surname residents of Texas are citizens of the United States, but many of their parents and grandparents emigrated from Mexico in this century.

There is increasing evidence, however, to suggest that many of the current illegal immigrants hope to stay permanently in this country and that the continuing economic and political problems of their home country will drive many more to the United States with the same intent. There is also evidence that Mexico's economic troubles are changing the traditional pattern of migration—today whole families are seeking to enter the United States illegally and to remain permanently. In fact, political conflict in several Central American nations in the 1980s has led to the same result. Yet the current cycle of Mexican and Central American immigration, like the cycles of the past, will depend above all on the job possibilities and other incentives arising from the American economy and on the success of U.S. immigration policies.

European Migration

By 1850 Texas already had a notable number of European-born migrants, largely from Germany and the Germanic regions of Austria and Switzerland. In fact, there were more German-origin than Spanish-surname residents in Texas at the time (Jordan, 1969). These people, constituting just over 5 percent of the total population, were settled in a belt from Galveston westward to the general San Antonio area. The largest German settlements were at New Braunfels and Fredericksburg. In fact, Texas gained more European immigrants during this period than any other southern American state. As late as 1900 the number of central European immigrants living in Texas rivaled that of Texans born in Mexico.

Especially the Germans, but also some of the other European immigrant groups, lived in relatively exclusive communities, maintaining their native culture and language to a considerable degree. Beginning in the 1920s the numbers of new arrivals fell off substantially, and, without reinforcement, the cultural separatism of these groups began to decline (Meinig, 1969:85). A few aspects of the old exclusivity and some of the regional distinctiveness of these groups remain, but these cultural traits are far weaker today than they were even a generation ago.

A Pattern of Cultural Diversity

This review of the settlement of Texas and subsequent population trends indicates why the state's core cultural values are derived from those of the southern United States. The South provided the bulk of Texas's early settlers and has continued to provide a notable number of new migrants to the present day. At the same time it is also clear that Texas's society is considerably more cosmopolitan than that of perhaps any other Southern state. The state's Southern immigrants represented two distinct cultural subgroups, and both European and Mexican influences were also important even before Texas became a state. Indeed, Texas has been culturally diverse since the earliest years of Anglo settlement. As an inscription on the base of the San Jacinto Monument reminds us about the soldiers who fought at the battle of San Jacinto (1836):

> *Citizens of Texas and immigrant soldiers in the Army of Texas at San Jacinto were natives of Alabama, Arkansas, Connecticut, Georgia, Illinois, Indiana, Kentucky, Louisiana, Maine, Maryland, Massachusetts, Michigan, Mississippi, Missouri, New Hampshire, New York, North Carolina, Ohio, Pennsylvania, Rhode Island, South Carolina, Tennessee, Texas, Vermont, Virginia, Austria, Canada, England, France, Germany, Ireland, Italy, Mexico, Poland, Portugal, and Scotland.*

In recent years the state's cultural variety has been enriched by especially large numbers of Mexican and Central American immigrants, Sunbelt migrants from other regions of the United States, and Asians and Middle Easterners from several different nations.

We must also recognize, however, that for most of the state's history there was little interchange among cultural groups. The rigid regionalization of settlement patterns precluded much contact. Figure 2–2, based on 1880 census data, indicates the extent to which this pattern separated the different cultures of the state. (In each county, the group indicated is the largest one in the population, excluding those born in Texas.) The only regions where different ethnic groups lived in any notable proximity in the 1800s were where blacks and Lower South Anglos shared portions of East and Southeast Texas. But strong ethnic prejudice against blacks militated against any social or cultural exchange between these two groups.

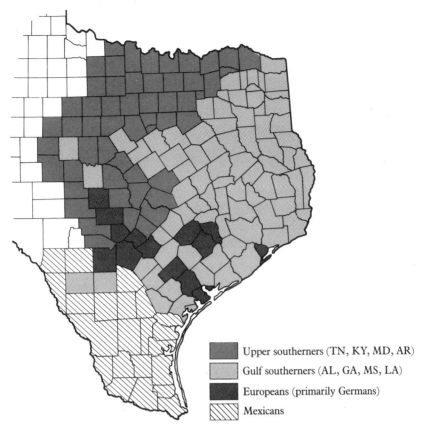

Upper southerners (TN, KY, MD, AR)

Gulf southerners (AL, GA, MS, LA)

Europeans (primarily Germans)

Mexicans

FIGURE 2–2   Origins of the Immigrant Population of Texas: 1880
Source: Jordan (1967:671)

THE FUTURE OF POPULATION GROWTH IN TEXAS

As we observed above, the population of Texas grew very rapidly in the 1960s and 1970s, and then the rate of increase declined in the 1980s. Nonetheless, a number of forecasts anticipate a growth rate in the state considerably higher than the national average and a total population of at least 20 million by the year 2000. If that projection proves to be accurate, it will represent about a *30 percent* increase since 1980.

Such rapid growth will pose major problems for both state and local political leaders. Increasing demands for public services; the accelerated wear and tear on public facilities like roads, schools, and parks; the impact on the quality of life in the state—these will be major issues for public action in the years ahead. The rapid growth of past decades, despite the recent slowdown, has already brought a number of these issues to the public agenda. Compared to states that are losing population, Texas is in an enviable position. Yet the challenges inherent in that position may prove to be difficult.

Population experts also observe that a significant shift in the ethnic composition of the state is now under way. The Anglo population has long been the overwhelming majority—even as long ago as 1850 as table 2–1 indicates. Yet the state's minority groups—and especially Hispanics—are now growing so rapidly, because of the large number of new immigrants and a high birth rate, that they will displace the Anglo majority early in the next century. One projection is that by the year 2015 Mexican-Americans will constitute 39 percent of the state's population, blacks 11 percent, Asians and other minorities 6 percent, and Anglos only 44 percent.

If these predictions are realized, they will have a host of far-reaching consequences for Texas politics. For one, the ethnic composition of the voting public will be dramatically reshaped. The demands this new electorate will press on government may be radically different, too, from those today. The new majority in 2015 may still harbor resentment for being the minority in times past. As we will show later in this chapter, the low income, educational, and occupational status of blacks and Mexican-Americans today can be expected to continue well into the future. Thus the political interests of the new majority in 2015 will be shaped by those social and economic circumstances.

MAJOR DEMOGRAPHIC CHARACTERISTICS

Beyond the variations in population size and ethnicity described above, there are several other characteristics of Texas's population that influence the state's political affairs in one way or another. The most important of these features concern patterns of settlement and residence of the population across the state, levels of education and income, and the occupational makeup of the state's work force. In the remainder of this chapter we will examine these characteristics in some detail, relying particularly on information from the 1980 census. That census makes it possible to separate the Anglo, black, and Spanish-speaking citizens of the state and to describe the distinctive social and economic positions of these ethnic groups. As we will see, the social and economic position of the state's minority ethnic groups is strikingly divergent from that of the Anglo majority.

Urbanization

One of the most dramatic changes in the state in the twentieth century has been the transformation of a heavily rural and small-town population to one that is predominately urban. In the nineteenth century the overwhelming majority of Texans lived in rural areas. In the 1850 census, for example, only 4 percent of the state's population was classified as urban, and an "urban" area was anyplace with a population larger than 1,000. Beginning early in this century, however, the "urban" population of the state began to grow quite rapidly. During the 1940s the number of such people first exceeded those living in rural areas. By the 1980 census about 80 percent of the state's residents were classified by the Census Bureau as urban-dwellers. Another indication of this radical shift in the residential status of the population is the fact that in 1980 only 2 percent of Texans lived on farms. And not only do most contemporary Texans live in urban instead of rural areas, but the very concept of what constitutes an urban place has undergone considerable transformation.

Over half the state's population in 1980, for example, lived in the Census Bureau-designated Standard Metropolitan Statistical Areas (SMSAs) of Houston, Dallas–Fort Worth, San Antonio, and Austin—all metropolitan areas with populations greater than 500,000. Thus Texas has experienced more than rapid urbanization. It has experienced the growth of huge urban areas with all the attendant social and political problems. No longer can Texans dismiss big city problems as those of the East Coast and West Coast. Today the majority of Texans face the same problems themselves. It is in this sense that "urban" life means something far different today than it did even a generation ago. And these big-city problems should become even more important in the years ahead.

Along with the appearance of large cities has come another development: the growth of large suburban communities as a portion of those cities. There is no precise definition of what constitutes a suburb; nor is there an ideal way to estimate the number of people who live in such places. Yet population researchers generally equate the suburban population with the number living in Metropolitan Statistical Areas but *outside* the central city portion thereof (Muller, 1981:5; Haar, 1974:27). By that measure 29 percent of Texas's SMSA population, or 24 percent of the total population in 1980, were suburbanites.

For a more compelling demonstration of the importance of suburbia in Texas, we can examine data on the growth of such places for Texas's six largest SMSAs between 1970 and 1980. Those figures, presented in table 2–2, illustrate the literal burgeoning of such areas in Austin, Dallas–Fort Worth, El Paso, and Houston. In all six of these SMSAs the suburbs grew at a higher rate than did the central city. Only in Corpus Christi and San Antonio did the central city growth rate approach that of the suburbs. This pattern of particularly rapid suburban growth characterizes almost all the metropolitan areas of the state.

Suburban areas create distinctive political demands and public service needs. While Texas already has a significant portion of its residents living in such areas, the number of such people will surely climb substantially over the next few decades. And in the years ahead their distinctive political interests and demands are certain to become more prominent in the state's politics.

Another development coincident with urbanization has been the dispersion of population across the state, at least in comparison to the situation in the 1800s. The western half of Texas remains much less densely settled, just as it was in the last century, but a significant movement of people to that region has occurred in recent decades. Figure 2–3, showing the location of the state's Standard Metropolitan Statistical Areas in 1980, illustrates some results of that movement. The El Paso, Amarillo, Lubbock, Midland, Odessa, Abilene, San Angelo, and Laredo SMSAs all are home to more than 100,000 people today. Some of these metro areas have been among the fastest-growing cities in the state in recent years. The growth of these cities is breaking down the distinctiveness of West and Central Texas, and it is bringing to those regions the same problems of large urban governments being faced elsewhere in the state.

TABLE 2–2   The Growth of Suburbs in Major Texas Cities: 1970–1980

City	Population 1970	Population 1980	Change (%)
Austin			
Central city	253,539	345,496	36
Suburbs	106,924	190,954	79
Total SMSA	360,463	536,450	49
Corpus Christi			
Central city	204,525	231,999	13
Suburbs	80,307	94,229	17
Total SMSA	284,832	326,228	15
Dallas–Fort Worth			
Central cities	1,237,856	1,289,219	4
Surburbs	1,139,767	1,685,659	48
Total SMSA	2,377,623	2,974,878	25
El Paso			
Central city	322,261	425,259	32
Suburbs	37,030	54,640	48
Total SMSA	359,291	479,899	34
Houston			
Central city	1,233,535	1,594,086	29
Suburbs	765,781	1,311,264	71
Total SMSA	1,999,316	2,905,350	45
San Antonio			
Central city	654,179	785,410	20
Suburbs	234,026	286,544	22
Total SMSA	888,179	1,071,954	21

Source: Census of Population (1981).

Yet another component of the urbanization trend concerns the patterns of residence of the state's two largest ethnic minorities. In the 1800s, both blacks and Mexican-Americans lived in rigidly defined and mostly rural areas. Blacks were heavily concentrated in rural East Texas, the area to which they were originally brought as slaves. Similarly, Mexican-Americans were mostly concentrated along the Texas–Mexico border, an obvious result of their own migration pattern and the availability of the agricultural and cattle ranching jobs they mostly assumed.

These regional patterns of ethnic location are still important today. The vast majority of black Texans still live in the eastern half of the state. And it is not uncommon for blacks to make up 20 to 35 percent of the population of many rural East Texas counties. Likewise, in rural counties along the border with Mexico, Spanish-surname Texans typically constitute 70 to 90 percent of the population. Yet focusing only on those places where ethnics compose very high percentages of the residents would lead one to misunderstand a second aspect of their current distribution in the state. For these two groups are also very heavily urbanized today, even more so than are the state's Anglo residents.

In 1980 some 86 percent of Mexican-American Texans and 88 percent of black Texans lived in urban places in comparison to 76 percent of Anglos. The largest numbers of Mexican-Americans live in, in order, San Antonio, Houston, El Paso, and Dallas, and the Mexican-American residents of these metropolitan areas constitute almost half the state's total. Similarly, over half of all black Texans live in the Houston and Dallas–Fort Worth metro areas alone, and there are other large groups of blacks in the "Golden Triangle" of Beaumont–Port Arthur–Orange and in San Antonio.

Income and Poverty Levels

The levels of personal income and wealth in the state are also of obvious importance to political life. Taken all together, Texans compare reasonably well to the national average in such matters. In 1986, the most recent year for which data are available, per capita income in the state was estimated to be $13,478, whereas the national average was $14,641. Yet the statewide average is particularly misleading because of the great variations, especially on the basis of ethnicity, that it obscures. More detailed figures from the 1980 U.S. census are necessary to illustrate these variations.

In each census people are asked about their individual and family incomes in the prior year. Table 2–3 presents these *family* income data for 1979 for Texas's three major ethnic groups. The table also shows the *per capita* income in 1979 for each group and the percentages of each of the groups whose family incomes fell below the federal government's "poverty threshold." The poverty

TABLE 2–3   Family Income and Poverty Among Texas's Major Ethnic Groups: 1979

Family Income Data	Anglo	Black	Spanish Origin	State Total
0–$4,999	5%	18%	15%	8%
$5,000– 9,999	11%	21%	21%	14%
$10,000–14,999	13%	17%	20%	15%
$15,000–24,999	29%	25%	27%	28%
$25,000–49,999	35%	18%	15%	29%
$50,000 and above	8%	1%	2%	6%
Median family income	$22,162	$13,064	$13,293	$19,618
Per capita income	$8,766	$4,512	$3,883	$7,205
Families with incomes below poverty line	6%	24%	25%	11%

Source: Census of Population (1983).

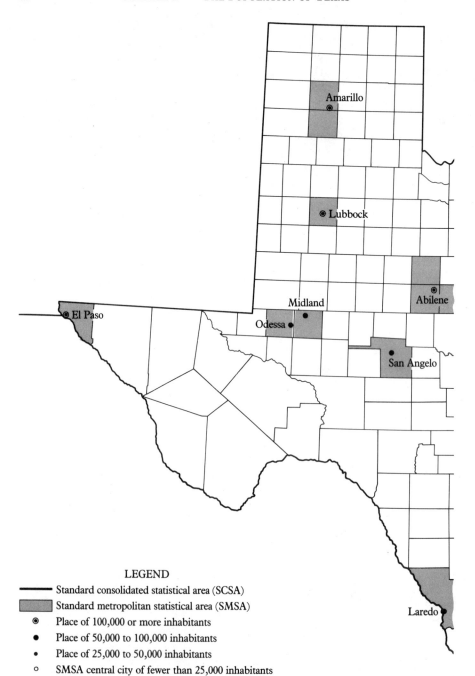

LEGEND

—— Standard consolidated statistical area (SCSA)

▨ Standard metropolitan statistical area (SMSA)

◉ Place of 100,000 or more inhabitants

● Place of 50,000 to 100,000 inhabitants

· Place of 25,000 to 50,000 inhabitants

○ SMSA central city of fewer than 25,000 inhabitants

SCSA and SMSA bounderies are as defined on June 19, 1981.

FIGURE 2–3   Standard Consolidated Statistical Area (SCSA) and Standard Metropolitan Statistical Areas (SMSA): 1981

Source: Bureau of the Census, 1981

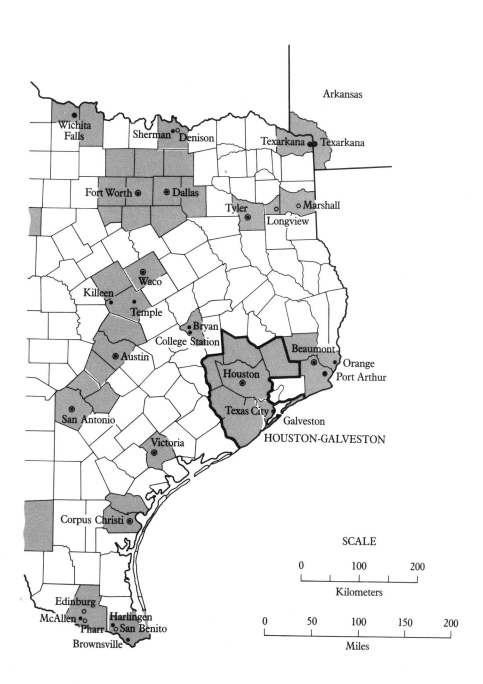

Arkansas

Wichita
Falls

Sherman
Denison

Texarkana Texarkana

Fort Worth Dallas

Tyler Marshall

Longview

Waco

Killeen

Temple

Bryan
College Station

Beaumont

Orange
Port Arthur

Austin

Houston

San Antonio

Texas City

Galveston

HOUSTON-GALVESTON

Victoria

Corpus Christi

SCALE

0   100   200

Kilometers

0   50   100   150   200

Miles

Edinburg

McAllen

Pharr

Harlingen

San Benito

Brownsville

threshold is based on the federal government's estimate of how much annual income families of different sizes must earn in order to be living "above the poverty line." Many observers argue, however, that the poverty threshold is quite low and underestimates the numbers of people actually living in poverty.

There are relatively poor and wealthy Texans in all three groups, but the two minority groups are heavily skewed toward the poor end of the income continuum. For example, almost 40 percent of black and Spanish-origin families earned less than $10,000 in 1979 compared with only 15 percent of Anglo families. Another good comparison is based on the median family income figures. In 1980 the minority groups' median incomes were only about 60 percent of the same figure for Anglo families. And, to make the contrast more compelling, the ratio of each minority group's income to the Anglo group figure actually declined slightly between 1969, the date of the previous census, and 1979.

The estimates of families living in poverty sharpen the contrast between the Anglo and the minority groups. Both ethnic minority groups have about four times as large a proportion in poverty as do their Anglo counterparts. And if one believes, as many do, that the poverty threshold does not really measure the number of people who are truly poor, then many more Texans would have to be included in that group. In fact, the federal government itself now implicitly concedes this criticism of its poverty threshold index and reports, as a second poverty estimate, the percentage of the population living below 125 percent of the standard poverty threshold. Using the latter figures, 33 percent of Spanish-origin families, 32 percent of black families, and 9 percent of Anglo families in Texas were living in poverty in 1979.

Education Levels

It is generally expected that in any large grouping of people there will be a substantial correlation between the income level and the education level of its members. Such is the case in Texas, particularly if we examine the levels of formal education within the three principal ethnic groups. Table 2–4 provides the statistics, again taken from the 1980 U.S. census.

In table 2–4 the two minority groups are skewed toward the low-education end of the continuum. The Anglo population, on the other hand, is skewed toward high education. Especially notable in the table are the large percentages of blacks and especially Mexican-Americans with an elementary education or less and the relatively small percentages of the same groups with college educations. Certainly the lower education levels of the two minority groups are, in part, the product of the particularly limited educational opportunities available to older members of those groups when they were of school age. Yet even in the current school-age population, particularly at the late high school and college levels, there is a notable gap between Anglo school enrollments and those of the two minority groups. A recent study, for example, found that the drop-out rates for Texas high school students over the period 1982–1986 were 27 percent for Anglos, 34 percent for blacks, and 45 percent for Hispanics!

TABLE 2–4 Formal Schooling for the Population 25 Years Old and Older: 1980

Schooling	%	Anglo	Black	Spanish Origin	State Total
Elementary or less		13	25	51	21
Some high school		17	22	13	17
Four years of high school		31	29	20	29
Some college		19	15	10	17
Four years or more of college		20	9	6	16

Source: Census of Population (1983).

Occupational Categories

As discussed in the preceding chapter, the Texas economy has been moving in recent decades toward a diversified manufacturing, service, and high-tech character, and the occupational structure of the state has, of course, been shifting in the same direction. Yet because of their differing education levels and general social positions, the state's ethnic groups do not all have the same opportunity to adapt with changes in the economy. Traditionally, members of the two minority groups were relegated to the lesser occupations in the economy, and that situation is still true for many ethnics today. To illustrate the current occupational structure of the state, table 2–5 presents employment figures for the state and the three major ethnic groups.

The categories of occupations in table 2–5 are broad, but they still reveal some compelling contrasts among the three ethnic groups. Of particular note are the differences between the Anglo and the minority groups at the highest occupational levels (professional, managerial, and professional employment) and at the lowest level for those whose jobs depend only on strong backs and hands (operators, fabricators, and laborers). Anglo Texans are concentrated as

TABLE 2–5 Occupational Categories Among Texas's Major Ethnic Groups: 1980

Occupation	%	Anglo	Black	Spanish Origin	State Total
Managerial and professional		26	12	11	22
Technical, sales, and administrative support		34	24	25	31
Service		8	25	16	12
Farming, forestry, and fishing		3	2	4	3
Precision production and craft		15	11	17	15
Operators, fabricators, and laborers		13	27	27	17

Source: Census of Population (1983).

disproportionately in the "higher" jobs as ethnic minority Texans are in the "lower" ones. These occupational differences should not be surprising, of course, in light of the educational and income differences that separate these groups.

CONCLUSION

This chapter has shown how Texas's original population and settlement patterns—based on rural and small-town settlements regionalized by ethnicity—have been substantially reshaped in recent decades. What has emerged in their place is a rapidly growing, highly urbanized, increasingly big-city and suburbanized population with considerable representation of all three of the state's ethnic groups in the major urban centers. This shift means that the state's political problems are increasingly those of growing big cities, as well. The remainder of this book will be concerned, therefore, with the efforts of Texas state and local governments in grappling with these problems.

The breakdown of the old cultural regions, the emerging ethnic diversity of the state's urban areas, and the rapidly increasing minority population also mean that Texans will be forced more and more to confront the differing interests and political demands of these different ethnic groups. Simple proximity, along with the heightened political activity of blacks and Mexican-Americans of recent years, will force such confrontations. One could also argue that this new situation offers an opportunity for cultural interchange and the sharing of cultural values in ways that might benefit the entire state—socially, economically, and politically. Yet this chapter has also described how the state's major ethnic minority groups occupy positions in Texas society far different from that of the Anglo majority. In the minority groups education levels are lower and occupational opportunities considerably more limited. As a result, the income and wealth of black and Mexican-American Texans are also lower, and the levels of poverty are much higher than among Anglos. These circumstances are, of course, considerable obstacles the state will have to overcome if it is to profit from the cultural diversity within its boundaries.

REFERENCES

Barrera, Mario. 1979. *Race and Class in the Southwest*. South Bend, Ind.: University of Notre Dame Press.

Benjamin, Gilbert G. 1908. "Germans in Texas." *German American Annals* 10 (January–February): 325–340.

Benjamin, Gilbert G. 1909. "Germans in Texas, Continued." *German American Annals* 11 (January–February): 103–113.

Census of Population, 1980, General Social and Economic Characteristics: Texas, PC 80-1-C45. 1983. Washington, D.C.: Bureau of the Census, U.S. Department of Commerce.

Census of Population, 1980, Supplementary Report: Standard Metropolitan Statistical Areas and Standard Consolidated Statistical Areas, PC 80-SI-5. 1981. Washington, D.C.: Bureau of the Census, U.S. Department of Commerce.

Fogel, Walter. 1979. *Mexican Illegal Workers in the United States.* Los Angeles: University of California, Institute of Industrial Relations.

Haar, Charles M. 1974. *The President's Task Force on Suburban Problems.* Cambridge, Mass.: Ballinger.

Hawley, Ellis W. 1979. "The Politics of the Mexican Labor Issue, 1950–1965." In George C. Kiser and Martha Woody Kiser (eds.), *Mexican Workers in the United States.* Albuquerque: University of New Mexico Press.

Jordan, Terry G. 1967. "The Imprint of the Upper and Lower South on Mid-Nineteenth-Century Texas." *Annals of the Association of American Geographers* 57 (December): 667–690.

Jordan, Terry G. 1969. "Population Origins in Texas, 1850." *Geographical Review* 59 (January): 83–103.

King, Allan G., and Rizo-Patron, Jorge. 1978. "Counting Illegal Mexican Aliens: Myths and Misperceptions." *Texas Business Review* 52 (June): 101–105.

Kiser, George C., and Silverman, David. 1979. "Mexican Repatriation During the Great Depression." In George C. Kiser and Martha Woody Kiser (eds.), *Mexican Workers in the United States.* Albuquerque: University of New Mexico Press.

McWilliams, Cary. 1949. *North from Mexico: The Spanish-Speaking People of the United States.* Philadelphia: Lippincott.

Meinig, D. W. 1969. *Imperial Texas: An Interpretive Essay in Cultural Geography.* Austin: University of Texas Press.

Muller, Peter O. 1981. *Contemporary Suburban America.* Englewood Cliffs, N.J.: Prentice-Hall.

Schwaller, Bob. 1983. "Here's Johnny-Come-Lately." *Texas Business* 7 (March): 24–29.

Yuen, Mike. 1987. "New Arrivals in Texas a Rarity." *Houston Post* (December 6): 1B.

TEXAS PEOPLE

3

THE POLITICAL
CULTURES OF TEXAS

This chapter will examine in some detail the attitudes of Texans toward their state and local government and the sources of their views. These attitudes have considerable relevance for several aspects of political life in the state—such as the goals Texans want their state to pursue through its policies and the extent to which individual citizens, themselves, wish to participate in government. Because of the many ties between these political attitudes and other aspects of state government, there will be occasion in later chapters to refer back to the material presented here. At the same time some of the most important sources of these political attitudes are the cultural and social roots of the groups whose migrations to Texas were chronicled in the last chapter.

Popular literature and journalism have for many years indulged in a caricature of the culture of the "typical Texan." Anyone who has lived for even a short period in the state has surely been exposed to this literature. In fact, the portrait of the typical Texan that arises in these writings is probably well known across the United States. D. W. Meinig (1969:89) has aptly summarized this portrait in the following way:

> The Texan emerges from these investigations as one who is strongly individualistic and egalitarian, optimistic and utilitarian, volatile and chauvinistic, ethnocentric and provincial, as one still very much under the influence of older rural and moral traditions. Such a person regards government as no more than a necessary evil, distrusts even informal social action as a threat to his independence, and accepts violence as an appropriate solution to certain kinds of personal and group problems. Material wealth is much admired for its own sake but industriousness has no particular value. . . . There is an easy acceptance of equality among one's own kind but a rigid sense of superiority over other local peoples, and a deep suspicion of outsiders as threats to the social order. The narrow moral strictures of Protestant fundamentalism are accepted as an ideal moral code but certain covert violations are routinely tolerated (such as the use of hard liquor).

No doubt some elements of this portrait are accurate for *some* Texans. Yet this superficial portrait, like all stereotypes, glosses over some important aspects of Texans' social and political attitudes. Above all, this stereotype obscures the existence of several distinct attitudes toward government that are held by different groups of Texans. To offer a more sophisticated rendering of political attitudes in the state and to take account of these different outlooks, we must turn to scholarship in political science on the subject of *political culture*.

THE CONCEPT OF POLITICAL CULTURE

Political culture refers generally to people's attitudes toward and evaluations of their government. But political culture has several specific components, as well.[1] Citizens' attitudes under this broad heading, for example, can be divided into three main issues:

1. The appropriate role of government in society—in other words, what should and should not be the responsibilities of government?

2. The appropriate role for the individual citizen in relation to government—in other words, what constitutes a citizen's duty, what level of participation in politics is to be expected of the average citizen, and what individual goals as opposed to community goals should the citizen pursue by means of that participation?

3. Evaluations of existing government institutions and officeholders—in other words, to what extent are these institutions and officials seen as legitimate expressions of the public will, to what extent are they held in esteem or mistrust, and to what extent are the policies enacted by these institutions thought to be satisfactory responses to citizens' desires?

At this point one might ask whether Texans do not simply hold the same political culture attitudes—under the three subheadings listed above—in which all American citizens are presumably instructed as a normal course of their civic education. In other words, do they not hold the attitudes presented in "civics text" discussions of such matters? There are several problems with such an assumption, but there is an element of truth in it, as well. Both the strength and the difficulty of this assumption can be illustrated by reference to the actual content of some typical civic education materials.

One civics textbook that has been widely used in Texas's secondary schools is *American Civics* by William H. Hartley and William S. Vincent. Hartley and Vincent (1970:38) offer an excellent example of typical civics text instruction in political culture values in the following passage:

> *American citizens have many responsibilities as citizens of our great nation. These responsibilities are the "shoulds" of citizenship. That is, American citizens are not required by law to carry out these actions. However, most Americans accept these*

responsibilities and carry them out because they are so important to the success of our government. These are the most important responsibilities of American citizens:

1. *American citizens should vote in all elections.*

2. *American citizens should be interested in their government and study the activities of their government.*

3. *American citizens should tell their representatives what they think about the problems facing their government.*

4. *American citizens should be willing to support the work of their government either as members of a political party or as independent voters.*

All Americans have probably been exposed to instruction like this at one time or another in their elementary and secondary education. Indeed, such teaching is one source from which Americans derive their political attitudes. Nevertheless, the actual political attitudes and behavior of many citizens deviate considerably from the standards posed for the "good citizen." Many Americans at times question whether their individual participation will in fact influence the government and therefore may come to question the importance of participation at all. At times some Americans may also doubt that the public interest is being served by this or that government official, agency, or policy. Such doubts can also lead to disillusionment with politics and with individual participation. Clearly not all citizens use their opportunities to participate in government—even by exercising the simple right to vote.

These observations should remind us of many instances in which our own political attitudes or those of our friends have differed sharply from the models established in civics texts. Yet these differences should not be surprising, for there are many sources from which one might learn such attitudes. The principal source is, of course, the family. At a young age children learn from their parents trust or cynicism or indifference toward government. Moreover, parents offer models for their children in their participation as well as their attitudes. Whether they vote regularly, participate actively in a political party or nonpartisan political organization, or otherwise involve themselves in political affairs will be a cue for their children's eventual political behavior.

And, of course, a person's own political experiences and evaluations become important as he or she matures. Personal experiences may reinforce what was learned from one's parents, or they may lead a person to question the value of that learning. Even the political environment in which a person lives will provide many subtle, or even not so subtle, influences that shape attitudes and behavior. The "organizational climate" of politics, particularly that managed by political parties, may offer strong encouragement or discouragement for citizen participation. In other words, the political party system of a state— whether it is a one-party or two-party state, whether parties encourage public participation, and so on—will influence individual attitudes and behavior.

Even such mundane matters as the voter registration system and the election calendar may influence citizen participation in politics. State laws regulating voter registration can depress voter turnout. (Chapter 5 will discuss several ways in which that was precisely the case in Texas as recently as the

1970s.) The timing of elections can affect voter turnout, too. If, for example, state and local elections are held simultaneously with national elections, such as that for the presidency and Congress, voting turnout will be especially high. If state elections are held at odd, separate times turnout will be considerably lower.

Finally, elected public officials can shape public attitudes and participation in government by controlling political party activities, setting particular voting requirements and election calendars, and simply encouraging and promoting democratic procedures. Public officials can set examples for individual involvement with government, and they can carry out their public duties in such a way as to inspire public trust and high esteem for government.

It should now be clear that political culture is shaped by many forces. Thus we should not be surprised to learn that individuals may differ in their specific values because of their unique family socialization and personal political experiences. At the same time it should not be surprising to learn that large numbers of citizens share many general political values. Indeed, we should expect to discover many such shared values because different people and their families share common social and cultural experiences and live in the same political environment.

We have seen, then, what political culture is and why both shared and differing political culture values might coexist in the same state. Yet the importance of this topic—not only for the study of Texas government but for any other level of government—has not been directly addressed. Before we turn to the specifics of political culture in Texas, however, one might ask why anyone should care about this subject in the first place. Is this merely an arcane topic of interest only to scholarly political scientists? Or is there some broader significance? There is, in fact, a strong case for the latter position. The importance of political culture can be illustrated by means of two examples.

One aspect of political culture involves citizen preferences about the role of government in society. That phrase may sound vague, yet it actually addresses quite down-to-earth matters. What Texan has not heard (or even participated in) arguments about whether the state is sufficiently generous—or, conversely, is too generous—toward the poor in its welfare programs? Likewise, arguments about such diverse subjects as capital punishment (whether the state is justified in taking human life as punishment for crime), the state's commitment to secondary and higher education, whether the state should outlaw abortions, or whether there should be a state "equal rights" amendment for women's rights—to name a few recent controversies—all revolve around different citizens' evaluations of the appropriate roles for government in society. This dimension of political culture is directly relevant to many deeply felt concerns of Texans about their government.

Similarly, another aspect of political culture involves citizen evaluations of what their personal role in politics should be. Presumably, therefore, once we know about the political culture of a state we will understand how active the citizens *as a collectivity* are likely to be in political affairs. More specifically, we might hope that a knowledge of political culture would help explain why only 47 percent of voting-age Texans turned out to vote in the 1984 presidential election while many states registered turnout in the range of 65 to 79 percent. The "civics text" explanation for democratic politics regards citizen partici- pation as fundamental to the healthy operation of the nation's government. While we may doubt whether the majority of citizens in any state fulfill the dictates of "civics text" democracy, surely a low-participation state like Texas is fundamentally different from high-participation states where 65 percent or more of the citizens regularly turn out to vote.

Political culture actually concerns many important everyday matters of politics and government. Political science research on this topic, it should also be noted, has uncovered a variety of other connections between state political cultures and the political attitudes, political behavior, and public policies of individual states (Kincaid, 1982). To understand how these connections arise, we must consider, first, the origin and dispersion of political cultures in the United States and then, second, the specific political cultures of Texas. The plural *cultures* is used quite explicitly with regard to Texas, as well, for there are several distinct political cultures in the state.

THE PATTERNING OF AMERICA'S POLITICAL CULTURES

One of the most compelling explanations for the patterning of American polit- ical cultures is that developed by Daniel Elazar in a book entitled *American Federalism: A View from the States* (1984). To explain the relevance of Elazar's view for Texas it is necessary first to recapitulate his general thesis. Elazar argues that three political subcultures have been of primary importance in the historical development of the United States. Each of these three subcultures was rooted in a particular social and geographic setting early in the history of the nation, and each has spread westward across the entire United States in a distinct pattern. Thus today each state is dominated by one or a particular combination of these subcultures. Evidence about the character of the domi- nant subculture can be found in several aspects of each state's politics.

The first of these subcultures Elazar calls *moralistic*. According to this perspective, government is one means to attaining the good society for all citizens. As Elazar (1984:117) says of this subculture: "Good government, then, is measured by the degree to which it promotes the public good and in terms of the honesty, selflessness, and commitment of those who govern." Politics is seen here as a concern of all citizens; thus public participation in politics is strongly encouraged.

Moralists hold that government service is public service, and it is expected that public officeholders will not derive special personal benefit from their positions. Political parties, while they might be seen as useful organizational devices, also are viewed distinctively here. Parties are merely means to larger and more important ends, such as the public good. Party loyalty, therefore, is less important than are those larger, more important ends.

Elazar traces the roots of the moralistic culture to the Puritans who, in settling New England, attempted to establish as religiously pure a society as possible. And government played an integral part in that effort. The descen- dants of the Puritans, coupled with groups of later-arriving Scandinavian immigrants with similar religious attitudes, pushed this cultural variant into the Great Lakes region of the Midwest and on into Minnesota, Iowa, Oregon, and Washington. Other carriers of this culture settled in smaller numbers in several other Midwestern and Western states.

The second subculture Elazar calls *individualistic*. In this culture citizens desire only a government with limited functions and goals. This is the laissez faire concept of government: Government should perform only limited and essential functions so that individuals can pursue their private (mostly economic) interests unfettered by governmental constraints. At the same time government is itself thought to be closely intertwined with this orientation toward individual economic opportunity. As Elazar (1984:115) expresses it:

> *The individualistic culture holds politics to be just another means by which individuals may improve themselves socially and economically. In this sense politics is a "business" like any other that competes for talent and offers rewards to those who take it up as a career. Those individuals who choose political careers may rise by providing the governmental services demanded of them and, in return, may expect to be adequately compensated for their efforts.*

In this conception, political officeholding becomes a "profession" that is better left to the specialists. Thus in a sense mass participation is not strongly encouraged. Yet on certain occasions participation and partisan loyalty are highly encouraged. Commensurate with this businesslike character of politics, political parties become instruments of the "business." In the fashion most commonly associated with "machine politics," government officeholders depend upon well-organized parties to maintain their positions and the rewards derived therefrom. There are those at every echelon in the party who are kept loyal by a flow of material rewards.

The individualistic subculture arose principally from the Germanic and non-Puritanical English settlers of the Middle Atlantic states. Among these groups the pursuit of individual opportunity was placed ahead of communal goals. The descendants of these settlers eventually moved westward in relatively distinct patterns just as those of the original moralistic Americans did. Elazar traces the movement of these people into a number of Midwestern and Western states, more or less within the middle third of the nation.

The final subculture in this scheme is *traditionalistic*. In the original version of this culture, government was just one element of an elitist, precommercial, social order. And government's principal function was to preserve that social order and the relative positions of different classes in it. Not surprisingly, then, politics is dominated by representatives of the social elite. In fact, Elazar argues that participation by nonelites is actually discouraged. It should also be obvious that the elite will benefit directly from politics as long as their position at the top of the social order is maintained. It is this *class* basis for the distribution of government benefits that distinguishes this system from the individualistic one.

As a final point of comparison, political parties are held to be of much less importance in this traditionalistic culture than in either of the first two. The principal reason is because parties are by their design intended to strengthen ties between the mass of citizens and their leaders. But those ties can come to imply that leaders should respond to grass-roots party members as well as to the elite. Equally unfortunate from the perspective of traditionalistic elites is the fact that political parties customarily encourage certain forms of mass political participation. Thus the development of parties is discouraged in this culture by the solidarity of the elite's interests and their fear of mass participation.

The traditionalistic culture originated, as one might have guessed by now, in the plantation-based agricultural system of the Old South. The plantation system created a social and political elite that was already well formed by the time of the American Revolution (and which in fact furnished many of the distinguished leaders of that revolution). Elazar argues that although this culture was most fully developed in Virginia and South Carolina, other Southern states were important homes for it, as well. Migration from these states carried this traditionalistic culture across all of the Southern states that eventually formed the Confederacy and into a few other Midwestern and Southwestern areas.

To illustrate the effects of migration patterns on the dispersion of these subcultures across the country, figure 3–1 reproduces Elazar's geographic representation of the locales of settlement of major streams of migrants. This figure indicates the principal regional homes of each of the three subcultures and a general sense of their separate streams of westward movement. One can also see that Texas is shown as having representatives of both the traditionalistic and the individualistic cultures. Elazar argues that the state's overall culture is a mixture of these two with the traditionalistic element predominating. This conclusion should not be surprising, of course, for the last chapter showed that the major source of migrants to Texas was the Southern United States, home of the traditionalistic culture.

Elazar recognizes that these subcultural values will be subject to some modification over time. One of the most important forces for such change has been continued migration among the various states. Certainly migration has been responsible for some mixing of cultures, and Texas, as we will see, has been particularly influenced in this fashion in recent decades. Another force for change has been internal evolution *within* certain subcultures. Of particular relevance to Texas is Elazar's argument (1984:133) that the traditionalistic culture has "tended to adopt individualistic elements as its traditional social bases have eroded." This kind of change may have reversed the relative importance of these two subcultural variants in the state.

POLITICAL SUBCULTURES IN TEXAS

With a general notion of political culture in mind, it is now possible to explore the specific political cultures of Texas in more detail. We will begin by focusing on the subcultures of the several groups of migrants that have come together to form the current residents of the state. First we will examine the *original* cultural pattern of each group; then we will consider what forces might be changing the composition of that original set of values.

Southern Anglo-Americans

Elazar argues that many of the Southern Americans who migrated to Texas brought with them the traditionalistic culture. Thus they would have upheld a preponderant role in political life for elite citizens, a modest role for the average citizen, and the maintenance of the social status quo (running from the elite at the top to slaves at the bottom) as principal objectives of government. The fact that Texas followed the rest of the South into the Confederacy is important evidence for this conclusion. Likewise, one can find other evidence (particularly relevant to the idea that government should preserve the social status quo) in both the role played later in Texas politics by landed elites and by the state's post-Reconstruction efforts to keep blacks in an inferior social and political position despite their emancipation.

Yet a more detailed study of Southern migration to Texas suggests that the individualistic culture may have been of near-equal importance from the earliest days of Anglo settlement. The last chapter discussed Jordan's research on the Upper South and Lower South origins of early Texans. (Recall that in 1850 these two regions had provided almost equal numbers of Texans.) According to Elazar's scheme, the Lower South migrants came from areas dominated by the plantation system and sustained by a traditionalistic culture. Much of the Upper South, on the other hand, had been settled by individualistic groups of Germans, Scotch-Irish, and non-Puritanical English (Jordan, 1967:667–668), many of whom had come from Pennsylvania, a core individualistic state according to Elazar.

The large numbers of Upper South immigrants in Texas surely gave prominence to individualistic values. Few of these people owned slaves, their support for secession in 1860 was mixed, and hence their commitment to a rigid social order must have been weaker than that of their fellow Texans from the Lower South. Thus there has long been an important strain of the individualistic culture in the state.

There are other reasons, as well, why one might question the primacy of the traditionalistic culture in Texas. Certainly the plantation system, and hence the landed social and political elite that was based on it, was ill developed in Texas compared to the Lower South where it had originated (Kousser, 1974:196). As Seymour V. Connor (1971:182–185) has written about 1860, "there were very few actual plantations in Texas and very few large slaveholders." While slaveholders might have been disproportionately influential in both social and political life, there had simply not been sufficient time for the traditionalistic elite to become as entrenched in Texas as elsewhere in the Lower South.

Also moderating the influence of the traditionalistic culture were the frontier spirit associated with the settling of much of the state and the individualistic ethic in the early years of the cattle and oil and gas industries in Texas (Meinig, 1969:86–89). Both these developments helped create new elites with social and political values somewhat different from the more rigid ones of the traditionalistic Lower South group. Surely these newer elites were the prototypes for much of the myth of the "typical Texan."

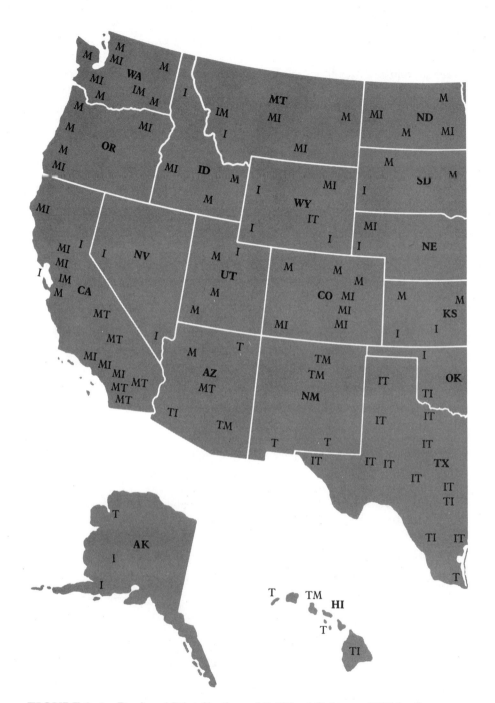

FIGURE 3–1   Regional Distribution of Political Cultures Within the States

Source: Elazar (1984: 124–125)

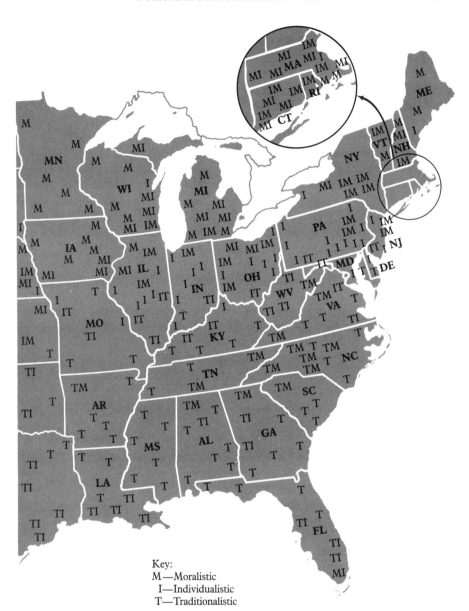

Key:
M—Moralistic
I—Individualistic
T—Traditionalistic

In summary, one could argue that the political culture of Anglo Texans has from the first been a mixture of traditionalism and individualism. At the same time there are several reasons for believing that the individualistic culture has been growing in influence over the history of the state, perhaps becoming the more important of the two. Yet there remained one component of the traditional culture that was accepted by the majority of all Anglo Texans well into the mid-twentieth century: the belief that those at the bottom of the social order, blacks and Mexican-Americans, should be kept at the bottom. As we will see, this fact had important consequences for the political cultures of these minority groups.

Mexican-Americans

What was the original political culture of Texans of Mexican origin? That culture, we must conclude, was a particular version of traditionalism. Mexican society in the early 1800s—whether in central Mexico or in the region that is now part of Texas—was a preindustrial one dominated by a landed elite and characterized by several features similar to those of the traditionalistic culture of the Lower South. (Mexico, however, did not tolerate a literal slave system among its indigenous people.)

Elements of this traditionalistic Mexican culture have remained vital well into the late twentieth century—both in Mexico itself (Almond and Verba, 1963:414–428; Needler, 1982:54–56) and in the United States among Mexican-Americans (Cortes, 1980:714–715; Vigil, 1977:75). A great respect for the extended family is one of those elements. A rigid role structure for family members, such as husbands and wives, is a second element. Adherence to the Catholic faith is a third. Indeed, some scholars have argued that Mexican culture still places considerably more emphasis on family and religious values than on individual achievement (Vigil, 1977:75–76).

There is evidence for the evolution and, at times, erosion of all these original values (Cortes, 1980:715; Moore and Pachon, 1976:137–138); yet they remain key cultural guideposts for many Mexican-Americans. And these values are traditionalistic in Elazar's terms. To the extent they remain important in the Mexican-American community, so does the traditionalistic political culture, even if to a lesser degree than in past generations. Indeed, some argue there is even a force that regularly strengthens these values. That force is the steady influx of illegal immigrants from Mexico, many of whom hold these values with particular tenacity (Cortes, 1980:715).

We must not, however, fall into the intellectual trap that ensnared many early students of Mexican-American culture. That trap was the conclusion that it was indigenous values *alone* which kept such people in a traditionalistic or "backward" role in American society (Garcia and de la Garza, 1977:34–39). There are undoubtedly traditionalistic elements in traditional Mexican-American culture. Yet the political and social culture of this group has been shaped, in part, by their experiences with Anglo society—and the characteristic features of those experiences have surely been Anglo discrimination, segregation, and exploitation of ethnic minorities.

From their earliest encounters, Anglo and Mexican relations were characterized by such features (DeLeon, 1983). Revolution from Mexico, the takeover of Mexican-owned lands by Anglos, and a variety of discriminatory public laws and private practices institutionalized the subordinate social position of Mexican-origin Texans well before the turn of the twentieth century. The demand for agricultural and other low-skilled workers throughout this century also reinforced a lower-class character and purely instrumental value for the Mexican people in the minds of many Anglos.

Thus Mexican-American Texans came to be locked into the lowest level of American society. They were physically encapsulated in rural or urban barrios separated from the areas where Anglos lived. They were denied equal educational opportunities which, along with Anglo prejudice, ensured they would remain in the lowest occupational positions in the society. In many cases they were co-opted into migratory work patterns and forced to follow the sequence of agricultural harvests from place to place or even state to state.

In light of these circumstances, one might conclude along with many students of Mexican-American culture that continued reliance on the extended family, maintenance of the Spanish language, and several other traditionalistic cultural features are *defensive* reactions to Anglo prejudice and discrimination (Moore and Pachon, 1976:135–136). Thus it can be argued that the character of ethnic relations is responsible for some portion of Mexican-American social and political values.

Blacks

The original culture of Texas blacks was traditionalistic, as well. Moreover, this was the culture of those who were literally enslaved at the bottom of a traditional society. Blacks were members by force, in other words, of the traditionalistic society of Lower South Anglo immigrants to Texas. In pre-Reconstruction Texas blacks had no political role and no reason to hope that they might rise from their slavery.

The Civil War and Reconstruction eradicated for a time the bonds of law and slavery that kept blacks in this subordinate role. Yet the end of Reconstruction and the return of state government to the hands of the Anglo majority eventually resulted in a reinstitution of many legal barriers to black social and political freedom. By means of the poll tax and the white primary and by violence and intimidation, black Texans were effectively precluded from political participation by about 1910 (Key, 1949:535). Further, the "Jim Crow" laws passed between 1870 and 1910 established racial segregation in schools, public transportation, and virtually all other public and private settings (Woodward, 1974; Kousser, 1974:196–209; Rice, 1971:140–150). These sanctions were, of course, only a few of the many prejudicial and discriminatory barriers erected by Anglo society against blacks. Many of these practices, one must remember, remained in force well into the 1960s.

The intent of these post-Reconstruction laws and practices was to keep blacks, like Mexican-Americans, at the bottom of Texas society. Slavery had been abolished, but in many practical ways the black's role was unchanged. In terms of social and economic advancement the results—as the prior chapter explained in detail—have been to restrict severely the educational, occupational, and material opportunities of black Texans. In political terms the result was to teach blacks that they could have no active role in the governing of the state (Meier and Rudnick, 1966:171–172). They could be, at best, mere *subjects* of the system; they would never be able to influence its leaders or policies by their own participation (Almond and Verba, 1963:214–229).

In short, while the Anglo society was evolving around them, blacks as well as Mexican-Americans were for many years kept in a social and political position much like that of their original, traditionalistic culture of pre-Civil War days. There could be only limited exposure to individualistic values because most avenues of opportunity were closed to blacks. And moralistic political notions must have been foreign to a people who could see the immorality of the way they were treated—even by government itself—simply because of the color of their skin.

As a result of their inferior social position, blacks came to adopt some of the same defensive cultural responses followed by Mexican-Americans. Similarly, some old traditionalistic values remained vital because of the limited opportunities for cultural evolution. Religion and the church played a particularly important role in the black community (Smallwood, 1981:96–108). To some extent, religion served a "compensatory" function, helping blacks suffer the burdens of the present world because of what the good Christian could expect in the next one (Sernett, 1975:165–167; Raboteau, 1978:305–314). There even developed in many black communities distinctive language dialects—in part because of the limited social interactions allowed outside the community and in part for defense against a hostile outside world (Baugh, 1983).

For most blacks as well as Mexican-Americans, therefore, the traditionalistic political culture endured well into the mid-twentieth century. But much of that culture was also a product of the inferior and circumscribed social roles forced on both minority groups.

Germans

Although the cultural distinctiveness of German Texans has declined considerably, a few remarks about the original political culture of that group are instructive for comparative purposes. The German immigrants to Texas in the nineteenth century had many of the characteristics Elazar identified with the individualistic culture. Their motivations to immigrate in the first instance centered around the search for individual opportunity in America (Geue and Geue, 1966:1–18; Jordan, 1966:38–59). Like many other individualistic groups, the Germans might best have been called ambivalent toward the issues of slavery and secession in the 1860s. The fact that few Germans owned slaves has been interpreted by some historians as a moral indictment of the institution on their part. Terry G. Jordan (1966:106–111), however, makes a good case for the argument that, much like the Upper South Anglo immigrants, it was also a lack of sufficient capital that accounted for the limited slaveholdings of this group.

Secession was itself controversial among German Texans. Some German areas voted heavily against it in the public referenda on the subject, while others voted in favor. Apparently a number of motives, some having nothing to do with slavery or states' rights (Jordan, 1966:182–185), account for these differences. Yet the Germans were labeled by many Anglos as abolitionists, and the resultant anti-German sentiment, along with the distinctiveness of German political views on some other issues, resulted in relatively high support for the Republican party among these people well into the mid-twentieth century (Key, 1949:275–276). With the decline of this group's cultural distinctiveness, however, their political distinctiveness has faded as well. Today the traditionally German regions of the state are no longer particularly notable for their Republicanism, and one must suppose that other aspects of this once-distinctive political culture are also vanishing.

CONCLUSION

This chapter has demonstrated how the political culture of Texas is in some senses a mixed one, much as the previous chapter showed the diversity of the population itself. In spite of this diversity, however, there have long existed key elements in the political culture of the state. At least from the time of the Republic of Texas, the culture of the state has been dominated by a mix of traditionalistic and individualistic values originating primarily in the two subregions of the American South. In that period and well into the middle of the twentieth century the political cultures of the state's two largest ethnic minority groups were also traditionalistic. These two cultures integrated relatively smoothly, therefore, with the dominant Anglo culture and found their places at the bottom of society set aside for blacks and Mexican-Americans.

The primary elements of this cultural mix were such that most Texans surely expected traditionalistic and individualistic elites to benefit personally from politics. Because both elite groups were politically conservative in most ways, government itself was expected to play a limited role in social and economic life. These limitations on government can still be seen today: in the relatively modest state regulatory structure, in the wide latitude given private business to pursue "individualistic" goals, and in the state's low taxes. These aspects of contemporary state government—all derived in part, once again, from the original political culture of the state—will be the subjects of extended discussion in later chapters.

In other areas, however, both the traditionalistic and individualistic elite groups expected government to be quite active—largely where such action might be necessary to preserve the power of the elites. In chapter 5 we will see, as examples, how a number of political party activities and public laws were developed to restrict popular participation in Texas government. Similarly, some government agencies have worked diligently to serve the interests of elite-dominated sectors of the economy.

Moralistic elements, as Elazar defined them, have from the first been rare in Texas's political culture. Instead, the goals of government were framed in terms of traditionalistic or individualistic objectives. And corruption, just like legal opportunities to derive personal benefit from government service, was easily tolerated and even, at times, envied.

Along with Elazar, we must recognize, however, that powerful, if slowly acting, forces are changing Texas's political culture. Industrialization and "postindustrial" development as described in chapter 1 are two of those forces. Moreover, urbanization has been a related agent of cultural change. Together, industrialization and urbanization have brought diversity to the Texas scene while creating new social and economic elites at the same time. In the process they have eroded the power base of the rural and traditionalistic elite.

A second force for change has been the steady in-migration of non-Southern Americans throughout the 1900s but particularly in the era of Sunbelt migration. Many of these immigrants came from moralistic states or from places where individualism was not associated with ethnic prejudice as has been the case in Texas. Surely these migrants will themselves experience some degree of assimilation to Texas values. But—recalling from the previous chapter the relatively well-educated, career-oriented, and professional character of most of these people—they may also be articulate and capable advocates of values new to Texas. One might speculate that, just as has been the case with industrialization and urbanization, these new migrants will weaken the remnants of traditionalistic culture, will strengthen the individualistic culture, and will be at least a modest force for the inclusion of more moralistic values in the state.

Finally, there are significant changes under way within the state's ethnic minority cultures. The eradication of all the legal obstacles and many of the social barriers to their participation in society at large—which will be explained in detail in the next chapter—has created a sense of opportunity among blacks and Mexican-Americans. Not only may they now participate in political life, but the political consciousness of both groups has been stirred to seize this new opportunity. One of the resultant cultural changes within these groups has been the adoption of certain individualistic values now that social and economic opportunities have been opened to them. Another change has been the adoption of certain moralistic values, at least in the sense that blacks and Mexican-Americans have come to demand government action to redress past inequities against their people. Thus progress among Texas's ethnic minorities will undoubtedly erode even further the traditionalistic culture, expand the individualistic culture, and emphasize certain moralistic concerns.

Political culture helps determine the structure of government, the character of government policies, and the nature of public participation in government. While this chapter has indicated some of the ways Texas government is linked with the state's political culture, many details of that linkage must await the extended discussions of later chapters. The principal conclusions of this chapter, however, constitute underlying themes we will encounter again and again throughout the book.

NOTES

1. The political science literature offers several distinct though interrelated approaches for the study of political culture. Representative discussions of this subject are provided in Almond and Verba (1963), Devine (1972), Elazar (1984), and Kincaid (1982). The empirical research on America's political cultures and their relation to other aspects of political life is reviewed in Kincaid (1982) and Savage (1981).

REFERENCES

Almond, Gabriel, and Verba, Sidney. 1963. *The Civic Culture*. Princeton: Princeton University Press.

Baugh, John. 1983. *Black Street Speech*. Austin: University of Texas Press.

Connor, Seymour V. 1971. *Texas: A History*. New York: Thomas Crowell.

Cortes, Carlos E. 1980. "Mexicans." In *Harvard Encyclopedia of American Ethnic Groups*. Cambridge, Mass.: Belknap Press of Harvard University.

DeLeon, Arnoldo. 1983. *They Called Them Greasers: Anglo Attitudes Toward Mexicans in Texas, 1821–1900*. Austin: University of Texas Press.

Devine, Donald J. 1972. *The Political Culture of the United States*. Boston: Little, Brown.

Elazar, Daniel J. 1984. *American Federalism: A View from the States*. 3rd ed. New York: Harper & Row.

Garcia, F. Chris, and de la Garza, Rudolph O. 1977. *The Chicano Political Experience*. North Scituate, Mass.: Duxbury.

Geue, Chester William, and Geue, Ethel Handel. 1966. *A New Land Beckoned: German Immigrants to Texas, 1844–1847*. Waco: Texian Press.

Hartley, William H., and Vincent, William S. 1970. *American Civics*. Rev. ed. New York: Harcourt Brace Jovanovich.

Jordan, Terry G. 1966. *German Seed in Texas Soil: Immigrant Farmers in Nineteenth Century Texas*. Austin: University of Texas Press.

Jordan, Terry G. 1967. "The Imprint of the Upper and Lower South on Mid-Nineteenth Century Texas." *Annals of the Association of American Geographers* 57 (December):667–690.

Key, V. O. 1949. *Southern Politics*. New York: Vintage Books.

Kincaid, John. 1982. "Introduction." In John Kincaid (ed.), *Political Culture, Public Policy, and the American States*. Philadelphia: Institute for the Study of Human Issues.

Kousser, J. Morgan. 1974. *The Shaping of Southern Politics: Suffrage Restriction and the Establishment of the One Party South, 1880–1910*. New Haven: Yale University Press.

Meier, August, and Rudnick, Elliott M. 1966. *From Plantation to Ghetto*. New York: Hill & Wang.

Meinig, D. W. 1969. *Imperial Texas: An Interpretative Essay in Cultural Geography*. Austin: University of Texas Press.

Moore, Joan W., and Pachon, Harry. 1976. *Mexican Americans*. 2nd ed. Englewood Cliffs, N.J.: Prentice-Hall.

Needler, Martin C. 1982. *Mexican Politics*. New York:Praeger.

Raboteau, Albert J. 1978. *Slave Religion*. New York: Oxford University Press.

Rice, Lawrence D. 1971. *The Negro in Texas, 1874–1900*. Baton Rouge: Louisiana State University Press.

Savage, Robert L. 1981. "Looking for Political Subcultures: A Critique of the Rummage-Sale Approach." *Western Political Quarterly* 34 (June):331–336.

Sernett, Milton C. 1975. *Black Religion and American Evangelicalism*. Metuchen, N.J.: Scarecrow Press.

Smallwood, James M. 1981. *Time of Hope, Time of Despair: Black Texans During Reconstruction*. Port Washington, N.Y.: Kennikat Press.

Vigil, Maurilio. 1977. *Chicano Politics*. Washington, D.C.: University Press of America.

Woodward, C. Vann. 1974. *The Strange Career of Jim Crow*. 3rd ed. London: Oxford University Press.

THE TEXAS
CONSTITUTION

B ecause the Texas Constitution was written in 1875 and ratified by the
voters in 1876, its history is intimately connected with that of some of
the other events of the nineteenth century discussed in earlier chapters.
Of particular relevance is the development of the political culture of the state.
The constitution was heavily influenced by some of the same forces that shaped
the political culture. In consequence, the material in this chapter builds upon
themes developed in previous ones.

At the same time this chapter looks forward to the remainder of the book.
Certainly the constitution has significantly influenced the character of Texas's
contemporary political institutions and policies. One might think of the constitution as an "architectural blueprint" for the state government. Yet it is not
simply the organizational form and arrangement of these structures that is
prefigured in the constitution. For the constitution is the source of several
strong-points and an even larger number of weaknesses inherent in the current
governmental system.

THE FUNCTIONS OF STATE CONSTITUTIONS

State constitutions are the fundamental laws of states. That is, they define the
powers of the state government, how those powers will be exercised, and how
they will be limited—subject only to the constraints on state governments
imposed by the United States Constitution, the supreme law of the nation. The
U.S. Constitution allots to the states what powers will be theirs—the so-called
residual powers left to the states after the enumeration of the federal government's own responsibilities largely in Article I of the federal document. Moreover, amendments to the U.S. Constitution have often defined more clearly or
limited more narrowly the powers of the states. The Fifteenth Amendment,
for example, made unconstitutional any state government actions that discriminated on the basis of race.

Decisions of the U.S. Supreme Court in the twentieth century have often served both to extend and to limit the powers of state governments, regardless of their own original constitutional provisions. Extensions of state power have arisen particularly from Supreme Court acceptance of new state regulatory powers. Limitations on state power have arisen most typically through court decisions on individual rights. An example of the latter kind of decision, discussed at length in chapter 5, was the Supreme Court decision in 1966 outlawing poll taxes as a requirement for voting in state or local elections. Examples like this illustrate that state constitutions exist within a larger legal environment delimited by the U.S. Constitution and that this environment and the limitations it imposes are dynamic and not static.

The principal manner in which state constitutions go about detailing the powers of the state government and how they will be exercised is by describing the various institutions of that government. Like the U.S. Constitution, state constitutions divide governmental power among an executive, a legislative, and a judicial branch. The major institutions within each branch are described at least in outline, and the powers and limitations of each branch along with the "checks and balances" among the branches are typically listed. Furthermore, state constitutions list the qualifications for serving in elected and certain appointed offices of government.

State constitutions also describe the political rights of their citizens. Most of these rights are set forth within a Bill of Rights section much like the Bill of Rights embodied in the first ten amendments to the U.S. Constitution. State Bills of Rights were necessary at one time because the individual rights guarantees of the federal document originally limited only the federal government itself. Several decisions of the U.S. Supreme Court, particularly in the twentieth century, have extended the provisions of the federal Bill of Rights and all of the U.S. Constitution to the states. Yet in recent years state Bills of Rights have taken on new significance, because they sometimes have been provided with individual rights guarantees that are more extensive than those in the U.S. Constitution. For example, Texas voters approved in 1972 an amendment to the state constitution that ensures one's civil rights regardless of "sex, race, color, creed, or national origin." The federal constitution, on the other hand, still has no so-called equal rights amendment (ERA) with reference to sex.

Another important component of every constitution is its provision for an amendment process. The principal means of amending the Texas constitution is by ratification by the state's voters of proposals initiated in the state legislature, as was the case with the ERA amendment noted above. Some of the shortcomings of the constitution to be described have made the amendment process—along with its own limitations—of considerable importance to Texas government.

There is one other typical characteristic of state constitutions—one that many critics believe to constitute a significant shortcoming. Most state constitutions include a large number of details about how state and local governments should operate, how specific government policies should be executed, and what limits are to be imposed on the government. In short, one might say that most state constitutions contain a considerable amount of "ordinary" instead of constitutional law—that is, they contain many provisions that should be in statutory law passed by the state legislature.

Including what one might call ordinary law in the constitution might not seem a bad idea at the time constitutions are written, because such provisions might accord well with public preferences and the political needs of the time. Yet fifty or a hundred years later, when public preferences and political needs may have changed dramatically, such detailed provisions may impose unfortunate limitations on government. Such has surely come to be the case in Texas.

One can get a vivid indication of just how common and how extensive are the ordinary law provisions of state constitutions simply by comparing their length to that of the U.S. Constitution. The latter document is about 8,700 words in length. The average state constitution is today about 26,000 words long, even though in recent decades some of the longest ones have been revised and shortened considerably. The Texas Constitution is, at 62,000 words, the fourth longest in the nation. Even before examining the text of the Texas Constitution, we can be sure we will find there many detailed, ordinary law provisions simply because of its length.

More than ordinary law provisions account for the length of the Texas Constitution, however. There is also quite an excess of unnecessary language. An illustration of the wordy, duplicative, obsolete language of the constitution can be drawn from any of the several proposed revisions of that document that have rewritten it into a simplified, reorganized, and nonredundant form—without any change in its substantive meaning. One such effort, prepared for the Constitutional Convention of 1974, reduced the then 52,000-word constitution to only 17,000 words and, again, with no change in its substance (Searcy, 1973).

Another sign of the character of the Texas document is revealed by the fact that it is not reprinted in the back of this book. Almost every text on the American national government routinely includes the U.S. Constitution as an appendix. That custom is practical because of the document's brevity. But it is also academically sensible because virtually every line of the U.S. Constitution is meaningful and profitable for study or discussion. Such is hardly the case with the Texas Constitution. Not only is it exceedingly long, it is also boring and extraordinarily tedious to read because of the amount of detail it includes. A brief perusal of the Texas Constitution would satisfy any reader that printing the full text of the document could be of only very modest profit either to the student of Texas government or to a publisher. (The most convenient source for the complete text of the state constitution is probably any biennial edition of *The Texas Almanac*, which is usually available in the reference section of public and university libraries.)

HISTORY OF THE TEXAS CONSTITUTION

Having outlined the principal purposes of state constitutions and having, as well, begun to hint at the character of the Texas Constitution, it is time to consider the latter document in some detail. First we will discuss the architects who drew up this blueprint for state government, the forces influencing their decisions, and the goals they envisioned for the government they were designing.

The present constitution of Texas is the fifth one under which the government has operated since the admission of Texas to the United States in 1845. The first of these constitutions was the one adopted in 1845 with statehood; the second was the 1861 Confederacy constitution; the third was that of 1866 when Texas reentered the Union; the fourth was adopted in 1869 under the relatively stringent Reconstruction criteria imposed on the state by the Radical Republicans in the U.S. Congress. The present document was written by a constitutional convention in 1875 and ratified by the voters in 1876 at the end of the Reconstruction era. The political and social circumstances of those times are clearly evident in the instrument.

The Intent of the 1875 Convention

The authors of the present state constitution were influenced by three principal forces arising out of the social, political, and economic circumstances of the times. These separate forces all worked, however, to influence the constitutional convention toward the same general architectural design for state government.

Ending Reconstruction Government   The first of these forces was a passionate desire to rid the state of all traces of the Reconstruction-era government. The white majority had found the entire period of Reconstruction a hardship, but the time between 1867 and 1874 had been especially unfortunate in the minds of most Texans. In the latter years the U.S. Congress imposed particularly explicit and, to most Southerners, harsh conditions for an eventual unqualified return to the full rights of statehood and the end of Reconstruction. The state was occupied and its government controlled by the Union army for much of this period. Blacks were enfranchised and given new social privileges. Many of the state's military officers and government officials from the Confederacy were initially imprisoned and then later, after they were freed, barred from holding public office or even voting.

To make matters worse, the civilian government of the state was run during the Radical Reconstruction period by a coalition of carpetbaggers, blacks, and long-time Union sympathizers. These people had reshaped the government— by means of the constitution of 1869 and by the so-called "Obnoxious Acts" passed in 1870 and 1871 by the state legislature—to ensure that they could dominate the political life of the state. In the 1869 constitution there was created a strong, central state government. The governor was given broad appointive and policy supervision powers. Local government was closely controlled by the central state authorities. Elections were carefully monitored and, some said, manipulated by the Republican regime. And taxes were considered by the white majority to be onerously high.

Moreover, certain policies of the Republican government came in for strong criticism. Much of the tax money went to support an extensive system of public elementary and secondary education that many Texans thought unnecessary and far too expensive. To promote the construction of a railroad system in the state, the Republicans had subsidized the rail companies—first with state bonds and later, when the bonds were declared unconstitutional by the state supreme court, with large gifts of state land based on mileage of rail lines completed. As a consequence of these and other expansive public policies, both the tax rate and the indebtedness of the state ballooned under Radical Republican rule.

While historical scholarship is divided on the validity of some of the criticisms of the Republican regime, those complaints were strongly felt by many Texans at the time (Connor, 1971:221–223). One might say, in the language of political culture, that the majority of Texans believed many of these activities to fall outside the "appropriate role of government in society." Additionally, of course, they believed that the government was controlled by people who did not represent the popular will. To use another political culture idea, the regime was seen as illegitimate.

In the minds of most Texans the low point of the Reconstruction era was the administration of Governor E. J. Davis in 1870–1874. Davis was the only Republican governor to serve under the 1869 constitution, and most Texans at the time would have probably said he used it to the fullest. Along with his Republican state legislature, Davis passed what his Democratic critics called the Obnoxious Acts, giving more executive powers to the governor along with control of a state militia to back them up. Davis used these powers vigorously, even going so far as to declare martial law at four different times in different counties in the state. The state militia itself was widely criticized as being more lawless than law enforcing. The spending proclivities of the Republican regime were also highly criticized. Davis's administration was responsible for much of the public debt incurred during Reconstruction, a point that can be well illustrated by a single comparison (Miller, 1910:107): The 1866 constitution had limited the public debt to $100,000; but under the 1869 constitution and in the years of Davis's governorship alone, the public debt of the state grew by more than $2,100,000!

Yet Davis and the Republicans' control of government was short-lived. They would have been opposed by most Texans regardless of their policies, but the policies they did pursue brought a fierce public reaction. In 1872, at the first election after Davis had assumed office, the Democratic party regained control of the state legislature. The new legislature quickly set about repealing the Obnoxious Acts and as much else of the Republican program as they could. Then, in the 1874 election, the Democrats won control of the governorship. The consolidated Democratic government, after struggling with the task of rewriting the constitution itself, called for a constitutional convention to do the job. Thus the first and most forceful motivation for a new constitution was to eradicate the Radical Republican blueprint from state government.

Responding to Farmers' Demands A second factor in the 1875 convention was the political agenda of the Patrons of Husbandry, better known as the Grange. The Grange was a society intended to further the interests of farmers and the rural population. Members of the Grange made up almost half of the constitutional convention, and they had some well-developed ideas about how state government should be structured and how it should be limited. The Grangers wanted to create a very economical government that could exist on a modest tax structure. At the same time they wanted the government to limit the powers of the banks and the railroads, the two private-sector institutions that most affected the livelihood of farmers. In consequence of these motivations, the Grange amounted to a second force at the convention that was pressing for a reduction in the power and expense of state government. Furthermore, just as the typical convention delegate wanted to eradicate the power of outside political forces over Texas government, the Grangers wanted to weaken the power of outside *economic* forces over their lives.

Responding to the Panic of 1873   The third force influencing the convention was the state of the economy. Texas, like the rest of the nation, was still in the midst of the Panic of 1873, an economic depression that began in the fall of 1873 and lasted well into 1878. In many respects this depression was just as severe as that of the 1930s. These similarities extended beyond economics to political life. Joseph Schumpeter (1939:337) has described the similarity between these two depressions: "The political complement was also similar—Granger movement, agitation for inflation, strikes, and riots being, if we take account of differences in social and political structure and attitude, more than fair counterparts of corresponding phenomena in the recent instance." The economic hardships brought on by the depression constituted, then, a third force encouraging economy in government.

When the convention met in 1875, these three motivations were foremost in the minds of the delegates. And the delegates themselves were representative of these interests. Some ninety delegates (three from each state Senate district) had been chosen to attend the convention by public election. Of these, seventy-five were Democrats broadly representative of the anti-Reconstruction majority of the population. Almost half the delegates were also members of the Grange, and thus there were more farmers than any other occupational group.

The New Blueprint for Government

It is not difficult, then, to imagine the kind of government that was designed by the 1875 convention. A principal motivation was for economy in government. To achieve that aim, the convention authored a host of changes from the existing system. These changes included reducing the salaries of state officials and legislators (including a 20 percent reduction in the governor's salary), stipulating biennial instead of annual legislative sessions, reducing the government's tax revenues and its spending commitments for "big ticket" items like public education, and fixing a constitutional limit of $200,000 on the state's debt.

One of the major changes was that in public education. The 1869 constitution had provided for a free public school system with a compulsory attendance law and sufficient taxes to support the system. But public education was opposed by the Grangers, and the new constitution provided for a quite limited and ill-funded school system with no compulsory attendance. These changes were controversial even at the time. Indeed, a Galveston newspaper commented that "the convention, after decreeing universal suffrage, had now also decreed universal ignorance" (McKay, 1942:105).

A second motivation was to weaken the central state government—in part as a reaction to Davis's autocratic governorship and in part to return more control to the public at large and to local officials. To achieve this aim, several state agencies were disbanded and control of their functions was returned to local officials. The governor was stripped of most of his appointive powers, and most of the offices he had previously filled by appointment were made elective. The terms of office of state officials were also shortened to keep those who were elected "closer to the people."

Finally, to ensure that their objectives would be met, the delegates went into considerable detail in the written text of the constitution to lay out explicitly their ideas for a limited government. Thus the great length of the document is in good part a product of their zealous effort to weaken the government and to make their intentions clear and unalterable.

Some of this explicitness served to fulfill the positive functions desired by the convention. The constitution writers ensured, for example, that the state would have the power to regulate banks, railroads, and private corporations (in accordance with Granger fears about those institutions). Similarly, a prohibition against "usurious interest" was included along with one to prevent the forced sale of a homestead for nonpayment of debts. The latter provisions also came from the Granger agenda.

Ratification of the New Constitution

When the draft of the new constitution was submitted to the voters in early 1876, it was approved by more than a 2-to-1 margin (with 136,606 votes for and 56,652 against). That the document would be accepted by the voters was surely to be expected. There was too much hatred for the Radical Republican government on too many different issues for the outcome to have been otherwise. Nevertheless, not all parts of the state favored the new document. Voter support was highest in the rural and small-town areas, and the proposed constitution was actually defeated in several of the bigger cities. Its rejection in urban areas was in some sense prophetic, because the limitations of the new constitution have probably come to affect urban areas most particularly. It is in the cities, after all, that nineteenth-century agrarian strictures against big government are felt most acutely by twentieth-century Texans.

REVISING THE CONSTITUTION

Agitation to revise all or part of the Texas Constitution began virtually from its initial ratification. At three different times this agitation has produced proposals from the state legislature for constitutional conventions to rewrite the document completely. The first proposal in 1917 died because of the opposition of Governor "Farmer Jim" Ferguson. A second in 1919 was defeated by the voters. The third, providing for a constitutional convention made up of state legislators to meet in the summer of 1974, was accepted by the voters in 1972.

The 1974 convention proved, however, to be at least a partial failure. Its committees produced a draft constitution, but full agreement on the draft could not be reached before the term of the session ended. Perhaps out of some embarrassment over this failure, the legislature took up this draft when it met in regular session the succeeding year. With a few modifications, the draft constitution was presented to the voters as a set of eight amendments that would have completely revised the 1876 document.

The proposed new constitution also drew considerable support from key groups in the state. As one observer has put it:

> The document drew the support of the deans of all eight Texas law schools, over 200 professors of government at 31 colleges and universities throughout the state, most of the state's major newspapers, respected authorities on constitutions, and a number of civic and political groups, among which were the Texas Municipal League (for the local government article), the Texas State Bar (for the judiciary article), the Junior Bar (for all the proposals), the AFL–CIO (for six of the eight proposals), the National Farmers Union, Common Cause, the League of Women Voters, the Texas Association of College Teachers, the American Association of University Women, and the American Association of Retired Persons. Barbara Jordan, Leon Jaworski, and Robert Strauss were among the well-known Texans in favor of the document. [May, 1977:66]

In spite of this impressive support, all eight amendments were soundly defeated by the voters in 1975. Postelection analyses suggested that the revision effort failed for three major reasons:

1. Lack of vigorous political leadership in support of the new document
2. The outright opposition of the governor to some of its provisions
3. The poor organization of the pro-ratification election campaign.

The constitution also provides for a process of item-by-item amendment of its separate provisions, and this second route has been used quite often since 1876. The amendment process requires that, first, proposed amendments must be initiated in the Texas Legislature and must be approved by two-thirds of the full membership of each house. Once so approved, a proposed amendment must be accepted by a majority of those voters actually voting in a general or special election. (The legislature decides which upcoming election ballot will present a given amendment.)

The use of the amendment process gives testimony to the extent to which the constitution gets further and further out of date with the passage of time. Over the life of the constitution, as table 4–1 illustrates, more and more amendments have been both proposed and adopted. In recent years Texas voters have been confronted with an election on proposed amendments almost annually, and it has not been uncommon for there to be eight to a dozen amendments on a given year's ballot.

TABLE 4–1 Constitutional Amendments Proposed and Adopted: 1880–1987

Decade	Number Proposed by Legislature	Number Adopted by Election
1880s	13	5
1890s	16	11
1900s	20	10
1910s	32	9
1920s	25	12
1930s	46	34
1940s	39	25
1950s	39	33
1960s	81	55
1970s	74	40
1980–1987	83	69
Totals	468	303

Sources: Marburger (1956:52–54); May (1972:21); and *The Texas Almanac* (various years).

Another perspective from which to consider the frequency of constitutional amendment in Texas is to compare it with the history of the U.S. Constitution. The latter document, ratified in 1789, is almost twice as old as the Texas Constitution. But the U.S. Constitution has only 26 amendments in comparison to the more than 300 that have been added to the Texas Constitution. Moreover, the first ten amendments to the U.S. Constitution (the Bill of Rights) were added together virtually as part of the process of original ratification. Thus one could fairly argue that the U.S. Constitution has been amended only sixteen times after the original agreement on it.

Voter Turnout for Constitutional Amendments

Proposed constitutional amendments generate little voter interest. When such proposals have been presented to the voters in *special elections* (when no races for public office are on the ballot), they have typically drawn less than 20 percent of the registered voters (and much less of the voting-age population) to the polls. Table 4–2, which is based on the most comprehensive study of

TABLE 4–2 Voter Turnout for Constitutional Amendments: 1951–1972

Type of Election	Registered Voters Voting (%)
Special elections (only constitutional amendments on the ballot)	16
Off-year general elections	39
General elections in presidential election years	51

Source: May (1972:20).

amendment voting available, indicates that turnout is higher in nonpresidential and particularly presidential *general election* years but only because of the pull of the latter races on the ballot.

Recent elections provide good illustrations of the low interest stimulated by constitutional amendments. In November 1984, Texas voters were presented eight constitutional amendments on the same ballot headed by the U.S. presidential election. About 5.3 million Texans, or 47 percent of the voting-age population, voted in the presidential race. Yet only slightly over 4 million of those same voters, or about 36 percent of the voting-age population, were interested enough or persistent enough to vote even on the constitutional amendment that got the most votes. The least "interesting" amendment drew the votes of about 3.3 million Texans, or 30 percent of those of voting age. The preceding figures alone indicate the low salience of amendments. Even further evidence for that low salience, however, is indicated by the fact that in 1985, on a special election ballot, just under a million Texans voted on the amendment that received the most votes on that date. This poor showing came even though a number of municipalities were also holding their own local elections at the same time, providing additional inducements for voter turnout.

Regardless of the kind of election, one must admit that voter interest in these amendments is not impressive. Furthermore, in low-turnout elections, those who do vote are particularly unrepresentative of the population at large. Those who go to the polls on these occasions are, on average, of much higher education, income, and social status, and they are much more likely to be Anglos. Thus it is a biased sample of Texans who will make decisions about most constitutional amendments.

Results of the Amendment Process

The most obvious result of the process outlined above is that it allows only piecemeal revision of a constitution that most observers would agree is in need of a comprehensive reworking. The passage of time alone has supplied evidence to support this conclusion—evidence from the increasing frequency with which the legislature must turn to the amendment process. But other factors exacerbate the problems with the constitution and even encourage more amendments which, in turn, make it a worse legal instrument.

On the one hand, the original detail in the constitution merely breeds more detail. The constitution's conservative authors went to great lengths to ensure that the government would be constrained in its powers. The result has been that succeeding generations of state leaders—largely a conservative lot, as well—have had to go back time and again to revise first this passage, then another, and yet another in an attempt to keep a highly specific legal instrument relevant to the governmental needs of a changing society.

Nor is detail the only problem. From the first, the constitution has been a place to secure one's special economic or political interests. Farmers and local businessmen in competition with out-of-state interests had their special concerns guaranteed in the constitution as it was first written. Yet these groups only served as examples to others who desired the same security. If one's position could be safeguarded by the constitution, instead of by mere statutory law subject to change by any session of the legislature, it would be far more likely to remain secure. Even a casual examination of the constitution reveals a multitude of such provisions. How else can we explain the presence in the document of the outlines of the state employee retirement system, the Veterans' Land Board, the Veterans' Land Fund, the State Medical Education fund to pay scholarships for medical students who promise to practice medicine in rural areas, or the section empowering the legislature to provide financial assistance to the survivors of law enforcement officers killed on duty? How else, as well, might we explain the special tax treatment in the constitution given to agricultural property including livestock and poultry and to solar and wind-powered energy devices? Regardless of how worthy such provisions might be, their presence in the constitution instead of in statutory law must be attributed to efforts by special interest groups to seek maximum security for state policies that favor their economic or social positions.

Another way we can evaluate the results of the amendment process is to ask what kinds of proposals have been more and less likely to receive majority voter support at elections. An analysis of this question for amendments voted on in the 1951–1972 period concluded that voters were mostly negative toward changes in the basic structure of the state government, toward state finance proposals, and toward tax exemptions for special groups. On the other hand, amendments in the fields of education, welfare, health care, and for revising the judicial branch were more likely to be successful (May, 1972:24–25). The fate of more recent proposed amendments appears to have been generally similar—with one qualification.

One can make a strong argument that the amendment process amounts to nothing more than a crapshoot for the average voter. That is, it amounts simply to a toss of the dice when it comes to the true intent of any given amendment and how the voter should vote on that proposal. Some of the time, but not all of the time, the special interest proposals are obvious. Some of the time, but again not all of the time, the proposals that relate to serious governmental problems are obvious. Yet rarely, even in the two preceding instances, is either the significance of the amendment itself or the importance of accepting or rejecting it made clear to the average voter.

This problem certainly arises, in part, because most voters do little to acquaint themselves with proposed constitutional amendments. After all, re-call how little interest such amendments stimulate among voters. In part the problem also arises because these issues typically receive little media coverage. Unlike races for elected office, there is not a human candidate to make speeches, kiss babies, and otherwise communicate directly with voters about these matters. Instead, voters must confront *ideas* in constitutional amendments—and that, for many people, is a far more difficult task.

The state government itself, however, does a poor job of educating the voter with regard to constitutional amendments. Proposed amendments must be published before the election in major newspapers in the state, along with a brief explanatory statement of the intent of the proposed change. The amendment and the explanation for it must also be posted in each county courthouse thirty days prior to the election. The legislature even publishes "pro and con" pamphlets analyzing upcoming amendments; yet one can be certain that none of these three "advertising" methods reaches very many voters. Surely many voters give their only detailed attention to proposed amendments when they first encounter them on an election ballot.

But consider what a voter will see on such a ballot. The proposed amendments appear last on the ballot and then only in simplified form. As examples of this procedure, the eight amendments presented to the voters in the 1984 election are reproduced in figure 4–1 exactly as they appeared on the ballot. While the average voter might fairly surmise that abolishing the office of county treasurer in Bexar and Collin counties is a minor change of no great significance to state government at large, that voter would have no clue to the importance of the other seven amendments based on what appears on the ballot alone. Thus voting on such amendments often becomes a toss of the dice for the average voter.

The problem is not simply that it is difficult to separate the trivial from the consequential in the amendment process. Under a constitution like the present one in Texas, the process is inevitably cluttered with both trivial and highly detailed proposed amendments. Special interest proposals will continue to appear from time to time. A highly detailed—and outdated to boot—constitution that has traditionally been seen as a haven for special interests breeds just such a process. Yet some proposed amendments appear trivial because they are intended to revise trivial-looking but often quite important elements of the constitution. Others, perhaps the majority, will appear highly narrow in their application, again because they are intended to alter specific provisions.

On the last point one might once again profitably compare the Texas Constitution with that of the federal government. Because it is written in broad rather than specific language, the U.S. Constitution invites amendments of considerable breadth. The implications of such amendments, while they still can be controversial, are more obvious and of more obvious importance than those that are typically put forward to revise a constitution like that of Texas. Recall, as just one example, the recent and long-running national debate engendered by the proposed Equal Rights Amendment to the U.S. Constitution. Both supporters and opponents of this proposal agree that it would have considerable importance if adopted (although they disagree on what all its consequences would be). Because people recognized how important the proposal was, it received considerable public debate and comment. We should not be surprised, in contrast, to see how little public attention is given to proposed amendments to the Texas Constitution. Nor should we be surprised to see that, in consequence, truly important amendments and even the general importance of the amendment process itself get little public recognition in Texas.

IMPACT OF THE 1876 CONSTITUTION

The 1876 constitution affects the present structure and operations of government in Texas in several ways. To summarize the most important of these

GENERAL ELECTION — ELECCION GENERAL
HARRIS COUNTY, TEXAS — CONDADO DE HARRIS, TEXAS
NOVEMBER 6, 1984 — 6 DE NOVIEMBRE DE 1984
Page 10

PROPOSITION NO. 1 — PROPOSICION NÚM. 1

"The constitutional amendment to provide state banks the same rights and privileges as national banks."

(La enmienda a la constitución para darles a los bancos estatales los mismos derechos y privilegios que tienen los bancos nacionales.)

| FOR (A FAVOR DE) | 239 |
| AGAINST (EN CONTRA DE) | 240 |

PROPOSITION NO. 2 — PROPOSICION NÚM. 2

"The constitutional amendment to create from general revenue a special higher education assistance fund for construction and related activities, to restructure the permanent university fund, and to increase the number of institutions eligible to benefit from the permanent university fund."

(La enmienda a la constitución para establecer de ingresos generales un fondo especial de apoyo para la instrucción superior, para propósitos de construcción y otras actividades respecto a eso, para reorganizar el fondo de universidad permanente, y para aumentar el número de instituciones elegibles para aprovecharse del fondo de universidad permanente.)

| FOR (A FAVOR DE) | 249 |
| AGAINST (EN CONTRA DE) | 250 |

PROPOSITION NO. 3 — PROPOSICION NÚM. 3

"The constitutional amendment authorizing the legislature to provide for payment of assistance to the surviving dependent parents, brothers, and sisters of certain public servants killed while on duty."

(La enmienda a la constitución autorizando a la legislatura para suministrar un pago para asistir a los sobreviviente padres, hermanos, y hermanas que dependen de ciertos empleados públicos que hayan muerto durante el cumplimiento de sus obligaciones oficiales.)

| FOR (A FAVOR DE) | 258 |
| AGAINST (EN CONTRA DE) | 259 |

Page 10

GENERAL ELECTION — ELECCION GENERAL
HARRIS COUNTY, TEXAS — CONDADO DE HARRIS, TEXAS
NOVEMBER 6, 1984 — 6 DE NOVIEMBRE DE 1984
Page 11

PROPOSITION NO. 4 — PROPOSICION NÚM. 4

"The constitutional amendment to abolish the office of county treasurer in Bexar and Collin counties."

(La enmienda a la constitución para eliminar el puesto oficial de tesorero del condado en los condados de Bexar y Collin.)

| FOR (A FAVOR DE) | 265 |
| AGAINST (EN CONTRA DE) | 266 |

PROPOSITION NO. 5 — PROPOSICION NÚM. 5

"The constitutional amendment authorizing the state senate to fill a vacancy in the office of lieutenant governor."

(La enmienda a la constitución autorizando al senado del estado para llenar una vacancia en el puesto oficial de vicegobernador.)

| FOR (A FAVOR DE) | 272 |
| AGAINST (EN CONTRA DE) | 273 |

PROPOSITION NO. 6 — PROPOSICION NÚM. 6

"The constitutional amendment to permit use of public funds and credit for payment of premiums on certain insurance contracts of mutual insurance companies authorized to do business in Texas."

(La enmienda a la constitución para permitir el uso de fondos y crédito público para pagar las primas sobre ciertos contratos de seguro perteneciendo a pagar las primas sobre ciertos contratos de seguro mutuales autorizadas para manejar negocios en Texas.)

| FOR (A FAVOR DE) | 280 |
| AGAINST (EN CONTRA DE) | 281 |

Page 11

GENERAL ELECTION — ELECCION GENERAL
HARRIS COUNTY, TEXAS — CONDADO DE HARRIS, TEXAS
NOVEMBER 6, 1984 — 6 DE NOVIEMBRE DE 1984
Page 12

PROPOSITION NO. 7 — PROPOSICION NÚM. 7

"The constitutional amendment relating to the membership of the State Commission on Judicial Conduct and the authority and procedure to discipline active judges, certain retired and former judges, and certain masters and magistrates of the courts."

(La enmienda a la constitución perteneciendo a los miembros de la Comisión Estatal Sobre Conducta Judicial y a la autoridad y procedimiento de castigar a jueces activos, a ciertos jueces retirados y a los que fueron jueces, y a ciertos asesores del juez y magistrados de las cortes.)

| FOR (A FAVOR DE) | 294 |
| AGAINST (EN CONTRA DE) | 295 |

PROPOSITION NO. 8 — PROPOSICION NÚM. 8

"The constitutional amendment to provide a per diem for members of the legislature equal to the maximum daily amount allowed by federal laws as a deduction for ordinary and necessary business expenses incurred by a state legislator."

(La enmienda a la constitución para disponer una asignación por día para miembros de la legislatura igual a la cantidad máxima que se permite diariamente por ley federal como un descuento de los gastos de negocio ordinarios y necesarios incurridos por un legislador del estado.)

| FOR (A FAVOR DE) | 303 |
| AGAINST (EN CONTRA DE) | 304 |

Page 12

FIGURE 4–1 Constitutional Amendments on the Election Ballot: 1984

effects, we can draw upon an excellent series of monographs on this topic prepared by the Institute of Urban Studies at the University of Houston during the early 1970s—the period of the last effort at comprehensive constitutional reform in the state. By summarizing the institute's conclusions with regard to the major institutional divisions of state government, we can appreciate the contemporary impact of the 1876 constitution.

Impact on the Chief Executive

Because of significant constitutional limitations on the governor's powers in all the separate areas of traditional executive responsibility (management of the executive branch, control of policy implementation, and the recommending of new policies and programs to name only a few), the Texas governor is one of the weakest in the nation. The governor's power is constrained in several ways: by a "plural executive" at the highest level of state government where the governor is only one of several officeholders elected separately by the people; by an executive system that relies heavily on agencies run by multimember boards or commissions that are independent of gubernatorial control; and by limited power vis-à-vis the legislature, thus greatly restricting the governor from fulfilling the role of "chief legislator" that has been assumed by many other state governors. Fred Gantt (1973:7) has summarized this situation with a little assistance from someone who knew the office firsthand: "Because of the governor's largely ceremonial role, in which genuine authority is held to a minimum and in which his discretionary powers are carefully limited, former Governor Allan Shivers commented, 'the Governor of Texas is something of a paper tiger.' "

Impact on the Executive Branch

Apart from its effect of weakening the governor's power, the plural executive diffuses responsibility for the operation of government in such a way that it is difficult for the public to know who or what agency is responsible for different government functions. Moreover, the plural executive leads to an inflexible executive structure (because it is established in the constitution and not in statutory law) that is difficult to change in response to shifting demands on government (Redford, 1973:73).

The use of the board and commission structure has similar effects. This structure, according to Redford (1973:88), "fragments administration and insulates it from the influence of the governor in coordination, planning, and budgeting. The constitutional status of boards, either by their creation or by reference to their duties or structure, reduces the ability of the legislature to reorganize the administrative structure of the state."

The management of the state's financial matters—whether in budget planning or implementation, in financial reporting, or in the procurement of goods and services—is similarly diffused among a large number of agencies and officials, once again making coordination, control, and even timely implementation difficult (Redford, 1973:97–113).

Impact on the Legislature

The consequences of the present constitutional system for the legislative branch are aptly summarized in the following passage:

> *Burdened by restrictions from another century, the legislature has been unable fully to rise to the challenges of the present age. Instead of a strong legislature performing its intended tasks of representation, problem resolution, and oversight of state administration, the present legislature is a weakened body constrained by limited biennial sessions, by its inability to review vetoed bills after adjournment, or to call itself into special sessions. These limitations together with constitutionally pre-scribed salaries, a senate presided over by an executive branch official (i.e., the lieutenant governor), and a multitude of constitutional legislation . . . restrict the legislature's power to act effectively. [Citizens Conference on State Legislatures, 1973:55]*

Impact on the Judiciary

Like the other branches of government, the court system suffers from having too much of its structure specified in the constitution, making it very difficult to adapt with changing demands on the system. The arrangement of Texas courts—with many different kinds and levels of courts, often with overlapping jurisdiction—is also unnecessarily inflexible, complicated, and confusing (Smith, 1973).

CONCLUSION

This chapter has surveyed the origin of the Texas Constitution and the con-sequences of that document for contemporary state government. Based on the foregoing survey, it would be fair to say that in some senses the authors of the constitution were highly successful. Their desire, in particular, to create a low-cost, weak, highly fragmented governmental system has certainly stood the test of time, for such is the kind of government Texas still has today. But that original conception of what government should do and how it should be organized was itself a product of an entirely different social and political era. Texas was then a predominately agrarian state with none of the social and economic problems of a large population, high urbanization, and extensive industrialization.

The constitution's authors could not foresee the serious problems that confront Texans today. Nor could they have anticipated that in the twentieth century Americans would radically shift their thinking about government's responsibility for such problems. In the mid-nineteenth century most Ameri-cans still held a laissez faire conception of the "appropriate role of government in society" (to recall a phrase from the vocabulary of political culture). That is, Americans wanted government to be responsible only for a limited set of social, economic, and security matters.

Yet in the twentieth century Americans have developed a desire for a quite different sort of government. Political scientists refer to this second type of government as the *positive state*—in other words, one where government has substantial responsibility for social and economic welfare. Even the majority of political conservatives today agree that government should have a major role in alleviating poverty in the nation, in guiding the economy to minimize recessions and prevent depressions, in promoting long-term economic growth, in reducing some of the most dangerous hazards of modern life like substantial crime and pollution, and in meeting the special needs of large urban areas in such matters as transportation, education, housing, and health care. Liberals and conservatives may disagree about exactly how big is government's responsibility in these areas, and they may disagree about the practical policies that ought to be pursued to achieve specific goals; yet they agree that government has a role in such matters and that role exists because the American public has demanded it.

What should now be clear, however, is that the Texas Constitution weakens the state's ability to respond to this new role of positive government. The authors of the constitution produced a document well suited to their interests and their times but very difficult to revise as public interests change. It is the citizens of the state, of course, who suffer most in this situation. State government is ill-equipped to do what Texans expect of it for these reasons. Elected officials are hampered in meeting public demands or even in carrying out some of their own too-ambitious campaign promises. Texas government is forced to practice a false economy, where simple cheapness is substituted for efficiency and effectiveness.

For these reasons the state of Texas is in dire need of a complete constitutional overhaul. Yet there is no serious interest in such change among the state's elected officials at present—and their leadership is certainly crucial as the 1972–1975 revision effort demonstrated. There is little likelihood, on the other hand, of strong public demand for such a change because the average Texan seriously misunderstands the character and impact of the state's constitution.

Many of the state's traditional elite groups—in other words, those groups whose interests were long ago provided for in the constitution and who therefore fear any change in the status quo—have promulgated the myth that changing the constitution would destroy the conservative and low-cost character of state government. There is no reason, however, why the state cannot have a modern, though still conservative, governmental system that is capable of addressing the state's problems both energetically and efficiently. In a state such as Texas with a predominately conservative citizenry, it is hard to imagine the public accepting anything but a relatively conservative government.

Yet the average Texan has apparently accepted the myth that constitutional change will bring higher taxes, governmental waste, and too-liberal policies. So far, no public official has come forward to explain the inaccuracy in this myth or the real implications of the current constitution as opposed to alternative arrangements. Thus Texans may well have to live with their present constitution quite a bit longer, getting, as a result, far less and far worse government than they expect or deserve.

REFERENCES

Citizens Conference on State Legislatures. 1973. *The Impact of the Texas Constitution on the Legislature.* Houston: Institute for Urban Studies, University of Houston.

Connor, Seymour V. 1971. *Texas: A History.* New York: Thomas Y. Crowell.

Gantt, Fred Jr. 1973. *The Impact of the Texas Constitution on the Executive.* Houston: Institute for Urban Studies, University of Houston.

Marburger, Harold J. 1956. *Amendments to the Texas Constitution of 1876.* Austin: Legislative Reference Division of the Texas State Library.

May, Janice C. 1972. *Amending the Texas Constitution, 1951–1972.* Austin: Texas Advisory Commission on Intergovernmental Relations.

May, Janice C. 1977. "Texas Constitutional Revision: Lessons and Laments." *National Civic Review* 66 (February):64–69.

McKay, Seth Shepard. 1942. *Seven Decades of the Texas Constitution of 1876.* Lubbock: Texas Technological College.

Miller, E. T. 1910. "State Finances of Texas During Reconstruction." *Quarterly of the Texas State Historical Association* 14 (October):87–112.

Redford, Emmette S. 1973. *The Texas Constitution: Its Impact on the Administration.* Houston: Institute for Urban Studies, University of Houston.

Schumpeter, Joseph A. 1939. *Business Cycles.* Vol. 1. New York: McGraw-Hill.

Searcy, Seth S. 1973. *The Texas Constitution: A Reorganization and Simplification Without Substantive Change.* Austin: Texas Advisory Commission on Intergovernmental Affairs.

Smith, Allen E. 1973. *The Impact of the Texas Constitution on the Judiciary.* Houston: Institute for Urban Studies, University of Houston.

TEXAS
ECONOMY

ELECTIONS IN TEXAS

Political Parties, Public Participation,

and Interest Groups

E lections in democratic societies are intended to be occasions where citizens choose their public leaders and endorse the policies of one set of candidates. Public participation in the election system—and the extent of the *opportunities* for participation—are therefore important concerns of this chapter. Political parties and interest groups, on the other hand, play a major role in shaping the opportunities for public participation. Yet the influence of political parties and the *system* of parties may not be well understood by the average citizen. Most Texans, for example, are well aware of the historical dominance of state politics by the Democratic party. Probably few citizens, however, are aware of the consequences of the one-party system for public participation and democracy in Texas.

To understand these consequences, we must first consider the role that political parties are supposed to play in a democratic society. Then, to assess the roles of elections and parties in Texas politics, we will review the origin of the one-party system in Texas and discover how that system has shaped opportunities for public participation in politics.

Interest groups, too, are centrally involved in the election process, and their involvement is shaped by the character of the political party system as well. It is useful to look at the role and importance of interest groups in Texas politics in conjunction with the election system. Yet interest groups work to achieve their goals at several points in the political process. To understand their role at these other points, we will consider interest group activities again in the chapters on the legislature, the executive branch, and metropolitan politics.

POLITICAL PARTIES IN A DEMOCRATIC POLITY

To understand the place of political parties in a democratic nation, we might begin with a definition of what a political party is. In the words of a leading scholar on the subject, a political party in a democratic nation "is a group that competes for political power by contesting elections, mobilizing social interests, and advocating ideological positions, thus linking citizens to the political system" (Eldersveld, 1982:11). Beyond that simple definition there are, as Eldersveld points out, some particularly notable aspects to the role of political parties. One of these aspects concerns their importance in the process of representing citizen preferences for government policy. The large size of modern nations like the United States precludes the operation of so-called direct democracy—all Americans cannot, for example, sit down together in the same room and take a majority vote on issues of government policy. But political parties make possible indirect public control of government.

Parties help maintain public control because, first, it is expected that competing parties will form to represent at least the major political interests among all those that inevitably arise in a large, diverse society such as the United States (or the state of Texas). These different parties will then develop proposed government policies intended to satisfy the interests of their followers. Second, parties actually ensure public control, according to this argument, because the leaders of rival parties must vie for majority public support in elections to be able to control the government and transform their proposals into actuality. Periodically, as well, the leaders of the party in power must stand for reelection where their efforts at policymaking can be reevaluated by the voters (and attacked by the leaders of the "out" party).

Parties perform many specific political functions in the process of carrying out the general ones just mentioned. They help recruit candidates for office. They assist candidates in organizing and paying for their campaigns. They run much of the apparatus of public elections. They attempt to negotiate with a variety of groups in society to create majority coalitions around mutual political objectives. Once a party controls a major part of the government (either by controlling the White House, the Congress, the governor's office, the state legislature, or the like), its elected leaders work together to shape public policy. But the two most critical functions of parties, and the ones that lie behind all these day-to-day political activities, are to represent the major political interests in the society and to provide a means for public control of at least the principal features of government policy.

FORMATION OF THE ONE-PARTY SYSTEM IN TEXAS

The Democratic party's dominance of Texas politics, still evident in the state today, was a product of the last twenty-five years of the nineteenth century, a period of intense political controversy and party competition. It is true that the Democrats had come to dominate the state shortly before the Civil War, coalescing out of a virtual no-party system early in the life of the state. Yet the Civil War and Reconstruction interrupted normal politics, with Northern military rule and even Republican party dominance existing for a time during the latter period. The termination of military occupation in 1870, however, foreshadowed the end of Reconstruction when control of government would be turned back to the white majority of the state. In 1874 the Democratic party regained control of the state's elective offices and began to eradicate many of the traces of Reconstruction government as discussed in the preceding chapter. But there remained several sources of competition for Democratic hegemony.

There were, first, considerable numbers of blacks along with some Unionist sympathizers and carpetbaggers who had formed the base of support for the Republican party. In the immediate post-Reconstruction period the Republican party could rally between a quarter and a third of the state's voters behind its candidates for governor, and in the so-called Black Belt areas blacks dominated local politics because of their majority position in the population (Rice, 1971:86–112). Yet white Texans, like the white majority in all the ex-Confederacy states, were not willing to allow blacks the political rights supposedly assured them now by the Fourteenth and Fifteenth Amendments to the United States Constitution. By a variety of methods—including violence, intimidation, and ballot box fraud—whites quickly began to curtail the political rights of blacks (Barr, 1971:193–208; Rice, 1971:112–150). The final stroke in this process of disenfranchisement, as we will see, did not come until after the turn of the century.

A second threat to Democratic dominance also emerged in the latter part of the nineteenth century. This second threat came from the various agrarian protest movements that culminated in the Populist movement in the 1890s. As early as 1875 similar interests had a telling impact on state government when members of the Grange, an early militant farmers' organization, played an important role in the state constitutional convention as described in chapter 4. Later in the century several protest political parties vied for the support of poor whites and dissident poor farmers against the more elitist Democratic party. Thus the Greenback, the Farmers' Alliance, and the Populist parties all fielded strong candidates for governor between 1880 and 1900. Moreover, the threat posed by these groups was heightened when the Republican party either ran a coalition candidate together with one of the latter parties or simply gave its official endorsement to one of their candidates and did not run a separate one.

The high tide of these second- and third-party movements peaked in the 1890s. In neither of the gubernatorial elections of 1892 or 1894 did the Democrats win even a majority of the votes cast. Indeed, their candidates won the office only because of the division of the remaining votes among the opposition parties. Moreover, voter turnout was at an all-time high during this period, in large measure because of the popularity of the causes espoused by these third parties. The threat posed by these parties convinced Democratic party leaders of the necessity for action.

The course of the Democratic party's action in Texas was the same as that followed in every other Southern state, all of which were experiencing the same surge of black and poor white political support for second and third parties. The Democratic party's response took a form that one scholar has called the "Bourbon Coup d'État," meaning a subversion of the electoral process by the dominant economic elites to ensure their own control of politics and to minimize the roles played by poor dissident groups whether black or white. While scholars differ on some of the details of how this "coup" came about, they are in agreement about its general consequences and its role in the formation of the succeeding one-party system (Bartley and Graham, 1975:1–11; Key, 1949:533–643; Kousser, 1974; Woodward, 1951).

The Bourbon Coup employed three tactics. First, the state Democratic party, just like the national Democratic party, co-opted certain policies of the Populist and then the Progressive parties to lure away some of their supporters. Beginning in the late 1880s, the Democrats created a number of state laws— in particular, to regulate more closely the activities of the railroads, the insurance companies, and various out-of-state corporations operating in Texas—to mollify Populist party voters. Many historians, however, have argued that these and similar reforms actually benefited only the middle and upper classes at best or only the established and wealthy elites at worst (Kousser, 1974:229– 231; Woodward, 1951:369–395). Certainly these reforms were, as C. Vann Woodward has put it, "for whites only." Moreover, they were for *local* whites only. Out-of-state corporate interests—railroads, insurance companies, oil companies—were principal targets of such reforms.

A second Bourbon tactic was to encourage (or simply ignore) the general white backlash against black political participation. Even though blacks constituted a smaller portion of Texas's population than was the case in many Deep South states, they still could pose a serious political threat to Democrats in the state. They were concentrated in a few geographic areas, as chapter 2 indicated, and thus they could wield particular power in those areas. Further, blacks provided the core of support for the Republican party in the state and, in coalition with other small parties, could pose a quite serious threat to Democratic control of state government as they did several times in the 1890s. Thus the white elite stood to benefit directly from the general antiblack sentiment among the Anglo population. By means of violence, ballot box fraud, and collaboration with the state government, local white political leaders had largely disenfranchised most Texas blacks by the turn of the present century.

The third Bourbon tactic was simply to change the rules of the political game—that is, to alter the laws regulating the right to vote in order to minimize participation of the poor and weaken the opportunities of minority parties. One such legal change came about when the poll tax was adopted as a requirement for voting by a constitutional amendment in 1902. Another important change in the rules came in the form of the "white primary." Under the white primary blacks were denied, by one means or another, the right to vote in Democratic party primaries. Beginning at least in the 1890s, this result was achieved by force and intimidation in a number of Texas counties. Eventually the whites-only feature of these elections was written not only into Democratic party rules but into state law. Certainly those blacks who paid their poll taxes and weathered white intimidation, or worse, could vote in the general election. After all, the U.S. Constitution guaranteed that right. But in the era of one-party Democratic dominance the "real" election was the Democratic primary, for that was the only point at which any significant competition existed among candidates. Thus effective participation in elections was denied blacks by the white primary.

The final rules changes came about when the state adopted the so-called Terrell Election Laws of 1903 and 1905. These changes put into statutory law the poll tax requirement, they restructured the party nomination system, and they imposed new organizational requirements on all parties. These requirements were particularly onerous on small, ill-developed parties—in other words, all parties except the majority Democrats (Kousser, 1974:208–209; Weeks, 1972:205–211).

CONSEQUENCES OF THE ONE-PARTY SYSTEM

The one-party Democratic system that arose from these developments dramatically reshaped Texas political life. The most drastic of its consequences was surely a reduction in public participation in politics. Table 5–1 offers vivid evidence on this decline. From its high point of almost 90 percent turnout of voting-age citizens in 1896, for example, participation in gubernatorial elections fell sharply to about one-third of the voting-age population in 1908. Voter participation was slightly higher, but not dramatically so, in the Democratic party primary that preceded each such election. This fact should not be surprising, however, for this primary was the only point where any real competition occurred in gubernatorial contests. The drop in turnout in presidential elections was equally dramatic, and only rarely did as many as a third of voting-age Texans vote in the presidential contests between 1904 and 1952.

The voter turnout declines in table 5–1 reflect the shift in political participation that occurred for all three of the state's ethnic groups. Yet the change was particularly dramatic for ethnic minorities. It has been estimated, for example, that as late as 1940 only 9 percent of black Texans were even registered to vote (Matthews and Prothro, 1966:148). While comparable estimates are not available for Texans of Mexican origin, V. O. Key's research (1949:271–274) indicates that these people were also often disenfranchised by the rules of the game under the one-party system. Moreover, the bulk of those Mexican-American Texans who did vote did so under the orders of a local boss or *jefe* who paid their poll tax and told them how to vote in exchange for a job or small favors. The boss himself received political favors from those he helped elect to office (Weeks, 1930).

Voter disenfranchisement like that described above was not unique to Texas but occurred throughout the South. In some of the other Southern states the

TABLE 5–1   Voter Turnout in Gubernatorial and Presidential Elections: 1880–1908

Election	1880	1884	1888	1892	1896	1900	1904	1908
			Voting-Age Population Voting					
Gubernatorial	69%	80%	69%	76%	86%	65%	36%	34%
Presidential	69%	80%	78%	79%	88%	61%	30%	34%

Sources: Kousser (1974:199); Bureau of the Census (1975:1071–1072); and authors' calculations.

decline in turnout was even more dramatic than in Texas. In Alabama, Georgia, and Mississippi, as examples, turnout in U.S. presidential elections under the one-party system often was in the range of only 10 to 20 percent of the voting-age population. Figure 5–1 offers another perspective on this aspect of the Bourbon Coup and the beginning of the period of disenfranchisement. The figure shows the trend in voter turnout in presidential elections for Texas alone, for all the ex-Confederacy states averaged together, and for five moralistic states averaged together. As figure 5–1 indicates, the South as a whole and Texas in particular compared favorably with the moralistic states in the late 1880s and early 1890s. Yet as the Bourbon Coup commenced, turnout fell dramatically in the South. There was a decline in the moralistic states as well, as the high tide of populism receded, but these states continued to have double the turnout of the South through all its years of Democratic one-party control.

The second major consequence of this political shift was the elimination of second and third parties as effective competitors in the state. After their peak in the 1890s, the agrarian and other protest parties were able to attract only tiny percentages of voters. Within two decades, most had vanished from the political scene. The Republican party continued to exist, but it lapsed into a minor, largely ceremonial role. In gubernatorial elections, for example, the GOP would go through the motions of running a candidate, yet that candidate would typically garner only between 15 and 20 percent of the vote. The outcome was never in doubt; the election was at best a formality. At the party's point of lowest political fortune during the midst of the New Deal and World War II, GOP candidates for governor sometimes polled only 2 to 5 percent of the total vote. Some have argued, in fact, that the sole reason for even the ceremonial

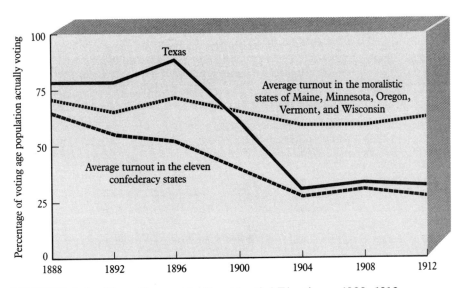

FIGURE 5–1   Voter Turnout in Presidential Elections: 1888–1912
Source: Bureau of the Census (1975:1071–1072)

existence of the party during this period was so that its state leaders could dispense what federal patronage might come to Texas when a Republican president was in office.

Finally, and most important, political life in the state was controlled during this period by the Democratic party alone. On the surface, the party often gave the appearance of at least some internal competition among its rival leaders, and this competition appeared to give voters some voice in party affairs. After all, they could choose among those leaders in primary elections. This appearance of competition was, however, misleading. Voter participation was itself quite low, as has already been indicated, because of the Bourbon Coup. Thus the extent of public control even in primaries was limited. Just as important was the fact that the apparent competition within the party was only a surface phenomenon.

There were often controversial and passionately fought primary election contests between rival Democratic leaders. But rarely did these contests have anything to do with public policy. That is, candidates seldom offered different policy positions among which voters could choose. Instead, candidates often based their campaigns on personality differences, on moral issues like Prohibition, or on symbolic appeals to religious, family, or agrarian values. Thus the governor's office housed such figures as the controversial "Farmer Jim" (or "Pa") Ferguson. Ferguson was a folksy demagogue who rallied rural voters with attacks on the educated and the "city slickers." But once in office he did little for his rural constituents. Ferguson was impeached from the office in 1917 for misuse of public funds and a number of other charges. He then twice successfully ran his wife, Miriam "Ma" Ferguson, for governor and directed her tenure in office from behind the scenes.

Another governor cut from a similar mold was W. Lee "Pappy" O'Daniel who first became popular as a radio country singer pumping the sales of his flour company's products with his band, the Light Crust Doughboys. O'Daniel successfully ran for governor in 1938 and 1940 on a platform advocating the Ten Commandments and the Golden Rule. O'Daniel's appeal was, as well, to the country vote, as typified in the campaign song he wrote himself, "Them Hillbillies Are Politicians Now" (Gantt, 1964:290–291):

> Been hangin' round the mountains all these years
> Singin' songs about the train-wrecked engineers.
> They've been pavin' all the cities
> With their pretty corn-fed ditties,
> And they've got the politicians all in tears.
> They come to town with their guitars
> And now they're smokin' big cigars—
> Them Hillbillies are politicians now.

Beyond the flamboyant governors there were the colorless and the incompetent ones. Among these surely was "Ma" Ferguson, who fronted for her husband for two terms. There was Charles Culberson, governor in 1895–1897, who perhaps should be best remembered for calling a special session of the state legislature to pass a law banning prizefights in the state. There were Joseph T. Sayers and S. W. T. Lanham, the last governors who had served in the Confederate army. These two men, governors in the period 1899–1907, are best remembered (if not remembered only) for the air of Old South gentility they brought to the governor's mansion. Even in very recent times the one-party system has produced several lackluster and do-nothing governors.

This competition on superficial and symbolic matters obscured the policy aims that united the Democratic party. Those aims included keeping government in the hands of a small, traditionalistic, and individualistic elite; maintaining a state governmental system that was favorable to the economic interests of such elites; and blocking the participation of groups who might challenge the favored position of these elites—such as the poor blacks and whites who had challenged that system in the 1890s. Clearly the Democratic party's operations under this system differed sharply from the ideal functions of parties in a democratic society.

WEAKENING OF THE ONE-PARTY SYSTEM

Although the Democratic party still dominates many aspects of Texas politics, there have appeared in recent decades several cracks in its formerly solid foundation. While the one-party system operated virtually undisturbed from the turn of the present century to perhaps the early 1940s, several forces have been operating to weaken the party and promote a competitive two-party system.

Socioeconomic Change

One of the major forces acting on the party system has been the socioeconomic change experienced in Texas during this century and discussed previously in chapters 1 and 2. Most relevant to the party system have been the in-migration of many non-Southerners to the state, the out-migration of blacks, the decline in the proportion of blacks in the total state population, the urbanization of the state, and the rise of the industrial economy.

A major consequence of these socioeconomic changes has been the rise of a new economic elite—primarily an urban and industrial elite—who have competed at times with the established rural, small-town, and agrarian leaders who traditionally controlled the Democratic party. The party has mostly been able to incorporate these new elite groups, in part because of its solid control of both the state government and elections for seats in the U.S. Congress. Yet in the process of co-opting these new groups, the party itself has become more diverse, more internally combative, and less able to maintain a united front on major policy issues.

At the same time, some of the new elite and some of the non-Southern migrants have provided new sources of support for the Republican party. Many of the new elite have found the ideology and membership of the national GOP more suited to their own political interests. Many of the non-Southern migrants have, as well, brought Republican party allegiance with them to Texas or have come from states where the party was well accepted and regularly competitive in state politics.

Among all the Southern states, economic issues like those arising from the foregoing changes have been particularly important in Texas. This is the case because Texas has experienced more rapid socioeconomic change in this century than has the typical Southern state. This fact, coupled with the relatively small proportion of the Texas population that remained black by the 1940s (in comparison with the typical Deep South state) meant that, first, the racial issue which could unite all whites under one party banner was relatively weaker in Texas and, second, new political issues arising out of economic transformation were relatively stronger.

The Impact of the New Deal

A second force also divided the Democratic party internally—the New Deal revolution in American national politics. Ironically, the nationwide political majority that President Franklin Roosevelt was able to create for the Democratic party carried with it the seeds for the eventual breakdown of the Democratic party in the South. This breakdown came about because of the economic and particularly the civil rights liberalism of the New Deal.

Texas remained solidly in the fold of the national Democratic party until about the 1940 presidential election. By that time the liberalism of the Roosevelt administration was clear, and many Southern political leaders were beginning vigorously to support rival presidential candidates. Southern Democrats in Congress even moved as early as 1937 into an informal liaison with Republicans (known as the "Conservative Coalition") to vote in opposition to many of Roosevelt's policy proposals. One of the most Republican-leaning of Democratic congressmen was "Pappy" O'Daniel, who left the Texas governor's office to run successfully for the U.S. Senate in 1941 (Key, 1949:361–362).

In 1944 the Texas Democratic party split sharply over the question of whether to support Roosevelt's reelection, and in 1948 a major break with the national party came in the form of the Dixiecrat party as a Southern splinter group. By 1952 the leader of the state Democratic party, Governor Allan Shivers, was campaigning openly for the Republican candidate for president, Dwight Eisenhower, under the banner of the "Shivercrat" faction. Shivers even ran for governor in 1952 as the candidate of *both* the Democratic and Republican parties. His campaign, like O'Daniel's Republican sympathies in the 1940s, is symbolic of the ideological upheaval of the times and demonstrates its influence on party politics in the state.

What had also transpired in Texas by the mid-1940s was the creation of a liberal wing of the Democratic party that followed the New Deal policies of the Roosevelt and Truman administrations and attempted to compete with the larger, traditionally conservative elements of the state party. The liberal wing, led at various times by such people as Lyndon Johnson, Ralph Yarborough, and Frances Farenthold, has remained a permanent if minority element of the party to the present day. It has scored occasional election victories, but it has never been able to wrest control of the party from the conservative element.

It was not just among the party leaders that the New Deal had a significant impact on Texas party politics. The liberalism of the New Deal proved too extreme of many of the party's rank-and-file followers, as well. Every Republican presidential candidate since Thomas Dewey in 1948 has received strong electoral support from Texas voters. More important, Republican candidates Eisenhower, Nixon, and Reagan carried the state in 1952, 1956, 1972, 1980, and 1984. Thus many Democrats in the state became what has been called "Presidential Republicans"—voters who remained Democratic in statewide elections but who were quite willing to vote for a Republican in the presidential race.

The Rise of the Republican Party

A third force has been the slow but steady increase in the power of the Republican party in state politics. There were the dramatic election victories such as John Tower to the U.S. Senate in 1961, Phil Gramm to the Senate when Tower retired, and Bill Clements to the governorship in 1978 and 1986. But the total number of local and statewide offices held by Republicans has risen more slowly than these dramatic victories might suggest. The party's progress has been greatest in the state legislature. As recently as 1970 Republicans held only 10 of 181 seats there. By 1987 they held 56 of 151 House seats and 6 of 31 Senate seats. But the party held few statewide elected offices and only about 14 percent of local ones (Stanley, 1987).

Whether Texas deserves to be labeled a two-party state is hotly debated, yet the Republicans have surely made great strides in recent decades. They field candidates for far more offices than they did in the heyday of the one-party system. They have sizable representation in the U.S. Congress and the state legislature. Their gubernatorial candidates have run strong races in every election since 1962. And they are making notable inroads in local races, especially in the party strongholds of Dallas and Houston.

Federal Government Intervention

A fourth force operating on the party system has been federal government intervention in the election "rules of the game." Beginning in the 1940s, a long series of federal court rulings and new legislation from Congress forced a transformation in the election system in Texas and every other Southern state. Most of these actions were motivated by the discriminatory aspects of the former election rules—aspects that worked to the particular disadvantage of ethnic minorities. Yet these changes have also struck down features of the old rules that limited the voting participation of whites as well as ethnics. In effect, the federal government has eradicated the old electoral system designed at the time of the Bourbon Coup whose purpose was to restrict mass participation in government regardless of race. Thus Texas has moved from a system that discriminated against all ethnic groups to one that should discriminate against none.

The first of these legal changes came about in 1944 when the U.S. Supreme Court struck down the all-white primary. In the case of *Smith* v. *Allwright*, which was a challenge specifically against the Texas all-white primary, the court ruled that this system violated the Fifteenth Amendment constitutional rights of blacks. As noted above, the all-white primary had appeared as early as the 1890s in some Texas counties and had been established in state law in 1923. An earlier Supreme Court ruling in 1927 had declared that such a primary system could not be a feature of state law, but in response the Democratic party had simply made the system a part of *its* rules and claimed the privilege to do so because it was a private and not a governmental organization. But in 1944 the Supreme Court rejected this argument, deciding instead that a political party was "an agency of the state" because it was so closely regulated by state statutes in carrying out its electoral functions. Based on that interpretation, parties were subject to the provisions of the Fifteenth Amendment, which precludes denial of the right to vote on the basis of race by any state or federal government action.

The second major federal action came again from the Supreme Court but not until 1962. In that year and in 1964 the court ruled in a series of cases (beginning with *Baker* v. *Carr* in 1962 and then with *Reynolds* v. *Sims* in 1964) that both houses of state legislatures should be regularly reapportioned so that each representative or senator would represent virtually the same number of constituents as every other representative or senator. In effect, the Supreme Court called for what has been termed "one man, one vote" apportionment—that is, a system in which each voter's vote has the same weight in every election district.

These court rulings were extremely important because in almost every state in the nation apportionment systems had, over a number of decades, become highly unequal and therefore discriminatory because of inequities in the number of citizens living in different districts. A study of the Texas Legislature in 1963, immediately after it had just been reapportioned on the basis of the 1960 census, for example, showed that there remained serious population inequalities among districts (Davis, 1965). Some 42 percent of the population could elect a majority of the members of the House of Representatives, and only 30 percent could elect a majority of the Senate. And it was the large, rapidly growing urban areas that were underrepresented by this system.

As a result of this older system of apportionment, rural and small-town areas of the state had greater representation in the Texas Legislature than did urban and rapidly growing areas. That is, rural Texans were able to elect a proportion of state legislators that was far greater than their own percentage of the state's population. Since rural and small-town areas were the heartland of the traditional Democratic party elite, as well, this system gave these elites disproportionate political power over political leaders from the growing urban and industrial centers. This situation was one major means, therefore, by which the traditional elites were able to retain control of both the party and state government even when their own role in the economy and society of the state had been considerably eroded.

The next round of federal intervention in the election system also began in 1964 when the Twenty-fourth Amendment to the U.S. Constitution was ratified, barring the poll tax as a requirement for voting in federal elections. Then in 1966 the Supreme Court ruled that poll taxes violated the Equal Protection Clause of the Fourteenth Amendment and were, therefore, unconstitutional even in state elections. Texas, like the three other Southern states that still employed this requirement, was forced to drop it as a prerequisite for voting.

Perhaps the most extensive federal involvement in state election rules was initiated by the Voting Rights Act of 1965. Recognizing the low overall voter turnout in the South, the particularly low voting of blacks, and the probable explanation for this situation in discriminatory state and local laws, the U.S. Congress passed this act to eradicate such discrimination. The act effectively eliminated all remaining discriminatory requirements like poll taxes and literacy tests, barred any other election laws or procedures that might restrict unfairly the right to vote, and subjected any change in voting or election procedures in the Southern states to prior federal government approval to ensure that such changes would not dilute minority voting strength. The act went so far as to provide for federal examiners and election observers to oversee voter registration procedures and elections. The Voting Rights Act was extended for five years without change in 1970. Then, when the act was extended the second time in 1975, Hispanics and several other language groups were also given protection under its coverage. Finally, the act was extended in 1982 for another twenty-five years. The results of the Voting Rights Act were to place all Texas election procedures under federal government scrutiny, to ensure that all remaining restrictive election laws and practices would be eliminated, and to encourage energetic voter registration efforts aimed at minority citizens of the state.

Finally, in 1971 a lower federal court found the system of voter registration in Texas in violation of the Equal Protection Clause of the Fourteenth Amendment. The culprits in this instance were the requirement for annual reregistration and the early deadline for registration (effectively, nine months before the customary November general election date). These requirements were found by the court to have discriminatory impacts on the registration of ethnic minorities. In response to this ruling the state has developed a system of virtually permanent voter registration with a far more lenient maximum waiting period of only thirty days between initial registration and ability to vote.

Changes in Public Participation

As a result particularly of the preceding changes in election and suffrage laws, public involvement in Texas politics has expanded significantly since the 1940s. Table 5–2 on voter registration and turnout in presidential elections documents this change. Quite clearly, Texans of all ethnic groups have benefited from these changes. While comparable estimates for Mexican-Americans are not available, the data for blacks and whites in table 5–2 support this contention. Black voter registration jumped almost fourfold between the Supreme Court's

TABLE 5–2   **Voter Registration and Turnout in Presidential Elections: 1940–1980**

Involvement	1940	1960	1980	1984
Voting-age white Texans registered	42%	43%	75%	82%
Voting-age black Texans registered	9%	35%	56%	72%
Total Texas voting-age population voting in presidential election	30%	42%	45%	47%

Sources: Bureau of the Census (1975:1071–1072); Bureau of the Census (1983:261,264); Bureau of the Census (1987:244,245); Matthews and Prothro (1966:148); and authors' calculations.

decision in *Smith* v. *Allwright* (1944) and 1960. White voter registration did not change in this period, but white voters were not, of course, affected by *Smith* v. *Allwright* and had not suffered unique discrimination in terms of access to the primary election as had blacks. After 1960, however, and with the banning of the poll tax and other restrictive aspects of the registration system, the registration of both groups increased dramatically.

In presidential elections the voting turnout of Texans has increased by about half since 1940. While this is a considerable improvement, the state still lags behind the national average. In the 1984 presidential election, for example, 47 percent of voting-age Texans voted, whereas the nationwide turnout was 53 percent and some moralistic states had turnout in the range of 70 to 75 percent. Although the turnout in Texas has been moving closer to the national average, it must be said that the nationwide voter turnout in presidential elections has itself been slowly declining since a peak of 63 percent in 1960. This decline has made Texas's relative performance look better. Public participation in elections in Texas has improved considerably in recent decades, but the state still rates somewhat poorly in comparison to the national average and, in particular, to a number of high-participation states.

REASONS FOR THE LOW VOTER TURNOUT IN TEXAS

Several explanations have been advanced to account for the continued low involvement of Texans in politics (in comparison to national averages). One of these explanations concerns the historical legacy of the traditionalistic political culture. For decades traditionalistic values framed Texans' thinking about politics. Public participation was not highly encouraged. Reliance on the wisdom of political elites, rather than the dependence of those elites on the public, was emphasized. And, as we have seen, political elites created a system of suffrage and elections that reinforced the values taught in the traditionalistic culture. Public involvement in politics was sharply limited. What participation was allowed was largely ritualistic: The party of the ultimately successful candidate was never in doubt, and no public policy matters of great consequence were to be settled by elections.

In the past the absence of two-party competition contributed to low public participation—as the limited extent of such competition does today. States with meaningful two-party competition consistently evidence greater public involvement in politics than do one-party states. Texas itself provides evidence for this conclusion, for public involvement was quite high in the state in the 1880s and 1890s when there were strong second and third parties. As noted earlier, a competitive second party helps mobilize opposition against the "in" party. It serves as the constant critic of the "in" group, as well, keeping its failures in the public eye. And second parties can appeal to those in society whose interests are being ignored by the dominant party. Thus the continued weakness of Texas's second party contributes to the low level of public involvement.

The potentially beneficial effects of two-party competition in Texas are themselves limited, however, by the fact that both the Democratic and Republican parties wish to appeal primarily to conservative voters. Both parties have traditionally offered little in the way of specific proposals to aid the liberals, the poor, or the minorities in the state. Hence what might generally be called the liberal interests in Texas have been given little attention as both parties play to the middle-of-the-road and conservative elements.

There is one final element that discourages public participation in politics in Texas: the demographics of the state's population. Research on political participation in the contemporary United States has demonstrated that certain kinds of people are more likely than others to vote and engage in political activities. For example, table 5–3 presents data on the percentage of Americans nationwide—broken down into relevant demographic categories—who reported having voted in the 1980 presidential election. Clearly those who were white,

TABLE 5–3   Participation of the National Electorate in the 1984 Presidential Election

Demographic Characteristic	Percent Reporting Having Voted
Age	
18–20	37
21–24	44
25–34	55
35–44	64
45–64	70
65 and over	68
Years of schooling	
8 or fewer	43
9–11	44
12	59
More than 12	73
Ethnicity	
Black	56
Spanish origin	33
White	61

Source: Bureau of the Census (1987:244).

older, wealthier, and better educated tended to vote in greater numbers. Research on other elections—including state and local ones—and on other forms of political participation confirms these findings.

It is generally argued that persons of higher education, wealth, and so on have been better socialized into moralistic and participatory values, regardless of the dominant political culture of the state where they reside. Similarly, such people show greater interest in politics and higher levels of what is called *political efficacy*, the belief that one's personal involvement can directly influence political outcomes. Such people typically have a set of political beliefs—a product of their socialization and life experiences—that supports the value of democratic political participation. In contrast, the poor, the less well educated, ethnic minorities, and even relatively young voters typically have less interest in politics and much weaker political efficacy. Thus the lower voting turnout of these groups can be explained in the same terms.

As chapter 2 demonstrated, the population of Texas has significant percentages of some of these low-participation groups. Most notably, about a third of the population is composed of ethnic minorities. The low participation of blacks and Mexican-Americans is itself, of course, explainable partly by the political role they were socialized to accept during the era of one-party government and partly by the fact that so many of them are relatively poor and poorly educated. Texas also has a notable number of poor and poorly educated whites who contribute to the low public participation in the state.

These demographic factors help explain the current levels of public involvement of Texans in politics. Yet one should not make too much of these factors or generalize them out of their context. They refer only to the character of participation in the contemporary United States. In Texas in the 1890s, as in most of the nation at that time, participation was very high among all groups, including the poor, the poorly educated, and the recently enfranchised blacks. The high participation in that earlier era was a product of a dramatic set of political issues, but it was also the result of a competitive party system and liberal suffrage laws. Thus demographic factors may be important today, but they are themselves influenced by the party system, the electoral system, and the nature of the political times.

OBSTACLES TO TWO-PARTY COMPETITION

Public participation in Texas elections has been dramatically transformed in the last thirty years. Competition between rival factions has increased in the Democratic party, and the Republicans have made significant inroads. Indeed, Texas could be fairly described as a two-party state, at least in presidential elections. Why, then, one might ask, has the progress toward two-partyism been so much slower in state elections? The answers to this question provide additional perspectives on the evolution of election and party systems.

One principal difficulty for the Republican party in all of the South has been the traditional conservatism of the local Democratic party. While the national Democratic party—both in the Congress and as represented in many of the party's presidential nominees—has been considerably more liberal since the New Deal, Southern Democrats have on the whole remained highly conservative on the issues of major interest to Southern voters. Thus the Democratic party in the South has occupied the ideological ground that the Republicans themselves would typically hold. Democratic leaders in the South have even made explicit their dissatisfaction with the liberal wing of their party, going so far at times as to openly support Republican nominees for the presidency.

The conservatism of the typical Southern Democrat makes Republican electoral strategy far more problematic. Republicans must make more sophisticated, and therefore more difficult, distinctions between themselves and the Democrats. They must pose as "better" conservatives or as different kinds of conservatives or as more honest or more capable leaders. Clearly such arguments are more difficult to substantiate and therefore may not prove convincing to many voters. It would be far easier for the Republicans if they were able simply to write off their opponents with a single verbal stroke as "nasty liberals" and then to occupy the conservative territory alone.

The long-time hegemony of the Democratic party and the traditional view that its primary constituted the "real election" for most state and local offices have also worked to the disadvantage of the Republicans. Many voters who might otherwise prefer to vote Republican probably feel that to have any influence on the outcome of state elections they must vote in the Democratic primary. Thus the GOP primary attracts far fewer voters and far less attention than it otherwise would. The Republican voter's best strategy at this point is also uncertain. Should Republicans vote for the most conservative candidate in the Democratic primary to help ensure, at the least, that a conservative will win the general election? Or should they vote for the more liberal Democratic candidate in the primary and then vote for the Republican in the general election (hoping, of course, that the general election will be between the liberal Democrat and a Republican more suited to the conservative temperament of the state)? Or should the Republican voter ignore the Democratic primary to participate in the GOP contest, knowing that a conservative Democrat will probably face a conservative Republican in the general election? The best choice among these strategies is not clear. It is probable that the potential force of Republican voters is dissipated in many elections because some choose one, some the second, and some the third alternative.

Yet another factor has limited the growth of the Republican party in Texas: the use of the *long ballot* in state and local elections. The term *long ballot* refers to a system whereby voters elect a large number of executive officers rather than electing a single chief executive who then appoints his or her principal subordinates. The most notable example of the long ballot is that for state executive officers. Texans elect, in separate races, not only the Governor but also the Lieutenant Governor, the Attorney General, the State Treasurer, the Comptroller of Public Accounts, the Commissioner of the General Land Office, the Commissioner of Agriculture, and the board members who head the Railroad Commission and the State Board of Education. One might contrast this system to that of the federal government where voters choose only among tickets of candidates for the presidency and the vice-presidency to head the entire executive branch. Once elected, a president then appoints all the Cabinet officers and a large number of other high-level executive branch officials, creating in the process an entire administration devoted to the pursuit of his policy goals.

The long ballot is particularly disadvantageous for small second parties attempting to compete with a large, well-established party such as the Democrats in Texas. It is quite difficult for the smaller party to find a sufficient number of attractive, experienced, or well-known candidates to run for all the positions on the long ballot. It is often difficult, as well, to attract the funds to pay for a large number of such campaigns. Thus when the occasional Republican scores a major campaign victory, he or she may stand virtually alone in a forest of Democrats elected to other posts. In effect, executive power is highly dispersed in such a system, and winning a single election places only a small portion of such power in the control of the second party.

An excellent example of the effects of the long ballot came about in 1978 when Bill Clements was first elected to the governorship. Republicans were jubilant, but all the other state executive offices and 85 percent of the seats in the state legislature were held by Democrats. Poor Bill Clements had almost no one even to talk to in Austin from his own political party! And one can make a strong argument that in the succeeding four years Texans learned nothing about what a Republican administration could really have accomplished. Clements had so little control over the executive branch of the state, despite occupying its highest office, that his power was severely limited. Unfortunately, Clements found himself in much the same situation when he was reelected to the governorship in 1986. (There are a number of other important consequences of the long ballot, beyond their impact on party politics, which are considered in detail in chapter 7.)

Some changes in the party system have likely been held back, too, through tinkering with the election calendar. Before the 1974 election, the governor and other chief state executive officers served two-year terms and ran for election in November of even-numbered years—on the same election day when the U.S. presidential race was held every four years and, in the intervening even-numbered years, when U.S. congressional elections were always held. Under this pre-1974 system there was particularly high voter turnout in every other state election—in those years, that is, when the "high stimulus" presidential election headed the ballot. In the intervening election years, when only congressional and senatorial races would be on the ballot along with those for state offices, voter turnout would average about 20 to 25 percentage points lower. The circumstance of coincident gubernatorial and presidential elections also meant that a very popular presidential candidate might generate a "coattail" effect by inducing many voters to vote for the state office candidates running under the same party banner. Thus state political races might get caught up in national political movements.

In 1971, however, the Democrat-controlled state legislature approved for submission to the voters what appeared to be an unrelated reform proposal: to give the governor a four-year instead of a two-year term of office. This proposal was primarily justified by the argument that the four-year term would give the governor more time to develop a program while having to spend less time running for reelection. This argument and related ones addressed the legitimate concern of many observers of state government that the two-year term unnecessarily restricted a governor's ability to meet the demands of the office. But the proposed amendment also stipulated that gubernatorial elections would be held every four years in the "off year" or nonpresidential election years. This schedule was justified by the argument, proposed by the Texas Legislative Council, a research arm of the legislature, that it would generate greater interest in state politics (Texas Legislative Council, 1972:26).

The proposed amendment was approved by the voters in the 1972 general elections and took effect with the 1974 state elections. But the effect of this reform was, contrary to the argument of the Texas Legislative Council, to ensure that voter turnout in these elections would remain at the traditionally lower level of off-year contests. The following figures illustrate the turnout decline that came about because of this change for all the subsequent gubernatorial elections:

Percent of Voting-Age Texans Voting in:				
1972	1974	1978	1982	1986
44%	20%	26%	30%	29%

While there was an increase in turnout in these elections up to 1982, the percentages still fall considerably below those in presidential years.

The precise motivations of those who proposed this reform are not known. Yet the net result was clearly twofold. The altered election calendar reduced the electoral role of poor and minority voters—the people shown by research on voter turnout to be the least likely to participate in low-stimulus, off-year elections. In effect, then, this reform eliminated some of the expansion of popular participation in elections that had been achieved largely under federal pressure since the 1940s. It thus helped the traditional leaders of the Democratic party regain some of the control over party affairs that had been threatened in the last several decades. At the same time this change meant that highly popular Republican presidential candidates could not induce "Presidential Republicans" in the state to become full-fledged Republicans on election day. Hence the prospects for continued Democratic control of state government were clearly enhanced.

INTEREST GROUPS IN A DEMOCRATIC POLITY

Interest groups are formal, private organizations that attempt to influence government decision making by involving themselves in election campaigns and by the direct lobbying of government officials. Like political parties, interest groups can play an important and positive role in the working of a democratic government. These groups can facilitate the communication between citizens and government by making known the political views of particular groups. In Texas, the interests of such diverse groups as accountants, farmers, oil companies, environmentalists, and Mothers Against Drunk Drivers (MADD) are introduced into political debates.

To represent the views of their members and sympathizers, interest groups do many things that political parties also do. They help recruit candidates for public office (who must, of course, become the nominees of parties). They contribute and encourage campaign funds for candidates. They also "advertise" their views on prominent political issues to the general public, in the hope of encouraging widespread support for those views. What an interest group does uniquely, however, is to lobby government officials to convince them, too, of the wisdom of the group's position. Thus nearly all elected officials and executives and even heads of executive branch agencies are routinely lobbied by such groups.

Lobbying also has promulgated a negative image for interest groups. At times it appears they try to persuade government officials to ignore the general public interest and adopt that of the particular, narrow group. At times lobbying has the appearance of buying political favors with campaign contributions and other benefits for public officials. Lobbyists sometimes appear to have easy access to sympathetic government officials when members of the general public feel those officials are distant and difficult to influence.

Thus, determined, well-organized interest groups of all kinds have at least the possibility of getting some response from government. A large membership, high professional expertise, or good organization can offset limited financial resources. Of course the larger, the more prestigious, and the better-funded the group, the more likely it will enjoy such political good fortune. Yet even small or ill-funded interest groups can be politically successful.

The negative image that interest groups endure is sometimes well-deserved. Yet these groups can, as we observed earlier, assist the democratic process. In large diverse societies there are many social, cultural, and economic interests which may be affected by government. As government grows in its power and responsibility, its influence on those interests becomes more and more prominent. For this reason many Texans might wish to have a voice in the making of government policy. At the same time, most of us will not take the time personally to carry through on that wish. Government is too distant and sometimes too complex for us to know how to make our views known effectively. And the time, expense, and energy necessary to do so prevent many of us from making any effort.

Many Texans are surely happy, then, that there are interest groups that share their political preferences and that regularly press those views on government. Those employed in the oil business, those concerned about environmental matters, and those who favor parimutuel betting—to name but a few of many possibilities—have been recent beneficiaries of such organized efforts. Thus we would readily agree that *our* interest groups are good and legitimate in their efforts to influence government. It is only those *other* groups which are the bad ones and deserve the negative image.

CHECKS ON INTEREST GROUP POWER

The contradiction in the preceding conclusion is readily apparent, but it also attests to the two-sided role interest groups can play in our government. They *can* be highly beneficial to the democratic process. They can also be highly detrimental to it if the broad public interest is subverted by their efforts. To ensure that such groups perform in only a beneficial way, there must be checks on their unique powers of organization, financial capability, and access to government officials. Those checks can arise out of the political culture, out of the number and diversity of (and hence competition among) interest groups, out of the political party system, or out of the activities of government institutions.

Socioeconomic Structure

One of the strongest influences on interest group power is the character of the socioeconomic structure of the state. States with relatively homogeneous economies have fewer but more powerful interest groups than do states with more diverse, complex, and "developed" economies (Zeigler, 1965).

Advanced economic development creates diversity in the economy and accords significant economic power to a broad range of economic sectors and interests. Homogeneity, on the other hand, typified by a state with an economic system highly dependent on only a few key industries, means that the leaders of those key industries have by far the highest economic and, hence, political status in the state. Homogeneity also means that there are few alternative centers of private power that might compete against the primary ones in efforts to influence state politics.

We have noted that throughout most of this century the Texas economy has relied on agriculture and on the extraction of natural resources like petroleum products. That period was one of economic homogeneity which ensured the political power of interest groups from agriculture and the oil and gas businesses. We have seen, too, that recent social and economic changes like advanced industrialization, "high tech" development, and urbanization have begun to diversify our economy and society. These changes mean that new centers of economic power are developing to compete with the old ones and with each other. Over time this process should mean the weakening of older interest groups and, perhaps, of all groups collectively.

Political Culture

A second check on the power of interest groups can arise out of the political culture of the state. Chapter 3 explained how the three basic political cultures looked upon the advancing of private interests through politics.

Individualistic   Under individualism it is culturally acceptable to advance one's private interests through political activity. That culture, in fact, has a particularly open and sympathetic attitude toward such efforts.

Traditionalistic   In the traditionalistic culture there is a similar but slightly restrictive attitude toward self-advancement. Under traditionalism it is only the social elites who are expected to advance their private interests through the political arena. Such private action is justified as the prerogative of the elite, or it is rationalized as actually being in the interests of the entire state.

Moralistic   In a moralistic society, finally, cultural norms discourage the earning of private gains through political action. Political activity in such a society is supposed to serve the broad public interest.

Texas, we recall, is a state with a mixed individualistic and traditionalistic culture with just a few strands of moralism. Thus there are few restraints on interest group power arising from political culture as there are in more moralistic states. Indeed, we must conclude that our political culture actually encourages interest group activity in the pursuit of narrow private interest.

Political Party System

A third characteristic of states that has been linked to the strength of interest groups is the nature of the political party system. States whose governments are regularly controlled by only one political party are typically ones which also have especially powerful interest groups (Zeigler, 1965). As we noted in our earlier discussion of the political party system in Texas, one-party dominance of state politics has inevitably meant that not all legitimate interests will be well represented in politics. The existence of two competing parties broadens the range of interests represented and creates competition among different points of view for influence over political decisions. A two-party system does not inevitably weaken the power of interest groups, but it means, at the least, there will be greater competition among the most influential groups and less likelihood that one or a small number of groups will dominate the state.

Another consequence of a one-party system lies in the possible influence of small interest groups in addition to that of the biggest and best-known organizations. In a one-party state, like Texas, a small and little-known group representing narrow interests can be quite influential simply by gaining the support of the leaders of the one major party. Such groups as the Texas Automobile Dealers' Association, the Texas Brewers' Association, and the Texas Association of Realtors, to name a few examples, can have considerable impact on certain aspects of government and policy. In a two-party system, by contrast, the power of small interest groups will at times be limited because the members of one of the two parties oppose a particular group's policy demands. For especially big and powerful organizations, the situation is somewhat different. Acknowledged powerful interest groups will typically get at least a hearing from both parties. Thus in a state like Texas a variety of interest groups can at times be quite influential with respect to government policy that concerns their members.

Naturally the long-time dominance of Texas politics by the Democratic party has meant that Texas has not enjoyed the benefit of this possible check on interest group power.

Character of the State Legislature

We observed earlier that checks on interest groups can arise out of the activities of governmental institutions. Such checks can take several forms, but a particularly important one for Texas concerns the level of "professionalism" of the state legislature. In general, the lower the level of legislative professionalism, the greater the likelihood that interest groups can sway the decision making of that governmental body. Unprofessional legislatures have members who are relatively ill-qualified for their positions, have high turnover of members, pay their members low salaries, and provide only limited technical and staff resources for legislative decision making. Such legislatures are more easily influenced by lobbyists than are professional ones, and in chapter 6 on the Texas legislature we will explain in more detail both why this is the case and what methods lobbyists use to exercise their influence.

Unfortunately, Texas has one of the least professional state legislatures in the nation. Again, the details which explain why this is so are presented in chapter 6. Yet we can conclude here that this is one other possible check on interest group power from which Texans derive no benefit. In fact, we are significantly disadvantaged because of the character of our legislature.

INTEREST GROUP POWER IN TEXAS

All the conditions just cited are ones that do not check, but actually strengthen, the power of interest groups in Texas. Indeed, throughout its history, Texas has been an excellent example of how interest groups can be especially powerful. One of the best early illustrations of this power comes from the Constitutional Convention of 1875 that wrote the state's present constitution. As explained in chapter 4, that convention was dominated by the political interests of the Grange, a powerful farmers' organization. The content of the new constitution, and thus the character of Texas government and public policy, was shaped to conform to the interests of the Grange. Agrarian interests remained important in Texas for many years, but the development in the twentieth century of the oil and gas industries produced powerful new rivals for the control of state government. These groups became so important that in the 1940s the chairman of the state's Democratic Party State Executive Committee admitted: "It may not be a wholesome thing to say, but the oil industry today is in complete control of state politics and state government" (Stilwell, 1949:315).

Economic homogeneity, Democratic party domination, restricted public participation in elections, and the character of the state's political culture also meant that it was particular kinds of interest groups which would be most powerful. Established business interests and professional groups linked to the dominant economic sectors—and favoring conservative, status-quo oriented policies—were overwhelmingly advantaged. The operations of parties, elections, and interest groups served to reinforce one another to keep this system in place to benefit these interest groups.

Socioeconomic development has been the only notable change that should moderate interest group power in Texas. Because this state has become more complex socially and economically, there now exist many new interests desirous of influencing governmental decisions. Although agriculture and the oil business remain quite powerful economically and politically their declining fortunes have weakened their political clout. The state's minority ethnic groups are becoming more outspoken and aggressive in pressing their demands on state government. In time these changes should moderate the degree to which the traditional establishment interests dominate state politics. Yet much of that change will come about by new groups displacing the old ones. In other words, interest groups could, in the future, remain very powerful collectively, but there will be some shifting in their relative power and some enhanced competition among them.

Two different research projects on the power of interest groups in state politics, executed years apart, confirm both the traditional and continuing power of such groups in this state. The first of these studies found that in the early 1950s Texas was one of twenty-four states having especially strong interest groups involved in state politics (Zeller, 1954). More recently, Morehouse (1981) found Texas to be one of twenty-two states in which interest groups were especially powerful. The only change from the previous study was that the list of powerful interest groups in the state was now lengthier. On that list were the Texas Chemical Council, the Mid-Continent Oil and Gas Association, the Independent (petroleum) Producers and Royalty Owners Association, the State Teachers' Association, the Manufacturing Association, the Texas Motor Transportation Association, medical interests, and insurance interests.

INTEREST GROUPS AND ELECTIONS

One of the major methods by which interest groups seek to influence government policies is by helping secure the election of candidates for office who are sympathetic to their views. Principally by means of campaign contributions to such candidates, interest groups hope to ensure that the government will be run by people with their concerns favorably in mind. Naturally, relatively wealthy interest groups with "well-heeled" members have considerable advantages. The influence of sizable campaign contributions has become especially critical in recent years because of the rising—and literally astronomical—costs of major election campaigns. Two recent examples will illustrate both the high costs of election campaigns and the key role played in defraying those costs by major interest groups.

Mark White, in his 1982 election to the governorship over the incumbent Bill Clements, spent almost $9 million in his campaign. While that figure alone seems staggering, Bill Clements spent over $13 million in his losing campaign. Even more interesting, however, is what happened after the election, for on election night in November 1982 Mark White was still in debt for almost $5 million in loans used to finance his campaign spending. Yet by the time he filed his final campaign finance report in January 1983, White's loans had been completely paid off. That debt of $5 million was eliminated in less than two months because of the rush of business lobbies and interest groups—many of whom had backed Clements before the election—to bring their presence and their interests to the attention of the newly elected governor (McNeely, 1983; *Texas Observer*, 1983). These groups sought this attention, of course, by being openhanded with contributions to help eliminate White's debt.

One might think this situation would arise only with a newly elected Democratic governor, but it was repeated in 1986 when Bill Clements ousted White from the governorship. On election day in 1986, Clements's campaign was $4.5 million in debt. Yet a large number of lobbyists, many of whom had supported White in the campaign, "jumped aboard the late train" after the election, making substantial contributions to Clements to help pay off his debt. We can conclude, then, that the long-time importance of interest groups to Texas politics is considerably reinforced today because of the role they can play in campaign finance.

CONCLUSION

One must conclude from this survey of the Texas electoral system that, for many years, Texas politics were not very democratic. Indeed, the party system and ultimately the government were dominated by conservative elites with only minimal and virtually ritualistic public involvement. One feature commonly thought to be standard in American democracy—that of regular two-party competition—simply did not exist in Texas or in the rest of the South after the Bourbon Coup. Even today, the extent of two-party competition in Texas state politics is low. Thus there is nothing inevitable or even indispensable about the two-party pattern, even though it has often been presented in just those terms in civic education courses in the United States.

Recent years have witnessed the operation of powerful forces both encouraging and retarding the breakdown of the one-party system. Democratic theory concerning the functions of political parties also suggests why a two-party system is preferable. Yet it should also be clear that change toward a two-party system in Texas is proceeding very slowly. To some extent, this change has been driven by social and economic changes in the state, but "outside" forces like federal government intervention have been equally important.

It appears that the Republican party will continue to grow, but it is equally likely that its growth will continue at a slow pace. Perhaps more important for Texas party politics in the near future, however, will be the internal struggles of the Democratic party. That party cannot be dominated as completely today by a narrow elite as it was even ten or twenty years ago. The state has become far too diverse and far too different from the social and economic circumstances that supported the old system. One result of that diversity has been the appearance of new elite groups whose interests are at times divergent from and at times common with those of the older elite.

Another important change for the Democratic party has been an increase in the political activity of the state's ethnic minorities. Blacks and Mexican-

Americans, who have traditionally been left at the bottom of Texas society, are now demanding more of the government—with the clout of large numbers of potential voters behind their demands. It may well prove that the Democratic party's success in resolving these internal divisions and responding to an increasingly diverse society in the state will decide the Republican party's future success.

REFERENCES

Barr, Alwyn. 1971. *Reconstruction to Reform: Texas Politics, 1876 1906.* Austin: University of Texas Press.

Bartley, Numan V., and Graham, Hugh D. 1975. *Southern Politics and the Second Reconstruction.* Baltimore: Johns Hopkins University Press.

Bureau of the Census. 1975. *Historical Statistics of the United States.* Pt. II. Washington, D.C.

Bureau of the Census. 1982. *Statistical Abstract of the United States, 1981.* Washington, D.C.

Bureau of the Census. 1983. *Statistical Abstract of the United States, 1984.* Washington, D.C.

Bureau of the Census. 1987. *Statistical Abstract of the United States, 1987.* Washington, D.C.

Davis, Clarice McDonald. 1965. *Legislative Malapportionment and Roll-Call Voting in Texas, 1961–1963.* Austin: Institute of Public Affairs, University of Texas.

Eldersveld, Samuel J. 1982. *Political Parties in American Society.* New York: Basic Books.

Gantt, Fred. 1964. *The Chief Executive in Texas.* Austin: University of Texas Press.

Key, V. O. 1949. *Southern Politics in State and Nation.* New York: Random House.

Kousser, J. Morgan. 1974. *The Shaping of Southern Politics: Suffrage Restriction and the Establishment of the One-Party South, 1880–1910.* New Haven: Yale University Press.

Matthews, Donald R., and Prothro, James W. 1966. *Negroes and the New Southern Politics.* New York: Harcourt Brace Jovanovich.

McNeely, Dave. 1983. "Lobbyists 'Buy Ticket on Late Train' or Risk Being Left Out." *Austin American Statesman,* January 23, p. C1.

Morehouse, Sarah McCally. 1981. *State Politics, Parties and Policies.* New York: Holt, Rinehart and Winston.

Rice, Lawrence D. 1971. *The Negro in Texas, 1874–1900.* Baton Rouge: Louisiana State University Press.

Stanley, Jeanie R. 1987. "Party Realignment and the 1986 Texas Elections." *Texas Journal of Political Studies* 9 (Spring/Summer):3–13.

Stilwell, Hart. 1949. "Texas: Owned by Oil and Interlocking Directorates." In Robert S. Allen (ed.), *Our Sovereign State.* New York: Vanguard Press.

Texas Legislative Council. 1972. *Fourteen Proposed Constitutional Amendments Analyzed.* Austin: Texas Legislature.

Texas Observer. 1983. "Political Intelligence." February 11.

Weeks, O. Douglas. 1930. "The Texas-Mexican and the Politics of South Texas." *American Political Science Review* 24 (August):606–627.

Weeks, O. Douglas. 1972. "Texas: Land of Conservative Expansiveness." In William C. Havard (ed.), *The Changing Politics of the South*. Baton Rouge: Louisiana State University Press.

Woodward, C. Vann. 1951. *Origins of the New South, 1877–1913*. Baton Rouge: Louisiana State University Press.

Zeigler, Harmon. 1965. "Interest Groups in the States." In Herbert Jacob and Kenneth N. Vines (eds.), *Politics in the American States*. Boston: Little, Brown.

Zeller, Belle. 1954. *American State Legislatures*, New York: Crowell.

6

THE LEGISLATURE

T
he Texas Legislature is the lawmaking institution of the state government. Yet the legislature has several important functions beyond simply making new laws. Its ability to fulfill any of these functions is profoundly affected by constitutional requirements for its structure and by other aspects of its procedures and practices as they have developed over the years. Before considering those procedures and practices, however, it is worthwhile reviewing the judgments of a number of other observers about the character of the Texas Legislature.

THE IMAGE OF THE TEXAS LEGISLATURE

The Texas state capitol—the meeting place of the legislature—was built between 1883–1888. To pay for the new statehouse, the legislature authorized one of the biggest "horse trades" in history: more than 3 million acres of land in the Texas Panhandle in exchange for the construction of the building. Some historians have argued that the state got quite a good deal out of the trade, since the eventual construction cost of the capitol far exceeded the value of the land at the time. Yet modern-day critics of the legislature might retort that this was perhaps the last good deal the legislature has secured for the state. And, they would add, the wheeling and dealing aspect of the exchange has characterized most of the legislature's work ever since. Nor would these be the only problems with the contemporary legislature in the eyes of its many critics. Writing as long ago as 1940, for example, the authors of a notable textbook on state government said of the institution:

The casual observer witnessing the day-to-day performance of an ordinary legislature receives an impression that the situation in Austin is all but hopeless. He sees what appears to be a maelstrom of impulsive opinions; a blundering procedure of chronic disorder and muddlings that culminate invariably in the wreck of construc-

*tive legislation, and [that] produce instead a maze of compromise and error which
the succeeding session will have to spend much time in undoing before proceeding
with its own work. [Patterson, McAlister, and Hester, 1940:59]*

The intervening half century does not seem to have brought notable improvement to the legislature. The indictment just cited has been echoed by
virtually every major textbook on Texas government that has been published
since that 1940 observation. Likewise, although the Texas Legislature has not
been the subject of a great amount of original research by political scientists,
those studies that are available typically confirm this dismal view of the institution in one regard or another.

Moreover, the legislature has periodically been the subject of journalistic
reports that paint a similar portrait of the body. The most notable of these is
the now-institutionalized assessment of the "ten best" and "ten worst" individual legislators that is published in *Texas Monthly* at the end of each regular
legislative session. The exploits of each session's "ten worst" members along
with the fierce competition for this dubious designation, while laughable and
entertaining, are also quite depressing when one considers their importance
for state government.

If the image of the legislature among these critics is less than admirable,
what exactly are its details? Most critics would agree that the Texas Legislature
reveals very little professionalism, that it is heavily influenced, if not controlled,
by special interest groups, mostly from the business sector, and that it has not
adopted very many of the modern procedures of more progressive state legislatures. In consequence, these critics would add, the work of the legislature is
often poorly carried out, and all too often the broad public interest is sacrificed
to that of powerful lobby groups.

These are serious charges that strike at the very purpose of the legislature.
Students of Texas government should be able to draw their own conclusions
about the accuracy of these charges, and to make that possible the present
chapter brings together the major research findings on state legislatures in
general and the Texas Legislature in particular. The chapter will, as well, offer
our own assessment of these matters in the conclusion. As a beginning point
for this subject, however, it is worth considering just what legislatures are
intended to do in the political system. Knowledge of the essential functions of
legislatures will provide a set of benchmarks against which to assess the performance of the Texas institution.

THE FUNCTIONS OF LEGISLATURES

Lawmaking The principal job of a legislature, as noted in the introduction,
is that of *lawmaking*. That is, a legislature is empowered by the constitution
with the writing of new state laws and the revising of old ones. Of course, the
legislature does not monopolize all of the lawmaking power; some of it is shared
with the governor because of his or her right to propose legislation and to veto
bills passed by the legislature.

Students of the lawmaking function should be familiar with the process that textbooks traditionally call "how a bill becomes a law." This phrase refers to the step-by-step institutional procedure through which a proposed law, or bill, must pass if it is to win the approval of the legislature and then the governor before becoming law. Figure 6–1 is a schematic diagram of the major aspects of that process in Texas. The diagram identifies both the principal "approval points" for bills and the order in which a bill must pass through those points. Lawmaking here—as in all American legislatures—is an elaborate, complicated process. Yet this aspect of the *process* of lawmaking is far less important to a legislature's performance than are several other characteristics—such as the nature of the membership and the leadership of the body, the professionalism and expertise in the legislature, and the dispersion of power within it. These matters are the concerns of the rest of this book.

Oversight　　The second major task of the legislature, after lawmaking, is one that political scientists have come to call *oversight* of the executive branch. Once the legislature has created new laws or government policies, they are implemented by the executive branch. An important task of the legislature then becomes overseeing the job done by executive (that is, administrative) agencies. Legislators want to know that their intentions as embodied in the original laws are being carried out. They also want to learn, in the exercising of their oversight, whether unanticipated difficulties have arisen in the process of policy implementation that call for a revision of the original law. Oversight, then, is an ongoing task of the legislature.

There are two other major tasks to be performed by this institution, but before describing them we should first note some important difficulties of lawmaking and oversight today. A useful perspective for understanding these difficulties is to contrast present-day legislative duties with those of the late nineteenth century—for example, shortly after the ratification of the constitution of 1876.

Chapter 4 explained how the authors of the 1876 constitution, like the majority of Texans at the time, wanted a very limited state government. They eliminated a number of state agencies that had been created under Reconstruction, and they returned a variety of powers to local governments. Moreover, through the nineteenth century and well into the present one, state governments throughout the United States were rather limited in their powers (at least in comparison to the powers they exercise today). One might say, once again, that state governments followed reasonably closely the political philosophy of laissez faire—the notion that government should be charged with only a very limited range of responsibilities.

Proponents of laissez faire would say that state government should provide only the most basic public services—those that cannot be efficiently or safely provided by the private marketplace. Among these services would be policing, probably some public health functions, limited protection of the state's natural resources, and a limited public education system. Beyond these and a few other essential services, such people would argue, it is preferable to rely on the private sector to fill society's needs.

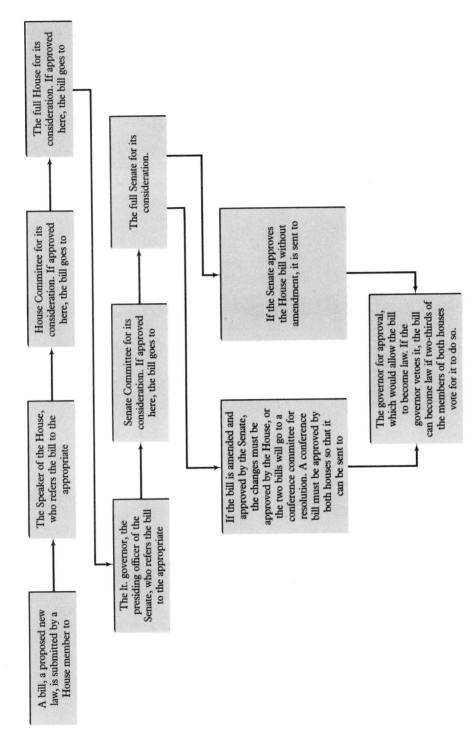

FIGURE 6–1 The Lawmaking Function: How Laws Are Made in Texas

Under a limited government like the one in Texas in the late nineteenth century the tasks of lawmaking and oversight are relatively simple. Compared to the present day, there were not many state agencies, not many laws, and not many challenging tasks facing government. Thus the time and effort required by legislative responsibilities in that period were themselves not very demanding.

Today, however, the state of Texas—like every other state—has moved far beyond laissez faire government. The social and economic problems of the twentieth century, the demands of the citizens of Texas for certain kinds of government action, and even demands from the federal government that states initiate certain kinds of action have brought about a fundamentally different state government. Today the state of Texas has taken on a wide range of responsibilities—in education, social welfare, environmental regulation, public health, crime control, and the regulation of business and the professions to name only the most obvious examples. Nor is it simply the range of responsibilities that is important here. Increasingly, the policy problems in many of these areas have become technically complex as never before. Just what kind of environmental control efforts are likely to be most successful and at what costs are complex questions about which even experts in the subject disagree. The same is true for problems in public education, social welfare, and all the other major policy areas now the responsibility of state government.

Political scientists refer to a governmental system that has taken on such a broad array of responsibilities as a *positive state,* meaning a government that has assumed positive—or activist—responsibility for the resolution of a large number of society's problems. Under such a system, the tasks of lawmaking and oversight become much more complicated than under the laissez faire system. In making new laws legislators must now attempt to master complex, often highly technical issues that may have far-reaching effects on the state. They must often contend with the conflicting judgments of different experts on some of these policy issues, for often the experts themselves disagree. Because *any* government policy in many of these areas will have considerable influence on the society or economy of the state, legislators also must contend with vigorous lobbying efforts by groups that stand to gain or lose by their decision.

Similarly, the job of the legislator has become more complicated because, under the positive state, there exists a much larger number of public agencies charged with the responsibility of executing state policy. Thus the oversight function becomes more challenging. And oversight, like lawmaking, itself often revolves around technical questions as legislators attempt to assess just how good a job executive agencies are doing at their assigned tasks. In short, the nature of the times in late-twentieth-century America has revolutionized the character of these first two legislative functions.

Representation   There are, as noted above, two more functions for the legislature. The third task is called the *representation* function. This is, of course, linked to the fact that legislators are popularly elected to make public policy decisions in the name of their constituents. Thus, in the processes of lawmaking and oversight, lawmakers should be representing those who elected them. Certainly in the era of the positive state this third task itself becomes more difficult. Facing a number of complex issues, even the most well-intentioned legislator might be uncertain about the preferences of his or her constituents on many of those issues. Moreover, because public opinion polls have typically shown that the average citizen often has very limited knowledge of many complicated policy issues, the constituency may actually have no clear preference on some of these issues to guide the legislator.

But the task of representation would be complicated under any circumstances because it can sometimes demand, simultaneously, entirely different actions on the part of the legislator. Political scientists have noted at least two representational roles of the legislator that may be contradictory. One is that of the *delegate*, the elected representative whose goal is to make policy decisions exactly as the majority of his or her constituents would prefer. The other role is that of the *trustee*, whose goal is to make the policy decisions that are in the best interests of his or her constituents, even if those constituents might not recognize the wisdom of such decisions.

Research on individual legislators has shown that some try to achieve one or the other of these two roles while some others attempt to move back and forth between the two roles depending on the policy issue at stake. Looking at this question from a slightly different perspective, one might guess that some legislators are merely driven by self-interest—attempting to make the decisions they think will best help them stay in office. At times legislators might do what they think the majority of their constituents desire. At other times, however, they might follow the interests of only those constituents who belong to their political party, or they might follow the interests of those groups or individuals who helped them most in getting elected in the first place. Whatever strategy legislators individually follow, the task of representation is never simple.

Public Forum   The last function of the legislature is in some sense a collective one that relates to the successful operation of democratic government. The legislature ought to be a public forum for criticism of existing government policy. In a democratic system, of course, it is anticipated that this criticism will come largely from the political party or parties out of power—that is, those not in a majority in the legislature or who are not represented by the governor. Yet disaffected or factional elements in the majority party may at times also provide some of this criticism. The importance of this out-group criticism for the healthy functioning of a democratic society cannot be overemphasized. It ensures that policy issues are fully debated before government action is taken; it helps expose shortcomings in proposed and existing policies; and it keeps the public far better informed about public issues and policies than they otherwise would be. In short, such out-group criticism simply keeps the in-party of government leaders on their toes.

Criticism of government policy does not, of course, have to arise only in the legislature. Yet this is a particularly important place for it to do so. This is the principal institutional forum where policy questions will, of necessity, be debated. It is essential that minority or out-party points of view be represented

in those debates. The legislature commands a number of institutional resources, such as research expertise, access to information, and legal authority
that can be used by minority interests to help publicize their cause. And this
institution is one that, because of its prominence, ensures that policy criticism
voiced here will receive media coverage and public attention. Thus whether
the public at large ultimately agrees or disagrees with criticism of government
policy on any given issue, the goals of democratic government are furthered
by its existence.

These four functions of legislatures—lawmaking, oversight, representation, and criticism—provide a starting point for our consideration of the Texas
Legislature. In the remainder of this chapter we will examine the aspects of
the legislature that assist it in the pursuit of those goals and the aspects that
constrain it. The conclusion will draw together the strands of evidence on these
matters, assess the overall performance of the legislature, and then relate that
assessment to the image of the legislature discussed earlier.

THE REALITY OF THE TEXAS LEGISLATURE

Since the four basic legislative functions are to some degree technical tasks,
we begin our review of the Texas Legislature by analyzing its technical competence as it relates to those functions. It is fortunate that there already exists
a comprehensive analysis of these matters which compares the Texas Legislature to those of all the other states. That analysis, completed in 1970 by a
nonpartisan group, the Citizens Conference on State Legislatures, and published in a book entitled *State Legislatures: An Evaluation of Their Effectiveness*
(1971), offers a fascinating comparison of the legislatures of the fifty states. We
will review those findings, detail some of the shortcomings of the Texas Legislature revealed in that study and elsewhere, and then offer a contemporary
assessment of how the Texas body rates in terms of technical competence.

The Citizens Conference on State Legislatures adopted five broad criteria
by which to evaluate individual legislatures:

1. *Functional capability*   The legislature should have adequate time, research and support staff, facilities, and managerial methods to carry
   out its duties with competence.

2. *Accountability*   The structure of the legislature ought to be publicly
   comprehensible and publicly accessible, information on the legislature
   and its decisions ought to be publicly available, and the leaders of the
   legislature ought to be accountable to the membership.

3. *Information-handling capability*   Legislators should have sufficient
   time, staff, and procedures to collect and analyze the information they
   need to discharge their duties.

4. *Independence*   The legislature should be able to determine its own
   agenda and meeting times, it should be sufficiently independent of the
   executive branch to function as a partner in the governmental process,

and by various procedures and public information processes the legislature should be freed from undue pressure by outside lobby groups.

5. *Representativeness* Members of the legislature ought to be sufficiently identified with their constituents, provided sufficient technical resources and legislative opportunities, and sufficiently diverse in their personal characteristics (age, profession, ethnicity, gender, and so on) to ensure that they do represent public preferences.

Rating the Texas Legislature

For each of these five criteria the Citizens Conference developed a long checklist of specific features that would strengthen the legislature's ability to perform that task. All fifty state legislatures were analyzed on these checklists and were then ranked from the most to the least well structured in the terms of each criterion. The major results of this research effort were, then, rankings of the fifty states on these five criteria of legislative capability along with a summary ranking based on the five individual ratings.

And how did the Texas Legislature compare? Table 6–1 presents all six rankings that came out of the Citizens Conference study. The results are certainly nothing to brag about: Texas ranked thirty-eighth overall and rated poorly on four of the five component scales. Texas's ranking was especially poor on functional capability, information handling, and independence. Only on the representativeness scale did the Texas Legislature score well in comparison to the legislatures of other states. If the Texas Legislature fared so poorly in this comparison in 1970, what were the major criticisms that led to this poor showing? And which of those criticisms still hold today?

Constitutionally Mandated Short and Infrequent Sessions Today the state constitution still limits, as it did in 1970, the regular sessions of the legislature to biennial meetings (once every two years) of only 140 days' duration. (Regular sessions begin on the second Tuesday in January of odd-numbered years.) This limitation is quite important because, with the growth of the positive state, the work load of the legislature has expanded both in size and in complexity. A 140-day session might have been adequate to carry out all the necessary business when the constitution was adopted in 1876, but today it seriously compromises the quality of lawmaking and oversight. Similar restrictions were common in many other states earlier in this century, but today forty-three states have annual legislative sessions with, therefore, considerably more working time available to handle these duties.

Inability to Call Itself into Special Session Only the governor can call a special session of the Texas Legislature, and the body can, in such sessions, only consider the issues the governor places on its agenda. Special sessions are also limited by the constitution to only thirty days' duration. Thus the legislature itself cannot use the device of special sessions to get around the limitation on regular session meeting times to devote more time to consideration of regular legislative business.

TABLE 6–1 Citizens Conference Rankings of State Legislatures

Overall Rank	State	Ranking on Functional Capability	Ranking on Accountability	Ranking on Information-Handling Capability	Ranking on Independence	Ranking on Representativeness
1	California	1	3	2	3	2
2	New York	4	13	1	8	1
3	Illinois	17	4	6	2	13
4	Florida	5	8	4	1	30
5	Wisconsin	7	21	3	4	10
6	Iowa	6	6	5	11	25
7	Hawaii	2	11	20	7	16
8	Michigan	15	22	9	12	3
9	Nebraska	35	1	16	30	18
10	Minnesota	27	7	13	23	12
11	New Mexico	3	16	28	39	4
12	Alaska	8	29	12	6	40
13	Nevada	13	10	19	14	32
14	Oklahoma	9	27	24	22	8
15	Utah	38	5	8	29	24
16	Ohio	18	24	7	40	9
17	South Dakota	23	12	15	16	37
18	Idaho	20	9	29	27	21
19	Washington	12	17	25	19	39
20	Maryland	16	31	10	15	45
21	Pennsylvania	37	23	23	5	36
22	North Dakota	22	18	17	37	31
23	Kansas	31	15	14	32	34
24	Connecticut	39	26	26	25	6

	State					
25	West Virginia	10	32	37	24	15
26	Tennessee	30	44	11	9	26
27	Oregon	28	14	35	35	19
28	Colorado	21	25	21	28	27
29	Massachusetts	32	35	22	21	23
30	Maine	29	34	32	18	22
31	Kentucky	49	2	48	44	7
32	New Jersey	14	42	18	31	35
33	Louisiana	47	39	33	13	14
34	Virginia	25	19	27	26	48
35	Missouri	36	30	40	49	5
36	Rhode Island	33	46	30	41	11
37	Vermont	19	20	34	42	47
38	Texas	45	36	43	45	17
39	New Hampshire	34	33	42	36	43
40	Indiana	44	38	41	43	20
41	Montana	26	28	31	46	49
42	Mississippi	46	43	45	20	28
43	Arizona	11	47	38	17	50
44	South Carolina	50	45	39	10	46
45	Georgia	40	49	36	33	38
46	Arkansas	41	40	46	34	33
47	North Carolina	24	37	44	47	44
48	Delaware	43	48	47	38	29
49	Wyoming	42	41	50	48	42
50	Alabama	48	50	49	50	41

Source: Citizens Conference on State Legislatures (1971:40).

Too Many Members in the House of Representatives The Citizens Conference believed the optimum size of the lower house of a state legislature to be one hundred members; beyond that number, it argued, the functional capability of a legislative body was compromised. By that standard the Texas House of Representatives with its 150 members remains much too large.

Shortcomings of the Committee System Not only the study by the Citizens Conference but a considerable body of other research also suggests that the committee systems of the Texas House and Senate are considerably outmoded. It is widely accepted that legislatures should have so-called standing committees with separate policy responsibilities (for education, law enforcement, natural resources, and so on). The task of these committees is to do the first-round review of proposed new laws when the legislature meets in regular session. Most students of legislatures believe, as well, that a well-structured committee system is essential to the effective working of the whole institution. A good committee system is particularly important for the technical quality of lawmaking and oversight. The Texas Legislature has standing committees and did so in 1970, but there were several problems both then and today with the ways in which those committees operate. (The standing committees of the 1987 legislative session are shown in table 6–2.

TABLE 6–2 Committees of the Texas Legislature: 1987

House of Representatives

Agriculture and Livestock	Insurance
Appropriations	Judicial Affairs
Business and Commerce	Judiciary
Calendars	Labor and Employment
Corrections	Liquor Regulations
County Affairs	Local and Consent Calendars
Criminal Jurisprudence	Natural Resources
Cultural and Historical Resources	Public Education
Elections	Public Health
Energy	Public Safety
Environmental Affairs	Retirement and Aging
Financial Institutions	Rules and Resolutions
General Investigating	Science and Technology
Government Organization	State Affairs
Higher Education	Transportation
House Administration	Urban Affairs
Human Services	Ways and Means

Senate

Administration	Intergovernmental Relations
Criminal Justice	Jurisprudence
Economic Development	Natural Resources
Education	Nominations
Finance	Rules
Health and Human Resources	State Affairs

The biggest problems with the committee systems of the Texas Legislature relate to how individual legislators get to be members of different committees and how the chairpersons of those committees are chosen. In the Texas Legislature both these matters are effectively controlled by the presiding officers of the separate houses. That is, the Speaker of the House and the lieutenant governor as the presiding officer of the Senate control the selection of both committee members and chairpersons. There does exist a limited *seniority* system that determines some of a member's committee memberships. In other words, legislators get to choose some of their committee assignments, and a rule of seniority (or length of service in the legislature) is employed to determine which members will get the most highly sought-after committee assignments. Yet the seniority system only determines a limited number of all committee assignments, and the bulk of those decisions remain in the hands of the presiding officers.

One consequence of leader control of committee assignments is that there is no guarantee of continuity of membership on the committees. As one example of how the presiding officers manipulate the committee system, at the start of the 1983 regular session the new Speaker of the House, Gib Lewis, reappointed the chairpersons of that body's thirty-three committees. He appointed only six chairpersons to keep the leadership of committees they had chaired in the preceding session. Ten other representatives who had chaired committees in the prior session were given different chairmanships. The remaining seventeen committees were chaired by entirely new leaders. Similarly, the membership as well as the leadership of the committees was shuffled at the start of the new session.

In 1985 Lewis retained eighteen of the twenty-two chairs he had appointed in 1983 and who were reelected to office. For the 1987 legislative session, however, he dumped eight committee chairs from the prior session. Some of these people reported in the press that they lost their positions—as they were told by Lewis or one of his assistants—for failing to support the speaker's legislative program in the 1986 special session.

Continuity of membership and leadership on legislative committees is important because it allows legislators to specialize in the issues handled by their committees. They can become more expert about the subject *and* more knowledgeable about government programs and policies. A good seniority system or some other method by which legislators can influence their own committee assignments can also redound to the quality of legislative work. On the one hand, when legislators can influence their own committee assignments, they are more likely to be placed on committees in which they have great interest and on which they will be willing, therefore, to work especially hard. On the other hand, committee assignment rules that allow the more senior members to get the most prestigious committee appointments create incentives to remain in the legislature. Thus experience and, one would hope, expertise in legislative work are rewarded.

A committee system with high turnover and one, as well, that is controlled by the presiding officers has several potentially unfortunate consequences. It becomes particularly difficult in such a system for members to develop expertise or even very much background knowledge of the subject matter of their committees. There will be little incentive even to attempt to do so, for in the next regular session one might be placed on an entirely new set of committees. The inability to choose one's own committee assignments means, as well, that there is little guarantee that members will get to serve on the committees whose subjects they already know well or care about the most.

Finally, the fact that the presiding officers control the committee system means that these two leaders can "stack" committees with certain members to control the decision making that goes on in those groups. Even the reforms that created the limited seniority system and brought about other changes in the committees in 1972–1973 have not cut appreciably into this power. Despite certain restrictions on the presiding officers' committee stacking powers, those powers remained quite strong even after the reforms (Moncrief, 1979). Indeed, changes in the internal rules of the House of Representatives in 1983 and 1985 increased the speaker's committee appointment powers even further (Price, 1985). Among the traditional powers of the presiding officers are the rights to determine the jurisdiction of individual committees, to assign bills to individual committees, to appoint the members of conference committees, and to control a number of other legislative resources important to the operation of the committee system.

The Citizens Conference cited a number of other problems in the committee structures of the two houses of the Texas Legislature. The details of those criticisms are not of great importance at present, but it is worth noting that only in one or two instances has any notable progress been made since 1970 in terms of responding to those charges. As for the major problems of the committee system, very little substantial change has been made since the Citizens Conference report—and some of the changes that have come about, like those strengthening the committee-control powers of the Speaker of the House, have aggravated rather than solved the problems of the committee systems.

Scheduling Problems   Another major problem cited by the Citizens Conference was the matter of scheduling debates over proposed legislation after it has been sent to the full House or Senate after approval by one of the committees. The Citizens Conference proposed that there be an automatic calendar guaranteeing that each bill would be debated and that the debate would occur on a certain date. The calendar existing in the Texas Legislature in 1970 and still used today is too complicated and is subject to manipulation by the presiding officers. In the House there are eight different calendars to which different bills can be assigned. But in both houses the presiding officer controls the assignment of bills to calendars, and both of these officials have a number of parliamentary powers that enable them to manipulate the calendars or simply ignore them.

At first glance this subject of the calendars might appear to be just a trivial detail of procedure. Yet two quite significant problems arise out of this issue. One is that without an automatic calendar—and under the time pressure of the short 140-day session—the legislature inevitably falls far behind schedule in working its way through each year's body of proposed legislation. The early days of the session are largely taken up with organizational work and then the initial committee hearings. Toward the end of the session, on the other hand, and particularly in the last few days, the pace of debating and voting on bills becomes frantic. There is always a logjam of legislation that must be considered in the final days. A large number of these bills are, therefore, pushed through the legislature with little time for debate. Bad bills—and even devious ones—can be approved in this atmosphere, because the quality of lawmaking is inevitably compromised under these conditions.

Moreover, because the presiding officers can manipulate the calendar these officials have enormous discretionary power over the ultimate fate of many bills. The speaker or lieutenant governor can ensure that they bring up for debate certain bills at the time when they are most or least likely to be passed—in accordance with their own preferences for the fate of the bill. They can hide controversial bills in the logjam of legislation that is rammed through the legislature in the closing days of the session. They can even kill a bill by seeing that it never comes up for debate. An excellent discussion of just one of the parliamentary powers that make this situation possible is offered in the editorial on pages 122–123. The character of the scheduling system, at first glance a seemingly minor institutional detail, has enormous importance both for the quality and for the kind of legislation that comes out of the Texas Legislature.

Inadequate Legislative Salaries   The Citizens Conference also argued that Texas, like many other states, paid its legislators salaries that were far too low. The conference argued that lawmakers ought to be paid something that at least approaches a full-time annual salary so that more people can consider running for the legislature and so that, once elected, legislators can devote all their time to that job.

The salaries of Texas legislators are set by the constitution and thus can be raised only by constitutional amendment—another problem in the eyes of the Citizens Conference because of the typical difficulties associated with the amendment process. In 1970 the Texas Constitution stipulated annual legislative salaries of $4,800 a year plus $12 a day for expenses when the legislature was in session. These salaries have been raised subsequently, but even today Texas legislators earn only $7,200 in annual salary plus a $30 per diem expense allowance for the first 120 days of regular sessions and for each day of a special session. In other words, legislators earn about $9,000 per year in total compensation.

The consequences of low pay should be obvious. Only certain kinds of people—the wealthy or those in unusually fortunate professional circumstances—can even contemplate running for the office. And many of those who are elected can devote only a limited part of their time to the job. Even when the legislature is in session, many of the members are forced to carry on their private professions at long distance from Austin, supplemented by weekend trips home to do as much business as possible. The time and effort that ought to be devoted to lawmaking, oversight, and so on are, of course, compromised.

FELTON WEST

SENATE SHOULD END CALENDAR TRICKERY

AUSTIN—Tourists briefly visiting Senate sessions this year may leave with the idea that creating a Texas-flag flower bed at the Capitol is the Senate's next item of business.

Right there at the top of the Senate calendar, printed daily in a little green booklet, is Senate Bill 123, by Sen. Roy Blake of Nacogdoches, "relating to the creation and maintenance on the grounds of the State Capitol a permanent flower bed depicting through appropriate design and flower selection the Texas flag."

Blake is chairman of the powerful Senate Administration Committee, so his bill—up there first in line to be considered by the full Senate—ought to move fast, right?

Wrong.

His bill is not going anywhere. By agreement with Lt. Gov. Bill Hobby, Blake will never try to pass it.

SB123 is just a serious joke, the session's blocking bill. Its whole purpose is to ensure that the calendar, which is officially the "regular order of business," or ROB, is never followed. Since Blake will not try to pass it, no bill beneath it on the calendar can be considered by the Senate unless its author has rounded up an extraordinary majority of votes to suspend the ROB.

A sponsor may have 16 or 18 votes committed for his very good bill—enough to pass it in the 31-member Senate—but it won't ever be passed unless he can muster a two-thirds majority of those present to suspend the ROB so it can be brought to the simple-majority passage vote. The two-thirds-of-those-present majority is 21 votes if there's a full house.

First the sponsor must get recognized by the presiding officer (the lieutenant governor) to make a motion to suspend the ROB. If he

Limited Staff Support   The Citizens Conference also argued that Texas legislators were provided insufficient staff support to carry out their duties appropriately. Legislators are provided monthly staff and office expense allowances, but most observers believe these funds are adequate only to cover basic office and clerical functions. They are not sufficient to allow legislators to hire professional research personnel to aid in the tasks of information gathering and analysis so important to lawmaking and oversight today. To compound this problem, the staff funds of the individual standing committees are themselves limited. In some states, by comparison, far more generous staff resources are provided both individual legislators and the committees.

The Lieutenant Governor Problem   Texas, like several other states, was also criticized because the lieutenant governor—a publicly elected executive branch is recognized and wins the two-thirds majority for his motion, his bill is brought up, explained, debated, possibly amended, and tentatively approved. Then, if the author can muster a four-fifths majority of the membership (25 votes) to suspend a constitutional rule requiring final passage on another day, the bill may be finally passed and sent to the House the same day.

If the four-fifths majority can't be achieved, then on another day the sponsor must get the ROB suspended again by a two-thirds majority, after which the bill may be passed by a simple-majority vote.

If you ask me, it's terribly undemocratic and the Senate should have a better way to regulate traffic. But this has been the Senate system for as long as anybody there can remember. Lieutenant governors and most senators like it. It enhances a lieutenant governor's control and helps senators obscure their stands on hot-potato bills. It "works both ways," preventing passage of bad bills as well as good ones, its admirers say.

But if a bill has simple-majority support, as long as it is not shown to be unconstitutional, it should become law. Merit, not tricky rules, should determine whether it is passed; this should not have to wait for years until the majority support has grown bigger.

Senate bill traffic could be regulated instead by having committees, which already study bills closely, decide which have enough merit to be voted on at all by the full Senate.

Blake, who seems fond of flower bills, used the same flower-bed bill to block the calendar in the regular legislative session in 1983. The State Purchasing and General Services Commission even wanted to help pass it—until Blake explained.

In 1981, he introduced a bill to prohibit importation of diseased camellias. But whatever dangers foreign camellias threatened us with, Texas evidently remains unprotected from them, because that was just the 1981 calendar-blocking bill.

Cute, eh? But such a system has a profound effect on our laws.

[*Houston Post*, 1985]

official in theory—wields considerable power as the presiding officer of the Senate. In effect, the lieutenant governor is a legislative branch, not an executive branch, official. He does not, like the vice-president of the United States, assist the chief executive in implementing policy and supervising administrative agencies. The only time that the lieutenant governor acts in this capacity is when he assumes the position of acting chief executive, in largely ceremonial fashion, when the governor is out of the state. Instead of assuming a significant role in the executive branch, the lieutenant governor works in the legislative arena to make laws and policy. And he is a very powerful official because of that position.

If Texans recognize the reality of the lieutenant governor's role, then at least they will not be misled by the arrangement. But many citizens probably do misunderstand the office, assuming the lieutenant governor is indeed just like the vice-president of the United States. Thus they misunderstand how independent and powerful the lieutenant governor is and do not realize that he is really a legislative more than an executive branch official. As J. William Davis (1967:18–19) has said:

> The analogy of the Vice President of the United States is not appropriate to the office of the lieutenant governor of Texas. The Vice President has similar constitutional functions, presiding over the Senate and succession to the presidency, but the realities of the office are quite different. The Vice President runs on the ticket with the President, as a member of the "team." They are elected together and are expected to work together at all times. At the President's request and direction, the Vice President may substitute for the President on many occasions and serve as his spokesman, not only in the Senate, but before the nation and the world. . . . This is not true of the lieutenant governor in Texas. He and the governor are elected separately, each running his own race. . . . Persons elected to the two offices may conceivably be of different political leanings. The lieutenant governor rarely substitutes for the governor as his representative or spokesman. Even though he may make many public appearances, he does so as the lieutenant governor, not as a spokesman for the governor. The governor and lieutenant governor usually work together in many ways, but they are not necessarily a part of the same team.

This arrangement means that the distinction between the legislative and executive branch is blurred and, moreover, that the Senate is not able to choose its own leadership. This situation is ill-understood by the average Texan, and many citizens are thereby misled about the actual distribution of power in state government. Beyond that, this arrangement weakens the traditional independence of the legislature in a way that many political observers believe to be objectionable.

Consequences of These Problems

Some implications of these various problems with the Texas Legislature have already been mentioned, yet the major difficulties bear reiteration because they are all related. One major impact is on the character and quality of the membership of the legislature. The low pay, the personal demands arising from spending about five months every two years in Austin—typically leaving one's family, friends, and professional life back home—and the limited opportunities for professional advancement and technical specialization in the current committee system mean that the people who are elected to the legislature are often little better than amateurs. There are too few incentives, in other words, to attract very many of the most highly qualified potential candidates. Indeed, the best people have far more attractive alternatives in both the private and the public sector. Furthermore, there are few incentives for those who are elected to stay in the body, so that turnover is relatively high. (Turnover, tenure, and related aspects of the membership of the legislature are discussed in more detail in the next section.)

Another consequence of Texas's legislative system is that the presiding officers of the House and Senate have become enormously powerful. Their control over the committee system and the calendar have already been discussed. Yet we should remember that, simply in their actions when presiding over debates, they have considerable additional power over the fate of legislation. The Speaker of the House and the lieutenant governor also control many of the research and staff resources of their respective houses. They even control the membership of conference committees that must meet to work out compromises between conflicting bills passed by the two bodies.

Based on the powers of the presiding officers and the relative weakness of the individual members, one can make a strong case—as many inside observers have—that the Texas Legislature is itself hardly a democratic body. Instead it is something like two feudal monarchies, dominated by the presiding officers who control the agenda and the majority of the members the majority of the time by their power to distribute favors and rewards to those who accept their leadership. Little that is opposed by the presiding officer will ever come out of either house. Some observers have even shown how the powers of the presiding officers have actually grown substantially since the time of the Citizens Conference analysis of state legislatures (Pettus, 1980; Price, 1985).

But the most important result of these various problems is that the quality of the legislature's functioning—whether in lawmaking, in oversight, in representation, even in policy criticism—is seriously compromised. The time for legislative work is too limited. The quality of the membership is too low. The incentives to remain a legislator are too meager to prevent high turnover. The resources available to the members for research, information gathering, and analysis are too limited. The committee system stifles the development of policy expertise. Finally, a number of the individual problems combine to increase the power of the presiding officers over that of the individual members.

Current Ranking of the Texas Legislature

The discussion to this point has relied largely on the 1970 comparative study of state legislatures. Even though the current situation in the Texas Legislature has been noted on a number of separate points, you might wonder how that body would fare today in an overall comparison. Although no such study has recently been executed, it is still possible to estimate with some certainty how the Texas Legislature would rate in such a study.

It is possible to make such an estimate because from approximately 1965 to 1980 there was considerable reform within state legislatures in the United States. The Citizens Conference study was itself only one example of the widespread criticism of existing legislative institutions and procedures. As a consequence of this widespread interest in reform, many states revised their legislative systems in one respect or another. In a number of states constitutional limitations on legislatures—on their meeting times, frequency of meeting, salary levels, and even on their lawmaking authority—were relaxed. Many states adopted annual instead of biennial sessions. Most raised legislative salaries. Staff and research resources were expanded dramatically in many states, and many adopted new scheduling systems to reduce logjams and streamline the flow of legislative work.

Texas, however, made only very modest changes in its legislature during this period. Most of its original constitutional limitations on the body have been left intact. Biennial sessions and very limited special sessions were retained. The system of strong presiding officers was retained and, as noted above, even strengthened further. The problems of scheduling and the end-of-session logjam remain. The incentives for professional legislative work are still quite low. There were, it is true, some positive achievements—an increase in legislators' salaries in 1975, some reforms in the committee system, some increases in staff support and in oversight activities. Yet Texas only made limited progress in modernizing its legislature—even in these areas where there were changes—while many other states were taking considerable strides. These facts suggest that if the Citizens Conference study were replicated today, the technical competence of the Texas Legislature would rate even *lower* now than it did in 1970 when compared to the legislatures of the other states.

THE LEGISLATORS THEMSELVES

We turn now to an examination of the elected members themselves, how they get elected, what sorts of individuals they are, and even the reasons they enter and leave the institution. The state constitution requires a member of the House of Representatives to be at least twenty-one years of age, a citizen of the United States, a qualified voter in the state, and a resident of the state for two years preceding the election and of the House district for one year. The requirements for Senate eligibility are essentially the same except that the minimum age is twenty-six and the state residency requirement is five years. Elections to the House are held in November of even-numbered years, and House members serve two-year terms once elected. Senators serve four-year terms, and half of them are elected in November of each even-numbered year. Beyond these formal requirements for membership, however, there are practical requirements that determine who will seek office in the legislature.

The Practical Requirements

The most obvious requirement is that one must have sufficient interest in politics to seek an office that will require campaigning for the better part of a year, suffering through both a primary and a general election, spending about half the year after the election living in Austin participating in the legislative session and possibly a special session, and then devoting the succeeding year and a half to at least some interim activities and service for constituents—all for about $9,000 a year in total compensation.

Yet this hurdle of interest in politics might be overcome for any number of reasons. In terms of political culture, some legislative hopefuls surely are motivated by something like the moralistic orientation of political life in the public interest. Others probably follow the individualistic idea that politics can aid one's personal career. The salary of a legislator will not itself make a great contribution to one's personal success, but some hope to use their experience in the legislature to seek higher and more lucrative political office. Others frankly hope to use their time in the legislature to make business associations, learn the ins and outs of state government, become acquainted with representatives of the major lobby interests, and then retire from the legislature into an enhanced private career. The latter route can be particularly useful for young professionals in business, law, insurance, and real estate. Finally, some legislative hopefuls probably get their ambition from family or friendship ties with others seriously involved in political life. Many people reared in a highly political family are socialized to believe that it is natural and even expected of them to enter that life. Thus sufficient interest in politics to get over this first hurdle can arise for a number of reasons.

A second practical requirement is that one must be a self-starter and probably even a "self-nominator." Political parties and other formal organizations are not as deeply involved in the initial recruitment of new candidates for the legislature as one might first guess. Many candidates recruit themselves to run for the office. Lawrence W. Miller (1977:123–125) found, for example, that in a study of individuals who entered and left the legislature between 1969 and 1976, some 43 percent said they were "self-recruited" to run for office. Only 13 percent said that political party organizations had recruited them. (The remainder were influenced in their decision to run for office by one or another private, nonparty organization.)

A third practical requirement is that one must be in a personal and professional situation that allows one to run for an office that pays so little and yet demands so much of one's time—even if pursued on a part-time basis. In short, a person must either be independently wealthy or have a job that can itself become a second part-time position while he or she is in the legislature. Besides people who are independently wealthy, those who are self-employed are typically better able to meet this requirement. The point is that the financial and time demands of a legislative career, even a short one, constitute a hurdle that only a small and select group of Texans will be able to get over.

One must also be able—by one's own wealth, by having the right connections, or by dint of hard campaign work—to raise sufficient funds to pay for a political campaign. A survey of campaign expenditure reports for the 1984 election year suggests that serious candidates for the Texas Senate probably spent at least $150,000 in their campaigns. Candidates in competitive House races typically had to spend at least $80,000. Even a veteran representative running unopposed for reelection in a small-town district would have probably spent $10,000 to $20,000 in his or her campaign. Each succeeding election year, of course, requires another round of such spending—and the search for campaign contributions necessary to support it.

Who Gets Elected?

From those who get over the practical hurdles and seek election to the legislature, what kinds of people are typically elected today? Table 6–3 offers information on that question by way of a breakdown of the demographic

TABLE 6–3   Characteristics of Members of the Texas Legislature: 1987

Characteristic	Senate (%)	House (%)
Sex		
Male	90	91
Female	10	9
Age		
20–29	0	1
30–39	26	27
40–49	35	42
50–59	32	18
60 or older	6	11
Education		
Less than college	0	3
Some college or bachelor's degree	32	57
Advanced or graduate degree	68	40
Ethnicity		
Anglo	77	81
Black	6	8
Mexican-American	16	11
Occupation		
Law	55	29
Business	39	46
Ranching or farming	—	9
Education	3	5
Medicine	3	3
Homemaker	—	3
Retired	—	3
Other	—	3

Source: Texas State Directory (1987).

characteristics of legislators in 1985. That information indicates that the legislature is overwhelmingly composed of male, Anglo, well-educated businessmen and lawyers. The only other notable demographic characteristic of the legislative body concerns the occupational data. The table lists the primary occupation reported by the lawmakers; yet a remarkable number of the attorneys and businessmen reported that they were also engaged in farming or ranching. This fact attests, on the one hand, to the breadth of the business interests of these people and, on the other hand, to the continuing salience of these traditional occupations among the state's elected leaders.

Why They Leave the Legislature

As is true in all state legislatures, the rate of membership turnover from election to election has been declining in Texas over most of the present century. In the last twenty or so years, average turnover at elections has been in the range of 20–25 percent in the Senate and 20–30 percent in the House. Yet these figures indicate only the percentage of "freshmen" elected in a given year. Average tenure in office is also important. After the 1986 elections, as an example, the average tenure in the Senate was 6.4 years and it was 5.0 years in the House. Thus the average senator had served only one and a half terms, and the average representative two and a half. These figures indicate that the typical member does not remain very long in the House or the Senate. If one thinks of the legislator's job as requiring the development of specialized knowledge and expertise, the average member will probably not have advanced far in those terms before he or she leaves the institution. This problem is, fortunately, moderated a bit by the fact that most freshman senators served in the House before election to the more senior body. Yet even in the Senate the average member does not have a long career.

Why is it that most members leave so soon, and what might we learn from their reasons for leaving? There has not been much research on this question for the Texas Legislature itself, but research on state legislatures in general suggests some probable answers. First, of course, some members will seek but fail to be reelected. Miller (1977:43–45) found that in the early 1970s about one-third of those who left the Texas Legislature did so because of failure to win reelection. But of even greater interest are those members who retire voluntarily. If we remember that most people enter the House with no prior experience in elected office, and keeping in mind the financial, personal, and time demands of the office, the likely reasons for voluntary retirement should be clear. (In Miller's study 25 percent of those who left the legislature during the period he examined did so voluntarily.)

The principal reason for voluntary retirement is probably the financial strain of the job. Miller (1977:67–69) found that two-thirds of those who retired voluntarily in the early 1970s reported this to be a major reason that determined their decision. And no other single reason was mentioned by even as many as 20 percent of these people.

Another probable reason for voluntary retirement might be called one of psychological fitness for political life. Since most legislators are serving in public office for the first time, it should not be surprising that some of them find they are unsuited for the demands of such a position. The rigors of campaigning, of continually during the campaign having to ask people for financial contributions, of enduring the occasional highly bitter election campaign, of having one's private life open to the scrutiny of the mass media and one's campaign opponent, of sacrificing one's career and family life to the demands of the office—some legislators will find these costs greater than the rewards.

Once again, the low pay and relatively low status and professional opportunities in the legislature mean the rewards that might offset some of these demands are particularly meager in Texas. Thus it should not be surprising that the average tenure in the House, particularly, is not very long. Even many of those who can put up with the costs of political life may not want to do so for very many years. By the fact of the higher status of their office—and because most of their number were experienced in politics before running for the Senate and thus understood the demands of the politician's life—senators typically are willing to serve a longer time in office—provided they continue to get reelected.

Another reason some retire is for *private* career ambitions. Some young professionals, as mentioned earlier, seek office in the legislature to serve a term or two to make business connections that will aid their careers. Their motivation for being in the legislature, therefore, has little to do with the job itself. One must be skeptical about how devoted such people are to the tasks of lawmaking, oversight, and representation if their primary interest is in their personal careers.

Some retire because of *public* career ambitions. That is, they wish to seek higher and probably better-paying public office. (Miller found that 42 percent of those who left the legislature in the early 1970s ran for another office.) The state legislature, particularly the House of Representatives, is a good starting place for a political career, and many people hope to use it to get to a Senate seat, a seat in the U.S. Congress, or even a local position in city or county government. The financial and other costs of membership in the legislature probably influence the decisions of such legislators, for even many local government offices pay far better salaries than does the legislature. This reason for retirement suggests that politically ambitious members will not want to remain long in the legislature. One might fairly suspect that these are often the most capable members.

Implications of the Patterns of Membership

If one considers the diverse reasons for recruitment and retirement, it is easy to draw a portrait of the typical state representative when first elected. That person will be a well-educated white male, either early in a business or professional career or at a later, more established career position. He will be inexperienced politically. His primary motivations will vary, and some of them will have little to do with the tasks of the legislature. The majority of these people will find little reason to remain long in the legislature. The combined effects of election defeat, voluntary retirement, and departure to seek higher and more attractive political office mean that most will stay only two or three terms.

While one can point to several different reasons why the typical representative will wish to retire voluntarily (either to leave politics entirely or to seek a more attractive public office), the work life, low pay, and other characteristics of the legislator's job are such that several of these reasons may interact to bring about a member's decision not to run for reelection. That is, the nature of the job imposes *all* these burdens on almost all the members of the House, regardless of their motivations to remain there and their stamina to put up with them.

Another important conclusion concerns the characteristics of the legislature that attract certain kinds of new legislators in the first place, particularly in the House of Representatives. The high costs and low rewards of House membership explain why it is relatively wealthy but also mostly politically inexperienced individuals who typically seek election there. Institutional features, characteristics of the institution, explain in large part why the legislature is very *unrepresentative* of the citizens of Texas and why the members—again particularly in the House—are relative amateurs. The same institutional characteristics help explain the high turnover and low average tenure in the body. The high costs and low rewards ensure that most people will not stay long and their limited experience will not be greatly enriched by many technical legislative skills acquired during their time in office. In this second instance, institutional characteristics weaken even further the technical competence of the members.

The typical state senator suffers under many of the same difficulties created by the institutional system. Yet most senators, at least, have served in the House before moving on to the Senate. They should have developed some of the technical skills and some of the detailed understanding of government policy that we would desire for legislators. Presumably they also understand the costs and rewards of continued membership in the legislature and have accepted those facts of political life. The higher prestige of Senate membership may explain part of this willingness to continue to serve in the legislature. At the same time we should also recall that the average tenure of senators is not significantly longer than that of representatives. Thus the rewards of service in the Senate may not, in fact, be particularly more attractive. One could well conclude, therefore, that the costs of time spent in the Senate must be much the same as those for the House.

SPECIAL INTEREST GROUPS AND THE LEGISLATURE

Another major concern of this chapter is the role that interest groups play in the legislative process. In discussing the image of the Texas Legislature, we noted that many critics believe special interests are very powerful in that body. If they are so powerful, how do they make their influence felt? There are five principal means that might be employed by interest groups to influence any legislative body. All five are now used, or have been used in the past.

Bribery

Many seem to believe that outright bribery is the principal means of influence. Certainly bribery has been important at times in all levels of American politics. In the nineteenth century and in the first half or so of the present one it may even have been the primary means of influence. Yet most students of the subject believe that the incidence of this practice has fallen off dramatically in recent decades—in part because of more aggressive journalistic reporting of bribery when it is discovered, in part because of changing public mores on the subject, and in part because of new and more vigorously enforced laws against it. One might also conclude that most lobbyists no longer need resort to bribery. Most have other resources that are not only more potent but legal, as well.

One should not discount the notion, however, that from time to time bribery still occurs. Just how serious such problems can be is indicated by the scope of the so-called Sharpstown Bank scandal, which was uncovered in 1971 by the U.S. Securities and Exchange Commission. Houston banker Frank Sharp, head of the Sharpstown Bank, attempted to influence state banking legislation by bribing a number of state officials with bank stock from which they could gain handsome profits. Governor Preston Smith, Speaker of the House Gus Mutscher, and some of Mutscher's closest supporters in the House were implicated. Mutscher and two other legislative officials were eventually convicted of conspiracy to commit bribery as a result of their role in the affair.

The "Social Lobby"

Another traditional means of lobby influence of legislators has been what is called the "social lobby." The social lobby refers to the regular practice of a number of interest groups and their representatives of entertaining state legislators. Many of these organizations maintain regular "hospitality suites" in hotels near the Capitol building where a legislator can get a "free" meal or a drink in a relaxed, informal setting *and* where someone from the lobby can casually discuss the organization's interest in pending legislation at the same time. The social lobby also provides a good number of "free" meals at lavish restaurants; gifts of food, liquor, or other things; and even weekend trips for deep-sea fishing, for hunting, or simply for a party at someone's ranch away from Austin.

Some may look upon the social lobby as a subtle form of bribery, and some legislators may even succumb to it just as if it were that. But above all it creates an implicit atmosphere of indebtedness on the part of many lawmakers. They have accepted favors and thus they cannot complain if favors are requested of them at a later time by the lobbyist. Moreover, the social lobby simply provides special opportunities—in relaxed, amiable settings tinged with a sense of indebtedness—for certain groups to press their political demands upon legislators.

The representative of a less well-heeled organization or the individual citizen wishing to advocate a particular point of view must fight for space on the crowded daily calendar of his or her legislator. Such a person might get only a few minutes of the legislator's time as he hurries from one meeting to another—or, worse, might get only a form-letter response written by a secretary in the legislator's office. Thus the social lobby creates a unique and especially favorable environment for communicating one's political interests—for those who can afford to pay for the opportunity.

Many observers have concluded that the social lobby is no longer as important, or as flagrant, as it once was. It is said that the days when the standard tools of this approach were "booze, blondes, and beefsteaks," have waned considerably. This judgment is probably accurate, if for no other reason than the fact that journalistic reporting of the practice has made lobbyists more circumspect. Yet the social lobby remains important. Inquisitive news reporters still turn up juicy examples of the practice (Ellis, 1981). Even in its more circumspect contemporary form, the social lobby still provides unique opportunities to influence the legislature.

One of the reasons the social lobby remains important is because of the unusual social circumstances in which lawmakers find themselves when the legislature is in session. The typical legislator has left at home his or her family, friends, and job—hence his or her regular social and professional life—to move to Austin from January through May at the least. Even though most legislators travel home for many weekends, their regular lifestyles are entirely disrupted. Many of them are also living in Austin on a modest budget because of their low pay as legislators and because of the professional sacrifices required to hold their elected position. They often live in inexpensive motels or join together in groups to share the rent of a house.

The relative poverty and the disrupted social circumstances of legislators in these conditions heighten the importance of the social lobby. Here are people offering a free drink, a free meal, free tickets to this sporting or cultural event, or a free weekend for barbecue and relaxation at someone's ranch in the hill country. Here are people, in other words, who offer a free and sometimes quite elaborate substitute for one's missing social life. It is not surprising, then, that the social lobby persists and that, even if subtly, it constitutes an important avenue of special interest group influence.

Campaign Contributions

Another powerful and legal means for influencing legislators is to assist them in meeting the expenses of running for office. Typical campaign costs were noted earlier, and it would be a rare individual who could pay them personally. Thus outside contributors are critically important to virtually every candidate.

State campaign finance laws have, since 1973, made it illegal for certain special interests, specifically corporations and labor unions, to contribute directly to candidates' election campaign funds. Yet this provision only means that the contributions of major special interest groups must be made either by individuals or by so-called political action committees (PACs). PACs are simply private organizations that constitute legal entities for channeling campaign funds to candidates. Most PACs are established by special interest groups to support candidates favorable to their cause. Individual members of the group contribute to the PAC, and then the PAC contributes to individual candidates for office. As an indicator of the importance of these groups, one study of campaign financing in Texas indicated that state senators received 50 percent of their contributions in 1983 from PACs (*Houston Post*, 1984).

Research Material on Policy Issues

Lobbies sometimes exert another, entirely different means of influence as an information and research source for legislators. The research resources of the legislators themselves are poor because of their limited professional staff, limited personal time, and the difficulties of developing expertise when turnover is high and seniority rules limited. Legislators frequently are unable to pursue, by their own resources, careful research into policy problems and solutions. But the better-funded interest groups have customarily provided information to fill this gap. Many of these groups maintain high-caliber, professional research staffs to carry out just such research. Many other interest groups can draw upon the technical expertise of their members or their member organizations to provide such research. Of course, such information always takes the point of view of the group that prepares it.

The legislator working on a major policy problem can always depend on both the availability of such information and its inevitable bias. If a legislator is favorably disposed toward the position of the interest group, of course, he or she will also have the same bias. Thus legislators who work closely with well-funded interest groups will have no shortage of well-prepared material to support their legislative arguments. Those who work, alternatively, for less wealthy or less well organized groups, or who simply want to adopt an entirely independent perspective on legislative questions, will have considerable difficulty in developing equally detailed material to support their point of view.

The weak research resources of the Texas Legislature, then, create an additional opportunity for certain interest groups to gain disproportionate influence. Many students of legislatures argue that this information-providing function has become one of the most important techniques of special interests. The era of the positive state and of technically complex policy problems has brought with it a serious need for sophisticated information to aid the lawmaking function. If a legislature cannot fill this need on its own, self-interested groups are both ready and eager to help it out.

"Going to the Top"

The last and perhaps most important technique of special interest group influence is to go straight to the top—that is, to spend a disproportionate amount of one's time and resources getting the most influential legislators, the lieutenant governor and the Speaker of the House, on one's side. This technique is effective because of the great power of these two officials, a situation well understood by sophisticated lobbyists. If a group has the presiding officers (and hence their teams of supporters) backing its interest, that group is in a strong position indeed. The presiding officers, then, themselves become the lobbyists for that interest group—for they use their clout in the legislature to persuade the other members to support that group's preferences, as well.

CONCLUSION

This chapter began by observing the low esteem in which the Texas Legislature is held by many political scientists and journalists. A detailed examination of this body—its institutional characteristics, its technical competence, its internal politics, its membership, and the special interest forces acting upon it— offers considerable evidence why that unfortunate reputation is well deserved.

The Texas Legislature is an amateur body. It is a body with poorly developed technical capabilities. It is highly controlled by its presiding officers, a situation that is certainly at variance from typical expectations about democratic institutions. This situation, as well, makes the work of the legislature highly dependent upon the skill, the honesty, the fairness, and the concern for government in the public interest possessed by the lieutenant governor and the Speaker of the House. Individuals of laudable character in these positions can shape laudable governmental policies. But those of lesser character will also have considerable power to create quite unfortunate policies.

A number of the institutional and membership characteristics of the legislature also strengthen certain kinds of special interest group influence on state government policy. It is a fundamental tenet of democratic government that citizens should have the right to lobby their government and attempt to influence its decisions. Yet the situation is such in Texas that wealthy establishment interests have especially disproportionate opportunities to do so. Other groups, often with equally legitimate interests, have far weaker opportunities to make their cases effectively before the legislature.

Finally, it should be clear how these various legislative characteristics compromise all four of the major functions of the Texas Legislature. Lawmaking, oversight, representation, and the providing of a forum for critical policy debates are all carried out in a far less satisfactory manner than is desirable. Regardless of whether one desires liberal or conservative policies from the state government, in other words, he will not be well served by the current legislative system. A few individual and group interests will no doubt be well served. But the public interest will often suffer in the process. One can only conclude that it is public misunderstanding of the Texas Legislature—along with a false sense of economy that equates cheap government with good government—that allows this situation to continue. Surely with the Texas Legislature the old adage is true that "you get what you pay for."

REFERENCES

Citizens Conference on State Legislatures. 1971. *State Legislatures: An Evaluation of Their Effectiveness*. New York: Praeger.

Davis, J. William. 1967. *There Shall Also Be a Lieutenant Governor*. Austin: Institute of Public Affairs, University of Texas.

Ellis, V. 1981. "Legislators Hunt Doves and the Chemical Lobby Pays." *Dallas Times Herald*, September 27, p. C3.

Houston Post. 1984. "Texas Officials Got $5 Million in Contributions." April 28, p. A6.

Houston Post. 1985. "Senate Should End Calendar Trickery." January 20, p. B2.

Miller, Lawrence W. 1977. "Legislative Turnover and Political Careers: A Study of Texas Legislators, 1969–1975." Unpublished Ph.D. dissertation, Texas Tech University.

Moncrief, Gary. 1979. "Committee Stacking and Reform in the Texas House of Representatives." *Texas Journal of Political Studies* 2 (Fall): 44–57.

Morehouse, Sarah McCally. 1981. *State Politics, Parties, and Policy*. New York: Holt, Rinehart and Winston.

Patterson, Caleb Perry, McAlister, Sam B., and Hester, George C. 1940. *State and Local Government in Texas*. New York: Macmillan.

Pettus, Beryl E. 1980. "Escape from Modernization: Legislative Institutions Out of Synchronization with Environmental Changes." *Texas Journal of Political Studies* 2 (Spring): 27–41.

Price, Jorjanna. 1985. "Texas House Amends Its Rules Despite Warning, Criticism." *Houston Post*, January 10, p. B7.

Rosenthal, Alan. 1974. "And So They Leave: Legislative Turnover in the States." *State Government* 47 (Summer): 148–152.

Shin, Kwang S., and Jackson, John S. III. 1979. "Membership Turnover in U.S. State Legislatures: 1931–1976." *Legislative Studies Quarterly* 4 (February): 95–104.

Texas State Directory. 1987. Austin: Texas State Directory, Inc.

Zeigler, L. Harmon. 1983. "Interest Groups in the States." In Virginia Gray, Herbert Jacob, and Kenneth N. Vines (eds.), *Politics in the American States: A Comparative Analysis.* 4th ed. Boston: Little, Brown.

Zeller, Belle. 1954. *American State Legislatures.* New York: Thomas Y. Crowell.

7

THE GOVERNOR

The governor is, of course, the highest elected official in the state executive branch. The holder of this office can fill a number of important roles we might not initially appreciate. Before proceeding to the details of those roles, however, it is useful to consider the images of the governor and the governorship held by the public at large and by scholarly students of the subject.

THE IMAGE OF THE GOVERNOR

If we were to ask the proverbial man or woman on the street what is the job of the governor, the most typical response would surely be that the governor is just like the U.S. president except that his powers are limited only to this state. In other words, our average citizen might respond, the governor is the head of the executive branch, the "boss," the leader of the civil servants who work in the executive branch agencies of the state government. A loquacious citizen might go on to say that the governor also has an important legislative role, just as the president does. This citizen would be thinking about the fact that in contemporary America the president has assumed a very powerful role in the lawmaking process. The president has been allowed by the Congress to *initiate* policy and the lawmaking process on many important issues. In fact, the Congress has come to expect that the president will adopt this role, although members of Congress still guard their own power to revise or expand upon the president's policy recommendations. Thus many average Texans surely assume that the governor of this state has an analogous relationship with the Texas Legislature. One's image of the governorship, in other words, is shaped considerably by the assumption that all governmental chief executives are much like the president.

The image of the governor described above is, however, seriously in error. As J. William Davis and Ruth Cowart Wright (1976: 112–113) have expressed it: "It is with regard to the power of the governor that the average Texan probably suffers the greatest misconception of his state government. The governor is highly visible. His election is hotly contested. It appears that he must be a powerful chief executive, the counterpart of the president on the state level. Not so." In reality, the governor of Texas is a quite weak public official with powers that fall far short of those the average citizen probably believes he has. This fact has been reiterated by scholars and critics of Texas government for decades.

As long ago as 1933 a state legislative investigation of the executive branch of government concluded.

> *It might be logically assumed that the duties of the governor, in his capacity as chief executive officer of the state, would closely resemble the duties of the general manager of a large business enterprise. This is not at all the case, however. There are a great number of independent agencies in the state government, and the executive heads of most of these agencies are beyond the scope of the governor's direct authority, due to the methods of selecting them. The pressure of routine business, most of it of detailed character, keeps the governor from devoting much time to duties of an executive nature. There are too many administrative departments, boards, commissions, and other agencies for him to keep in touch with them all. [Joint Legislative Committee on Organization and Economy, 1933: 2]*

More recent scholarly discussions of the governor's role have pointed out that *all* his formal powers, not just those of a strictly administrative nature, are quite limited. And many governors themselves have complained of this situation. Consider, as examples, the remarks of four men who held the office in the twentieth century:

> *The governor of Texas, under the present apportionment of governmental responsibility, hardly has the opportunity to form a policy and is without power to enforce departmental efficiency. [Dan Moody]*
>
> *If the governor asks them [a state executive branch agency] to do something they don't want to do, they can tell him to go jump into the lake. [W. Lee O'Daniel]*
>
> *The governor of Texas is something of a paper tiger. [Allan Shivers]*
>
> *Nobody works for the governor. They all work for their boards. Administrators won't volunteer anything—I never know anything except by hearsay. They volunteer nothing. [John Connally]*

A major task of this chapter will be to explain why the preceding remarks are correct. In the process we will also examine the role that governors can play in state politics and discover the resources that determine their success in that role. Before proceeding to the details of how this office operates, however, it will be helpful to consider the functions of governors and executive branch agencies more generally and learn how public expectations for those institutions have changed.

THE FUNCTIONS OF GOVERNORS

The role of an American governor in the politics and administration of his or her state is the result of several separate factors: public expectations about governmental responsibilities at different times in the history of the state, efforts to expand or to limit those responsibilities through constitutional reform, and alternating periods of competition and cooperation with the state legislature over how much power that body would allow the chief executive. Obviously the history, development, and politics of each state have been sufficiently distinctive to mean that the governorship may have assumed a somewhat distinctive character in every state. Yet one can detect common patterns of state political development, as well. By tracing the historical evolution of those patterns, we can see quite clearly the ways they have affected the governorships of almost all states.

The evolution of what we might call the *public philosophy* that defines the role of governors—indeed, that defines in some sense the role of the entire administrative branch of government—was brilliantly described by Herbert Kaufman (1956). The idea of a public philosophy about chief executives and executive systems may sound highly abstract and academic. Yet when we explore exactly what is meant by this phrase, we find that it refers to quite practical and important matters about how government is to be run.

Representativeness　Kaufman noted three different historical eras when different public philosophies were dominant. In the first of these eras, lasting roughly from the founding of the American nation to the late nineteenth century, the dominant philosophy stressed a goal of *representativeness* to be served by the executive branch of government. That is, this philosophy sought great public control over the executive branch. The practical results of the pursuit of this goal were, first, that state governors were—very early in the history of the United States—typically given a position subordinate to the legislature, itself the preeminent representative body. The governor's weak position was weakened even further during the first third or so of the nineteenth century when a second dimension of representativeness was widely adopted. This second feature was the expansion of public control of executive officials by making the majority of their positions elective. Thus many states adopted a *plural executive* whereby not just the governor but most major state offices were filled in separate elections.

Texas's first state constitution, that of 1845, gave the governor more power than any of its successors, although even here a stringent limit was placed on the number of terms a governor could serve in office. Each successive new constitution adopted more constraints on the office in keeping with the philosophy of representativeness (Gantt, 1964: 15–39). Even the 1869 Reconstruction constitution was in this tradition, but the Republican-dominated legislature gave a wide array of statutory powers to the governor that offset the general orientation of the document. It was the abuse of these statutory powers by Governor Davis and their association with Republican rule—as described in chapter 4—that led to the even more restrictive constitution of 1876. Put another way, it could be said that the 1876 constitution was the product of a desire to rid the state of the "unrepresentative" Republican leaders and to weaken the powers of the governor so that no future incumbent could be the autocratic ruler that Governor Davis had been. Even today the office of the governor is greatly constrained by the provisions of the Texas Constitution of 1876.

Late in the nineteenth century, however, some of the institutional features established in the pursuit of representativeness fell into disrepute nationally. One reason for this disenchantment was the abuse of power by political bosses who controlled state or city administrations with political party machines. In many eastern seaboard cities such machines were based on the manipulation of new immigrants, as machine officials would supply jobs or other favors to the immigrants in exchange for their votes at election time. Yet widespread corruption among elected political leaders, in legislatures as well as in the executive branch, and a sense that elected officials often lacked the technical competence to carry out important governmental tasks, also led to a new public philosophy. Kaufman called this second philosophy the search for *neutral competence* in government. That is, reformers sought to place control of many governmental functions in the hands of professional experts who were themselves insulated from political influence.

Neutral Competence   At the level of state government, neutral competence was sought by the creation of a variety of independent boards and commissions given the power to carry out specific governmental functions. These agencies were to be staffed with specialists whose expertise would shape agency decisions. Typically, these agency heads would be appointed by the governor with the approval of the legislature. But once these officials were in office, the governor could not control their policy making and he could not fire them either. Typically the terms of office of the members of these boards and commissions did not coincide with that of the governor. Rarely would a single governor have the power to appoint even a majority of the members of a board. These various institutional arrangements, it is easy to see, did in fact insulate the experts who headed such agencies from very much political control by either the governor or the legislature.

Thus in the late nineteenth century a variety of such agencies was created, particularly those sparked by the regulatory commission movement. In Texas a number of these agencies were created in the period 1890–1920. Most of them were intended to regulate either a single business field—like banking or insurance—or a single profession—like law or medicine.

As Kaufman argued, neutral competence remains a highly valued goal for public bureaucracies. It is seen in the development of merit systems for public employment, in the desire to eliminate "patronage" employment systems, in increasingly advanced educational requirements for public jobs, and in periodic controversies over elective versus appointive systems of choosing executive officials. The 1984–1987 controversy in Texas over whether the State Board of Education should be appointed or elected is an excellent contemporary example of the latter situation. In 1984 the legislature passed a law converting the board from an elected to an appointed one. The intention of the law was to allow a new team of "neutrally competent" board members to oversee the initiation of the sweeping educational reforms passed in 1984, which came to be known under the label "House Bill 72." Proponents of the appointed board had argued precisely that the existing, elected board was not competent for this task. The 1984 law mandated this change in the board for only four years, but a referendum on the 1987 election ballot allowed voters to indicate their preference between the two systems. The majority endorsed the election alternative. Representativeness prevailed over neutral competence.

Even many of the supporters of the philosophy of neutral competence admit to problems that can arise in government because of this system. In fact, such problems have been hotly debated in the twentieth century as more and more government agencies were structured under this philosophy. The creation of a variety of independent boards and commissions under no central authority led to fragmentation in governmental effort. The multiple, elected executive system created in the search for representativeness has had similar effects, and the independent agency movement exacerbated this tendency. Thus the coordination of policy efforts across agencies became quite difficult. At times different agencies in the same state worked at cross-purposes. Neither elected chief executives nor the public at large nor even the legislatures that created these agencies had as much influence over them as they often desired.

The lack of coordination became more pronounced and far more important as state governments moved steadily away from laissez faire toward positive state responsibilities as described in previous chapters. Government was becoming much more powerful, it was attempting to regulate many more aspects of social and economic life, and each separate governmental function was becoming ever more expensive. In these circumstances it is hardly surprising that governors and state legislatures desired to curb the independence of many agencies and integrate all their activities.

Executive Leadership This disenchantment with the worst aspects of the independent agency system in the twentieth century led to the spawning of a third public philosophy for executive systems. Kaufman called this third philosophy the desire for *executive leadership*—meaning control and coordination of the entire executive branch by a single chief executive. Progress toward this third goal—which requires greatly increased gubernatorial power—has been slow in many states because of legislative fears about losing power to the executive as well as the resistance of independent agencies to "political" control. Yet in this century a number of reforms have extended the authority of the governor in many states. The earliest of these measures increased the length of the term of office, allowed governors to run for more than a single term, and gave that official greater appointive, budgetary, and policy coordination powers. In the last two decades, the period of extensive reform of state legislatures, the powers of many governors were also greatly extended, in particular by granting them new organizational powers over the executive branch (Beyle and Muchmore, 1983; Sabato, 1978: 63–96).

In Texas, only a few of the reforms associated with the drive toward executive leadership have been accepted. The constitution of 1876 had no restriction on the number of terms a person could serve in that office, but its requirement for only a two-year term was changed to a four-year term by amendment in 1972. However, none of the other major reforms consistent with the notion of executive leadership has been adopted in this state. Yet Texas is not entirely alone in its reticence to pursue this philosophy. The executive systems of many states still retain features of all three philosophies cited by Kaufman. Features of each new system were typically adopted piecemeal so that the net result has been an administrative hodgepodge with no single dominant rationale. The result for states like Texas is that the most recent philosophy, executive leadership, is the least well represented.

Despite the slow evolution of the philosophy of executive leadership, some states have advanced quite far in the pursuit of such a system. In these states there is considerable truth in the analogy between the powers of the president and those of the governor. Such states have accepted the idea that, in the era of positive government, control of the state's executive branch should be concentrated in the hands of a single chief executive who is accountable to the people through elections and through the legislature. Furthermore, to give that executive the ability to carry out the leadership tasks the public expects today, these states have expanded the formal powers of their governors in several vital areas—over policy making, over budgeting, and over the activities of the executive branch.

THE REALITY OF THE TEXAS GOVERNOR'S POWERS

The powers that have been bestowed on governors in states wishing to strengthen executive leadership are *formal* powers prescribed either in the constitution or in statutory laws passed by the legislature. Virtually all governors have some powers in each of those areas, of course; it is the relative extent of their authority in each area that distinguishes the weak from the strong. Yet because every governor's formal powers are set out in state law, they can be easily compared with those of the governors of other states. Thus one can assess the relative position of the governor of Texas vis-à-vis the powers of other governors and against the theoretical standard of executive leadership.

Rating the Governor's Principal Formal Powers

The most recent assessment of the relative powers of American governors is that offered by Gray, Jacob, and Vines (1983: 454–459) following in the tradition of earlier work by Beyle (1982), Beyle and Dalton (1981), Ransone (1982: 27–47), and Schlesinger (1965). All these authors distinguish five separate aspects of gubernatorial power.

1. *Tenure potential* based on the length of the term of office allowed the governor and the limitations, if any, on the possibilities of reelection to the office

2. *Appointive powers* based on the percentage of major offices filled by gubernatorial appointments and the extent to which such appointments are limited by other arrangements (such as a requirement that the governor's nominees must be approved by the legislature)

3. *Budget powers* based on the extent of the governor's control over the budget-making process

4. *Organization powers* based on the extent of the governor's power over executive branch agencies (which might range from the ability to direct the programs and policies of agencies to the power to reorganize large portions of the administrative system)

5. *Veto powers* based on the governor's power to veto bills by the legislature and the legislature's power, in turn, to override such a veto

In each of these five areas Gray and her colleagues rated the fifty governors and assigned each a score of from 1 to 5—the higher the score, the greater the power in the particular area. In addition to these individual power scores, they also calculated a summary index of power based on all five component areas combined. How did the governor of the great state of Texas compare, one might ask? Table 7-1 offers the results.

Out of a possible total score of 25, the governor of Texas received only 11 power points. And that rating means Texas's governor is the second weakest in the entire nation in terms of formal powers. Why, one might ask further, does the chief executive of this state rate so poorly? What are his formal powers in each of the five component areas covered in table 7-1?

Tenure Potential   On this first attribute the governor of Texas was rated "very strong" along with the heads of seventeen other states, principally because there is no limit on the number of terms an individual can serve. In theory a governor can, if reelected, remain in office long enough both to learn the ropes and to carry out an extended policy program. Yet the actual execution of such a program depends on other powers besides just tenure, and in these other areas the office is far weaker.

Appointive Powers   Gray and her colleagues rated the governor of Texas among the eight weakest in the ability to appoint heads of major state agencies. The power to hire and fire such agency heads, as the president of the United States has with a large number of federal agencies, would give a governor considerable control over the policies of those agencies. But the governor is severely limited here because, first, several of the most important agency heads are separately elected, including the lieutenant governor, the comptroller of public accounts, the treasurer, the commissioner of the General Land Office, the attorney general, the commissioner of agriculture, the members of the Texas Railroad Commission, all state judges, and the members of the State Board of Education.

TABLE 7–1 Combined Index of the Formal Powers of the Governors: 1981

State	Tenure Potential	Appointive Powers	Budget Powers	Organization Powers	Veto Powers	Total Index
New York	5	5	5	4	5	24
Hawaii	4	5	5	4	5	23
Maryland	4	4	5	5	5	23
Massachusetts	5	5	5	5	3	23
Minnesota	5	5	5	3	5	23
New Jersey	4	4	5	5	5	23
Pennsylvania	4	5	5	4	5	23
Utah	5	4	5	4	5	23
California	5	5	5	2	5	22
Connecticut	5	3	5	4	5	22
Illinois	5	5	5	2	5	22
Michigan	5	2	5	5	5	22
South Dakota	4	3	5	5	5	22
Wyoming	5	4	5	3	5	22
Arizona	5	3	5	3	5	21
Colorado	5	3	5	3	5	21
Delaware	4	4	5	3	5	21
Idaho	5	3	5	3	5	21
Iowa	5	4	5	2	5	21
Alaska	4	1	5	5	5	20
Maine	4	4	5	5	2	20
Montana	5	3	5	4	3	20
Tennessee	4	4	5	3	4	20
Missouri	4	1	5	4	5	19

Nebraska	4	4	5	1	5	19
Ohio	4	3	5	2	5	19
Virginia	3	4	5	4	3	19
Wisconsin	5	3	5	3	3	19
Florida	4	1	5	3	5	18
Georgia	4	2	5	2	5	18
Kansas	4	2	4	3	5	18
Kentucky	3	4	5	2	4	18
Louisiana	4	4	4	1	5	18
North Dakota	5	1	5	2	5	18
West Virginia	4	3	5	2	4	18
Alabama	4	3	5	1	4	17
Arkansas	2	4	5	2	4	17
New Mexico	3	4	5	2	3	17
Oklahoma	4	2	5	1	5	17
Washington	5	2	5	2	3	17
Indiana	4	5	5	1	1	16
Oregon	4	1	5	3	3	16
Rhode Island	2	4	5	3	2	16
Vermont	2	4	5	3	2	16
Nevada	4	3	5	1	2	15
New Hampshire	2	1	5	4	2	14
North Carolina	4	5	3	2	0	14
Mississippi	3	2	1	1	5	12
Texas	**5**	**1**	**1**	**1**	**3**	**11**
South Carolina	4	1	1	1	3	10
Average score	4.1	3.2	4.7	2.9	4.1	19.0

Source: Gray, Jacob, and Vines (1983:458–459).

The only major offices the governor can fill by appointment are the secretary of state, the adjutant general, the executive director of the Department of Community Affairs, and the director of the Office of State–Federal Relations. The secretary of state is a glorified keeper of certain state records; the adjutant general is the head of the Texas National Guard. The executive director of the Department of Community Affairs coordinates a number of joint federal–state programs and administers certain federal programs run by the state. The director of the Office of State–Federal Relations is the state's lobbyist in the nation's capital. What is striking, of course, about this list of the governor's "major" appointees is that none of them has, in fact, a major policy-making position and none of them heads a truly major state agency.

The governor has the power to appoint the members of more than one hundred boards or commissions; yet this power is severely limited in accordance with the intentions of the philosophy of neutral competence. Some of these appointees must be drawn from certain professions or particular regions of the state; all of them serve overlapping terms of office of over four years to limit the number of members of any given agency that a single governor might appoint; and once in office they are outside the control of the chief executive.

Budget Powers   Gray and her colleagues rated the governor of Texas among the three weakest in the nation in terms of budget-making power. Although the constitution requires that the governor submit a proposed budget to the legislature at the beginning of each session, the Legislative Budget Board (LBB)—an agency created in 1949 and controlled by the presiding officers of the legislature—prepares and submits to the legislature its own budget. And the LBB document has become by custom the definitive budget for legislative action.

Organization Powers   In this area the governor of Texas was once again rated as being very weak—in fact, as one of the twelve weakest such offices in the nation. The governor has virtually no power to reorganize or consolidate either agencies or their functions, nor does he even have clear authority to control the actions and policies of individual agencies. The constitution implies that the governor should have some control over executive branch agencies.[1] In practice, however, he has very little control because of the independent constitutional status of so many agencies and because of his limited power to hire or fire agency heads.

Veto Powers   Here the governor of Texas scored a moderate power rating. He has from the constitution the power to veto bills passed by the legislature and to veto "line items" in appropriation bills. For a bill to become law over the governor's veto it must be approved by two-thirds of the members of each house of the legislature.

Beyond the explicit constitutional details of the veto power, there are practical circumstances which both strengthen and weaken that power. Often the mere threat of a veto, if argued with enough force by the governor, can result in amendments to a bill before it is passed by the legislature. As the preceding chapter indicated, getting a bill through the legislature can be difficult enough in the first place, and the pressures of time can be so severe as to limit the prospects of getting it through both houses a second time should it be vetoed. Thus a sufficiently creditable threat of veto can often lead to a successful compromise that amounts to a victory for the governor.

The veto power is also strengthened by the fact that so many bills are passed in the last few days of the 140-day legislative session. Many bills arrive on the governor's desk for approval, therefore, after the legislature has closed down and its members have gone home for another year and a half. Should the governor veto one of these bills, the legislature cannot override the veto simply because it is not in session. Thus the legislature's inability to keep to a timely schedule, a problem discussed at some length in chapter 6, limits its ability to control the lawmaking process vis-à-vis the governor. His veto can be absolute with all these end-of-session measures. A study of the use of the governor's veto power from 1876 to 1968, it should be noted, indicated that over two-thirds of all vetoes exercised by governors during this period came after the legislature had adjourned (Gantt, 1969).

Finally, certain practical matters *limit* the governor's veto power over appropriations items. For example, his veto must be "all or nothing." The governor cannot say, "I believe this item is 10 or 15 percent too high, so I will reduce it by that amount." Instead he must accept it entirely or veto it entirely. Often this means the governor must accept line items that he believes are too generous because at least some level of spending on that item is critical to the functioning of the agency concerned. This fact means, as well, that agency heads may be able to circumvent the item veto by clever budgeting practice. By combining controversial and noncontroversial items or by otherwise lumping together items—and getting them through the legislature, of course—they can often avoid the threat of a veto.

Other Formal Powers

Beyond the formal powers considered by Gray and her colleagues there are three others accorded the governor that deserve some discussion: military powers, intergovernmental relations powers, and legislative powers.

Military Powers   The constitution designates the governor as the "commander in chief of the military forces of the state" and empowers him with calling "forth the militia to execute the laws of the State, to suppress insurrections, repel invasions and protect the frontier from hostile incursions by Indians or other predatory bands." Barring the likelihood of a border war with Mexico or a sudden uprising of the state's few remaining Indians, this power is not very consequential. The state militia may prove useful from time to time in helping preserve order after natural disasters, but the fact that the governor has these military powers does little to help him run the state government or shape its policies.

Intergovernmental Relations Powers   Of far more consequence are the powers granted the governor in relations with other states and the federal government. The constitution charges the governor with conducting the state's business with these other governments, and his position as broker or spokesman with the federal government can be critical. If the governor is an effective spokesman for the state in its relations with the federal government, his credibility and prestige with the people and the legislature will rise.

Of even more practical consequence under this heading is the fact that the governor is a key figure in dispensing funds to local governments that are provided by federal or state programs. Indeed, a number of federal programs and grant distribution policies require the governor to act as the state's central planning and grant-dispensing officer. The governor's office directly administered over $30 million in such monies in 1988 (mostly for criminal justice and regional planning activities) and is somehow involved in the planning, funding, or implementation of local government activities in a variety of other ways.

Legislative Powers   The constitution gives to the governor four major powers that involve him in the lawmaking process:

1. It directs him to deliver a message to the legislature at the start of each legislative session on the "condition of the state."
2. It empowers him to "recommend to the Legislature such measures as he may deem expedient."
3. It allows him to convene the legislature in special session and to set the agenda of such sessions.
4. It allows him to veto bills passed by the legislature (along with the item veto over appropriations measures) subject to an override if two-thirds of the members of both legislative houses overturn the veto.

These legislative powers are undeniably important. They illustrate the fact that American constitutions typically provide for the sharing of legislative, executive, and judicial power among the branches of government rather than a literal separation of powers. Yet the formal legislative powers given the governor of Texas have not evolved as far as have those of the president or those of some other governors. The legislature has seldom been willing to regard the governor's ideas as more than mere recommendations. And unlike the relationship that exists between the president and Congress, the Texas Legislature has shown little willingness for the governor to initiate policy proposals. In other words, the status of the governor's proposals is far lower in the eyes of Texas legislators than is that of the president's proposals in the eyes of members of Congress. As we will see later in this chapter, the governor must rely heavily on his *informal* powers to heighten the status of his proposals. Even using those informal powers, many governors must work very hard simply to get a serious hearing in the legislature for their ideas.

THE GOVERNOR'S STAFF

To assist in the execution of his responsibilities, the governor is provided—in the Office of the Governor—a professional staff of notable size. In fiscal year 1988, for example, the Office of the Governor under Bill Clements was budgeted $5.2 million and 161 full-time personnel positions for its principal operations. A typical "organization chart" for the office is provided in figure 7-1 under the tenure of Mark White in 1985.

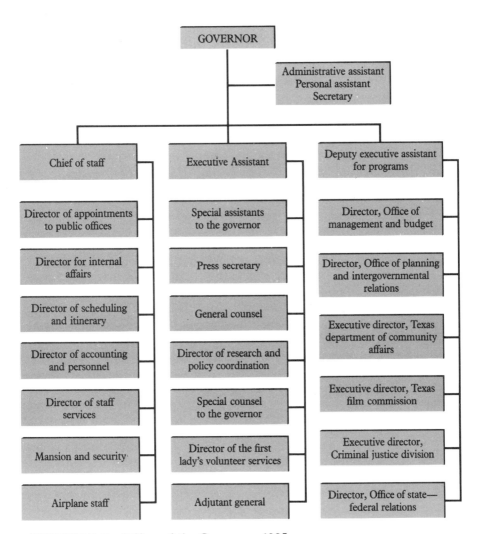

FIGURE 7–1   Office of the Governor: 1985

THE GOVERNOR'S INFORMAL POWERS

In addition to the powers fixed in law and described above, there are a few informal sources of political strength on which governors can draw. The most important of these informal powers are those that arise from the governor's duties as *"chief of state,"* from his position as leader of his political party, and from the strength of his political personality.

Chief of State

The role of the governor is enhanced beyond that implied in his formal powers simply because he is the highest elected official in the state and that position carries considerable public and political prestige. Some of this prestige arises because the governor functions as the chief of state. Fred Gantt (1973: 25) has described this aspect of the governor's job in the following passage:

> *In his role as head of state (which Constitution writers in 1876 viewed as what probably should be his major role), he represents the state on ceremonial occasions. He shakes hands with thousands of persons each year; he travels tens of thousands of miles to appear at public functions; he makes hundreds of speeches; and he is photographed with scores of groups or individuals. His presence at any meeting adds a sense of importance and dignity that would be lacking if he were not there, for he symbolizes the state and its authority. He issues numerous proclamations, calling upon citizens to observe such diverse occasions as Blackeyed Pea Week, Buy-It-Made-in-Texas month, Multiple Sclerosis month, and Save Your Vision Week—thus adding his prestige and backing to the observance.*

Acting in the role of chief of state the governor has the opportunity to develop an important informal source of power. Such is the case because many citizens may confuse appearance with reality. That is, they may assume that the *appearance* of power—as it arises in the role of chief of state—implies that the governor has equally prominent political and administrative power in the government at large. If people *think* the governor is powerful or if they *think* him important, then even if his formal powers are weak he will be able to draw upon that misplaced prestige if he is a skillful politician. Even other public officials over whom the governor has little or no formal power must grant him at least some deference because of the prestige of his office.

Some of the governor's formal powers—such as his position as spokesman in Texas's relations with the federal government and with other state governments—arise because he is chief of state. In exercising those formal powers the governor can gain even more prestige. Again, if he is seen by the public and other state officials as carrying out prestigious duties in negotiating with these "outside" powers, he will become more important in their eyes.

Head of Party

By tradition the governor has been seen as the nominal head, at least, of his political party. That is, he is the chief spokesman for the party. He has typically led the party's delegation at state and national political conventions. And he has been important in the fund-raising efforts of the party. Once again, this is a role that has developed informally and is not required of the governor. Yet most governors have desired the opportunity to lead their party because of the potential benefits to their own position and career. Just as is the case with the chief of state activities, party leadership enhances the prestige, visibility, and apparent importance of the governor.

These benefits arise, as well, even though many of the governor's party leadership activities are more ceremonial than anything else. This is the case because the party organization itself plays so limited a role in campaigns and elections. It does not monopolize the recruitment of candidates to run for office. It does not monopolize fund-raising efforts. (Most candidates, as we have noted, raise the bulk of their funds independently.) Nor does the party force candidates who run for office under its banner to accept a common set of policy positions. Despite these limits to the organizational powers of the major parties, they retain considerable prestige and importance that are bound to be shared by whomever is seen as their leader.

Political Personality

The main source of informal power the governor can draw upon—indeed, some would say, the most important source of *all* his powers—is his personality. In other words, it is the governor's personal political skills and his desire to use them to accomplish his political objectives that determine his impact on state government. It is the governor's personal abilities as a politician—his powers of persuasion, his ability to sell his ideas to the public and to other officials, his ability to negotiate with powerful figures whether they are other public officials or representatives of major interest groups—that determine how effectively he will employ both his formal and informal powers.

A governor's political personality is of special importance in Texas because of the severe restrictions on his formal powers. If the office were accompanied by strong administrative, budgetary, and policy-making authority, then even a governor of limited personal political abilities could leave his mark on state government. In the absence of such powers, however, every governor must work diligently and resourcefully if he desires to leave a record of notable accomplishment. Personal political skill constitutes, therefore, the most important asset upon which any governor in this state can draw.

THE GOVERNORS THEMSELVES

The remarks of the preceding section about the personal political abilities of governors lead naturally to a discussion of other factors relevant to that office—concerning, above all, the requirements for the office and the kinds of people elected to it. Just as is the case for membership in the legislature, the constitution prescribes certain requirements that must be met before one can hold the office. The candidate must be at least thirty years of age, be a citizen of the United States, and must have lived in the state for at least five years immediately preceding the election.

The constitution also establishes certain terms and requirements of service as governor, although some of these conditions have been changed by amendment over the state's history. The constitution, as accepted by the voters in 1876, prescribed a two-year term of office and set an annual salary for the governor of $4,000. In 1936 the salary was raised to $12,000 by constitutional amendment, and then in 1954 the voters accepted an amendment that allows the legislature to fix this salary. By 1986 the legislature had raised the salary to $94,350, one of the highest governor's salaries in the nation. As noted earlier, another constitutional amendment passed in 1972 changed the term of office to four years.

Practical Requirements for Election

Beyond these formal requirements, there are also practical limitations that determine what kinds of people can realistically hope to be elected to this office. If one considers the people who have successfully campaigned for the position since World War II, several practical requirements are obvious.[2] The first of these has been—with the one exception for Bill Clements—that the person must be a member of the Democratic party. Another essential attribute has been extensive experience either in the legislature or in another elective state office. Seven of the nine postwar governors have had such experience. The exceptions—John Connally and Bill Clements—had served in high-level administrative positions in the federal government in Washington. Third, every successful candidate for the office since the late 1930s has either been long associated with the conservative "establishment" elite of Texas or has favored sufficiently conservative policies to have been readily accepted by that elite (Green, 1979: 3–21).

Another practical requirement for the office—yet one easily met by those who have already passed the three cited above—is the ability to attract a large amount of campaign funds. At least since the end of World War II contemporary observers have lamented the high cost of campaigns for this office. An estimate of the cost necessary to "assure election" in the late 1940s was a minimum of $300,000 (Stilwell, 1949: 320). That figure translates into about 30 cents per general election vote cast for the winning candidate in the 1948 election.

By the mid-1960s Gantt (1964: 279) estimated that a hard-fought campaign would cost each candidate at least half a million dollars, which translates into 35 to 40 cents per general election vote for successful candidates in that period. This "typical" total spending figure, however, was itself far exceeded when John Connally reported spending $699,000 in his successful 1962 campaign.

The most striking increase in costs began in 1978 with the campaign of millionaire businessman Bill Clements. Clements was willing to spend his own money—and quite a lot of it—along with his outside contributions in order to get elected. In his 1978 campaign Clements spent more than $7.1 million, or about $6 for each general election vote he received. Then, in the 1982 campaign, challenger Mark White spent $8.9 million—or about $4.20 per general election vote in defeating Clements. In the same race, it should be noted, Clements spent some $13.3 million—or $8.94 for each vote he received—in his losing effort. The final White-Clements "rematch" in the 1986 election saw the combined expenditures of the two candidates top $25 million and those of winning candidate, Clements, average $6 per general election vote. The campaign spending figures for these recent races provide ample evidence for the importance of this last "practical requirement" for seeking the office of governor.

Who Gets Elected?

The importance of these practical requirements can be seen in the personal characteristics and backgrounds of recent Texas governors. Table 7-2 summarizes the backgrounds of the post–World War II incumbents in that office. Every person to hold the office during this period—as well as the overwhelming majority of prewar governors—was a middle-aged Anglo male with substantial business and public-sector experience. All the governors in the postwar era have been college educated and many—the attorneys—have held advanced professional degrees. Most had served in some kind of state elective office before seeking the governorship. All had been successful businessmen or attorneys, as well. All of them save one were elected under the banner of the Democratic party, and all of these Democrats were associated with the party's conservative wing.

The Fate of Ex-Governors

To paraphrase an old axiom, ex-governors never die, they just fade away. One might think that experience in the governorship would be an important stepping-stone to higher office. It is undeniably an office with high prestige, and one might think that service there could embellish any political career. Moreover, most governors have left the office in their middle to late fifties—still at a quite appropriate age to seek higher office. Yet such has rarely been the case in Texas. Of the twenty-six individuals who served in this office since 1876 and who did not die in office (as only one did), only fourteen subsequently ran for higher elective office or even for reelection to the governorship. Only five of these fourteen were successful, the most recent being Bill Clements. Clements was reelected to the governorship in 1986 after losing an earlier reelection bid in 1982 when he was the incumbent. Before Clements, the last governor to seek higher office successfully was W. Lee "Pappy" O'Daniel in the 1930s! O'Daniel served in the U.S. Senate after his stint in the governorship, as discussed in chapter 5. Less than a third of all twenty-six ex-governors have held *any* other elective or appointive public offices subsequent to their tenure as governor (Gantt, 1964: 64–68; Phares, 1976).

It seems fair, then, to draw certain speculative conclusions about post-gubernatorial careers. One is that the office is so limited in power—and, hence, political opportunity—that it rarely affords an individual the political success or public esteem necessary to seek higher office successfully. The second conclusion is that sophisticated politicians recognize the limitations of the

TABLE 7-2 Personal Backgrounds of Post–World War II Texas Governors

Governor	Age at Election	Public Experience in			College Education	Profession
		Texas Legislature	Other Elective State Office	Federal Elective or Administrative Office		
Coke Stevenson (1941–1947)	53	✓	✓		✓	Banker, rancher
Beauford Jester (1947–1949)	54		✓		✓	Lawyer
Allan Shivers (1949–1957)	42	✓	✓		✓	Lawyer, businessman
Price Daniels (1957–1963)	47	✓	✓	✓	✓	Lawyer
John Connally (1963–1969)	46			✓	✓	Lawyer, businessman
Preston Smith (1969–1973)	57	✓	✓		✓	Businessman
Dolph Briscoe (1973–1979)	50	✓			✓	Rancher, businessman
Bill Clements (1979–1983)	62			✓	✓	Businessman
Mark White (1983–1987)	43		✓		✓	Lawyer
Bill Clements (1987–present)	70		✓	✓	✓	Businessman

office as a stepping-stone to higher ones. Therefore, such politicians seek other routes to satisfy their ambitions and leave the governorship to the less ambitious and perhaps the less able. Either conclusion, if correct, would be a telling affirmation of just how important is the governor of this state.

CONCLUSION

Early in this chapter we discussed the public's image of the office and role of the governor; the public view was one of a powerful chief executive. Yet the remainder of this chapter has demonstrated how very different from that public image the office is in reality. The formal powers of the office are very limited. While there are informal sources of gubernatorial power, none of them are unique to this state nor are they of unusual importance to Texas governors. Hence the office is weak both in an absolute sense and in a relative one when compared to the governorships of other states. One must conclude, then, that this office is very different from what the average Texan believes it to be. It may well be very different, too, from what the average candidate for the office believes it to be in his or her election campaign. Many candidates make campaign pledges they simply will not, if elected, have the power to fulfill because of the limitations of the office.

First, the weakness of the governorship in Texas can be explained by the influence of the philosophy of representativeness on the state's constitution (and, hence, on the rest of our governmental system). Second, the late-nineteenth-century philosophy of neutral competence, in expanding into the regulatory commission movement, fragmented control of the executive branch. The result, of course, is an administrative system with little central control.

It is also clear that the most contemporary public philosophy—that of *executive leadership*—has had the least impact on the office of the governor in Texas. One can fairly conclude that this state is attempting to achieve late-twentieth-century governmental objectives with an administrative system rooted largely in the early nineteenth century. One should not be surprised if many difficulties arise in that effort.

These conclusions also emphasize the importance of the informal powers and the political personality of the governor of Texas—at least if the governor wishes to leave his mark on the state's public policies or administration. To have such an impact, a governor will have to be personally very skillful as a politician and use the informal sources of power boldly. Yet even the most skillful and resourceful of governors should not expect to have enormous influence on the direction of state government. This same set of circumstances explains why individuals with weak personalities and limited political skills are overwhelmed by the office. Such individuals—and Texas has certainly had its share of them as governors—will be little more than figureheads exercising no real authority and, in effect, giving over control of the executive branch to the legislature and to the independently powerful heads of individual state agencies.

NOTES

1. The constitution does not include a detailed explanation of the governor's executive powers. It does, however, along with a number of other specific grants of power, confer upon the governor the title of "chief executive officer of the State" (Article IV, Section 1) and charge that "he shall cause the laws to be faithfully executed" (Article IV, Section 10).

2. For an analysis of the patterns of ascension to the Texas governorship roughly between the end of Reconstruction and World War II, see Schlesinger (1957: 74–87).

REFERENCES

Beyle, Thad L. 1982. "The Governor's Power of Organization." *State Government* 55,3:79–87.

Beyle, Thad L., and Dalton, Robert. 1981. "Appointment Power: Does It Belong to the Governor?" *State Government* 54,1:2–13.

Beyle, Thad L., and Muchmore, Lynn R. 1983. "Governors in the American Federal System." In Thad L. Beyle and Lynn R. Muchmore (eds.), *Being Governor: The View from the Office*. Durham, N.C.: Duke University Press.

Davis, J. William, and Wright, Ruth Cowart. 1976. *Texas: Political Practice and Public Policy*. Dubuque: Kendall/Hunt.

Gantt, Fred Jr. 1964. *The Chief Executive in Texas: A Study in Gubernatorial Leadership*. Austin: University of Texas Press.

Gantt, Fred Jr. 1969. "The Governor's Veto in Texas: An Absolute Negative?" *Public Affairs Comment* 15 (March): 1–4.

Gantt, Fred Jr. 1973. *The Impact of the Texas Constitution on the Executive*. Houston: Institute for Urban Studies, University of Houston.

Gray, Virginia, Jacob, Herbert, and Vines, Kenneth N. (eds.). 1983. *Politics in the American States: A Comparative Analysis*. 4th rev. ed. Boston: Little, Brown.

Green, George Norris. 1979. *The Establishment in Texas Politics: The Primitive Years, 1938–1957*. Westport, Conn.: Greenwood Press.

Joint Legislative Committee on Organization and Economy. 1933. *The Government of the State of Texas: General Executive and Administrative Agencies; and the Militia, Texas Rangers, Highway Patrol, and Examining Boards*. Austin: Von Boeckmann-Jones Co.

Kaufman, Herbert. 1956. "Emerging Conflicts in the Doctrines of Public Administration." *American Political Science Review* 50 (December): 1057–1073.

Phares, Ross. 1976. *The Governors of Texas*. Gretna, La.: Pelikan.

Ransone, Coleman B. 1982. *The American Governorship*. Westport, Conn.: Greenwood Press.

Sabato, Larry. 1978. *Goodbye to Good-Time Charlie: The American Governor Transformed, 1950-1975*. 2nd ed. Washington, D.C.: CQ Press.

Schlesinger, Joseph A. 1957. *How They Became Governor: A Study of Comparative State Politics*. East Lansing: Governmental Research Bureau, Michigan State University.

Schlesinger, Joseph A. 1965. "The Politics of the Executive." In Herbert Jacob and Kenneth N. Vines (eds.), *Politics in the American States: A Comparative Analysis*. Boston: Little, Brown.

Stilwell, Hart. 1949. "Texas: Owned by Oil and Interlocking Directorates." In Robert S. Allen (ed.), *Our Sovereign State*. New York: Vanguard Press.

Bill Clements, Governor
Tom Phillips, Chief Justice

Jesus Moya, Activist

Ann Richards, State Treasurer

Bill Hobby, Lt. Governor

Barbara Jordan, Professor

Jim Hightower,
Agricultural Commissioner

Jim Mattox,
Attorney General

THE BUREAUCRACY

I t took Mrs. Harold Thiele about 24 hours and dozens of calls to seven public and private agencies before she got a skunk out of her kitchen. The first call was to the Austin police. Officers feared a shot at the animal cowering behind an oven might hit a gas pipe. The next call was to Austin Animal Control. They did not answer the telephone on Saturday night so Thiele forced the skunk into a small cage. The woman called animal control officers again Sunday morning, but employees there refused to come out and get the captured skunk. Next up on Thiele's telephone list was the Texas Department of Health followed by the Austin City Sanitation Department and Austin Humane Society—all without luck. . . . [Finally] Austin City Manager Jorge Carrasco . . . ended the situation by sending an employee from animal control with instructions to "eliminate the problem."

—Associated Press

The average citizen might think that it would be a relatively easy task to get local government to keep the weeds cut. Nothing, however, could be further from the truth. In Houston, don't even ask the city bureaucracy to cut the weeds in the ditch next to your house. They won't do it. A city ordinance requires the homeowner to control the weeds up to fourteen feet outside his property. The city *will* mow the weeds on esplanades. However, it will take a determined effort to find out which agency is responsible. In Houston, that task falls to the Parks and Recreation Department because esplanades are defined as miniparks. If the weed problem is on a street corner concealing a stop sign, however, the citizen would be foolish to call Parks and Recreation because they will refuse to accept responsibility. Is it then a problem for the Public Works Department? Nothing as rational as that. Who then? As it turns out the Traffic and Transportation Department is the agency to call. If the weeds in question are on an overgrown or abandoned lot rather than in a ditch or on an esplanade or street corner you have to contact still another bureaucracy: the Health Department. If there is an abandoned house on the lot then you have to call the Code Enforcement Division of the Housing Conservation Section, Dangerous Building Branch, Public Works Department—unless the property with the weeds is owned by a city agency. In that case call that department to take care of the problem. (*Houston Post,* July 20, 1987)

It is likely that many Texans have had a similarly negative experience with the bureaucracy. At the same time, many citizens appear to be fairly well satisfied with the outcome of their encounters with bureaucrats (Elling, 1983:246). The significant point is that the average Texan is quite dependent upon the bureaucracy On a day-to-day basis, it is the most prominent and crucial branch of government. By way of illustration, there are fewer than two hundred state senators and representatives, a handful of statewide elected officials, and several thousand mayors, city councillors, and school board members. There are more than 169,000 state bureaucrats, however, and over 500,000 local government employees in Texas.

Only infrequently does the average citizen deal with an elected public official. One is much more likely to come into contact with a bureaucrat, and when he or she does, the transaction is apt to involve a matter of importance to the citizen. Bureaucrats do not, so far as the citizen is concerned, deal with abstract policy. Instead they make specific decisions about the services that are most essential: education, law enforcement, health, water supply, fire protection, transportation, and recreation.

This chapter examines the bureaucracy in Texas from several perspectives. First we will consider the role of the bureaucracy in a democratic society. How can appointed public officials be held accountable? Next we will examine the historical development of the bureaucracy and the ways in which the state bureaucracy in Texas reflects changing philosophies of government. We will also be analyzing the conflicts between objectivity and responsiveness, efficiency and effectiveness, and independence and accountability.

BUREAUCRACY IN A DEMOCRATIC SOCIETY

What should be the proper relationship between elected officials and administrators? How can bureaucrats be held accountable? Should they be an independent force in government? Even democratic theorists disagree on the appropriate function for the bureaucracy.

Herbert Finer (1941:342) maintains that "the servants of the public are not to decide their own course: They are to be responsible to the elected representatives of the public, and these are to determine the course of action of the public servants to the most minute degree that is technically feasible." According to Finer, bureaucrats should be closely supervised and directed by elected officials. Appointed administrators should be allowed as little discretion as possible. Whenever possible, the judgment of the elected official rather than the judgment of the bureaucrat should prevail on policy issues.

Carl Friedrich (1940) places greater trust in the ability of the administrator to make wise policy choices. Consequently, he would provide the bureaucracy with considerable latitude in the discharge of its duties. The test of a "responsible" decision would be the extent to which it is responsive to technical expertise on the one hand and to public preference on the other. According to Friedrich (1940:17), a bureaucratic policy can be called irresponsible "if it can be shown that it was adopted without proper regard to the existing sum of human knowledge concerning the technical issues involved. We also have a right to call it irresponsible if it can be shown that it was adopted without proper regard for existing preferences in the community, and more particularly its prevailing majority."

Friedrich would give the bureaucrat a significant degree of independence from elected officials. He would then expect them to make policy choices on the basis of their professional expertise. Their decisions would be limited only by the requirement that they be generally compatible with the preferences of the majority.

Still another perspective is offered by Joseph Schumpeter (1950:68), who argues that the bureaucracy must be "strong enough to guide and, if need be, to instruct the politician. . . . In order to be able to do this it must be in a position to evolve principles of its own and sufficiently independent to assert them. It must be a power in its own right." Schumpeter's perspective is fascinating because it is not only a statement of what ought to be but an accurate description of reality as well. That is, many critics of the bureaucracy charge that the bureaucracy *is* a power in its own right and that it has achieved virtual independence from elected officials. As a result, it is alleged to be both unaccountable and unresponsive.

These three differing perspectives on the appropriate role of the bureaucracy reflect a basic ambiguity about how much independence and power the administrative branch of government should have. Americans have a deep distrust of appointed officials. They fear bureaucratic power because too easily that power can degenerate into abuse and arrogance. Our society agonizes over how bureaucrats are to be held accountable and made responsive to the will of the people.

At the same time, the extraordinary complexity of modern society requires the dedicated attention of career specialists. These experts should be protected from political interference so that they can perform their duties competently, fairly, and impartially.

This confusion over how to protect the bureaucracy—and how to protect the people from the bureaucrat—can be seen in Texas state government. Basically there are three types of state agencies.

1. The first type consists of departments whose directors are appointed by the governor. These agencies come closest to the executive control model, whereby the bureaucrat is accountable to a chief executive.

2. The second type is the state agency headed by an elected official. Since these elected administrators, at least in principle, are directly account-

able to the voters of the state, responsiveness to the public is allegedly maximized.

3. The third type of agency is the appointed board or commission. This bureaucratic structure is most compatible with the notion that bureaucrats should be independently powerful and insulated from interference by elected officials.

The bureaucratic structure in Texas state government that most closely resembles Herbert Finer's ideal is the elected department head. Finer, we recall, would allow administrators as little discretion as possible and would make them directly and immediately accountable to elected officials. In Texas, the system whereby the voters elect various department heads (land, agriculture, treasurer, attorney general) closely parallels Finer's ideal bureaucratic type. The presumption is that the administrator responsible for a particular function or program will be directly accountable to the voters, and individual bureaucrats within the agency will be accountable to the elected department head.

Carl Friedrich's notion of an administrator who strikes a balance between professional expertise and public preference in making policy decisions is reflected in those Texas state agencies where the director is appointed by and responsible to the governor. Such administrators are given considerable discretion in making decisions based on their technical training, superior information, and experience, but they are always limited by the need to take public preferences into account. The fact that they are appointed by and accountable to the chief elected official in the state ensures sensitivity to public preferences.

The extreme position taken by Joseph Schumpeter is best represented in the variety of boards and commissions in Texas state government. It is Schumpeter's perspective that the bureaucracy should be an essentially independent force in government. If anything, it should use its superior knowledge to instruct public officials rather than be guided or directed by them. State boards and commissions by and large meet those criteria. They are largely independent of the governor and the legislature, they are essentially unaccountable to the public, and they are an important force in policy making.

In Texas, therefore, the state bureaucracy is composed of three distinct organizational types. Each of these types reflects a different theory as to how much power the bureaucrat should have, what the role of the elected official should be, and to whom the bureaucrat should be accountable.

CHANGING PHILOSOPHIES OF GOVERNMENT

The three basic types of state bureaucracy also reflect the historical evolution of practice and thinking about power in the public sector. As discussed in the chapter on the governor, this evolutionary process moved through three distinct periods. The first period, from the beginning of the republic to the late nineteenth century, emphasized *representation*. There was a deep distrust of executive power. Consequently, power was concentrated in an elected legislature at the expense of the executive. A subordinate executive was weakened even further when the notion of the plural executive was widely adopted. This change emphasized the election of several executive officials in addition to the governor.

A second philosophy of government was the search for *neutral competence*. This period began in the late nineteenth century and was prompted in large part by the excesses of the political machine in many eastern cities. The widespread corruption in politics, in combination with the growing perception that elected officials lacked the technical competence to perform many public tasks, contributed to the rapid growth of an independent corps of professional bureaucrats. One outcome of this era was the growth of boards and commissions to perform a variety of governmental tasks. These boards and commissions stimulated the development of career experts who came to rely upon a body of professional knowledge and a set of professional values to make many policy decisions. Eventually these administrators developed a considerable degree of independence from elected officials. The establishment of civil service merit systems for public employees was a major factor in this process of insulation from political control.

The third public philosophy was known as the search for *executive leadership*. This philosophy was concerned with granting the governor a greater measure of control over the bureaucracy—by strengthening his appointment and removal powers, by eliminating independent boards and commissions, and by abolishing the plural executive. This movement gained ascendancy during a period when state governments were expanding their regulatory functions and providing a wider and wider array of increasingly complex and expensive services. This greatly expanded scope of governmental activities convinced many observers that the multitude of independent boards and commissions, the fragmentation and overlap of state agencies, and the limited powers of the governor all violated principles of sound management. They sought to make the state bureaucracy more efficient, more effective, and more accountable to the chief executive.

All three philosophies are reflected in state government in Texas. The emphasis upon *representation* can be found in a weak governor and the plural executive. The search for *neutral competence* is reflected in the variety of independent boards and commissions that exist in profusion. And the movement toward *executive control* is found in recent efforts to strengthen the governor's appointment powers and concentrate certain departments under his control.

CHARACTERISTICS OF BUREAUCRACY

All bureaucracies have several characteristics in common. They include the following:

1. An emphasis on accomplishing goals efficiently and effectively
2. Hierarchy
3. Chain of command
4. Division of labor and specialization of labor
5. Promotion on the basis of performance

Bureaucracy is a form of organization that concentrates upon goal accomplishment. This observation is true no matter what the particular goal may be. Some bureaucracies produce automobiles, others produce toys or breakfast cereals, and still others produce services such as education, defense, or banking. But whether the task is to educate students or to defend the society or to make and market aspirin, the goal remains the same: to accomplish the task as efficiently and effectively as possible.

Experience has shown that several organizational features enhance the efficient and effective accomplishment of goals. One such feature is hierarchy. In a hierarchy, there are superiors and subordinates. There are people at the top, in the middle, and at the bottom. Bureaucracies also have a chain of command. Everyone has a boss and each employee is responsible to a superior in the organization. There is no such thing as democracy within a bureaucracy.

Bureaucracies also divide labor and emphasize specialization. This division and specialization of labor can be seen in every large-scale organization. There are departments of production, manufacturing, marketing, personnel, advertising, administration, public affairs, research and development, accounting, maintenance, purchasing, and legal affairs. Within these departments, there are blue-collar workers, supervisors, executives, clerks, secretaries, computer programmers, accountants, economists, lawyers, researchers, engineers, scientists, personnel specialists, office managers, janitors, electricians, and plumbers.

In the ideal bureaucracy, all promotions are on the basis of merit or production. Those who produce are rewarded. Advancement up the bureaucratic ladder is dependent upon the worker's contribution to accomplishing the goals of the organization. Incompetents are weeded out. Productive employees are promoted. In reality, of course, incompetents are sometimes rewarded and the best workers may be passed over or even penalized. Therefore, it should be emphasized that the preceding definitions are for the ideal bureaucracy. In operation, most organizations do not even approach this ideal.

Bureaucratic Decision Making

To understand the role and influence of the state bureaucracy in Texas, we need to know something about how bureaucracies make decisions. Research reveals that the *process* of decision making within all large organizations is remarkably similar (Perrow, 1972). Organizations recognize that it is impossible to be completely rational in making decisions. Rationality has to do with setting goals, comparing costs and benefits, gathering and evaluating evidence, and making reasoned choices on the basis of objective analysis and careful deliberations.

Such rationality in decision making is impossible to achieve, however, because of three powerful limitations that affect all organizations.

1. Bureaucracies cannot predict the consequences of their actions. They do not know what will happen as a result of making one decision rather than another. They can only estimate the possible impacts of their choices.

2. Bureaucracies do not have information on alternative courses of action available to them. In order to be rational in decision making, a bureaucracy would have to be able to pick and choose from among all alternatives. Because of limitations imposed by time, information, and resources, however, decision makers never know *all* the reasonable alternative courses of action. And since some alternatives are never allowed to come up for consideration, the decision that is actually made may not be the one that is most rational.

3. Bureaucracies cannot be rational in their decision making because they find it impossible to rank their goals and priorities. And unless the decision is goal-oriented, it is irrational and pointless. But beyond certain clear and immediate goals, it becomes exceedingly difficult for bureaucracies to specify their objectives and then rank them according to priorities. An automobile company knows that it wants to produce and sell more cars more efficiently. A university knows that it wants to educate its students as effectively as possible. Beyond an expression of immediate priorities, organizations find it tough to pick and choose from among a variety of complex and sometimes conflicting goals.

Because of these three limitations on rationality, bureaucracies have to settle for something less than the best decision. What they settle for is a decision that works. These workable decisions do not just happen, however. They have to be carefully planned. What the organization seeks is to make decision making a routine, controlled, and predictable process. It wants a decision that works and satisfies the needs of the organization. To obtain such decisions, bureaucracies rely upon standard operating procedures and indoctrination.

Standard operating procedures (SOPs) help the bureaucracy ensure predictable decisions by specifying what action employees are to take in certain instances. By telling workers what decisions to make under a particular set of circumstances, SOPs standardize and routinize decision making. They minimize the influence of individuals.

Training and indoctrination are also essential. Bureaucracies try to standardize decision making by hiring employees who already think and behave in ways that are compatible with the perspectives of the organization. When a company hires an engineer, it obtains an employee who is likely to approach problems in a fairly predictable way. Training and indoctrination of workers by the schools as well as on the job ensure that there will be few surprises when it comes to decision making.

The bureaucracy relies upon SOPs and training to guide the search for workable solutions. That is, an organization searches its past in an effort to find a previous problem that corresponds to the present one. If the decision invoked in that past instance worked, then there will be a powerful tendency to make the same decision again. Therefore, today's decisions generally bear a remarkable resemblance to past decisions. The best predictor of next year's decisions is last year's decisions. And when the past serves as a guide to the present and future, change tends to be very slow.

Some of the most vigorous criticisms of the bureaucracy stem from its decision-making process. Bureaucrats are accused of being slow to act and afraid to take risks. They are criticized because they resist change and favor the status quo. In their defense, however, it should be pointed out that the limitations on rationality in decision making make deviations from past behavior very risky indeed. The safest decision is to pursue a course of action that has worked in the past. Rapid and comprehensive change, rather than incremental change, is fraught with danger. Thus, one should not expect much innovation from the bureaucracy.

CONTRADICTIONS OF BUREAUCRACY

Much disenchantment with the bureaucracy stems from the fact that its critics probably expect too much. Moreover, the things they expect are sometimes contradictory. Citizens want their bureaucrats to be fair and impartial, for example. They want them to administer the law and public programs competently, consistently, and fairly. In order to accomplish these goals, bureaucracies try to hire professionals who will apply their expertise, the best management tools and scientific knowledge, and the most sophisticated technology.

Americans also want their bureaucrats to be responsive, however. When citizens call or write to complain about a problem, they expect the bureaucracy to take prompt and effective action. That is, they expect them to be responsive. Unfortunately, bureaucrats cannot be fair and responsive at the same time. Fairness implies evenhanded treatment of people. Fairness suggests that each case is handled on its merits. Fairness means no favoritism. If the bureaucracy is to be responsive, however, it has to play favorites. It cannot be responsive to everyone on an equal basis. To be responsive means to pick and choose among competing demands and give certain ones preferential treatment. Responsiveness comes into conflict with fairness because there are many different and competing demands, and to respond to some means to ignore others.

Unfortunately for bureaucrats, the citizen does not distinguish between fairness and responsiveness. Bureaucrats are expected to accomplish both. When they prove unable to do so, the public is often dissatisfied.

The public also expects efficiency and effectiveness. Efficiency is defined as accomplishing a goal with a minimum expenditure of resources. Effectiveness is defined as accomplishing the goal successfully. Often there is a contradiction between efficiency and effectiveness. Many citizens are concerned with high crime rates, for example. They want the police to provide better protection and catch more criminals. However, they may be unwilling to shoulder the additional tax burden necessary to fund dramatic increases in police patrols. In this instance, effectiveness (lower crime rates and better police protection) clashes with efficiency (resources required to do the job). Similarly, citizens want better streets and highways and education, but they are frequently opposed to paying more in order to obtain them. They want effectiveness and efficiency at the same time, and they want them painlessly. When citizens find there are trade-offs between efficiency and effectiveness, they tend to blame the bureaucracy for its inability to achieve both goals simultaneously.

The difficulty involved in measuring and achieving efficiency in bureaucratic operations is illustrated by the history of the Texas Commission on Economy and Efficiency. In 1985, State Representative Charles Evan (R–Hurst) successfully sponsored a bill to create the Commission and give it a life of four years. Evan became one of the Commission's fifteen members. In September 1986, however, he attacked the Commission for having accomplished nothing and essentially forced it to go out of business. In essence, he accused the Commission on Efficiency of being inefficient. Its last official act, however, was probably the most economical and efficient task it accomplished in its short life. The executive director announced that $50,000 of the original budget of $185,000 would be returned to the state treasury.

Professionalism and independence, on the one hand, and accountability on the other, pose yet another contradiction. Most citizens want bureaucrats to be independent. They want them to be insulated from "political meddling." They want them to be objective rather than subjective, to be fair rather than to show favoritism. They want them to be professionally trained and equipped with the most modern technology. They want them to apply their technical competence and professional values to the solution of public problems. They want that effort made in an environment free from interference by elected officials and pressure groups.

On the other hand, citizens also want bureaucrats to be accountable to the public. Nothing is more likely to anger the average citizen than the perception that bureaucrats are arrogant and unconcerned with the people's wishes. But if we establish an independent bureaucracy to ensure professionalism and impartiality, we also run the risk of creating a group of powerful public officials who are essentially free to chart their own course. An independent bureaucracy protected by job security is more likely to be accountable to its own professional values than to any concept of the public interest.

The Texas Department of Human Services, which is responsible for providing welfare services to the poor, provides an example of how this public anger can develop. The state's record in caring for its needy citizens is somewhat less than admirable. Texas ranks forty-sixth in the nation in welfare payments to the poor. It contributes only $57 a month to each child receiving Aid to Families with Dependent Children. One would assume, therefore, that the department's slim budget would be stretched thin and would provide only for the bare essentials. In 1987, however, it was discovered that agency executives had spent $130,000 on a few items of furniture. A single conference table alone cost $6,619 and the chairs to go around it cost $606 each. A custom-made credenza for the Commissioner's office cost $3,638. Two "executive" chairs were purchased for $1,129 each and two walnut desks cost $1,607 each. The Commissioner, Marlin Johnston, defended the purchases and observed that "in the welfare business, we're not second-class citizens." He further noted that "we don't have posh furniture." However, a bureaucrat at a neighboring bureaucracy, the Texas Railroad Commission, gleefully pointed out that his agency had purchased "executive" desks and chairs for only $415 each and $145 each, respectively. One state representative called the furniture purchases "obscene." The Department of Human Services spent more money on individual chairs for each executive than it contributed in aid payments for an entire year to one child. The public outrage in response to the disclosure of the furniture scandal is certainly understandable. It is noteworthy, however, that no public official characterized the state's treatment of the needy as obscene. Official wrath is reserved for bureaucratic incompetence, waste, and self-indulgence. Gross disparities in the distribution of burdens and benefits in the state are almost universally ignored.

THE POWER OF THE BUREAUCRACY

The bureaucracy is a powerful branch of state government in Texas. Its power derives from several sources. First, bureaucrats are essential. They are everywhere. Government cannot operate without them. They are crucial to the administration, enforcement, and implementation of thousands of state laws, regulations, programs, and policies. The typical citizen's encounter with state government is most likely to take place through an appointed bureaucrat.

Bureaucrats are powerful figures in government because of their expertise, as well. Many administrators spend their entire career in government, sometimes in the same agency or department. Because of this experience, they become more knowledgeable about their area of operations than anyone else. This knowledge is a source of power because others who are less experienced and less knowledgeable must often defer to their judgment on policy issues.

Moreover, expertise provides another source of power. Bureaucracies emphasize division and specialization of labor. They also encourage technical competence and detailed knowledge. This creation of specialists establishes a body of esoteric knowledge that is extremely difficult for an outsider to challenge.

Another major source of bureaucratic power is the discretion that administrators enjoy. Most state laws and programs provide many opportunities for the exercise of such discretion. Few laws are so precisely written that they do not leave a great deal of room for bureaucrats to exercise their own judgment with respect to enforcement. In fact such discretion in enforcing laws and regulations is the norm rather than the exception. Texas highway patrol officers, for example, have essentially unlimited discretion with respect to whether they will rigidly enforce the speed limits and whether they will issue a ticket or simply a warning. Bureaucratic discretion also exists when it comes to the enforcement of banking and insurance regulations, the delivery of services, and the implementation of a variety of state programs and policies. One extreme example of bureaucratic discretion recently came to light. In December 1984 it was learned that the Austin State Hospital was sending a van loaded with former mental patients to Houston twice a week. The patients were unloaded at a Greyhound bus station in a rundown part of the city and were left to fend for themselves. Reports indicate that some were victimized by criminals in the area. The Texas Department of Mental Health and Mental Retardation, which has jurisdiction over mental hospitals in the state, justified this exercise of discretion by noting that the department is under court order to reduce the patient population because of overcrowded conditions.

Bureaucrats find yet another source of power in the support of clientele groups. Every bureaucracy has clients. These are the people and groups that use the services provided by the board or commission or agency or department. Depending on the bureaucracy the clientele group may be bankers, farmers, real estate agents, schoolteachers, doctors, or the oil or insurance industry. The highway lobby, for example, is one of the most powerful clientele groups in the state. These groups have a direct and vested interest in the decisions of "their" bureaucracy. They closely monitor its activities. Key members of the clientele group, whether that group is oil, insurance, highway contractors, or schoolteachers, develop close personal relationships with top administrators in the agency.

The Public Utilities Commission illustrates this relationship. Since the PUC approves or rejects requests from the utility companies for rate increases, it is easy to see why they go to great lengths to influence decisions. The three PUC commissioners and their staffs are visited hundreds of times each year by executives of the utility giants—AT&T Communications, Houston Lighting and Power, Southwestern Bell Telephone, General Telephone, Central Power and Light of Corpus Christi, and Texas Utilities Electric of Dallas. Although the utility representatives are prohibited by law from discussing specific cases that are under review by the commissioners, their constant interaction with commission staff members provides numerous opportunities to influence policy outcomes.

Utility company executives also interact with commissioners and their staffs at business conferences. Frequently, the utility companies finance these meetings and conferences and pay part of the expenses of state officials in attendance. Since rate increases can easily translate into hundreds of millions of dollars in additional profits, these meetings are taken very seriously indeed.

Frequently the public interest takes a back seat to the narrow but much more forcefully expressed interests of the clientele group. When that happens, one can say that the bureaucracy has been "captured" by its clientele group. This capture is most likely to occur when a bureaucracy has responsibility for the regulation of a certain occupational group or industry.

The State Board of Morticians, which regulates the funeral industry, offers a good example of the capture of a state agency by the industry it was established to regulate. Five of the nine board members are associated with the funeral industry. Recent decisions reveal the board's pro-industry bias. For example, the board has applied to the Federal Trade Commission for exemption from enforcement of national regulations that apply to funeral homes in Texas. In addition, the agency has failed to comply with state law that requires it to employ a private investigator who is not associated with the funeral business to investigate complaints. It has hired embalmers and funeral directors as investigators.

Additional evidence of the board's bias is revealed in its decision to refuse to act on charges of illegal activity brought by a board member. In August 1984, a nonindustry member attempted to present the results of an investigation he had conducted. Specifically, his investigation of twenty-four funeral homes concentrated upon the extent of compliance with a state law which requires that the funeral home furnish customers with the prices of goods and services. He found that only one of the twenty-four was in full compliance with the law. However, the board president ruled that the violators would not be subject to further investigation.

The close association between the board and the funeral industry is further illustrated by the fact that the State Board of Morticians rents office space from and shares facilities with the Texas Funeral Directors Association. Although appearances can be deceiving, they are probably not deceptive in this instance.

Some bureaucracies are very adroit at exploiting the clientele relationship. Just as clients use the bureaucracy, bureaucrats also use the clientele group. If the agency's powers, jurisdiction, or budget is threatened, it will call upon its clientele to rally to its support. If this support is sufficiently energetic, it may persuade the legislature to change its plans. This point is discussed in more detail later in the chapter.

STATE EMPLOYEES: THEIR NUMBER AND SALARIES

Texas has more than 169,000 state government employees. Employees at Texas colleges and universities accounted for the single largest share of these workers (41 percent). Table 8-1 presents information on the number of state employees by function and their average monthly earnings. Note that the top five services in terms of number of workers are higher education (69,566 employees), hospitals (33,900), highways (13,925), welfare (11,666), and natural resources (8,033). These five services account for 81 percent of all state government workers.

TABLE 8–1   Texas State Employees by Service and Earnings

Service	Number of State Employees	Average Monthly Earnings Per Employee
Higher education	69,566	$1,670
Hospitals	33,900	$1,184
Highways	13,925	$1,548
Welfare	11,666	$1,350
Natural resources	8,033	$1,579
Corrections	6,759	$1,452
Health	6,452	$1,505
Miscellaneous	5,760	$1,489
Financial administration	5,201	$1,541
Social insurance administration	4,483	$1,548
Judicial, legislative, executive	1,814	$2,327
Law enforcement	1,708	$1,693

Source: U.S. Department of Commerce, Bureau of the Census, 1981.

The single highest-paid category of workers are those employed by the judicial, legislative, and executive branches of state government. The next highest-paid workers are those in state law enforcement and higher education. Hospital and welfare employees earned the lowest wages.

It should be pointed out that the majority of government workers in Texas are not state employees. Of the 855,233 public employees, 169,267 (19.8 percent) are state workers, 149,215 (17.4 percent) are federal employees, and 536,751 (62.8 percent) work for local governments in Texas.

Texas Compared with Other States

Texas employs fewer state workers on a per capita basis than most other states. Table 8-2 presents information on the states with the highest and lowest ratios of state employees to population. The table reveals several interesting findings. First, the states with the fewest employees per 10,000 population tend to be among the largest states in the country. California has fewer state workers per capita than any other state. Moreover, the states that staff state government with the fewest workers also tend to be highly industrialized. Industrial states such as Ohio, California, Texas, Pennsylvania, Illinois, Massachusetts, New Jersey, Indiana, and Michigan all rank among the states with the fewest employees per capita.

From another perspective, the states with the most state workers per 10,000 population tend to be small, rural, and less industrialized. Alaska employs almost four times as many state workers per capita as does Texas. In

TABLE 8–2   Comparison of State Government Employment: 1981

State	Number of Employees Per 10,000 Population	1981 Population
California	101.9	24,196,000
Florida	104.5	10,183,000
Pennsylvania	105.0	11,871,000
Illinois	106.3	11,462,000
Ohio	106.6	10,781,000
Texas	114.6	14,766,000
New Jersey	116.5	7,404,000
Indiana	120.3	5,468,000
North Dakota	189.5	658,000
Wyoming	194.9	492,000
Vermont	212.0	516,000
Rhode Island	217.7	953,000
New Mexico	247.0	1,328,000
Delaware	274.6	598,000
Hawaii	377.9	981,000
Alaska	437.6	412,000

Source: U.S. Department of Commerce, Bureau of the Census.

fact, Texas employed fewer state workers per capita in 1981 than it did in 1976. In 1976 there were 128 state employees for every 10,000 Texans. By 1981, this figure had dropped to 114.6 bureaucrats for every 10,000 residents. This figure compares to a nationwide state average of 135 employees per 10,000 population.

It is a myth, therefore, that the state bureaucracy in Texas is growing by leaps and bounds. Indeed, the number of state workers on a per capita basis has not even kept pace with the growth in population. There are considerably fewer state workers in Texas today in per capita terms than was the case several years ago.

How Much Do State Bureaucrats Cost?

Table 8-3 presents data on the states with the highest and lowest expenditures per capita for state government workers. The table reveals that forty-three states have higher per person costs for their state employees than Texas. State workers cost each Texan $17.37 in wages and salaries. The comparable figure in Alaska is $97.28, in Hawaii it is $57.63, in Delaware $37.49, and in New Mexico $33.66. The nationwide average cost of supporting a state employee is $26.41 per citizen.

The average state worker in the United States in 1981 was paid $1,507 per month. This figure ranged from a high of $2,233 in Alaska to a low of $1,167 in Mississippi. The average monthly salary for state workers in Texas was $1,515. This salary was lower than the one paid in nineteen other states and placed Texas just above the national average of $1,507.

We can conclude several things from this comparative examination of the Texas bureaucracy. First, Texas employs relatively few state workers on a per capita basis. There are only 114.6 state employees for every 10,000 Texans.

TABLE 8–3   Comparison of Per Capita Costs of State Government Employees: 1981

State	Per Capita Cost
Florida	$14.19
Missouri	$14.62
Ohio	$14.79
Pennsylvania	$15.75
Illinois	$16.84
Massachusetts	$17.12
Texas	$17.37
North Dakota	$29.90
Rhode Island	$33.29
Wyoming	$33.51
New Mexico	$33.66
Delaware	$37.42
Hawaii	$57.63
Alaska	$97.28

Source: U.S. Department of Commerce, Bureau of the Census.

That number places Texas forty-fifth among the fifty states. It should also be pointed out that most public employees in Texas are employed by levels of government other than the state government. There were 536,751 local government workers in Texas in 1981, for example, but only 169,267 state employees. Further, the per capita costs of the state bureaucracy are comparatively low in Texas. Each Texan pays only $17.37 to provide the wages and salaries of all state workers—far below the per capita costs in many other states. Finally, the majority of all state workers are employed in the delivery of only three public services. Seven out of every ten state bureaucrats are employed by public colleges and universities, state hospitals, and the highway department.

REORGANIZING THE TEXAS BUREAUCRACY

The state bureaucracy is frequently criticized for its alleged inefficiency, lack of accountability, duplication of effort, and domination by clientele groups. One reform that is often advanced as a solution to these problems is the reorganization of state administration. Proponents of reorganization see several advantages.

First, reorganization would eliminate the inefficiency and duplication of effort inherent in prevailing administrative practices. Currently several different boards, commissions, and departments are responsible for the delivery of the same or related services. Reorganization would consolidate these various agencies and make a single department responsible for service in a particular area. One agency would assume responsibility for water, for example, another for natural resources, and still another for transportation.

According to its advocates, reorganization would also enhance accountability. Under a reorganized administrative system, individual department heads would be appointed by the governor and would be responsible to him. Under the current system, some of the most important department heads are elected, and for other agencies the governor's appointment and removal powers are limited. With power over the bureaucracy concentrated in the hands of the governor, the public would know whom to hold accountable for inadequate performance. Department heads would answer to the governor, and the governor would be accountable to the voters.

Many believe that reorganization would contribute to greater efficiency and effectiveness. Under the present arrangement, various agencies, boards, and departments are free to chart their own course. Consequently, different bureaucracies sometimes work at cross-purposes to each other. There is little agreement with respect to goals and objectives and priorities. The absence of a common purpose, in combination with the absence of uniform personnel and financial practices and procedures, works against the efficient use of resources. Many observers claim that reorganization of the state bureaucracy would change all this. The governor and his staff would set broad policies, and the department heads and agency directors would implement them. Goals and priorities would be clearly articulated, and the various state agencies would work together to achieve them. Setting goals and establishing chains of command and lines of authority, the argument runs, would contribute to both the achievement of the goals and the efficient use of resources in pursuit of policy objectives.

Another alleged advantage of administrative reorganization is that it would reduce the influence of clientele groups. In the present fragmented bureaucracy, there are many opportunities for narrow interest groups to develop a preferential relationship with the state board or agency responsible for regulating them. The capture of a state agency by a clientele group ensures that the broad public interest will not be well served. But proponents of reorganization claim that the consolidation of scattered agencies, boards, and commissions into broad policy areas, in combination with the concentration of power in the hands of the governor, would lessen, if not eliminate altogether, the direct influence of clientele groups. Bureaucratic officials would then be accountable to the governor rather than to a narrow vested interest.

Barriers to Reform

If there are so many criticisms of the fragmented, unaccountable state bureaucracy, and so many advantages inherent in reorganization, why does the state administrative system continue to operate without significant reform? The state constitution is not wholly to blame. Although the constitutional obstacle is indeed one barrier to reform, there are other, more powerful, forces at work.

One source of potential opposition is the legislature, or at least some members of the legislature. Reorganization plans generally propose to strengthen the governor's control over the bureaucracy and reduce the role of the legislature in state administration. It is obvious, therefore, why the legislature may be unenthusiastic about proposed reforms. Moreover, many legislators enjoy close relationships with key bureaucratic officials. These professional associations and personal friendships operate to the advantage of the bureaucrats when efforts are made to reorganize the state administrative machinery.

And, of course, bureaucratic officials themselves frequently resist reform. This opposition is almost certain to occur when the proposed reorganization would eliminate some state agencies and drastically curtail the operations of others. Bureaucrats can prove to be effective opponents. They have the information, experience, and expertise to support their arguments. They maintain that the professionalism of state government will decline and efficient service delivery will suffer if the proposed reforms are implemented. Since bureaucrats can legitimately lay claim to expert status, their warnings cannot be taken lightly. Career bureaucrats can rely upon their numerous contacts in and out of government to quietly but effectively lobby behind the scenes against reorganization plans.

Some of the most vocal opposition to reorganization comes from elected officials. Any attempt to eliminate or consolidate the administrative functions presided over by the treasurer, comptroller, land commissioner, agricultural commissioner, or railroad commissioners would almost certainly arouse powerful opposition from the incumbents of these offices. And unlike appointed bureaucrats, these elected officials could make their appeals for support to a statewide constituency.

Another source of opposition is the clientele group. Groups that have labored long and hard for decades to develop a relationship with a state board or agency to ensure preferential treatment are highly unlikely to accept fundamental change in that relationship without a fight. Clientele groups are frequently composed of powerful, highly organized, and well-financed business interests. Therefore, their opposition to administrative reorganization is likely to be particularly effective. Given the widespread opposition to bureaucratic reform, then, it should not be surprising that reorganization efforts are frequently feeble and ineffective.

Would Reorganization Work?

There are so many critics of the state bureaucracy that one might think any change would be for the better. But would it? In fact, the evidence from reorganization efforts made in other states suggests that the results are not always as expected. Kenneth Meier (1980) studied sixteen states that undertook a reorganization of their bureaucracies and compared them with a like number of states that did not reorganize. He found that the reorganized state bureaucracies did not spend less money than the ones that failed to reorganize. Other studies support this conclusion.

Moreover, there is no evidence that reorganized state bureaucracies are more efficient and effective than ones that do not reorganize. Effectiveness, we recall, is defined as successfully accomplishing goals and objectives. An efficient organization accomplishes goals with a minimum expenditure of resources (money, personnel, equipment, effort). The problem with the concepts of efficiency and effectiveness is that they are exceedingly difficult to measure. Before we can determine whether a state agency is efficient in the expenditure of resources, we have to determine whether it is effective. That is, does it successfully accomplish its goals? But before we can determine whether an organization has accomplished its goals, a judgment has to be made about what those goals actually are. And organizations seldom have goals that are clearly expressed.

This problem is revealed when one asks bureaucratic officials what the goals of their organization are. They are apt to respond with a broad statement to the effect that their goal is to deliver a particular service or a set of services to the public at the lowest possible cost to the taxpayer. But that goal is so vague as to be essentially meaningless. When one probes more deeply, he quickly discovers that each agency and department has a variety of different goals. There are long-term goals and short-term goals. There are operational goals and symbolic goals. There are goals for the top-level administrators and goals for the employees. There are goals for the organization as a whole and goals for the individuals who make up the organization. Moreover, different offices within the bureaucracy pursue different goals. The governor and his staff may have one set of goals for the agency while the director and his staff perceive a different set. The problem of determining the true goals of the organization is further compounded by the fact that these various goals may prove contradictory.

Although one should not belabor this point, it is essential to emphasize how hard it is to measure the concepts of efficiency and effectiveness. It is often alleged that consolidation of the bewildering array of boards, commissions, and agencies into a much smaller number of departments, with control concentrated in the governor's hands, would greatly improve efficiency and effectiveness. But if we cannot accurately assess efficiency and effectiveness for the reasons previously discussed, how can we be so certain that reorganization would actually improve them?

SUNSET LEGISLATION

One feeble effort at reform has recently been made. In 1977 the legislature passed a sunset review law, which provides for the evaluation and termination of agencies unless renewed. The legislation created a Sunset Advisory Commission composed of four senators and four representatives. The commission's task is to evaluate at least twenty state agencies each year and recommend to the legislature whether the agencies should be continued or abolished. Although the agencies to be evaluated each year are left to the discretion of the commission, at least twenty must be reviewed annually so that all state agencies can be evaluated by 1989. Agencies included in the annual review are abolished unless the legislature decides to renew them for twelve years. All agencies are evaluated with the exception of agencies of higher education and those created by the state constitution.

The results of the first sunset review cycle suggested that the new requirements might significantly influence the growth and direction of the state bureaucracy. Of the twenty-five agencies evaluated, eight were abolished, another was discontinued and its activities taken over by another agency, and two others were combined with existing agencies. In the second review cycle, however, only two of twenty-eight agencies were allowed to die and three others had their functions taken over by existing agencies.

The subsequent recommendations of the Sunset Commission confirm the observation that the review process has not in fact had a significant impact upon the state bureaucracy. The number of agencies abolished each cycle has remained low. More important, the agencies terminated have never been among the most significant and influential. For example, one agency terminated during the 1985 review cycle was the Texas Health Facilities Commission. Agencies abolished in earlier evaluation periods included the Pink Bollworm Commission, the Board of Tuberculosis Nurse Examiners, the Texas Navy, the Stonewall Jackson Memorial Board, the Board of Examiners of Social Psychotherapists, the Burial Association Rate Board, and the Board of Library Examiners.

Most of the agencies abolished have either been insignificant or inactive. Sometimes they are both. A tuberculosis nurse has not been graduated in the state since 1961, for example. Indeed, the only school that trained such nurses shut its doors that year. Therefore, elimination of the Board of Tuberculosis Nurse Examiners (which licensed tuberculosis nurses to practice) cannot be considered a major reform of the bureaucracy. In fact, the Sunset Commission has even maintained some agencies that should have been abolished. The Burial Association Rate Board had its functions transferred to another board, it is true, but the Burial Rate Board had not even met in fourteen years!

In an earlier section we noted that bureaucrats and their clients can offer powerful resistance to efforts to abolish or alter an existing agency. This seems to be the case with respect to the reform goals of the Sunset Review Commission. Powerful, well-entrenched agencies can employ a variety of resources to escape termination. It is the inconsequential agencies that serve no useful purpose, that have few employees, and that enjoy the support of no powerful clientele group that will be scheduled for elimination.

In short, it cannot be known with certainty whether reorganization and consolidation would improve the administration of state government. One can only speculate that it might.

TYPES OF STATE BUREAUCRACIES

The Texas state bureaucracy defies description if approached from the perspective of a coherent administrative unit. Instead bureaucratic power, authority, and responsibility in state government are divided and scattered about. There are several different types of bureaucracies at the state level: boards and commissions, appointed department heads, and elected department heads.

Boards and Commissions

There are several different types of boards and commissions. Basically they can be classified, according to function and method of selection, as either elected, appointed, or ex officio boards.

One of the *elected* commissions is among the most powerful agencies in state government. The Texas Railroad Commission is of great significance to both the government and the economy of the state because of its jurisdiction over the oil and gas industry. Its three commissioners—elected in statewide elections to staggered six-year terms—have responsibility for the regulation of oil and gas drilling activities, the setting of production quotas, the regulation of oil and gas pipelines, and the regulation of coal and lignite mining. Originally established in 1891 to regulate the railroads, the commission continues to oversee the transportation sector within the state. In addition to railroads, it also regulates the trucking industry.

The *appointed* boards and commissions are vital to the administration of state government. Much more numerous than elected boards, their membership consists of appointments by the governor or some combination of appointments made by the governor, appointments made by other state officials, and ex officio appointments. The members of these boards are appointed to staggered six-year terms. They appoint a chief administrator who is responsible to the board for the direct day-to-day operation of the organization. There are approximately two hundred boards and commissions in state government. They are active in the following broad policy areas outlined.

Agriculture   There are a number of boards and commissions under the general heading of agriculture. A prominent state commission in this functional area is the Texas Animal Health Commission. As its name implies, its main task is to administer programs to fight diseases in livestock. Typically the law specifies that various groups and geographic regions be represented. For example, the nine members of the Animal Health Commission (appointed by the governor with the consent of the Senate to staggered six-year terms) must include in their number hog, poultry, cattle, and horse raisers.

Education   A major group of state boards in this policy area are the seventeen boards of regents who set policy for the public universities in the state. In addition to these boards of regents, another state agency is important in establishing and monitoring educational policy. The eighteen members of the Coordinating Board, Texas College and University System, have responsibility for administering state aid to community colleges and federal grants to colleges and universities. In addition, the board approves degree programs and has various responsibilities for construction programs and projects.

Health and Hospitals   A nine-member board sets policy for the Department of Mental Health and Retardation. The board appoints an administrator to direct the operations of the department. The department's responsibilities include the operation of various schools, hospitals, outpatient clinics, and rehabilitation centers for the mentally ill and retarded. The department also has licensing authority over mental hospitals in the private sector.

Natural Resources   A major board in this area is the Water Development Board. Composed of six members (again appointed by the governor with the consent of the Senate to six-year overlapping terms), the board sets policy for the Texas Department of Water. The board also appoints a director to head the department. An important component of the Department of Water is the Texas Water Commission. Although part of the Water Department, the Water Commission is an independent commission with three full-time members appointed to six-year staggered terms by the governor. The Water Commission counts among its responsibilities the adjudication of water rights and disputes, the establishment of water districts, and the authorization of water use permits.

Examining Boards   A variety of state boards exist to regulate and certify qualifications for various occupations and professions. Prospective practitioners of certain trades or professions must obtain the license issued by the board before they can engage in the occupation. Examples of these examining boards are the State Board of Medical Examiners, State Board of Morticians, and State Board of Barber Examiners.

Other Boards A variety of other important state boards also exist. They include the State Board of Insurance, Public Utilities Commission, Texas Employment Commission, the Board of Pardons and Paroles, and the Parks and Wildlife Commission.

Apart from the elected and the appointed boards and commissions, there is a third type of board whose members hold the office by virtue of their occupancy of some other position in state government. These are the *ex officio boards*. For example, the Natural Fibers and Food Protein Commission consists of the presidents of the University of Texas, Texas A&M, Texas Tech University, and Texas Woman's University. Another example of an ex officio board is the Legislative Redistricting Board, which consists of the lieutenant governor, the Speaker of the House of Representatives, the attorney general, the land commissioner, and the comptroller of public accounts. This board has the responsibility to redraw the state representative and senate district boundaries after the census if the legislature fails to do the job.

Appointed Department Heads

Another type of state bureaucracy in Texas government is the agency head appointed by the governor. There are five of these agency heads.

Secretary of State The secretary of state is the state's chief election official. Other duties include the issuing of charters of incorporation for businesses and the publication of administrative rules and regulations.

Executive Director, Department of Community Affairs This agency head is responsible for directing and coordinating various programs at both the state and federal level that are relevant to local governments in the state.

Director, Office of State–Federal Relations This department has responsibility to watch out for the interests of the state in Washington, D.C. The chief function of the director is to provide information to the governor on federal aid and grant programs and on national legislation that is of importance to state and local governments in Texas.

Adjutant General The adjutant general commands the Texas State Guard and the Texas Army and Air National Guard.

Labor Commissioner The labor commissioner directs the operations of the Texas Department of Labor and Standards. This agency regulates a variety of economic activities from private employment agencies to boxing matches. It also monitors child labor, labor safety and health practices, and the standards and requirements imposed on the mobile home industry. Moreover, it collects, maintains, and publishes a variety of information and statistics on labor activities.

Elected Officials

Some important state agencies are headed by elected rather than appointed officials. These officials include the attorney general, the comptroller of public accounts, the land commissioner, the commissioner of agriculture, and the state treasurer.

Attorney General   The attorney general performs two major functions. First, he responds to requests for legal advice and opinions from the legislature and from all state agencies, boards, commissions, and departments. Although his interpretations of laws, rules, and regulations are not legally binding, they do carry significant weight. Therefore the attorney general exerts a major influence on the operations of state government through his evaluation of the legality of proposed or actual policies, rules, laws, and regulations. The attorney general is also the chief lawyer for the state. He represents the state in civil and criminal cases and, moreover, prosecutes violations of state law.

Comptroller of Public Accounts   The comptroller is a powerful state official because he directs the collection of taxes and, before each legislative session, issues an evaluation and estimate of anticipated state government revenues. These estimates (which are issued monthly during the legislative session) are vital to the appropriations process because the legislature is prohibited from spending more than expected revenues provide. The comptroller is more than an auditor, accountant, and tax collector. He is also a key figure in the appropriations process.

Commissioner of the General Land Office   The land commissioner's duties include control over the leasing of state lands (the state either owns or has mineral interests in 22.5 million acres) for grazing and oil and gas exploration. This official also operates the Veterans Land Program whereby Texas veterans can purchase land with money borrowed from the state. These low-interest loans are made possible through bond sales approved by the voters.

Commissioner of Agriculture   The commissioner of agriculture performs a variety of duties. He enforces laws relating to agriculture. He provides various educational and research services. He maintains standards of weights and measures. He promotes the agricultural products of the state. He regulates the use of pesticides. He administers consumer protection laws. He enforces disease and pest control programs and policies. And, finally, he provides food inspection services.

State Treasurer   The state treasurer is an important financial officer of state government. The treasurer's duties include the following: custodian of state funds; pays the state's bills; sells cigarette and alcoholic beverage excise tax stamps; custodian of state securities and county and municipal bonds. The state treasurer is also an ex officio member of the State Depository Board, which decides which banks will receive deposits of state funds, and an ex officio member of the State Banking Board, which reviews charter applications for new banks.

MINORITIES IN GOVERNMENT EMPLOYMENT

Critics of public bureaucracies are often concerned about the extent to which they provide equitable employment opportunities to minorities. When all government employees in Texas (both state and local workers) are considered, the state fares rather well with respect to its level of black employment. In fact Texas, along with most other states, overrepresents blacks in state and local government positions. One way to calculate an index of black representation is to take the black percentage of the state/local government work force and divide that figure by the black percentage of the state's population. A score of 1.0 would mean that blacks have the same percentage of government jobs as they have of the state's population. If blacks have 10 percent of the jobs and account for 10 percent of the total population, for example, their score would be 1.0.

When such calculations are made, Texas and forty other states score higher than 1.0 on the index of black job equality. Texas has a score of 1.367 while the scores for some other states are 1.507 in Florida, 1.605 in Illinois, 1.5 in Indiana, 1.313 in Louisiana, 1.110 in Maryland, 1.410 in Massachusetts, 1.519 in Michigan, 1.397 in New Jersey, 1.067 in North Carolina, and 1.716 in Pennsylvania. On the basis of this evidence, therefore, one might conclude that Texas and most other states do not penalize their black citizens with respect to employment in state and local government (Elling, 1983).

It should be pointed out, however, that information on the number of black employees does not provide a complete picture of minority employment patterns. Are black workers disproportionately clustered in clerical and menial positions while whites dominate the professional and managerial positions? Although the data to address this issue are not available, we can compare black employees' salaries to the salaries of white employees. If we divide the median annual salary of black state and local employees by the median annual salary of white employees in a state, a score of 1.0 would mean that the median salaries of blacks are the same as those of white employees (Elling, 1983). When such calculations are done, the results reveal that black public employees are substantially underpaid in comparison to white government workers.

In fact, Texas has the lowest score of any state in the union. Its score of 0.738 means that its black public employees are paid *less* in comparison to its white employees than is the case for any other state. It should be noted, however, that all but a handful of states (Minnesota, Montana, Nebraska, Oregon, Pennsylvania) pay their black workers a median annual salary that is also less than the median annual salary paid whites. Texas is one of a group of southern states (Alabama, Florida, Louisiana, Mississippi, South Carolina) that ranks at the low end of the range on the black/white salary comparison.

WOMEN IN GOVERNMENT EMPLOYMENT

When equality scores are computed for females employed by state and local governments, the results reveal that *no* state has a score of 1.0 or better. A score of 1.0, we recall, means that the percentage of jobs held by women is equal to their percentage of the state's population. Indiana has the highest score (0.918) and Vermont (0.465) and Delaware (0.554) have the lowest. Texas's score of 0.787 ranks it somewhere near the middle. A large number of states have higher scores and a significant number have lower ones.

No state achieves a score as high as 1.0 with respect to the salaries of female employees. A score of 1.0, once again, means that the median annual salary of female state and local government workers is the same as the median annual salary of male employees. In Texas that score is 0.738, which is identical to the salary score of black employees in the state. The Texas score for female salaries places it in the bottom third of the fifty states.

Blacks and Hispanics also earn less at the local level. Black city employees in Houston earn an average of $1,462 per month, while Hispanics earn $1,618 and whites are paid $2,138. Seventy-two percent of the white workers earn more than the average monthly check of $1,814, while only 21 percent of black and 35 percent of Hispanic employees receive a salary that exceeds the average. Minority female workers fare even worse. Only 10 percent of black female employees and 12 percent of Hispanic females were paid better than average salaries. The corresponding figure for white females was 33 percent.

CONCLUSION

An examination of the bureaucracy in Texas reveals that the state's administrative system reflects the impact of three philosophies of government. The emphasis upon *representation* can be found in a weak governor and plural executive. The search for *neutral competence* is reflected in the profusion of independent boards and commissions. The movement toward *executive control* is found in recent efforts to strengthen the governor's appointment powers and concentrate at least a few departments under his control.

Also, we have considered the structure of bureaucracies. Bureaucratic characteristics include an emphasis on goal accomplishment, hierarchy, chain of command, and division and specialization of labor. The power of the bureaucracy in government derives from its knowledge, its expertise, and its independence in the interpretation and implementation of policy. Another source of power is found in the support provided by clientele groups.

The state bureaucracy in Texas is frequently criticized for its alleged inefficiency, lack of accountability, duplication of effort, and domination by clientele groups. Thus, advocates of reform would like to see a reorganization of the bureaucracy. Different boards and commissions responsible for the delivery of the same or related services would be consolidated into a single department. Department heads would be appointed by and responsible to the governor. As a result, the reformers claim, efficiency would be increased, accountability would be improved, and the influence of clientele groups would decline.

There are several barriers to reform, however. One of the leading opponents of reorganization is the legislature, which is unenthusiastic about strengthening the governor's hand and weakening its own role in state administration. Other sources of opposition include clientele groups and bureaucrats themselves.

That any effort to reform the state bureaucracy is probably doomed is illustrated by the impact (or lack thereof) of sunset legislation. A Sunset Review Commission established by the legislature to review state agencies—and to abolish those that cannot justify their existence—has had no significant effect on the direction of state administration. The only agencies to be terminated are those that are inconsequential, inactive, or both. It should be pointed out, however, that for all the alleged advantages that would result from reorganization, there is no substantial evidence from scholarly studies to demonstrate that these improvements would in fact occur.

REFERENCES

Elling, Richard C. 1983. "State Bureaucracies." In Virginia Gray, Herbert Jacob, and Kenneth Vines (eds.), *Politics in the American States*. Boston: Little, Brown.

Finer, Herbert. 1941. "Administrative Responsibility in Democratic Government." *Public Administration Review* 1 (Summer): 335–350.

Friedrich, Carl J. 1940. "Public Policy and the Nature of Administrative Responsibility." *Public Policy* 1: 3–24.

Meier, Kenneth J. 1980. "Executive Reorganization of Government: Impact on Employment and Expenditures." *American Journal of Political Science* 24: 396–412.

Perrow, Charles. 1972. *Complex Organizations*. Glenview, Ill.: Scott, Foresman.

Schumpeter, Joseph A. 1950. *Capitalism, Socialism, and Democracy.* New York: Harper & Row.

9

THE COURT SYSTEM

T he judicial system of Texas has surely come a long way since the days when Judge Roy Bean would open court in his courtroom-cum-saloon in Langtry in the 1880s with the following announcement (Lloyd, 1967:63): "Hear Ye! Hear Ye! This honorable court is now in session, and if anybody wants a snort before we start, step up to the bar and name your poison." This chapter reviews the present character and operations of the state's court system with particular emphasis on how the functioning of the system corresponds with the public's understanding of it. Before beginning that review, however, it will be useful to consider the role of the court system in the overall state government.

THE FUNCTIONS OF STATE COURT SYSTEMS

The Texas Constitution says that the "judicial power" of the state shall be vested in its court system. This power is principally one of applying the constitutional and statutory laws of the state to civil and criminal disputes. That is, private citizens who believe that disputes arising in their civil affairs fall under provisions of state law and officers of the state charged with enforcing civil and criminal laws bring claims into the court system to be settled. The courts provide the institutional setting where such claims will be heard. Judges sit as arbiters, presiding over the hearing of these disputes. And juries—panels of ordinary citizens—may be employed to evaluate the facts, the resolution, and the settlement appropriate to each dispute.

Much of the courts' work is quite routine application of the law to specific cases. An individual is or is not guilty of a traffic violation or burglary or violating the local building code. A divorce should or should not be granted a particular couple. A deceased person's will is probated according to established procedures. By number, the overwhelming majority of court cases are of this routine character—although, of course, any such case can be of great consequence to the parties involved.

185

Other judicial decisions, though certainly only a very small percentage, are far from routine. The law itself may be unclear at some points. The facts of some cases may be sufficiently complicated to obscure whether they indicate illegal behavior. And some laws may conflict with constitutional provisions. The courts are called upon to resolve such intricate matters. Court decisions in such instances can have far-reaching consequences that are hardly routine. When the courts decide how to unravel the law's tangles they are deciding, in effect, what the law is. When they decide whether certain complicated facts fall within the purview of the law, they are defining the limits of the law's applicability. When they resolve conflicts between two or more laws, they are also deciding which law should prevail. In other words, in all these instances the courts can literally make law and public policy in the process.

THE IMAGE OF THE COURT SYSTEM

The nonroutine aspects of the judicial function are certainly the ones most widely discussed in the mass media and in scholarship on the courts. They are, after all, the more interesting aspects of the judicial role. The public probably has greater interest in the nonroutine aspects of the judicial system (except when members of the public find themselves involved in a "routine" legal dispute). A preoccupation with the sensational side of the judicial system has important consequences for our understanding of the system as a whole. It leaves Americans with certain images or perceptions of the courts.

First, there is the widespread perception that judges are impartial, "professional" umpires in the system—that is, technical experts of a certain kind. Thus the average citizen probably expects all judges to be technically qualified and to be isolated from "politics" so that their decisions might not be biased by partisan leanings or ideological disposition. Then, in their perceptions of the court system, most people accord to judges a crucial role in the system. These are, after all, the neutral technical experts who sit at the very center of court decision making. Finally, the average citizen probably believes that the nonroutine aspects of judicial decision making described here are the most important ones. Thus that citizen would focus attention on the highest courts in the system, the so-called supreme courts, because of the belief that more of the nonroutine and, hence, more important decisions take place there.

There is good reason to question the accuracy of these and many other public perceptions of the courts. A recent nationwide poll has shown, for example, that Americans admit they are less familiar with the courts than they are with the two other branches of their government (Bennack, 1983). That same survey also revealed some quite fundamental misperceptions of the operations of courts that are widely held by Americans. In this chapter we will consider the accuracy of these perceptions of the court system as they might apply in Texas. While there is some truth in all of them, each one can also lead to a misunderstanding of how this state's courts really operate. After examining the structure and operations of Texas courts, we will reconsider these public perceptions and their relevance for the reality of the court system.

ORGANIZATION OF THE TEXAS COURT SYSTEM

One's understanding of the court system ought to begin with the basic structural details of the system of courts, the geographic distribution of courts in the state, the method of selecting judges, and the role of juries.

Basic Structure of the System

The court system of Texas shares certain features in common with those of all the states. The system is a kind of hierarchy in which higher courts handle appeals from lower ones. In this arrangement the lower-level courts are ones with *original jurisdiction*—that is, the authority to hear the initial legal action in certain kinds of disputes (depending on the subject matter handled by each court). In other words, it is in these courts of original jurisdiction that witnesses are heard, evidence is presented, and verdicts are rendered.

The higher-level courts in the system are *appellate* courts, usually with no original jurisdiction and only with the authority to hear appeals of decisions of lower-level courts. The appellate courts of Texas have been described:

> *Appellate courts do not try cases, have jurors, or hear witnesses. Rather, they review actions and decisions of the lower courts on questions of law or allegations of procedural error. In carrying out this review, the appellate courts are usually restricted to [reviewing] the evidence and exhibits presented at the trial-court level. [Office of Court Administration, 1984:16]*

Within this general framework Texas, again like every other state, has a fairly elaborate set of courts. The most important of these bodies, along with their relationships to one another in the court hierarchy, are portrayed in figure 9-1. The three lowest of the courts in figure 9-1 are the ones with *limited* original jurisdiction. The two very lowest courts, the justice of the peace court and the municipal court, have jurisdiction limited to minor civil and criminal actions. Municipal courts, for example, hear traffic cases and those under city ordinances for zoning, fire safety, public health matters, and the like. The criminal jurisdiction of the justice of the peace courts is limited to offenses where the maximum punishment is by fine alone and that not to exceed $200.

Typically these two lowest courts are not *courts of record*. That is, there is no transcript of the actual court proceedings that is maintained for future reference (as in appeals of the decision). Court records at this level include only the nature of the original charge or complaint, the names and addresses of the parties involved, the plea of the defendant, and the final decision of the court.[1]

The second level in the system is that of the *county courts*. The Texas Constitution requires that there be one county court in each county, but the legislature is also empowered to create more of these courts "as it may deem necessary." Thus by 1985 there existed the 254 "constitutional" county courts and 132 "statutory" county courts created by the legislature. Most of the statutory courts are located in major metropolitan areas because of the heavy

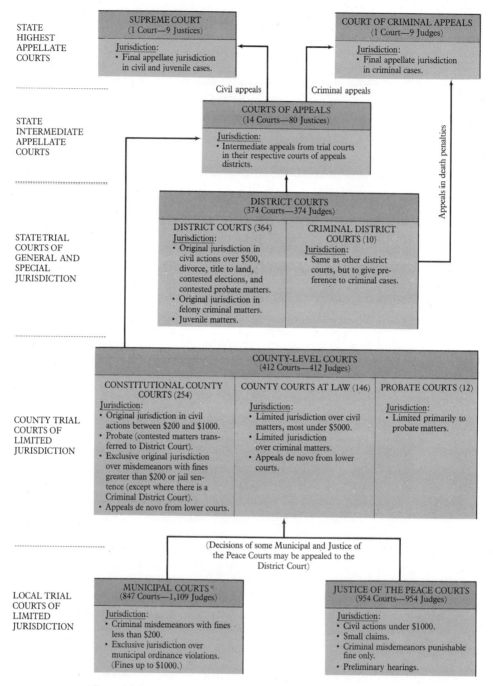

STATE
HIGHEST
APPELLATE
COURTS

SUPREME COURT
(1 Court—9 Justices)

Jurisdiction:
• Final appellate jurisdiction
  in civil and juvenile cases.

COURT OF CRIMINAL APPEALS
(1 Court—9 Judges)

Jurisdiction:
• Final appellate jurisdiction
  in criminal cases.

Civil appeals   Criminal appeals

STATE
INTERMEDIATE
APPELLATE
COURTS

COURTS OF APPEALS
(14 Courts—80 Justices)

Jurisdiction:
• Intermediate appeals from trial courts
  in their respective courts of appeals
  districts.

Appeals in death penalties

STATE TRIAL
COURTS OF
GENERAL AND
SPECIAL
JURISDICTION

DISTRICT COURTS
(374 Courts—374 Judges)

DISTRICT COURTS (364)
Jurisdiction:
• Original jurisdiction in
  civil actions over $500,
  divorce, title to land,
  contested elections, and
  contested probate matters.
• Original jurisdiction in
  felony criminal matters.
• Juvenile matters.

CRIMINAL DISTRICT
COURTS (10)
Jurisdiction:
• Same as other district
  courts, but to give pre-
  ference to criminal cases.

COUNTY TRIAL
COURTS OF
LIMITED
JURISDICTION

COUNTY-LEVEL COURTS
(412 Courts—412 Judges)

CONSTITUTIONAL COUNTY
COURTS (254)
Jurisdiction:
• Original jurisdiction in civil
  actions between $200 and $1000.
• Probate (contested matters trans-
  ferred to District Court).
• Exclusive original jurisdiction
  over misdemeanors with fines
  greater than $200 or jail sen-
  tence (except where there is a
  Criminal District Court).
• Appeals de novo from lower courts.

COUNTY COURTS AT LAW (146)
Jurisdiction:
• Limited jurisdiction over civil
  matters, most under $5000.
• Limited jurisdiction
  over criminal matters.
• Appeals de novo from lower
  courts.

PROBATE COURTS (12)
Jurisdiction:
• Limited primarily to
  probate matters.

(Decisions of some Municipal and Justice of
the Peace Courts may be appealed to the
District Court)

LOCAL TRIAL
COURTS OF
LIMITED
JURISDICTION

MUNICIPAL COURTS *
(847 Courts—1,109 Judges)

Jurisdiction:
• Criminal misdemeanors with fines
  less than $200.
• Exclusive jurisdiction over
  municipal ordinance violations.
  (Fines up to $1000.)

JUSTICE OF THE PEACE COURTS
(954 Courts—954 Judges)

Jurisdiction:
• Civil actions under $1000.
• Small claims.
• Criminal misdemeanors punishable
  fine only.
• Preliminary hearings.

* Ten municipal courts are courts of record. Appeals from those courts are taken on the record and not by
  trial de novo.

FIGURE 9–1   Court Structure of Texas: 1986

Source: Office of Court Administration

caseloads in such places. Many of these statutory courts are also specialized bodies handling only civil, criminal, probate, or juvenile cases.

Constitutional county courts have jurisdiction over certain civil and criminal matters as set out in the constitution, while the jurisdiction of each statutory court is defined in the legislation that created it. Essentially, however, county courts also handle relatively minor legal disputes—only misdemeanor criminal cases, for example. In civil disputes over monetary matters their jurisdiction is limited to cases where the amount in dispute is $1,000 or less for constitutional county courts and $5,000 or less for statutory courts. County courts also hear appeals of rulings from municipal courts and justice of the peace courts. County courts, like all those above them in the Texas system, are courts of record.

The third, and most important, level of trial courts is that of the *district courts*. These bodies have original jurisdiction in all felony criminal cases and in a number of civil areas. Generally, one can say that district courts have original jurisdiction over the more important legal disputes.[2]

The number of district courts has been increased over the history of the state in an effort to keep pace with the increase in caseloads. By 1986 there were 374 such courts, all limited in their authority to specific geographic areas. In certain large metropolitan areas, as well, some of these courts are specialized bodies hearing only selected kinds of cases. Despite the increased number of such courts, it has still been difficult for them to keep up with the growing volume of judicial business. In Harris County in 1985, for example, it was projected that the time between the filing of a civil suit in a district court and the case actually coming to trial would be thirty-seven *months* (Kennedy, 1985).

The first level of appellate courts in Texas is that of the *courts of appeals*. There are fourteen such courts, each with responsibility for a specified geographic area. There are eighty judges who serve at this level. Each of the fourteen separate courts has one chief justice and from two to twelve associate justices. These courts hear only appeals from district and county courts (with the exception that appeals of death penalty verdicts in the district courts go directly to the court of criminal appeals above this level). Hearings in the courts of appeals are decided either by all the judges on a given court sitting together or by three-judge panels.

Above the courts of appeals Texas has an unusual system in that there are two "supreme" courts. The literally named *supreme court* hears only civil and juvenile case appeals of decisions made in the courts of appeals. The supreme court is a nine-member body whose entire membership sits together to decide each case before it. One of the judges is elected to the position of chief justice; the others are designated justices.

The *court of criminal appeals* hears appeals of criminal case decisions of the courts of appeals and death penalty appeals from the district courts. This second "supreme" court also has nine judges who hear cases in Austin. Capital punishment cases are heard by the full court; others may be heard by three-judge panels.

The supreme court has some organizational control over the entire Texas court system. It develops the rules of civil procedure—that is, the procedural rules under which civil cases are processed by Texas courts. It also formulates rules for the administration of various lower courts, manages the case distribution of the several courts of appeals to equalize their work loads, supervises the State Bar and its rules, and oversees the disciplining of judges for misconduct.

Geographic Distribution of Courts of Original Jurisdiction

There are a great many courts and a greater specialization of courts in metropolitan areas because of the larger volume of legal disputes in such places. The response of the court system to its ever-expanding caseload is considered in detail later in this chapter, but the simple location of various courts is an important element of that response. Thus it is useful at this point to illustrate the differences between the separate court systems of different parts of the state. Table 9-1 shows the state and local courts that exist in three quite different Texas counties: Blanco County, an almost entirely rural county west of Austin; Lubbock County in the lower Panhandle, which is the location of the city of Lubbock; and Harris County in southeast Texas, which includes most of the Houston metropolitan area.

As table 9-1 indicates, the court systems of the two less populous counties have relatively small numbers of courts and judges. Even in Lubbock County with its two dozen judges, the bulk of these individuals serve in the relatively less important justice of the peace courts and municipal courts. In Harris County, by way of contrast, there is a large number of courts at all levels and

TABLE 9–1   The Court Systems of Three Texas Counties

Type of Court	Blanco County (Rural and Small Town)	Lubbock County (with a Medium-Sized City)	Harris County (Highly Urbanized)
Courts of appeal	None	None	1st and 14th Districts–18 courts of appeal judges
District courts	1	5	25–civil 22–criminal 9–family law 3–juvenile
County courts	1–constitutional	1–constitutional 2–county courts at law	4–civil 14–criminal 4–probate 1–constitutional
Justices of the peace	2	7	16
Municipal courts	1	9 in 8 cities and towns	94 in 33 cities and towns
Total number of judges	5	24	210

Source: Office of Court Administration (1986).

there is greater specialization among those courts. In light of the number and variety of courts in large metropolitan areas like Harris County, it is easy to understand why many people admit to limited familiarity with the court system.[3]

Selection of Judges

All judges in Texas, with the exception of municipal court judges, are elected in partisan elections held on the November ballot in even-numbered years. District court judges and all other elected judges below them serve four-year terms and are elected by the voters in their geographic district. Appellate judges serve six-year overlapping terms and are elected on statewide ballots. When vacancies occur in district court or higher positions—typically because of death or retirement—they are filled until the next election by nominees of the governor who must be confirmed by the Senate in its next regular session.

Partisan election of judges was favored in many states during the period of Jacksonian Democracy of the middle 1800s with its desire for "representativeness" in government—as described in chapter 7 on the governor. In the twentieth century, however, a variety of other selection systems have been promulgated with the hope of isolating the judicial bench from partisan politics and increasing the number of professionally competent judges. Thus in some states the legislature appoints judges to office based on their professional abilities. Even more popular in recent times have been various systems whereby governors appoint judges from lists approved by a nonpartisan review committee intended to screen candidates according to their merit and competence. In some of these systems the appointed judges must, to retain their posts, run for voter "approval" in an unopposed election after a certain initial term of office. Thus the public is allowed the opportunity to evaluate such judges on their records. It should be noted, however, that about a dozen states continue to use partisan election systems and that a nearly equal number use nonpartisan elections (Farthing-Capowich, 1984:154–155).

Partisan elections, in particular, have been widely criticized in recent years for several reasons. It is thought that such election systems discourage the candidacy of many highly qualified individuals who are averse to getting involved in politics and the rigors of election campaigns. Indeed, some have argued that the individuals attracted to these aspects of the system might be the very people one would *not* wish to see on the bench.

It has also been argued that the focus on party labels and the general partisan atmosphere of elections divert the voter's attention from what ought to be important: the professional qualifications of judicial candidates and the actual judicial records of incumbent judges. The typically low voter turnout in such elections—in part a result of the "rolloff" described in chapter 5—is said to undermine the degree of public control through the "representative" electoral mechanism. Yet it should be noted that *all* the various systems of judicial selection have their critics (Dubois, 1980:3–35) and that political science research on their character and consequences has not been able to demonstrate that any particular system is either clearly superior or inferior to the others.

In Texas the system of partisan elections has been criticized from time to time for all the reasons indicated above. Some of that criticism has become particularly sharp recently. Public interest in this issue has typically been quite low; yet some members of the legal profession, in particular, have been actively promoting a change in the method of selecting judges. A 1983 poll of members of the State Bar, with about half of the membership responding, found overwhelming support for changing to a nonpartisan election system (*Texas Bar Journal*, 1983:463). (The only choices offered in the poll were keeping partisan elections or changing to nonpartisan ones.) The state legislature held hearings on the subject in 1984 and 1985 but adopted no changes in the existing system. Then in 1986 several prominent state officials, including then-Supreme Court Chief Justice John Hill and Lieutenant Governor Bill Hobby endorsed a plan for judicial appointments by the governor from lists provided by a nonpartisan review panel. Despite such support, many members of the bar and many sitting judges continue to favor and lobby for the current system.

Grand Juries

All charges for felony offenses must arise out of a grand jury's deliberation over the facts of the potential case (although the accused can waive his or her right to the hearing and accept an indictment forthwith). Grand juries are twelve-member panels of lay citizens who serve individual district courts to review such cases, typically for a three-month or six-month term. These juries deliver an indictment when at least nine of their members believe sufficient evidence is available to proceed with indictment and trial. If at least nine members are not so persuaded, the grand jury will issue a *no bill* and no indictments will be issued.

Grand juries are intended to provide a point in the legal system where average citizens can play a role to ensure the quality of justice. Grand juries throughout the United States, however, have come under notable criticism in recent years (Frankel and Naftalis, 1975). While not much is known systematically about grand juries in Texas because of the limited research on them, two of the concerns cited by Frankel and Naftalis were found to be of great relevance to Harris County grand juries in a fascinating case study by Carp (1974). One of those concerns was that grand juries are seldom representative of the community at large; instead they are dominated by high-income, high-status individuals. Carp found that Harris County grand juries were overwhelmingly composed of male, Anglo, middle-aged, high-income businessmen and other professionals. In other words, these bodies were far from representative of the Houston community.

Moreover, grand juries have often been criticized as being controlled by district attorneys—whose recommendations about whether or not to indict often are the predominant influence on the jury's decisions. Carp found that in 1971 the various Harris County grand juries sitting in that year spent an average of only five minutes on each case in deciding whether or not to indict! And this period included the time necessary for the prosecuting attorney to present the case and the evidence. This finding, along with several others that emerged in the study, led Carp to conclude that these juries were heavily controlled in their decision making by the prosecuting attorneys and their representations. Typically the grand jury moved very quickly through the facts of each case, simply rubber-stamping the prosecuting attorney's recommendation about whether or not to bring an indictment. To the extent that a similar pattern of decision making characterizes other Texas grand juries, one would have to conclude that they provide little public control of the judicial process. One would also have to conclude that the prosecuting attorney, instead, turns out to be the key figure in the indicting process and that his opinion of individual cases is seldom constrained by this public body.

Trial or Petit Juries

Criminal defendants and disputants in civil proceedings are constitutionally guaranteed a trial before a lay jury if they desire it. If the criminal defendant or both parties in a civil case agree, however, the case can be heard by the judge in a so-called *bench* trial. In the latter instance, the judge determines both the final decision and whatever criminal penalty or civil settlement is appropriate. District court juries are twelve-member panels. Petit juries in the county and lower courts are six-member panels.

THE WORK LOAD OF TEXAS COURTS

To understand fully the character and operations of state courts, in addition to a knowledge of their structure, one needs a sense of the kinds and amount of business they do—the work load or caseload of various courts. Several aspects of the work load are of relevance here.

Cases Heard by Courts of Original Jurisdiction

Since it is the lowest courts that hear legal cases at their inception, the courts of original jurisdiction are of particular interest. Indeed, the work load of the appellate courts is, to a large degree, a product of what occurs in these lower courts. The very lowest courts in the Texas system—the justice of the peace courts and municipal courts—have caseloads heavily weighted with traffic offenses. For example, about 90 percent of municipal court cases arise from parking and traffic citations. Justice of the peace courts also hear large numbers of traffic cases along with a variety of others for misdemeanor crimes, small claims suits, foreclosures, and recovery of possession of personal property. County courts, too, have work loads heavily oriented toward relatively minor legal matters. These courts hear, as prominent examples, large numbers of cases involving traffic offenses, driving while intoxicated, bad checks, personal injury, and debt claims.

As indicated earlier, the district courts are the most important trial courts because they hear the more serious cases. Figure 9-2 presents a breakdown of the composition of the cases heard at this level in the most recent year for which complete data are available. While all cases involving serious criminal

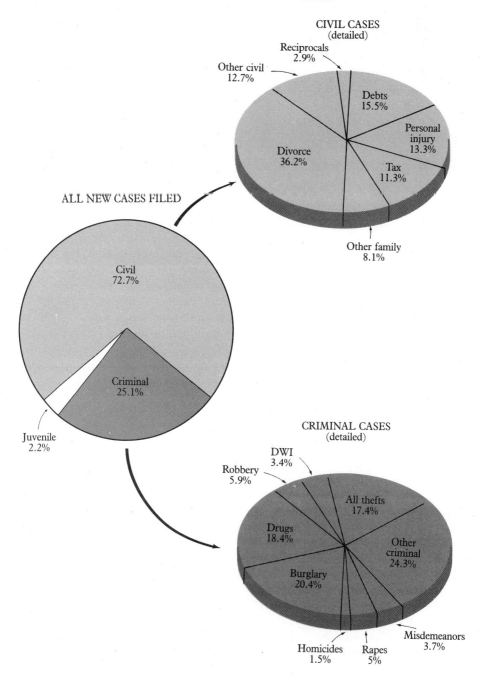

FIGURE 9–2   Cases Added to District Courts: 1986

Source: Office of Court Administration

offenses are heard in district courts, criminal cases constitute only about a quarter of their total work load. In fact, more divorce cases than criminal cases are heard in a typical year. Among the criminal offenses, as figure 9-2 indicates, the most typical ones are for theft, burglary, and robbery.

Growth of the District Court Caseload

Another important aspect of court work loads—and one that has caused considerable strain in all court systems—has been the great increase in the numbers of cases in recent decades. While this phenomenon has arisen for all levels of courts, it can be most appropriately illustrated for the district courts, again primarily because of their importance to the overall system.

Table 9-2 illustrates how the district court caseload has burgeoned in the last twenty years. The state of Texas has tried to keep pace with this growth by increasing the number of judges at this level, yet even with a near doubling of the judges during the period covered in the table, the number of new cases filed annually per judge has itself increased by over a third. Thus judges are forced to hear more cases per year in an effort to keep pace with the ever-rising number, and one has to suspect that the quality of justice might often be compromised under this kind of pressure.

How are district court judges able to handle the growing volume of work? If the typical judge worked five days a week for fifty weeks in 1986, he or she would have had to dispose of over six cases per day on an average to meet his or her share of the 1,624 cases settled per judge that year. Obviously, the average case must not have required much of the judge's or the court's time for resolution. And one might fairly wonder about the quality of this fast-moving justice.

Most cases that begin at this level of the court system also end there. That is, only a small proportion of district court decisions are appealed to a higher court. By way of example, in 1986 there were filed with the courts of appeals— the appellate court immediately above the district courts—some 7,832 cases. Moreover, thirty-five death penalty appeals went directly to the court of criminal appeals. These two sets of appeals taken together, however, represented

TABLE 9–2   Growth of the District Court Caseload: 1965–1986

Caseload	1965	1970	1975	1980	1986
New cases added to docket	191,653	260,171	346,081	427,871	581,902
Cases disposed of	190,699	249,829	322,623	373,355	607,571
Cases pending at year-end	212,695	259,847	337,641	473,191	605,552
Number of judges	182	211	261	310	374
New cases per judge	1,053	1,233	1,326	1,380	1,556
Cases disposed of per judge	1,048	1,184	1,236	1,204	1,624

Source: Annual Report of the Texas Judicial System (various years).

only a tiny fraction of the one million or so cases settled annually by the district and county courts in recent times. Thus, once again, the character of district court decision making becomes of special interest because the district court is, in fact, the "supreme court" for most cases.

Disposition of District Court Cases

We can see how the district courts get through their voluminous work load by examining in detail the ways in which cases are disposed of at this level—as indicated in table 9-3. For criminal cases, the table indicates that virtually all defendants were either found guilty or their case was dismissed. About half of all the criminal cases settled ended in convictions or guilty pleas (deferred adjudication is granted in selected cases where a defendant pleads guilty and the judge places the person on a rigid "probation" and defers the entering of a guilty verdict). Almost a third of all the cases were ones dismissed or revoked, but this figure is somewhat misleading. Many of the latter cases were ones in which the defendant had been convicted of another charge. (This circumstance arises because these statistics are kept on the basis of "cases"

TABLE 9–3 Disposition of District Court Cases: 1986

Disposition	Number	Percentage
Criminal Cases		
Total dispositions	139,265	100
Convictions	66,668	48
Placed on deferred adjudication	14,171	10
Acquittals	1,317	1
Dismissed or revoked	43,011	31
Other dispositions	14,098	10
Number of convictions where the defendant pleaded guilty	65,245	
Guilty pleas as a percentage of total convictions		98
Civil Cases		
Total dispositions	455,849	100
Judgment after jury trial	3,709	1
Judgment after bench trial	129,484	28
Default judgments	33,345	7
Agreed judgments	39,342	9
Summary judgments	6,600	1
Dismissed for lack of prosecution	102,407	22
Dismissed by plaintiff	64,165	14
Other dispositions	76,797	17

Source: Office of Court Administration (1986: 126–127)

instead of persons charged, and some individuals are charged with several "cases" in this system.)

Most notable of the statistics in table 9-3, however, is the fact that only 1 percent of all district court criminal cases ended in acquittal. The explanation for this remarkable fact lies in a second statistic: the percentage of guilty pleas among all cases that were not dismissed. As considerable research on other states has also demonstrated, in the overwhelming majority of criminal "trials" the defendant pleads guilty at the start and is quickly sentenced. There is literally no trial as one might think of it in the conventional way—that is, as an adversarial hearing before a jury with both sides presenting independent evidence.

It is difficult to know precisely how this pattern of the disposition of criminal cases affects the quality of justice. It might signify that the criminal justice system pursues only cases in which the evidence is entirely clear and overwhelming. In other words, all those individuals convicted in the district courts in 1986 were undoubtedly guilty if this speculation is correct. Of course, there might have been many truly guilty individuals among the third of the cases that were dismissed, perhaps because of the weakness of the prosecution's evidence.

Many critics of the criminal justice system question the universality of these conclusions. These critics point to the widespread use of the plea bargaining system whereby prosecutors bargain with defendants to induce them to plead guilty, usually to a reduced charge, to avoid the time and expense of a full trial. The critics believe that many defendants are not fully informed of the consequences of accepting a plea bargain. As Glick and Vines (1973:74) note, as well:

> There is no element of due process in the system, and the defendant is convicted without formal procedures or checks guaranteeing constitutional protections. . . . There is no judicial review of the propriety of the bargain, and not only does the process take place clandestinely, but in the sentencing stage there is often a pretense that no bargaining took place in order to reach the guilty plea.

Whether this system is just or not in most instances, it certainly helps explain why most cases end at the district court level. Since the overwhelming majority of those convicted of criminal offenses plead guilty in the first place, they have few grounds on which to support an appeal of their own conviction.

A similar pattern is evident for civil cases, as well. Only 29 percent of these cases were settled by complete trials in 1986. Over one-third of all civil cases were dismissed, often after the parties had reached out-of-court settlements. And the remainder of these cases were also settled in ways that required little court time or effort.

The preceding observations surely indicate how the court system is able to handle the volume of cases that it does—even though the backlog of pending cases still is rising in Texas district courts. These observations are important in another sense, as well. They indicate that in only a minority of cases does the court system operate in the way the average citizen probably assumes it does. One could say the average citizen probably accepts the "Perry Mason" model of the justice system, where every defendant is innocent until proven guilty. He gets his day in court. He gets to confront his accusers before a jury of his peers—and with the privilege of brilliant counsel.

Yet the typical state court case proceeds in a far different fashion (Blumberg, 1967; Eisenstein and Jacob, 1977). Both criminal and civil cases are more likely to be settled out of court by private negotiations between parties. There is, in other words, no adversarial confrontation before an impartial court and jury. For criminal cases, the pattern of actual decision making indicates, as well, that the prosecuting attorney is far more important to the outcome than is the judge—for it is the prosecuting attorney who arranges the plea bargain, just, one should recall, as it is the same individual who dominates the grand jury and the indicting process. Finally, once an out-of-court settlement is reached, there is no appeal of its terms. The criminal defendant who pleads guilty effectively gives up that right, and the civil litigant who settles privately must do so, as well, as a condition of the settlement.

Appellate Court Caseloads

While it has been argued here that the court of original jurisdiction is, in reality, the "supreme court" for most cases, it is still important to consider at least briefly the work load of the appellate courts. Every defendant who loses a case in the district or county courts is guaranteed by the state constitution the right to have an appeal of the outcome heard by the courts of appeals. As we noted above, currently only a very small percentage of these lower-level court decisions are so appealed.

Courts of Appeals   In the 1970s the backlog of as-yet-unreviewed criminal appeals grew considerably—because of more liberal rules about defendants' rights and because many more individuals convicted of criminal offenses were encouraged to appeal. Before 1981 these appeals went directly to the court of criminal appeals. In other words, the intermediate court of appeals heard only civil cases. Yet the growing criminal appeals backlog forced the state to reorganize the system. By a constitutional amendment that took effect in 1981, criminal as well as civil appeals were first directed to the newly expanded courts of appeals.

Since that reorganization, the courts of appeals have made steady progress toward reducing the backlog of unreviewed cases. In 1986, for example, these courts disposed of more than eight thousand cases and ended the year with a backlog about 6 percent smaller than it had been at the first of the year (although the end-of-the-year backlog still amounted to more than five thousand cases waiting to be reviewed). Of additional interest are the actual results in the eight thousand or so cases settled. In 54 percent of the appeals the decision of the lower court was affirmed. In only 13 percent was the lower court decision reversed in any way. (The remainder of the cases were dismissed or otherwise settled without a decision by the courts of appeals.) Thus most of the time the courts of appeals accept the decision of the lower courts as appropriate.

Court of Criminal Appeals   After the 1981 reorganization, individuals convicted of criminal offenses whose appeals were not found to be meritorious by the courts of appeals could request another rehearing by the court of criminal appeals. The latter court has discretion, however, in what cases it chooses to hear. That is, those appealing to this court are not guaranteed the right of a rehearing there.

The caseload statistics for 1986 offer a typical portrait of court of criminal appeals decisions since the 1981 reorganization. In 1986, the court received 1,360 petitions to review lower court decisions, 35 death penalty appeals, 2,074 applications for writs of habeus corpus, and 1,193 other motions as for the rehearing of appeals denied earlier. The court added only 356 of these cases to its docket for consideration of the lower courts' decisions, and it disposed of 409 such cases.

Supreme Court   Since 1981 the supreme court of Texas has heard only civil appeals from decisions of the intermediate courts of appeals. As a result its work load, while growing steadily, has been more manageable than that of the court of criminal appeals. By way of example, in 1986 the supreme court received 1,044 appeals of lower court decisions. The court accepted 139 such cases and disposed of 140. Notably, in 83 percent of the latter cases, the lower court decision was reversed in whole or in part. Finally, the court received over a thousand other applications for various writs and motions in the same year.

THE JUDGES THEMSELVES

At the beginning of this chapter we observed that most Texans probably accord a particularly important role in the court system to judges. We have by now, of course, pointed out some ways in which this view is both inaccurate and misleading. Yet no survey of the court system would be complete without a more detailed review of the requirements of judgeships, the processes of judicial selection, and the resultant character of the bench.

Statutory Requirements for Office and Salaries

State law prescribes certain qualifications necessary to run for election for some of the judgeships available in Texas. To qualify for a district judgeship or higher, one must be an American and Texas citizen, be licensed to practice law in the state, and have spent a certain number of years either in legal practice or serving as a judge (with the experience requirement increasing for the higher positions). To run for election to one of the constitutional county courts, it is only required that a candidate "be well informed in the law." In other words, formal legal training and a license to practice law are not necessary. Service on a statutory county court may, however, require professional legal experience if it was written into the law creating the court in question.

There are no formal educational or experience requirements that justice of the peace candidates must fulfill *before* seeking election. Yet in 1973 the state legislature required that nonlawyers newly elected to these positions must take forty hours of college study in the law within one year and then twenty more hours annually as long as they hold office. The educational requirements for municipal judges vary from city to city. But the majority of judges at this level—just like the majority of both county court judges and justices of the peace—are not trained in the law or, therefore, licensed to practice law.

The base salaries of the district court and higher-level judges are set by the state legislature. Counties where courts of appeal and district courts hold session may, however, supplement the base salaries of judges at these two levels, and many counties do so with widely varying supplemental amounts.[4] Salaries at the lower-level courts are set by the appropriate local governmental jurisdiction and, hence, also vary widely. Table 9-4 presents 1987 base and supplemental salary information for these various positions.[5]

The salaries of Texas judges compare reasonably well with those of the judges in other states. In a recent comparative survey the salaries of Texas Supreme Court associate justices ranked sixth in the nation among all state "supreme" courts (Lim, 1986). Texas District Court judge salaries ranked only thirty-first, but that comparison was made only on the base figure for the Texas judges. Texas District Court judges earning the higher salary supplements indicated in table 9-4 would have ranked among the very top trial court judges in the nation.

A more important salary comparison, however, is that with the professional colleagues of these judges who have remained in private practice. In the 1987 salary survey sponsored by *Student Lawyer* magazine, the average nonpatent law firm partner in Dallas earned $180,000 annually while the average Houston partner earned $215,000. One must suspect, of course, that the especially capable and successful law firm partners in Texas—those who are professionally well above the average—earn far above these average income figures, too. Thus

TABLE 9-4   Judicial Salaries in Texas: 1987

Court	Salary	Comments
Supreme court and court of criminal appeals		
Chief justice	$79,310	
Justices	$78,795	
Courts of appeals		
Chief justices	$71,379	Some counties supplement these
Associate justices	$70,916	salaries with an additional $4,000–$7,000 per year
District courts	$56,135	Some counties supplement these base salaries with as much as $21,000 more per year
County courts	Varies by each county	Determined by each county
Justices of the peace	Varies by each county	Determined by each county
Municipal courts	Varies by each city	Determined by each city

Source: Office of Court Administration (1986: 9–12)

if one hopes that Texas can attract highly capable legal professionals to its state judgeships, it is also clear that the state's judicial salaries fall far below what such capable individuals can earn in private practice.

Judicial Elections and Appointments

Very little research has been carried out on the typical election and campaign experiences of candidates for judgeships in Texas. As an example, there is little systematic information about how competitive or how expensive these races are. Nor is it known how the typical candidate decides to run, or is recruited to run, for office. Certainly these are quiet elections typically featuring modest campaign budgets, low public interest, and low voter turnout. The turnout is low for these races because they are usually listed far down the election ballot and many voters "roll off," or quit voting, before they reach these positions on the ballot.

For the mid-1950s, Henderson and Sinclair (1964:22) have shown that about 90 percent of the elections for district and higher judges were ones in which the Democratic party candidate ran unopposed. That figure attests, as well, to the low political salience of these posts. By the 1982 election, it should be observed, some 83 percent of the judicial candidates were still running for election unopposed. Yet in Dallas and Houston, where the Republican party is particularly strong, 51 percent of these races featured two-party competition (Bush and Coffee, 1982:1512). Thus in recent times the Republican party has begun to field a far more vigorous campaign effort in some parts of the state, but only in some parts. We are reminded, once again, of the difficulties faced by the Republican party in its efforts to expand and provide a viable alternative to the dominant Democratic organization.

Characteristics of Judges

If more research on the election process were available, it might indicate some of the informal requirements for judicial positions. Yet it is possible to learn some of those informal criteria, and a good deal more besides, by examining the information in table 9-5 on the personal backgrounds of Texas judges collected by the Texas Judicial Council.

There are several revealing pieces of information in this table. First, it provides a good summary of the typical state judge. Clearly women and younger individuals are quite rare on the bench, especially above the two lowest-level courts. The overwhelming majority of the district or higher-level judges are middle-aged males who have spent some time in private practice and in either a lower-court judgeship or a prosecuting attorney post. While the data from the Judicial Council do not include information on ethnicity, in Texas black and Hispanic judges are rare.[6]

Positions in the three lowest courts are also predominantly filled with middle-aged white males. At the same time, table 9-5 indicates just how rare are lawyers in the lowest courts. Other data from the Judicial Council indicate that fewer than half of the judges in these three courts even graduated from college.

TABLE 9–5 Personal Characteristics of Texas Judges

Characteristic	Supreme Court	Court of Criminal Appeals	Courts of Appeals	District Courts	Constitutional County Courts	Justices of the Peace	Municipal Courts
Number on the bench	9	9	80	354	254	949	1,073
Average age	58	52	57	52	53	55	52
(Percentage of total reporting age)	(100%)	(100%)	(100%)	(96%)	(85%)	(78%)	(66%)
Sex							
Male	100%	100%	97%	94%	94%	80%	80%
Female	0	0	3	6	6	20	20
Percentage law school graduates	100%	100%	100%	98%	28%	9%	40%
Percentage licensed to practice law	100%	100%	100%	100%	29%	9%	39%
(Percentage of total reporting education data)	(100%)	(100%)	(100%)	(88%)	(58%)	(70%)	(66%)
Percentage reporting previous experience as							
Prosecutor	11%	44%	35%	42%	NA	NA	NA
Private attorney	88	77	87	85	NA	NA	NA
Lower court judge	66	44	38	28	NA	NA	NA
Percentage who came to present judgeship by							
Election	11%	33%	57%	67%	22%	41%	NA
Appointment	89	67	43	33	78	59	NA
(Percentage of total reporting how they entered present position)	(100%)	(100%)	(100%)	(100%)	(100%)	(82%)	NA

Source: Office of Court Administration (1984: 10, 524–672)

Another quite interesting statistic here is the large percentage of judges who first gained their positions by appointment. The percentage varies across the various kinds of courts, but it is of notable magnitude for all of them. Since judges are publically elected, as observed earlier in the chapter, one might be puzzled by these figures. Their explanation lies in the relative frequency with which the governor gets to fill vacancies on the bench. Gubernatorial appointees must, of course, if they desire to remain on the bench, seek reelection at the next regular election date. Yet they are by that time incumbent judges who can profit from public exposure, incumbency status, and—if they are competent—a positive reputation among other lawyers and judges.

No research has been done on judicial retirements and the motivations that lead judges to retire and, hence, create the possibility of so many gubernatorial appointments. Yet one might speculate that at least two factors are at work in the process. Since so many judges are in their middle age or later, many of them may be ready to retire completely after eight or ten years on the bench. On the other hand, some judges may decide that they cannot afford to remain on the bench very many years. When they compare their state salaries to those available in private practice, many may choose to return to the more lucrative alternative after a few years. Certainly a highly competent attorney could work only part-time in private practice and still earn more than many judges. And that alternative might look more and more attractive to aging judges, tired of the heavy work load, inflexible hours, and repetitiveness of their duties on the bench.

CONCLUSION

Early in this chapter we considered the average citizen's image of the court system. Such a citizen probably thinks of judges as professional, nonpolitical experts, believes that judges and juries are crucial figures in the settling of all legal disputes, and thinks of the appellate courts as the most important courts in the system.

While these images of the court system are accurate to some degree, they are also misleading. In light of the actual structure and operation of the Texas court system, several qualifications must be noted with regard to those images. The "professional expertise" of many Texas judges is only that which they have gained by experience in the office—because many of the lower-level judges are not trained as lawyers. Furthermore, almost all the state's judges are inevitably caught up in politics and partisan influences since they must stand for election on partisan ballots. Nor does the election system, as was explained earlier, contribute much to the voter's ability to evaluate candidates for judgeships on their professional merit and ability.

While the preceding remarks about Texas judges are important, the present chapter has also indicated why judges are not as central to the outcome of most legal disputes as many citizens think. The burgeoning caseload, the pressure on criminal defendants to plea bargain, the pressure in civil cases for out-of-court settlements, and the powerful role of the prosecuting attorneys all indicate why the part played by either the judge or the jury is often quite limited—or even virtually nonexistent.

Finally, this chapter has suggested why one should not place too much emphasis on the role of the appellate courts either. The vast majority of cases begin and end in the very same place: in the court of original jurisdiction. The nature of the typical legal outcome—with mostly guilty pleas in criminal cases and out-of-court settlements in civil cases—also helps explain why these cases *cannot* be appealed. The right of appeal is effectively given up when one settles a legal dispute in either of those fashions. These findings indicate why all the components of the courts of original jurisdiction—the professionalism of their judges, the fairness and concern for justice of their prosecuting attorneys, and the time spent in settling individual cases—are critically important to the quality of justice in Texas.

NOTES

1. None of the state's justice of the peace courts is a court of record. Only 10 of 828 cities—Austin, El Paso, Houston, Longview, Lubbock, Marshall, Midland, San Antonio, Sweetwater, and Wichita Falls—maintain their municipal courts as courts of record. This circumstance becomes important when someone appeals a decision of one of these courts to a higher level. When the appeal is of a decision of a non-court-of-record body, the case must be completely retried, or tried *de novo*, in the higher court. This fact, and the added expenses associated with such rehearings, means that in most appeals from such courts the case is dismissed by the original judge so that his or her jurisdiction can avoid these expenses.

2. There is a certain overlap in the jurisdictions of the county and district courts: in civil suits with financial matters in controversy where the dollar amount at issue is between $500 and $1,000. The district courts have jurisdiction when the dollar amount at issue is $1,000 or higher.

3. Public understanding of the complete American court system is surely complicated, as well, by the existence of both the state and local system described in this chapter *and* the federal court system, which is not covered here.

4. These salary supplements are limited by state law so that the maximum possible annual salary for judges at one court level is always at least $1,000 less than those of judges at the next level.

5. There is no single official source that lists the salaries of all lower-court judges in Texas. Toombs (1983), however, has shown that the salaries of justices of the peace, many of whom are only part-time officials, are rather low, especially outside major metropolitan areas. In 1979, according to Toombs's data, almost half of all justices of the peace earned annual salaries of less than $7,000. Only 15 percent of them earned as much as $16,000 or more.

6. This portrait of the typical contemporary judge is virtually identical to that drawn by Henderson and Sinclair (1964) for the typical Texas judge of the mid-1950s.

REFERENCES

Bennack, Frank A. 1983. "The Public, the Media, and the Judicial System." *State Court Journal* 7 (Fall): 4–13.

Blumberg, Abraham S. 1967. *Criminal Justice.* Chicago: Quadrangle Books.

Bush, Bob, and Coffee, Gordon. 1982. "The Partisan System and the Search for Alternatives." *Texas Bar Journal* 45 (December): 1511–1513.

Carp, Robert A. 1974. "The Harris County Grand Jury—A Case Study." *Houston Law Review* 12 (October): 90–120.

Dubois, Philip L. 1980. *From Ballot to Bench: Judicial Elections and the Quest for Accountability.* Austin: University of Texas Press.

Eisenstein, James, and Jacob, Herbert. 1977. *Felony Justice: An Organizational Analysis of Criminal Courts.* Boston: Little, Brown.

Farthing-Capowich, Daina. 1984. "The State of the Judiciary." In *The Book of the States, 1984–85.* Lexington, Ky.: Council of State Governments.

Frankel, Marvin E., and Naftalis, Gary P. 1975. *The Grand Jury: An Institution on Trial.* New York: Hill & Wang.

Glick, Henry Robert, and Vines, Kenneth N. 1973. *State Court Systems.* Englewood Cliffs, N.J.: Prentice-Hall.

Henderson, Bancroft C., and Sinclair, T.C. 1964. *Judicial Selection in Texas: An Exploratory Study.* Houston: University of Houston Public Affairs Research Center.

Kennedy, Tom. 1985. "Individual Docket May Aid Case Load." *Houston Post*, March 18, p. B1.

Lim, Marcia J. 1986. "State of the Judiciary," pp. 146–174 in *The Book of the States, 1986–87.* Lexington, Ky.: Council of State Governments.

Lloyd, Everett. 1967. *Law West of the Pecos: The Story of Roy Bean.* San Antonio: Naylor Company.

May, Janice C., and Goldman, Nathan C. 1983a. "Judicial Selection: An Analysis." *Texas Bar Journal* 46 (March): 316–321.

May, Janice C., and Goldman, Nathan C. 1983b. "Judicial Compensation." *Texas Bar Journal* 46 (April): 450–457.

Office of Court Administration. 1984. *Texas Judicial System Annual Report, 1983.* Austin: Texas Judicial Council.

Office of Court Administration. 1986. *Texas Judicial System Annual Report, 1986.* Austin: Texas Judicial Council.

Texas Bar Journal. 1983. "State Bar Activities: Referendum Results Announced." 46 (April):463.

Toombs, Dennis L. 1983. "The Part-Time Lay Justice of the Peace in Texas." *Public Affairs Comment* 29 (May): 1–7.

White, David J. 1984. "The Tenth Annual Salary Survey." *Student Lawyer* 13 (November): 32–43.

10

GOVERNMENT AND POLICY IN TEXAS CITIES

I n this chapter we will concentrate on the characteristics, structures, and budgets of city governments in the state. Our principal concern will be how municipal and state governments differ and how those differences influence urban policies. The chapter will also analyze the diverse forms of government in Texas cities and comment on the impact of these different governmental systems upon policy outcomes. Finally, we will consider the priorities of Texas cities with respect to their revenues, taxes, expenditures, and debt.

CITY AND STATE GOVERNMENT COMPARED

Citizens probably think that city government in Texas is just a smaller version of state government. Certainly there are similarities in terms of function. Both city and state governments tax, write budgets, spend money, and pass laws. There are, however, some fundamental differences. Because of these differences, the job of governing Texas cities is more difficult and complex than that of governing the state. Local government officials find it more difficult to solve problems and respond to citizen demands (Yates, 1976).

One of the distinctive characteristics of Texas cities is that public services are delivered daily and frequently involve an encounter with a public employee. Garbage collectors pick up the trash, police officers respond to calls for service, and teachers interact with students. The citizens can *see* the service they are getting or not getting. They have a continuous opportunity to evaluate the quality of the service being delivered—and, therefore, the performance of local government. Thus citizens are likely to have opinions about public services. This is less likely to be the case at the state level. Although citizens may see a state highway patrol officer now and then, the services delivered by state government are generally much less conspicuous.

Another characteristic of local government in Texas is the essential nature of the services provided. Society simply cannot do without the police, fire, and education services. They are vital to the public safety, well-being, and hopes for the future. Issues of war and peace and the state of the economy may dominate the national political debate. At the local level, however, the crucial issue on a day-to-day basis is the quality of the public services provided. Many citizens are deeply concerned about these services. Therefore, they are more inclined to make demands upon government in an effort to influence their delivery. Public services provided by the state are simply not as prominent and urgent.

Another distinctive characteristic of local government is the citizen's proximity to public officials. Government that is close to the people may not necessarily be the best government, but it is certainly the most accessible. If citizens have a complaint about local government, they can express their discontent directly to the appropriate officials. They may visit a council meeting or a government office, telephone a bureaucrat, engage in a conference with a teacher, or organize a march on city hall. It is much easier, therefore, to communicate with public officials at the local level than at the state level. Unless he or she lives in Austin, a citizen who has a gripe about state government has to travel a considerable distance just to present a case. State government is far removed and even alien territory. The typical citizen feels far more familiar with local government. Consequently, citizens are more inclined to try to influence local government activities.

Local government is also distinguished by the element of bureaucratic discretion. For many local services, the bureaucrat *is* the service. The teacher in the classroom, the police officer on the street, and the building inspector investigating code violations are the heart of the public service being delivered. One problem for supervisors is how to keep an eye on these "street level" bureaucrats (Lipsky, 1980). Much of the time, no doubt, these public employees are doing an adequate and even superior job. But how does one know that? What is the teacher teaching and how well is he or she doing it? Which laws does the police officer enforce and which ones are ignored? What if the department head wants these employees to change their approach? How can he ensure that they respond? In recent years, some large cities in Texas (Houston in particular) have experienced problems with their police departments. Citizen complaints include charges of police brutality. But when a service such as police protection is delivered on the street by an employee far removed from control or even observation by supervisors, it is one thing for public officials to recognize a problem. It is another to resolve it. Because of the discretion of street-level bureaucrats, the job of local government officials is more difficult. When they try to change the behavior of public employees in response to citizen demands, they may find that the solution is as difficult as the problem.

Another distinctive characteristic of local government is that citizens may express different demands for the same service. Some citizens may want the police to do one thing (more neighborhood patrols, for example) while others want them to do another (place more emphasis on the traffic problem). Different groups also have different expectations for the public schools. Although they all want "quality education," they may well disagree on how to define it and how to achieve it. Because of these conflicting expectations and contradictory demands, the public official finds it is impossible to satisfy all citizens.

Still another characteristic that distinguishes local government from state government is the extent to which cities are influenced and limited by other levels of government. The national government, for example, has intervened and forced changes in the electoral structure of Texas cities (from an at-large scheme to a district arrangement). On the other hand, the city often does not have authority or jurisdiction in certain matters because they are the responsibility of the county or state. The state limits the power of the city in numerous ways—ranging from the types and levels of taxes that can be imposed to the training and control of public employees. Because of these limitations, local public officials find it difficult if not impossible to deal with many problems.

Because of these distinctive characteristics, policy making at the local level is far more complex than at the state level. Since the public services delivered at the local level are essential, citizens are more likely to make demands upon government. Moreover, the immediacy of local government encourages citizen involvement. Public officials find it difficult to respond to these demands, however. Not only are the public's expectations often in conflict, but the behavior of street-level bureaucrats is hard to control and, in many cases, the city lacks jurisdiction over major policy areas. Thus many problems remain unsolved.

State government is different. Because of the services it delivers, it is insulated from widespread citizen involvement. The average citizen is much less likely to care what the state government is up to. Its services may appear less crucial and prominent. And when state officials are required to deal with problems, they are in a better position to do so by virtue of their greater power and authority.

FORMS OF CITY GOVERNMENT

There are three basic forms of municipal government in Texas: the *mayor–council system*, the *manager–council form*, and the *commission*. Each of these government structures derives from one of two basic traditions in municipal government: *reformed* and *unreformed*. In order to understand city government in Texas today, it is necessary to review the development and impact of these traditions.

When the U.S. Constitution was written, the country was a rural, agrarian society. The largest city had fewer than fifty thousand residents. The nation's constitutional arrangements reflect that rural bias. For example, there are only three parties to the federal partnership as expressed in the U.S. Constitution: the national government, the state government, and the people. No mention is made of cities. City governments, therefore, are creations of their respective state governments.

Municipal government was of little concern until the onset of industrialization. An industrial economy required a vast and cheap supply of labor. The migration of the Irish and eastern and southern Europeans supplied much of that labor. These ethnic groups concentrated in cities. They found themselves in an alien environment where everything was different: language, religion, government, customs, and traditions. Any agency that provided them with assistance in getting a job, finding a place to live, and educating their children would have a strong claim on their loyalties. Today there are hundreds of government bureaucracies at all levels whose function is to provide help with employment, disability, health, social security, education, welfare, work conditions, and discrimination. A century ago, however, they did not exist. Not only was the role of government extremely limited, but newly arrived ethnics would have been among the last to effectively press their claims upon government.

Urban Political Machine   Thus a completely new form of local government developed in response to the needs of working-class ethnic Americans: the urban political machine. The machine had the following characteristics:

1. Official power was in the hands of a popularly elected mayor.
2. Power was also shared with machine bosses who operated behind the scenes and might not hold elected office.
3. The machine was highly responsive to its constituent groups. In return for voter loyalty, it provided the ethnic communities with material rewards in the form of jobs with municipal government, assistance with police authorities, help in finding a place to live, and stipends to the families of disabled and deceased workers.
4. The machine was a very personal form of government that emphasized a web of mutual obligations between voters and public officials. Its critics, however, charged that the price of personal government was favoritism, gross inefficiency, and corruption.

Unreformed Governments   Although the political machine in its pure form has vanished from the urban landscape, one can still see its remains in some Texas cities. These cities have what is known as *unreformed government.* A completely unreformed city government would have the following characteristics:

1. Executive authority is in the hands of a strong mayor who is elected by popular vote. He appoints and removes bureaucrats, has budgetary powers, and can veto acts of the city council.
2. The city council is selected by wards. The city is divided into geographically defined districts or wards and a council member is selected from each district. Therefore, different ethnic, racial, and income groups are guaranteed at least some representation on the council.
3. Political parties are active and contest every election. This partisanship is reflected on the ballot where candidates are identified according to party affiliation.

4. Patronage is an important resource of the party in power. Key jobs in city government are parceled out to reward party workers and supporters. Getting a job in municipal government depends more on one's political connections than on training and qualifications.

The political machine was an extreme form of an unreformed city government. It eventually generated intense opposition, however, from native-born Americans. These white Anglo-Saxon Protestants saw the corruption and ethnic domination of the machine as some of the worst features of the new industrial age. The explosive growth of the city with its worker slums and corrupt political bosses was a far cry from the town meeting version of local government where neighbors got together to solve political problems. Although this recollection of how things worked in an agrarian republic was idealized, it served as a point of reference for what historians have labeled the reform movement. The reformers were opposed to many things. Certainly they were against corruption and inefficiency in local government. But there is also evidence that they sought to wrest political control from the ethnic groups (Hays, 1964).

In order to accomplish their goals, the reformers seized upon the following notion as their rallying cry: "There is no Republican or Democratic way to pave a street." This sentence provides a clear and concise statement of the reformers' intent. They wished to remove politics and conflict from city government. To them, the primary task of municipal government was housekeeping: Pick up the trash, police the streets, put out fires, maintain the roads, educate children, provide sanitation, collect taxes, enforce laws. What was political about sweeping the streets and building a sidewalk? To the reformers the answer was self-evident. Since they saw nothing inherently political about those tasks, they asked why we should have politicians (and corrupt ones at that) do what a trained housekeeper could do much more efficiently and effectively.

Reformed Governments   The reformers sought to run the city as a business corporation. That is, they sought to remove political conflict from the city and operate it according to modern principles of business management. Their emphasis was on efficiency, effectiveness, and the "public interest" rather than favoritism, responsiveness, and strictly local interests. This urban reform movement was, then, part of the broad drive toward neutral professional competence in the executive branch of government described earlier in this book. The reform movement was, as well, highly successful. Today many Texas cities are considered "reformed" cities. They have the following characteristics:

1. Executive and administrative authority is in the hands of a professional city manager. This manager, who is appointed by the council and serves at its pleasure, appoints the department heads and other city administrators. The manager, who is frequently trained in a graduate school of public administration, administers the city according to "professional" rather than political values.

2. Policy making is vested in a city council. If the city manager is the chief executive and operating officer of the corporation, then the council members are the directors. They select the manager, set general policy, and leave it to the manager to execute that policy. The council does not interfere in the day-to-day administration of the city. If it becomes displeased with the manager's performance, its recourse is to find another manager. In turn, the manager does not (at least in principle) participate in the setting of policy.

3. Elections are nonpartisan. In an effort to remove political conflict from the operation of city government, political parties are not recognized. Although political factions may support slates of candidates (as the Good Government League used to do in San Antonio), parties as such are not organized and active. Candidates are not identified on the ballot by party.

4. An at-large electoral arrangement prevails. Instead of electing members of the council from wards as in unreformed cities, candidates are voted upon by the entire electorate. They run at-large and have no allegiance to a particular community or geographically defined district. The intent is to ensure that the council members represent the entire city or "public interest" rather than a narrow community within the city.

5. City employees are hired on the basis of merit rather than patronage. Performance on written examinations in conjunction with experience, background, training, and education determine successful applicants.

Among this state's major cities, only Houston and El Paso do not operate under the manager–council system, and even these cities cannot be considered completely unreformed. Houston, for example, has a mixed at-large and ward arrangement for selecting council members, whereby some are elected at-large and others represent geographic districts. In fact, all council members were selected at-large until the city was required to change its system by the federal government. Another characteristic of a reformed government in Houston is civil service protection for municipal employees and the hiring of many employees on the basis of merit rather than patronage. The mayor–council form of government is by no means nearing extinction in Texas, however. More than 700 Texas cities still operate under this plan (although these tend to be the smaller cities).

It should be pointed out that the mayor–council form of government is two different types, strong and weak. Under the strong mayor–council plan, the mayor is the chief executive with the power to appoint and remove department heads, prepare the budget, and veto council decisions. In the weak mayor–council system, the mayor's powers are much more limited. For example, he or she cannot appoint and remove administrators. No major city in the state uses the weak mayor–council plan.

The Commission Another form of city government in Texas is the commission. The commission was first used in Galveston after a hurricane killed more than 7,000 people in 1900. In response to the economic and social devastation that resulted, the city adopted the commission, which provides for the election of several commissioners. This form of city government is unique in that the commissioners combine legislative, executive, and administrative responsibilities. The commissioners jointly serve as the city council while individually they are heads of major departments such as public works and public safety. This form of government rapidly spread throughout Texas and the nation after its adoption in Galveston. Today, however, the strong mayor and city manager forms are much more prevalent in both Texas and the rest of the country.

In addition to classifying cities according to their form of government, they can also be categorized by whether they are general-law or home-rule cities. General-law cities operate under a uniform set of laws and restrictions established by the state government. Their tax rate limits, for example, are specified by the state. Cities of over 5,000 population may adopt their own charters subject to voter approval. Although these so-called home-rule cities cannot pursue courses of action that would violate the state constitution or laws, they have considerably more flexibility than general-law cities with respect to the conduct of their affairs.

Of the more than 700 Texas cities in 1979 that had mayor–council governments, only 14 were home-rule cities. Cities under 5,000 population are much more likely to use the mayor–council plan than larger municipalities. Of the 372 cities that had the manager–council plan in 1979, 201 were home-rule cities. These larger cities express a distinct preference for reformed government institutions while smaller cities (general-law cities) are much more likely to adopt a mayor–council system.

DOES THE FORM REALLY MATTER?

What difference does it make whether a city has a mayor–council or a manager–council form of government? Too often scholars discuss only the structure of government and ignore the impact. Does it make any difference to the citizen whether a mayor or appointed manager is in charge? The evidence from national studies suggests that the form of government does make a difference. Unreformed governments (mayor–council) tend to spend more and tax more than reformed ones. There is also evidence that blacks and other minorities are better represented on city councils in unreformed cities because of the ward rather than at-large electoral arrangement. Unreformed cities are also thought to be somewhat more responsive and accessible to the variety of groups and interests that make up the city. Because political parties are active and organized, the demands of different groups are more likely to be articulated. Because the chief executive is elected rather than appointed, and because the members of the council are accountable to individual wards, municipal government is alleged to be more responsive to group needs and demands (Lineberry and Fowler, 1967).

Do these findings apply to Texas cities? It is not possible to say with much certainty. For one thing, most of the larger cities have the manager–council form while most of the small ones are mayor–council. Because, in other words, most cities of comparable size have the same form of government, it is not possible to make many comparisons on the basis of different forms.

One can, however, speculate about certain impacts. For example, mayor–council cities do not appear to spend and tax more than manager–council cities in Texas. In fact, if we look at the largest cities we find that only one (Houston) out of the four top spenders on a per capita basis has the mayor–council form. Similarly, the mayor–council cities (Houston and El Paso) generally have lower property tax rates than the manager–council cities.

The ward versus at-large election system does seem to make a difference. When San Antonio and Houston switched from at-large to district council systems, the level of minority representation on the city councils increased. But does greater minority representation make a difference in terms of the public policies that are produced? That is a much more difficult question to answer. One would certainly think that more minority representation on city councils would ensure additional programs designed to respond to minority needs. However, there is, as yet, insufficient evidence to reach that conclusion.

One major difference that is frequently alleged to exist between mayor–council and manager–council cities revolves around the issue of efficiency. Because unreformed cities are run by popularly elected mayors whereas reformed cities are governed by professional city managers, it is generally thought that reformed cities are more efficiently managed. It is often pointed out, for example, that Dallas has a more efficient municipal government than Houston. It should be emphasized, however, that it is much easier to *claim* that one government is more efficient than another than it is to demonstrate it. If we wanted to prove that the municipal government in Dallas is more efficient than the one in Houston, how would we go about the task? Frequently, alleged differences in efficiency are based more on personal impressions than on any systematic evidence. Moreover, even if it can be shown that one city government in Texas is more efficient than another, it does not necessarily mean that the *form* of government is the cause of that difference.

In any event, much of the political conflict in Texas cities continues to be a fight between the reformers and those who would be willing to sacrifice some degree of efficiency in government for a more open and responsive government. One historian has argued that the reform movement was dominated by powerful business interests. The goal of those interests was to wrest control from neighborhoods and place it in the hands of "professionals" who would govern the city in the "public interest." To them, however, the public interest was business interests (Hays, 1964). Much of the political battle in Texas cities today is still a confrontation between citizens' groups on the one hand and, on the other, those who believe that the real business of city government is business.

It should be pointed out that the absence of political parties in the city does not mean that there are no active political organizations. In fact, political alliances often develop to support slates of candidates for mayor and city council seats. One prominent example is the Good Government League in San Antonio. From its formation in 1954 until 1973, the GGL won 78 of 81 city council elections. Although not a political party in a strictly legal sense, the GGL performed many of the functions of a party. It ran slates of candidates, raised and spent large sums of money to elect them, maintained a permanent organization, and had a stable leadership. One observer has called it an "upper-class political machine" that sought to gain and hold power for white, upper-class groups in San Antonio. Liberal and conservative coalitions have also appeared from time to time in Houston to support candidates for public office.

City Budgets and Expenditures

One useful way to compare cities and their policies is by reference to their priorities as indicated by expenditure levels. To determine how Texas cities spend their money, we can examine data on expenditure patterns for fifteen of the largest cities in the state. These general-fund operating expenditures are shown in table 10-1. The general fund is the budget that is used by cities to pay the day-to-day operating expenses for police and fire, garbage collection, and parks and recreation. Table 10-1 reveals that in every city police protection is the largest single item of expenditure. Houston, Dallas, and Waco spend at least 25 percent of their operating budget for police while Arlington, Amarillo, Irving, and Abilene spend less than 20 percent. The average in the cities is 22 percent.

Fire protection takes the next largest share of the budget. This service accounts for 20.5 percent of the budget in Lubbock and 12.5 percent in San Antonio. Police and fire protection together account for over 40 percent of the entire operating budget in Houston, Dallas, Lubbock, Beaumont, and Waco.

TABLE 10–1   Percentage of Budget Accounted for by Different Functions for the Largest Texas Cities: 1983

City	Police (%)	Fire (%)	Parks and Rec. (%)	Library (%)	Streets (%)	Sanitation (%)
Houston	26.5	19.0	4.8	2.6	3.4	5.9
Dallas	25.0	16.1	8.3	3.4	6.2	7.4
San Antonio	22.7	12.5	8.5	3.0	6.7	7.4
El Paso	24.3	15.1	7.1	2.3	4.0	8.6
Fort Worth	22.7	16.9	6.2	2.7	—	—
Austin	21.5	13.6	8.7	4.0	—	—
Corpus Christi	22.1	12.7	8.6	2.3	10.3	—
Lubbock	23.4	20.5	10.6	1.9	6.0	—
Arlington	19.7	15.2	7.3	2.9	—	—
Amarillo	19.3	13.7	8.0	3.6	11.4	9.1
Garland	22.2	15.4	8.2	3.8	7.3	8.8
Beaumont	24.1	20.0	5.7	3.2	11.4	—
Irving	14.0	13.0	8.0	4.0	—	5.0
Waco	25.7	20.4	—	3.6	10.2	11.5
Abilene	18.8	14.1	7.5	3.0	7.9	7.3

Source: Data obtained by authors from city budgets.

Waco spent 46.1 percent of its general fund for police and fire services while Houston spent 45.5 percent.

Only five services account for a lion's share of municipal budgets in Texas's largest cities. Police, fire, parks and recreation, streets, and sanitation consume 68 percent of the operating budget in Waco, 62 percent in Dallas, Garland, and Amarillo, 60 percent in Houston, 59 percent in El Paso, 58 percent in San Antonio, and 56 percent in Abilene. Spending priorities are similar in each city. As noted, police and fire protection are the major service priorities. One city spends as much as 11 percent on parks and recreation (Lubbock) and only one city spends less than 5 percent (Houston). Only two cities spend as much as 4 percent on libraries (Austin and Irving) and only Lubbock spends less than 2 percent.

Another way to look at the city budgets is to determine how much spending they reflect on a per resident basis. Table 10-2 presents the figures for the fifteen cities examined above. In total dollar amounts, Houston spends more than any other city. On a per capita basis, however, Dallas spends the most ($407 for each citizen) followed by Austin ($376). Houston spends $352 per person, Fort Worth spends $351, and Beaumont spends $318. Several cities spend much less. Waco spends only $199 per person while the corresponding figures in Garland, El Paso and Lubbock are $205, $218, and $219. Note that Dallas spends over twice as much per citizen as Waco and almost twice as much as Garland, El Paso, and Lubbock.

When we look at the per capita figures for individual services, we also find considerable variation among these cities. Dallas spends $102 per person for police, for example, Houston spends $93, and Austin spends $81. Yet Irving spends only $41, Amarillo only $47, and Garland only $45. The same pattern holds for fire expenditures. Houston and Dallas spend $67 and $66 respectively for fire protection while El Paso spends only $33 and Garland spends only $32.

Analyzing these per citizen expenditures for government services gives us an indication of how priorities differ among cities. Dallas and Austin not only spend more per person than any other city, but how they spend it is also interesting. For example, these two cities spend twice as much on parks and recreation as Houston ($17 per capita in Houston as opposed to $34 in Dallas and $33 in Austin). Similarly, Dallas and Austin also spend more than any other cities for libraries ($14 and $15 respectively), while El Paso and Lubbock spend the least ($5 and $3).

Another way to look at the public services purchased with budget expenditures is to compare personnel levels from city to city. The number of police officers and firefighters per 10,000 population, it could be argued, is a better measure of the level of police and fire protection provided the citizens than is the amount of money spent in these areas. Although Houston ($93 per capita) and Dallas ($102 per capita) spend much more on police than Irving ($41 per capita), it may be that the difference in the number of police officers on a per capita basis is not that great.

To help us compare employee levels across municipalities, table 10-3 presents information for police and fire employees in ten cities. The table reveals that personnel levels correspond fairly well to expenditure levels. The police

TABLE 10-2 Operating Expenditures Per Capita for the Largest Texas Cities: 1983

City	Total Per Capita Expenditure ($)	Per Capita Police ($)	Per Capita Fire ($)	Per Capita Parks ($)	Per Capita Library ($)	Per Capita Streets ($)	Per Capita Sanitation ($)
Houston	352	93	67	17	9	12	21
Dallas	407	102	66	34	14	25	27
San Antonio	290	66	36	25	9	19	22
El Paso	218	53	33	16	5	9	19
Fort Worth	351	79	59	22	9	—	—
Austin	376	81	51	33	15	—	—
Corpus Christi	265	59	34	23	6	27	—
Lubbock	219	51	45	23	4	13	—
Arlington	281	55	43	21	8	—	—
Amarillo	246	47	34	20	9	28	22
Garland	205	45	32	17	8	15	18
Beaumont	318	76	64	18	10	36	—
Irving	290	41	38	—	10	—	16
Waco	199	51	41	—	7	20	23
Abilene	286	54	40	21	8	23	21

TABLE 10-3   Number of Police and Fire Employees Per 10,000
Population in Ten Cities: 1983

City	Number of Uniformed Police Employees	Number of Uniformed Fire Employees
Houston	17.1	15.3
Dallas	20.8	15.9
San Antonio	13.3	12.3
Fort Worth	17.6	16.6
Amarillo	10.6	13.0
Beaumont	14.6	19.7
Garland	9.6	11.5
Irving	11.0	13.0
Lubbock	13.6	14.6
Abilene	13.5	13.2

Source: Data obtained by authors from city departments.

employees column indicates that Dallas has 20.8 police officers per 10,000 population, Houston has 17.1, and Fort Worth has 17.6. On the other hand, Garland has only 9.6, Amarillo 10.6, and Irving 11.0. The cities that spend the most for police also have the highest employee levels. It should be recalled that Dallas spends $102 per capita and Houston spends $93. The corresponding figures in Irving, Garland, and Amarillo are only $41, $45, and $47. A similar pattern is found for fire protection. Houston, Dallas, Fort Worth, and Beaumont have the highest per capita expenditures and the highest employee levels as well.

Budget and employee levels may not, however, tell us everything we wish to know about city policies. Frequently the average citizen's information about the operation of city government is limited to the budget—which is, of course, the major document of local government and the central focus of elected officials and the media. Certainly the budget can tell us how much government spends and what it spends it for. It tells nothing, however, about how effectively the money is spent. Similarly, the number of employees in a particular service tells us nothing about how well they are doing their job.

A city may spend a great deal of money on police protection, for example, and have a high number of police officers per capita. The city may even have increased its police budget for the past several years and yet crime rates might remain high and even be on the rise. Police officials respond that even more money is needed in order to fight rising crime. More money and more police raise citizens' expectations that something will be done about crime.

The problem for citizen and public official is one, in large part, of perception and expectation. If people see that a great deal of money is being spent to solve a problem, they expect the situation to get better. If their expectations are based on an analysis of city budgets, however, they could be wrong. Just because a city spends a great deal of money on its police and has a large number of police officers per capita does not mean that they will necessarily be used in the most efficient and effective manner. Moreover, there is evidence that the number of police may not have much of an impact on crime rates (Kelling, 1974). Some cities may have fewer police officers per capita and spend less money for police protection than others but have a lower crime rate. We cannot assume, then, that more money and more public employees guarantee superior service.

Despite these reservations, city budgets are important documents. They tell how much local governments spend and what they spend for. For example, our analysis has indicated that Texas cities emphasize police and fire protection and spend very little on health and social welfare. Some cities spend much more than others and have higher employee levels. At the same time, large numbers of dollars spent and employees hired are no guarantee of superior or even satisfactory service. Budgets cannot tell us how efficiently public employees do their jobs or how effective the service is in solving the problems it was intended to address. Furthermore, budgets do not tell us who gets the service purchased with government dollars. Do some neighborhoods get better police, fire, and library services than others? This issue will be considered in a later chapter.

Sources of Revenue

Another way to consider city government policies is to examine the sources of their income and see which citizens bear heavier and lighter burdens in providing that income. Surprisingly, considering their traditional importance for local government, property taxes accounted for only one out of every four revenue dollars in the ten largest cities in Texas in 1981. Although the property tax is the single largest source of revenue for the operating budget, it by no means provides a majority of revenues. In fact, the property tax is closely followed by charges and fees as a major revenue category. This source, which accounts for almost one out of every five revenue dollars, includes the money citizens pay for municipal services such as electricity, water, sewer, and garbage collection. Another major revenue source that accounts for nearly one out of every five dollars is federal aid. The federal aid category is followed by miscellaneous taxes (14.5 percent of operating revenues) and sales taxes (13.9 percent). Significantly, aid from state government is a very minor source of revenue. It acccounted for only 1.8 percent in 1981.

Important changes have occurred over the past several years with respect to revenue in the state's largest cities. Table 10-4 reveals that the property tax has declined significantly in terms of importance. In 1975, this tax generated 35 percent of operating revenues. By 1981, the property tax accounted for only 26 percent. Similarly, federal aid has also dropped in importance. In 1979, its budgetary share was 21.4 percent; by 1981, it had declined to only 17.9 percent.

Some taxes have accounted for a constant share of revenues during the period. State aid, for example, has grown only slightly. It contributed 1.5 percent in 1975 and 1.8 percent in 1981. Similarly, the sales tax accounted for 13.2 percent in 1975 and 13.9 percent in 1981. The decline in the importance of the property tax has been made up for by three revenue sources. The charges and fees category grew from 15.1 percent in 1975 to 18.8 percent in 1981, while

TABLE 10-4 Sources of Revenue for the Ten Largest Texas Cities

Source of Revenue	1975	1979	1981
Property taxes	35.0%	28.0%	26.2%
Federal aid	16.9%	21.4%	17.9%
Charges and fees	15.1%	18.2%	18.8%
Sales taxes	13.2%	14.5%	13.9%
Miscellaneous taxes	12.8%	11.0%	14.5%
Selective sales taxes	4.2%	3.7%	5.8%
State aid	1.5%	1.8%	1.8%
Other taxes	1.3%	1.4%	1.1%

Source: U.S. Department of Commerce, Bureau of the Census.

the miscellaneous and selective sales tax categories increased from 12.8 percent and 4.2 percent to 14.5 percent and 5.8 percent respectively.

Another important piece of information in table 10-4 is the extent to which the largest cities in Texas rely upon regressive taxes such as property and sales tax. *Regressive* taxes take larger shares of the incomes of poorer persons; *progressive* taxes (such as the income tax) take larger shares of the incomes of wealthier people. For example, a citizen with an income of $10,000 who pays $600 per year in property and sales taxes has 6 percent of his or her income taken by these taxes. On the other hand, the person with an income of $100,000 who pays $3,000 a year in taxes pays only 3 percent of his or her income to government. Table 10-4 reveals that most of the operating revenues are generated by regressive taxes. Even the charges and fees category is regressive because it consumes a larger share of the income of poorer persons.

Because there are no income taxes in Texas cities, low-income citizens carry a greater financial burden for government than richer citizens, a circumstance to be explored in detail in chapter 14. In fact, the only progressive revenue source at the local level, federal aid, is declining in importance. Federal aid accounted for a smaller share of the operating budget in 1981 than in 1979, again because of the Reagan administration's budget cuts. Therefore, it is likely that the difference in city revenues will be made up by increasing the burden on regressive taxes.

Some cities also rely more heavily upon certain revenue sources than others. Houston obtained 30 percent of its operating revenue from the property tax, for example, and Dallas received 32 percent. However, Austin obtained only 20 percent. Austin, on the other hand, used the charges and fees category for 35 percent of its income. El Paso and San Antonio obtained the largest percentage of their revenue (more than 30 percent) from federal aid.

TEXAS PROPERTY TAXES COMPARED

Ever since California's "Proposition 13" tax movement in the mid-1970s, property taxes have been highly controversial subjects. Although Texans frequently complain about their property taxes, two points should be noted. First, property taxes in Texas cities are generally lower than in many other cities in the country. Second, these taxes could be much higher than they actually are. According to the state constitution and state law, cities under 5,000 population can levy up to $1.50 per $100 assessed valuation. Cities over 5,000 can levy a property tax of up to $2.50 per $100 assessed valuation. Significantly, no large city in the state comes anywhere near this maximum tax rate.

Table 10-5 reveals that of the twenty largest cities in the state, Fort Worth levies the highest property tax. Even in that city, however, the rate is only $0.85 per $100 of assessed valuation. The lowest rate is found in Laredo ($0.37), while the average of the twenty cities is $0.59. This rate is much lower than the $2.50 legal limit. Even so, several cities tax at a level that is considerably lower than this $0.59 average. The rate in Austin is only $0.56, in Dallas it is $0.51, and in Houston it is $0.495.

Even though all twenty cities tax at a relatively low level, the property tax bite is much higher in some than in others. The rate in Fort Worth is 75 percent higher than in Houston, for example, while San Antonio's rate is 50 percent higher than Houston's and almost 100 percent higher than cities such as Garland and Irving. It is ironic, however, that several of the cities that impose the

TABLE 10–5   1983 Tax Rates Per $100 Assessed Valuation
in Twenty Largest Texas Cities

City	1983 Population	Valuation Per Capita	Property Tax Rate	Total Assessed Valuation
Fort Worth	396,850	$18,415	$0.850	$ 7,307,907,190
Odessa	100,568	11,716	0.760	1,178,255,095
San Antonio	786,023	8,589	0.758	6,750,840,940
Pasadena	113,000	13,947	0.756	1,576,024,900
Beaumont	122,000	20,852	0.750	2,543,921,008
Wichita Falls	94,201	19,212	0.693	1,809,803,267
Waco	102,773	16,182	0.660	1,663,030,999
Lubbock	178,282	18,085	0.610	3,224,270,010
Arlington	183,334	21,483	0.598	3,938,637,528
Corpus Christi	232,000	19,569	0.568	4,540,000,000
Austin	367,550	25,221	0.562	9,270,074,503
El Paso	460,000	15,557	0.531	7,156,364,262
Amarillo	149,167	15,333	0.520	2,287,112,399
Dallas	916,050	38,253	0.513	35,041,557,370
Houston	1,820,000	33,446	0.495	60,872,295,410
Abilene	102,767	21,986	0.480	2,259,435,000
Plano	84,000	37,423	0.455	3,143,548,133
Irving	112,000	40,447	0.400	4,530,039,730
Garland	147,800	30,447	0.388	4,500,000,000
Laredo	91,449	14,289	0.370	1,306,682,894

Source: "Texas Municipal Taxation and Debt—1983," Texas Municipal League.

heaviest tax burdens have *less* to spend on their citizens for services than cities that tax at lower levels. Houston, Dallas, and Austin all levy rates that are much lower than those found in Fort Worth and San Antonio. It is significant, though, that Houston, Dallas, and Austin all had higher per capita general revenues. In 1981, revenue per person was $532 in Austin, $472 in Houston, and $450 in Dallas. It was only $404 in Fort Worth and $350 in San Antonio.

How can it be that some cities tax at a higher rate but generate less revenue? Part of the answer lies in how wealthy the city is. Fort Worth and San Antonio simply have a lower tax *base*. Table 10-5 reveals that the per capita value of taxable property is $18,415 in Fort Worth and $8,589 in San Antonio. It is much higher in Dallas ($38,253), Houston ($33,446), and Austin ($25,221). Wealthier cities can generate more revenue with a lower tax rate simply because they have a bigger tax base.

THE CAPITAL BUDGET

Generally, attention is focused on the operating budget. The operating budget, as described above, deals with the traditional housekeeping functions of municipal government: police, fire, sanitation, parks and recreation, and libraries. Most operating expenditures are consumed by employee salaries and benefits and by the purchase and maintenance of equipment. However, there is another budget. The *capital budget* is for the construction of facilities such as roads, airports, and water and sewer lines. Because these facilities are very expensive, they cannot be funded from the operating budget. Therefore, the city goes into debt to obtain financing. It does this by selling tax-exempt bonds to investors.

There are two types of debt that Texas cities assume to generate revenue for the construction and improvement of capital facilities. *Revenue debt* is used for facilities such as water and airports paid for by user charges. *General obligation debt* is backed by all taxpayers.

Because of rapid growth, Texas cities have had to assume considerable debt in the past several years in order to provide roads and major utilities. Table 10-6 reveals that total per capita debt in the ten cities increased 23 percent from 1979 to 1981. Their average per capita debt is 32 percent higher than the U.S. average. Austin at $2,717 per capita and San Antonio at $1,479 per capita have the highest level of debt. It should be pointed out, however, that much of the debt of these two cities can be traced to the fact that both own electric power systems.

ECONOMIC PROBLEMS

The economic crisis in the state has also had an impact upon city government. A study by the Texas Municipal League (*Texas Town and City,* 1987) found that 43 percent of all cities anticipated a drop in revenues, while 58 percent have raised user fees for city services and 47 percent have delayed capital improvements. In addition, 45 percent raised property taxes, and 50 percent either froze hiring, froze wages, laid off employees, reduced or eliminated services,

TABLE 10-6 Per Capita Debt in Texas Cities

City	1979	1981
Houston	$ 696	$ 881
Dallas	609	693
San Antonio	1,063	1,479
El Paso	140	140
Fort Worth	497	533
Austin	2,064	2,717
Corpus Christi	387	381
Lubbock	368	333
Arlington	931	1,090
Amarillo	210	304
Ten-city average	696	855
U.S. average	563	648

Source: "Fiscal Notes," State Comptroller's Office, November 1983.

or did more than one of these things. Faced with a $26 million budget deficit San Antonio instituted a hiring freeze and cut some services. In response to a deficit of $13 million, Houston fired some workers and instituted a hiring freeze and service cuts. Although, to a considerable extent, Dallas's diversified economy has protected it from falling oil prices, it has not been immune to the state's economic woes. Declining revenues have caused the city to make cuts in personnel, parks and recreation, libraries, and health and human services.

CONCLUSION

Texas cities emphasize similar priorities in their operating budgets. Most budget expenditures go for such essential public services as police and fire protection, streets, and sanitation. Very little is spent for health and social welfare programs. These spending priorities reflect the essentially conservative nature of city government in the state. Some cities, though, spend much more than others—Dallas, Austin, and Houston spend the most on a per capita basis—and some cities employ many more police officers and firefighters than others.

Texas cities rely heavily upon the property tax, user fees, and service charges to generate revenue. These taxes are regressive because they place a heavier tax burden on poor citizens than on wealthier ones. Federal aid also provides a significant percentage of city revenues, and some cities such as San Antonio rely more upon federal aid dollars than others.

Local governments are limited in terms of the taxes they can levy—and the *rate* at which they can be levied—by the state. Cities in Texas cannot impose an income tax, for example. Moreover, the rate at which the property tax can be assessed is restricted. Different rates are allowed for home-rule cities and general-law cities. Yet no city assesses a property tax rate anywhere near the legal ceiling. In comparison to other states, Texans pay a relatively small proportion of their income in local taxes.

REFERENCES

Hays, Samuel P. 1964. "The Politics of Reform in Municipal Government in the Progressive Era." *Pacific Northwest Quarterly* 55 (October): 157–189.

Kelling, George L. 1974. *The Kansas City Preventive Patrol Experiment*. Washington, D.C.: Police Foundation.

Lineberry, Robert L., and Fowler, Edmund P. 1967. "Reformism and Public Policies in American Cities." *American Political Science Review* 61 (September): 701–716.

Lipsky, Michael. 1980. *Street Level Bureaucracy: Dilemmas of the Individual in Public Services*. New York: Russell Sage.

Yates, Douglas. 1976. "Urban Government as a Policy-Making System." In Louis Masotti and Robert Lineberry (eds.), *The New Urban Politics*. Cambridge, Mass.: Ballinger.

Texas Rangers, 1892

State Capitol, 1896

"Pappy" O'Daniel and the Hillbilly Boys, 1938

TEXAS HISTORY

"Pa" and "Ma" Ferguson, circa 1942

Wockmatooah, Comanche, 1896

THE POLITICS
OF METROPOLIS

To understand Texas cities, it is not enough just to know something about their form of government. We also need to know about the interaction among technology, economics, and urban structure. In that way we will not only be in a better position to understand the historical development of cities in the state, but we will also be able to speculate about their future.

THE CHANGING SHAPE OF THE CITY

The shape and behavior of the city are influenced, in large part, by the economics of the time. The great industrial cities of the Northeast and Midwest—Pittsburgh, Chicago, Cleveland—during the nineteenth and early twentieth centuries looked fundamentally different from the way they look today. That is because the economic conditions of the country were dramatically different. As chapter 1 on the Texas economy discussed in detail, the national economy was industrial then.

The cities of industrial America reflected the requirements of the age. All major elements—and people—had to be located in close proximity to each other. Workers, management, transportation, capital, and raw materials had to be nearby. Both raw materials and finished products were heavy and took up space. Plastics and lightweight alloys were not available, and transportation systems for the movement of materials were limited. Interstate freeways, trucking, and jet travel were nonexistent. Industrial centers were heavily dependent upon water and rail transport.

Because the age of the automobile, freeways, and suburbs had not yet dawned, workers had to live close to the factory. Because of the nature of assembly-line production, management had to be nearby to supervise and control labor. The limited communications system ensured that banking, marketing, and distribution services and facilities would be located in close prox-

226

imity to production and manufacturing centers. In short, the industrial city was much more compact than cities today. The limitations of transportation, communications, and technology demanded a close-knit and geographically concentrated urban area.

The modern city is vastly different. A drive through one of the great cities of Texas reveals very few factory smokestacks. Instead there are mazes of freeways, unending suburbs, and towering glass and chrome skyscrapers. The Texas city reflects the changing economy. Although there is still some manufacturing and production (petrochemicals, for example), Houston, Dallas, Austin, and San Antonio are increasingly centers for economic activity other than industry. These activities are concentrated around the processing of information in education, financial management, banking, high technology, communications, computers, research and development, medical services, insurance, government, and tourism. The modern Texas city is highly decentralized and geographically dispersed rather than concentrated.

Several developments account for these changes in the shape of the city. One major force was the automobile and the extraordinary mobility it provided. The car and the freeway made the suburbs possible. Now people could work in the central city and live in communities located at great distances from the city. Another major force was the changing economy. Texas cities no longer have a central business district. Instead they have several centers of economic activity distinguished by groups of skyscrapers clustered here and there against the skyline. This dispersal of economic activity was made possible by the extraordinary advances in communication and transportation. Now labor can be located in one place (even in a foreign country), management in another, capital in another, raw materials in another, and research and transportation in still another. Leaps in technology make possible the control and coordination of all these dispersed functions.

The changing shape of the city has had a variety of impacts. In this chapter we will explore those effects on political participation, suburbanization, fragmentation, and intergovernmental relations. Our emphasis will be upon entire urban areas rather than just the central city. The various municipalities within the great urban regions of the state are dependent upon one another as well as in sharp competition. The Dallas–Fort Worth metropolitan region, for example, includes not only Dallas and Fort Worth but Richardson, Plano, Irving, Denton, Arlington, Mesquite, and urban counties as well. To understand the changing nature and impact of fragmentation and participation within the city, we must concentrate upon the entire urban area.

METROPOLITAN TEXAS

As chapter 2 indicated, the population growth in the urban areas of the state during the past decade has been phenomenal. The metropolitan population in Texas grew by almost 30 percent from 1970 to 1980, compared to a national rate of 9 percent (Thomas, 1983). Table 11–1 presents the population changes for the twenty-five metropolitan areas in the state. Note the dramatic growth

TABLE 11-1   Population Changes in Texas Metropolitan Areas:
1970–1980

Metropolitan Area	1980 Pop.	1970 Pop.	Change	% Change
Dallas–Fort Worth	2,974,878	2,377,623	+ 597,255	+ 25.2
Houston	2,905,350	1,985,031	+ 920,319	+ 46.4
San Antonio	1,071,954	88,179	+ 183,775	+ 20.7
Austin	536,450	360,463	+ 175,987	+ 48.9
El Paso	479,899	359,291	+ 120,608	+ 33.6
Beaumont–Port Arthur– Orange	375,497	347,568	+ 27,929	+ 8.1
Corpus Christi	326,228	284,832	+ 41,396	+ 14.5
McAllen–Pharr–Edinburg	283,229	181,535	+ 101,694	+ 56.1
Killeen–Temple	214,656	159,794	+ 54,862	+ 34.3
Lubbock	211,651	179,295	+ 32,356	+ 18.0
Brownsville–Harlingen– San Benito	209,680	140,368	+ 69,312	+ 49.5
Galveston	195,940	169,812	+ 26,128	+ 15.4
Amarillo	173,699	144,396	+ 29,303	+ 20.3
Waco	170,755	147,553	+ 23,202	+ 15.7
Longview–Marshall	151,752	120,770	+ 30,982	+ 25.8
Abilene	139,192	122,164	+ 17,028	+ 13.9
Wichita Falls	130,664	128,642	+ 2,022	+ 1.6
Tyler	128,366	97,096	+ 31,270	+ 32.2
Texarkana	127,019	113,488	+ 13,531	+ 12.0
Odessa	115,374	92,660	+ 22,714	+ 24.5
Laredo	99,258	72,859	+ 26,399	+ 36.2
Bryan–College Station	93,588	57,978	+ 35,610	+ 61.5
Sherman–Denison	89,796	83,225	+ 6,571	+ 7.9
San Angelo	84,784	71,047	+ 13,737	+ 19.4
Midland	82,636	65,433	+ 17,203	+ 26.3
TOTALS	11,372,295	8,765,389	+ 2,607,006	+ 29.7

Source: Houston Chamber of Commerce, *1980 Houston Region Census Data*, Part I.

that has taken place. The Dallas–Fort Worth urban area added 597,255 persons, San Antonio grew by 183,775, Austin increased its population by 175,987, and the Houston urban area grew by almost a million. Two areas—Houston and Dallas–Fort Worth—were responsible for a majority of the population growth in the entire state and for 58 percent of the growth in metropolitan areas.

The population changes in the central cities of these metropolitan areas reveal some interesting patterns. Table 11–2 shows that two of the twenty largest cities in the state actually lost population (Fort Worth and Wichita Falls). Others experienced only moderate growth rates. Waco grew by 6.2 percent, Beaumont by 0.5 percent, and Dallas by 7.1 percent. Several others, however, had dramatic population increases. Brownsville grew by 62 percent, Garland by 71 percent, Arlington by 78 percent, and Austin by 36 percent. In fact,

TABLE 11–2   Population Changes in Texas Cities: 1970–1980

City	1980 Pop.	1970 Pop.	Change	% Change
Houston	1,594,086	1,233,535	+ 360,551	+ 29.2
Dallas	904,078	844,401	+ 59,677	+ 7.1
San Antonio	785,410	654,153	+ 131,257	+ 20.1
El Paso	425,259	322,261	+ 102,998	+ 32.0
Fort Worth	385,141	393,455	− 8,314	− 2.1
Austin	345,496	253,539	+ 91,957	+ 36.3
Corpus Christi	231,999	204,525	+ 27,474	+ 13.4
Lubbock	173,979	149,101	+ 24,878	+ 16.7
Arlington	160,123	90,229	+ 69,894	+ 77.5
Amarillo	149,230	127,010	+ 22,220	+ 17.5
Garland	138,857	81,437	+ 57,420	+ 70.5
Beaumont	118,102	117,548	+ 554	+ 0.5
Pasadena	112,560	89,957	+ 22,603	+ 25.1
Irving	109,943	97,260	+ 12,683	+ 13.0
Waco	101,261	95,326	+ 5,935	+ 6.2
Abilene	98,315	89,653	+ 8,662	+ 9.7
Wichita Falls	94,201	96,265	− 2,064	− 2.1
Laredo	91,449	69,024	+ 22,425	+ 32.5
Odessa	90,027	78,380	+ 11,647	+ 14.9
Brownsville	84,997	52,522	+ 32,475	+ 61.8
TOTALS	6,194,513	5,139,581	+ 1,054,932	+ 20.5

Source: U.S. Bureau of the Census, *Advance Reports, Texas.*

Arlington added more people (70,000) between 1970 and 1980 than Dallas (60,000).

Although most central cities experienced population growth, recall from chapter 2 that *suburbanization* is a major population trend. The incorporated Dallas suburbs of Arlington and Garland grew at a much faster rate than Dallas itself—indeed, Arlington gained 10,000 more citizens than Dallas. Because of this suburban growth, rural counties are rapidly becoming urban. Collin County and Denton County, both north of Dallas, either doubled their population during the decade or approached doing so. Collin County had 144,490 residents in 1980 (an increase of 116 percent), while Denton County grew by 89 percent from 1970 to 1980. Similarly, Montgomery County near Houston grew from 49,479 to 128,487 (an increase of 160 percent), while another Houston area county, Fort Bend, grew from 52,314 to 130,846 (an increase of 150 percent).

This suburbanization process is even more pronounced than it would appear. Houston, for example, accounted for much of its population increase during the decade by annexing new suburban growth that had occurred outside its boundaries (Thomas, 1983). It can also be expected that the suburbs will remain white and wealthy while the central cities will become poorer, blacker, and browner. Dallas was 41.5 percent black and Hispanic in 1980 while Houston's population was 45.2 percent black and Hispanic. It is likely that both cities will have majority black and Hispanic populations by 1990.

It is projected that the Hispanic population in many urban areas will grow at a particularly rapid rate. The Texas Department of Health forecasts that the number of Hispanics in Harris County (Houston) will increase by 161 percent between now and the year 2000—from 510,873 in 1985 to 1,335,766 by the turn of the century. It is also predicted that the Hispanic population during this same time period will grow by 119 percent in Dallas County (Dallas), 103 percent in Travis (Austin), 89 percent in Tarrant (Fort Worth), and 75 percent in El Paso (El Paso).

Texas has several top ten urban areas in the United States in terms of Hispanic population. The San Antonio area has the fourth largest concentration of Hispanics in the nation with 889,300. The Houston area ranks seventh with 706,000, McAllen–Brownsville is eighth with a Hispanic population of 588,300, and El Paso is ninth with 477,900. Hispanic students account for 36 percent of the total enrollment in the Houston Independent School District.

PARTICIPATION IN URBAN AREAS

The great growth of urban areas has had several important political consequences. One major impact has been upon the effectiveness of different types of political participation.

Voting as Participation

There are a variety of ways for citizens to participate in politics at the local level. One of the most widespread forms of political participation is voting. Yet municipal and other strictly local elections attract relatively few citizens. Most people stay away from the polls on these election days. To indicate the percentage of citizens who bother to vote in important local elections, table 11–3

TABLE 11–3 Percentage of Registered Voters Voting
in Mayoral Elections in Texas Cities

City	Number of Registered Voters	Total Votes Cast	Percentage of Registered Voters	Election Date
Houston	779,409	271,562	35%	1981
Austin	195,044	64,015	32%	1983
El Paso	144,459	39,020	27%	1983
Corpus Christi	113,167	29,250	26%	1981
Dallas	406,711	81,711	20%	1983
San Antonio	341,780	60,257	18%	1983
Lubbock	73,507	12,205	17%	1983
Amarillo	67,027	11,169	17%	1983
Abilene	46,463	4,008	9%	1983

Source: Data obtained by authors from individual cities.

presents data on turnout for mayoral elections in several cities. The table reveals that in no city does the election for mayor attract more than 35 percent of the registered voters. The range is from a high of 35 percent in Houston to a low of 9 percent in Abilene. The average turnout is 22 percent.

Low Turnout   It should be pointed out that the number of potential voters is much higher than the number registered to vote. Therefore, the actual turnout is considerably lower than the percentages shown. Voter turnout is even lower for other local elections, such as bond elections. A bond election elicits voter approval of the sale of municipal bonds to finance the construction of roads, buildings, airports, water, flood and sewer systems, parks, or transit facilities. An examination of some recent bond elections reveals that frequently only a few thousand citizens decide the fate of tens of millions of dollars in proposed bonds. Recently only 5,000 citizens decided $92 million in bonds in Irving, 14,000 voters decided upon $45 million in Corpus Christi, 10,000 Lubbock citizens passed judgment on a $43 million issue, and 14,000 voters in Fort Worth decided the fate of $130 million in bonds. Frequently less than one out of every ten registered voters will decide the outcome of such local elections. Since the number of registered voters is considerably lower than the number of potential voters, the turnout of *eligible* voters is, of course, much lower than that.

Reasons for Low Turnout   Why is voting turnout generally lower in local elections than in state elections? There are several reasons. First, state elections are thought to be more important. They involve the selection of the governor, lieutenant governor, attorney general, and other major statewide officials. Second, these elections are more prominent. In large part, this is due to media coverage. Major newspapers and television stations devote considerable coverage to state elections and stimulate citizen interest in the campaign. Another factor is the role played by the political parties. Increasingly the Republicans are challenging the Democrats for state offices. The party organizations raise and spend money, contact voters, and stimulate debate and interest in issues and candidates. These various activities have the effect of raising the level of voter turnout.

A final factor is the role played by interest groups such as labor unions and business organizations. Their political action committees are more likely to be highly active in state elections than in local ones. There are good reasons for this. These interest groups generally perceive that their interests are more directly affected by state government than by local government. Public employee unions such as the Texas State Teachers Association (TSTA) are very active in state elections, for example, but play no role in city elections. When interest groups do not support candidates and encourage their members to vote, turnout declines.

The average citizen simply does not think that local elections are as important as the election for governor and other state officials. Moreover, the reduced level of television and newspaper coverage, the limited activity of interest groups, and the absence of political parties all combine to depress voting turnout in city elections. On the latter point, national studies have indicated that the level of voting is higher in city elections where political parties are active than in those where they are not (Alford and Lee, 1968). Most Texas cities do not have active political party organizations.

Impact of Low Turnout What difference does it make if only a small percentage of citizens bother to cast a ballot in major local elections? Above all, public policy is probably much more conservative than it would be if more citizens decided to participate. Although we have been focusing on the factors that account for low overall turnout in city elections, it is also important to analyze the composition of those who do vote. Research indicates that conservative voters dominate the local electorate (Hamilton, 1971). Liberal voters are much less likely to participate. Since government officials respond to those who participate actively, local public policy tends to be conservative (Verba and Nie, 1972).

Furthermore, political participation in general is class-biased. The higher a citizen's income, education, and social status—recalling the discussion of elections and parties in chapter 4—the more likely it is that he or she will participate. In turn, the elements that account for higher turnout in state elections—media coverage, party activity, and interest group activity—have the greatest effect upon low-income voters. When those factors are not at work, the people most likely to vote for the more liberal candidates drop out of the electorate. The absence of political parties in local campaigns is particularly detrimental, for example, to the working-class citizen. These citizens rely upon the party for information about issues and candidates. In nonpartisan elections where candidates are not identified by party label, such information is not available. Wealthier and better-educated citizens do not rely as heavily upon party as a cue to voting. They have access to alternative sources of information. As a result, the electorate tends to be dominated by conservative voters.

In the preceding chapter we found that the budgetary and tax policies in Texas cities are very conservative. Municipal governments spend very little on health and social welfare programs. Moreover, they rely upon regressive sources of revenue (those taxes that take a larger share of the income of poorer persons such as sales taxes, property taxes, and user fees). Given the low turnout in local elections and the domination of the electorate by conservative voters, the conservative nature of urban public policy should not be surprising.

Contacting as Participation

Another major form of participation in Texas cities is personal contacting—that is, when the citizen phones, writes, or complains in person to a government official about a problem. The contact can be about a missed garbage pickup, a pothole in the street, a broken sewer line, trash on the sidewalk, drug problems in the schools, crime, a loud party next door, an obstructed drainage ditch, flooding after a rain, or stray animals in the neighborhood. There are literally hundreds of these problems that citizens complain to local government about. In fact, contacting may be the most widespread form of political participation at the local level. It is a very personal and very important form of political activity for the individual citizen. Because most contacting is done by telephone, it could be called "direct dialing democracy."

What do citizens contact about and how well does government respond to their political demands? To answer these questions, suppose we consider the results of a study of citizen contacts in Houston (table 11–4). This sample of citizen complaints reveals that people in Houston contact government about routine problems. Complaints about flooding and drainage account for one out of every five contacts with government, while problems with water maintenance account for another 20 percent of the sample. Citizens in Houston contact city government about problems that have a direct, personal, and immediate impact upon their daily lives.

Another study of citizen contacting in Dallas revealed that residents there also express a concern with basic municipal services in their contacts with public officials (Vedlitz and Dyer, 1983). The major problems in Dallas were refuse, street maintenance, and utilities and sanitation.

How well does city government respond to citizens who have a grievance about a municipal service? Table 11–5 presents the results of an examination of responsiveness to individual contacts in Houston. Only one out of every three citizens who contacts city government can expect a satisfactory response. Some 81 percent of the stray animal, 44 percent of the overgrowth and debris, 56 percent of the water maintenance, and 50 percent of the garbage-related problems were resolved. The same outcome occurred for only one out of every three sewer problems, however, and one out of every ten drainage and street-related complaints. Although drainage and street repair problems account for one-third of all contacts in the sample, they accounted for only one out of every ten satisfactory responses.

It appears that government's responsiveness to citizen contacts depends on the level of resources necessary to solve the problem. Since it is a relatively

TABLE 11–4   Number of Citizen-Initiated Contacts in Houston by Service

Service	Number	Percentage of Total
Drainage	121	22.5%
Water maintenance	113	21.0%
Overgrowth	63	11.7%
Debris	57	10.6%
Sewer	56	10.4%
Street maintenance	47	8.7%
Stray animals	26	4.8%
Garbage	20	3.7%
Other	19	3.6%
Traffic	16	3.0%

Source: Mladenka (1977).

TABLE 11-5   Percentage of Satisfactory Responses
to Citizen Contacts in Houston

Type of Contact	Satisfactory Response (%)	No Response (%)	Total Number
Drainage	10.0	90.0	22.3
Sewer	33.9	66.1	10.4
Stray animals	81.0	19.0	4.8
Overgrowth	44.4	55.6	11.7
Debris	43.9	56.1	10.6
Water	55.8	44.2	21.0
Streets	12.8	87.2	8.8
Traffic	37.5	62.5	3.0
Garbage	50.0	50.0	3.7
Other	57.9	42.1	3.5
Percentage	37.4	62.6	100.0
Total number	201	336	537

Source: Mladenka (1977).

simple task for the municipal bureaucracy to collect a missed garbage pickup or chase a stray animal, a satisfactory response is forthcoming in a majority of these instances. Yet some problems are much more difficult to solve. Houston, for example, is beset by widespread flooding problems. To provide adequate protection against flooding, huge amounts of money as well as the cooperative effort of several different units and levels of government would be required. Therefore, individual complaints about the flooding problem are ignored. Similarly, complaints about city streets are not responded to because of the small amount of money available for street repair.

Interest Groups

Another important avenue for citizen participation is through interest groups. In earlier chapters we considered the roles of interest groups in state politics in general, in state elections, and in influencing the state legislature. Yet there are hundreds of interest groups involved in Texas urban government, too. Some of them, such as chambers of commerce, are well financed and influential. Others, such as associations of police officers, represent municipal public employees. Still others are branch chapters of national organizations (the NAACP, for example) and represent racial minorities. But most interest groups at the local level are not as well organized and as prominent as these. Instead they represent loose-knit collections of citizens who are organized around neighborhood concerns. These neighborhood "protective" or "improvement" associations are primarily concerned with ensuring that zoning and deed restrictions in their subdivisions are enforced. They are also interested in the level of public services they receive. When they have a complaint about police protection or trash in the neighborhood, they report it to the mayor's office or a city department. These organizations serve as watchdogs for their neighborhoods and are the most prevalent type of interest group in the city.

Other than indicating the different types of interest groups that exist in the state's cities, there is not much that one can say about them. The necessary research has not been conducted. One might fairly assume, however, that business interests are the most effective political organizations at the local level. Certainly such groups have the most money. Money allows them to establish and maintain an organizational structure. They can afford office space, clerical and research support, and lobbyists. Their access to vast resources also allows business groups to effectively press their claims upon government. They can provide financial support to candidates in political campaigns, they can mold opinion through media advertisements—and they can supply politically relevant information. Public officials need information in order to make decisions. Because of the expense involved in gathering, packaging, and presenting it, business groups such as a city's chamber of commerce are often in a preferred position. Certainly these organizations have recognized that information can influence local decisions and therefore devote a significant share of their resources to research and analysis of major issues affecting local government.

There is another reason why organizations that represent business interests are generally the most effective. They enjoy status and legitimacy. Business groups are identified with stability, prosperity, fiscal conservatism, jobs, and economic growth. The business of the city, to many, is business. Public officials also find much common ground with representatives of business organizations. Both are well-educated and upper-class. Both are in favor of low taxes and economic growth. Because of these common goals and backgrounds, business interests enjoy a special relationship with public officials.

One example of a powerful nonbusiness interest group at the local level is San Antonio's Communities Organized for Public Service (COPS). COPS represents the Hispanic neighborhoods in the city and was founded in the 1970s to protest the inadequacy of basic essential services such as flood control. From the beginning, COPS relied upon a strategy of confronting public officials and demanding action. Group members held rallies, marched on city hall, and shouted down their opponents.

Such behavior is not unexpected from an organization that seeks change and yet represents a group that lacks significant resources. Well-established and wealthy organizations do not need to rely upon parades, demonstrations, pickets, and other forms of protest to effectively press their claims upon government. Instead, they depend upon more conventional tactics such as lobbying to achieve their goals.

The protest strategy employed by COPS was successful. By most accounts, city services have improved in Hispanic areas. Ironically, this success has entailed certain costs. With a growing reputation as a major force in city politics has come a recognition that a failure to modify previous behavior may antagonize other influential groups. COPS is now accepted by the business community and public officials as an influential group in the policy process. Their position on major issues is heeded in policy deliberations. If they continue to behave as an outsider group, they run the risk of losing some of their influence in establishment circles.

The structure of groups in Texas cities has changed considerably over the past twenty-five years. Although traditionally powerful business groups such as builders, developers, and chambers of commerce continue to play a major role, they now share the local political stage with groups that were either ignored or unheard of two decades ago. Black and Hispanic organizations are much more active and influential in city politics. The gay community has become a significant force in local politics in several cities. In fact, the gay community claims credit for the election of Mayor Kathy Whitmire and other public officials in Houston. Municipal employee unions are also a relatively new and powerful group. In particular, police and firefighter associations are active and organized. Their political activities include support of candidates for public office. In addition, they sometimes conduct advertising campaigns in newspapers and on television to mobilize public support on behalf of demands for improvements in pay and working conditions.

Finally, the structure of the business community itself has also changed. Increasingly, the executives of major corporations are relative newcomers to the state. They generally have little interest in local politics. Their political attitudes are more tolerant and cosmopolitan than those of the old guard bankers and oilmen. This new breed of corporate managers has a greater stake in national and international politics than in city and county affairs. Therefore, they are not very active in local politics.

Sometimes minority groups and the business community even form temporary alliances in support of certain issues. In 1986, for example, San Antonio voters defeated a proposition that would have limited the growth of city spending to an amount equal to the inflation and population growth rates. The measure was supported by military retirees and middle-aged, middle-class citizens. It was opposed by the Hispanic community and business leaders. The business community feared that the ceiling on spending would retard economic growth, while Hispanic opposition focused on the almost certain cuts in service that would occur as a result.

Protest as Participation

Another form of political participation in the city is protest. There are two types. Nonviolent protest occurs when citizens join together and demonstrate, parade, sit in, picket, or strike on behalf of a political goal. Such events are peaceful and frequently rely on television coverage to dramatize an appeal for the sympathy and support of other citizens who are unaware of the protestors' grievances. A variety of issues may generate a protest—ranging from inadequate municipal services in a neighborhood to alleged racial discrimination or police brutality. Generally, protest is resorted to only after conventional forms of political participation such as voting, contacting, and group activity have proved ineffective.

Violent protest deliberately employs violence to achieve a political goal. As such it is highly unconventional and is seldom seen in Texas cities. Riots have occurred in the state in the past, however, and this form of political activity certainly could occur again in the future. Since violence is a rare and highly unorthodox form of political participation, we can discount its importance. Moreover, it is not likely to be effective given the conservative political environment in Texas.

Exiting as Participation

One widespread but seldom noted form of political participation is exit from the city. When a citizen is upset with what his government is doing or failing to do, he can respond in one of three ways. He can do nothing. In fact, that response is the typical reaction for most citizens faced with a political problem—either because they are apathetic or because they do not believe that taking action would do any good. Another choice is to engage in the types of political activities we have already discussed—voting, contacting, joining an interest group, protesting.

But there is a third option open to the citizen and one that has proved to be very popular with many Texans. They can move. They can solve their political problems by moving away from them. This phenomenon has itself aggravated another major problem of Texas cities—that of fragmentation, which is discussed later in the chapter. Central cities in Texas are surrounded by both incorporated and unincorporated jurisdictions. Therefore, if a resident of the central city is displeased with taxes, crime, or the quality of public services, he can simply move to another jurisdiction. For those citizens who can afford it, this is a highly effective form of political participation.

The Effectiveness of Participation

Some types of political activity are more effective than others. Yet we should be clear whether we are talking about effectiveness for an individual or for a group. The vote, for example, is not an effective form of political participation for the individual. The citizen's vote is only one vote out of many. The vote can be successful for a group, however, if that group votes as a bloc and supports a victorious set of candidates. Yet even then the group may not get what it wants. Other groups will also make demands upon public officials, and resources or the power to use them may simply not be available to deliver on campaign promises. If the individual citizen wants prompt and effective action from government, he should not expect the vote to provide it. The vote, if it works at all, works slowly.

Contacting can be an effective form of participation for the person who has a relatively minor demand to make upon government. We have seen, for example, that city government tends to respond to contacts about missed garbage pickups, debris, and stray animals but ignores demands that would require a major investment of resources (such as flooding).

Neither violent nor nonviolent protest is likely in most cases to elicit a positive response from government. Since protest is used only after conventional forms of participation have proved ineffective, the protestors tend to be politically powerless. The protest is an attempt to gain public support and sympathy. The protestors seek an ally who will champion their claims upon government on their behalf. It is an effort that depends for its success upon establishing a coalition with others. It is seldom successful.

Interest groups can be highly effective. As we have noted, however, success is directly dependent upon the group's control over resources. Therefore, business groups are the most influential at the local level.

Exiting is perhaps the most effective form of participation for the individual. The citizen simply moves away from his problems. Exiting gives the individual a great degree of control over the situation since he is not dependent upon government to respond to his demand for action. Such mobility within an urban area is closely tied to the person's wealth and income, however. Poor citizens do not enjoy the exit option.

FRAGMENTED GOVERNMENT

A principal consequence of the growth of the modern, decentralized city has been the fragmentation of urban government. In other words, political power is fragmented in the metropolitan areas of Texas. No single unit of government has responsibility for the problems that beset urban areas or the power to solve those problems. Instead, governmental jurisdiction is divided up among dozens and sometimes even hundreds of different political units. In 1977, there were 368 different local governments in the Dallas–Fort Worth metropolitan area alone. This number included 11 counties, 171 municipalities, 76 special districts, and 110 school districts. The Houston area was divided into 488 different governments—6 counties, 86 municipalities, 343 special districts, and 53 school districts. By 1982, Dallas–Fort Worth had 392 governments and Houston had 622 governments.

What difference does this political fragmentation make for the urban areas of Texas? There are, in fact, lengthy arguments that fragmentation is a good thing; there are also lengthy arguments that it is a bad thing.

One alleged advantage is that it enhances the citizen's freedom of choice. If a person is upset with the governmental jurisdiction in which he lives, he can relocate to another nearby. He and his family may move to escape high taxes and crime or to find better schools for the children.

Another alleged advantage of fragmentation is that it creates competition among governments within an urban area. This competition forces them to become more efficient and responsive. According to this perspective, citizens shop among different governmental jurisdictions until they find the right package of housing, taxes, and services at the right cost. Government officials recognize that citizens are discerning shoppers. They realize that if they are to be successful in attracting them in a highly competitive environment, they will have to provide the best possible services at the lowest possible cost. Therefore, governments are forced to become both more efficient and more responsive.

According to the advocates of fragmentation, government is generally inefficient and unresponsive to its citizens because it enjoys a monopoly. It has no incentive to improve. In a fragmented system, however, it loses its monopoly. One government is forced to compete with other governments for preferred customers. This competition requires it to modify its behavior. The citizen benefits from the process.

The critics of fragmentation reject all these arguments. They contend that fragmentation itself is responsible for many of the problems found in urban areas in Texas. Specifically, they charge that fragmentation causes a disparity between needs and resources. Only the wealthy can afford to move to the suburbs. Exiting, in other words, is a class privilege. Therefore, as the city ages it increasingly becomes a "reservation" for the old, the poor, and racial minorities. These citizens have a greater need for government programs and services and therefore place heavy demands upon central city government. Because of fragmentation and exiting, however, the resources necessary to solve problems and finance programs have moved out to the suburbs. Moreover, the wealthy residents of the suburbs may continue to work in the city but pay no taxes.

Its critics also charge that fragmentation encourages the citizen to pursue narrow self-interest. If a person does not like what the government is doing, he or she can solve the political problems (crime, taxes, bad schools) simply by moving to another jurisdiction. There is less incentive, as a result, to stay and work to make things better. Yet only wealthier citizens can afford to pick and choose among neighborhoods and governments. Therefore, intense class and racial segregation occurs within the metropolitan region. The most intense competition develops in the struggle to attract upper-class citizens. The needs of the poor are ignored in this process.

Some believe that this competition among governments for citizens has negative consequences. Rather than forcing governments to become more efficient and responsive in an effort to attract "preferred customers," the critics of fragmentation maintain, this competition produces a lack of cooperation among governments with respect to urban problems. Many if not most urban problems affect the entire region rather than just the central city. Crime, for example, may be disproportionately reported in the central city but it has negative consequences for the entire urban area. High crime rates in the central city also make life more dangerous for the suburban resident who works downtown. More crime requires more courts, judges, jails, sheriffs, and prosecutors. Crime, in short, makes life unpleasant for everybody. The entire community pays for it in terms of declining social trust and greater expenditures.

According to the critics of fragmentation, however, there is no incentive for governments to work together to solve these area-wide problems. In a fragmented system things may even appear to get better for some governments as they get worse for others. As crime rates rise in the central city, residents will have a greater incentive to move to a jurisdiction where crime is lower. And these governments will have a continued incentive to maintain low crime rates—by attempting to attract the middle- and upper-class citizen and excluding the poor and racial minorities.

The critics of fragmentation argue that both individual citizens and governments are encouraged to pursue their own narrow self-interest in a fragmented system. In such an environment the prospects for cooperative problem solving are dim indeed. In fact, neither the supporters nor the critics of fragmentation would expect serious attempts by urban governments to work together to resolve major issues.

Councils of Governments (COGs) are one mechanism that has been used to bring some order to the planning process in metropolitan areas. However, they have not been successful in addressing the problems of urban areas in the state. The reason is that COGs have no power. They are voluntary associations of the several governments in a particular metropolitan region, and none of these governments is willing to give up any of its own power. Therefore, COGs are primarily planning and coordinating bodies. Although COGs have conducted a number of useful studies of flood control, transportation, and land use, their impact on major problems and issues has been minimal.

THE POLITICAL ECONOMY OF TEXAS CITIES

In his book *City Limits*, Paul Peterson argues that three elements are crucial to the behavior of the city: labor, capital, and land. Of these three, the city exerts significant control only over land. Labor and capital are highly mobile. They are free to move wherever they choose within a fragmented metropolitan area. The city cannot prevent people, money, resources, and business from exiting the city to locate in another city or neighboring suburban jurisdiction. However, the city is heavily dependent upon business and industry and middle- and upper-class citizens. The business community provides jobs while well-employed and better-off citizens pay taxes and make relatively few demands upon government. The city's primary interest is in economic growth. Growth creates new jobs, provides revenues to support essential services, and keeps taxes low. Growth is also crucial to the continued health of the city because it contributes to the maintenance of the city as an attractive location for existing and potential businesses and people.

According to Peterson, this perspective helps us understand the behavior of the city. Since cities have an overwhelming interest in economic growth, they are most concerned with *developmental policies*. Examples of developmental policies include the construction of a new sports stadium complex to attract a professional franchise, the development of a civic and convention center, the construction of a new airport and transportation network, and tax, land, and credit incentives to attract new industry. Since developmental policies stimulate economic growth they are perceived to be in the best interests of all. As a result, the support for these policies is widespread on the part of both political and economic elites.

Redistributive policies, on the other hand, will be strongly opposed. A *redistributive policy* is one that takes resources from the haves and gives them to the have-nots. Examples would include a new public housing project for the poor and increased city expenditures for social welfare programs. Cities resist redistributive programs because they harm economic growth. If a city invests significant resources in public housing, it will contribute nothing to economic development. No new jobs will be created. Funds for the project will have to come from tax revenues. Taxes may eventually have to be increased. The availability of public housing units will also attract more poor people to the city. They, in turn, will place further demands upon government. As a result, the city will become a less attractive location for both existing and prospective business and industry. Economic decline will follow.

Peterson's interpretation appears to apply well to Texas cities. We saw in the preceding chapter that the large cities in the state spend very little on redistributive programs. Public housing and other social welfare programs and services for the needy are almost totally ignored. Instead, economic growth and development is the major priority. For example, the Houston Economic Development Council is financially supported by city government. The Council, which is affiliated with the Houston Chamber of Commerce, works closely with Mayor Kathy Whitmore to attract business and industry to the city. The Council recently spent $500,000 on a campaign designed to attract businesses interested in space ventures. City leaders in both Dallas and Houston boast about modern civic centers, convention complexes, and world-class art museums and cultural exhibits. They emphasize the economic advantages that will accrue. These complexes and institutions will allegedly attract more conventions, more tourism, and more business and industry. Economic growth will be the primary benefit.

In Austin, the city's interest in economic growth was manifested in the competition for Sematech, a research consortium of fourteen of the nation's largest semiconductor firms. The intense national competition for Sematech was illustrated by the fact that Boston offered incentives valued at $400 million. However, Austin won with a package that included $8 million in discounts on home loans for company employees, tax exemptions, and $250,000 in cash. In addition, the University of Texas provided another $50 million in incentives. Mayor Henry Cisneros and San Antonio have been among the most competitive in seeking new jobs. Cisneros seldom delivers a speech in which he calls for higher taxes and more government spending to support expensive redistributive programs. Instead, he emphasizes jobs, growth, new industry, diversification, and economic development. He travels the nation and the world in his quest to lure new industries and jobs to San Antonio. San Antonio has long been heavily dependent upon tourism and military spending. The five military bases add $3.2 billion to the economy while tourism provides another $1 billion. Cisneros seeks to diversify the city's economy by making the area a center for the emerging biotech and bioscience industry.

ANNEXATION

Although the critics of governmental fragmentation point out a number of its negative features, the situation would be even worse if it were not for the broad annexation powers state government grants to Texas cities. Prior to 1963, there were essentially no limits on the power of a home-rule city to annex unincorporated areas. Even with the new law, however, those powers are still significant. A city has what is known as *extraterritorial jurisdiction*. This jurisdiction extends from 0.5 to 5 miles (depending on the city's population) from the city's boundaries. The city may annex areas within this jurisdiction up to a total of 10 percent of its land area. It may even exceed the 10 percent limit if the landowners and citizens of an unincorporated area request it. If it does not use up the 10 percent allotment in a given year, it may carry over the unused portion up to a total of 30 percent of its total land area.

Cities such as Houston have used their annexation power to minimize the effects of suburbanization. When new middle- and upper-class suburban areas develop outside the central city, Houston annexes them. Some of these annexed areas such as Alief and Clear Lake have vigorously protested their annexation. They argue that they are required to pay city taxes but do not receive adequate municipal services (although the law requires that such services must be provided). Because the annexation law gives great power to the central city, these annexation disputes are seldom resolved in favor of the suburb.

Nevertheless, we can anticipate two consequences as suburbanization and "white flight" continue. First, new suburban development may be pushed even a greater distance from the central city as these communities seek to escape the extraterritorial jurisdiction of the central city. Second, as suburban representation continues to increase in the state legislature, the broad annexation powers currently exercised by central cities may well be curtailed.

FEDERALISM

Two forces have had a major impact upon the dramatic growth of urban areas in the state. The first is economic change and development; the second is the role of federal aid. Federal aid accounted for only 18 percent of operating budget revenues in 1981 for Texas's ten largest cities. It would be a mistake, however, to assume that the federal government has played a minor role in the development of the state's urban areas. Instead it can be argued that federal involvement has been extraordinarily important in the development of urban Texas.

Houston serves as an excellent example of the significance of federal aid. Although a great deal of attention was given during the 1960s and 1970s to the city's refusal to accept federal money for its police department, the rhetoric concealed a fundamentally different reality: The city has always relied upon federal money to finance projects crucial to its economic growth. At the turn of the century, Houston began to use federal funds to finance the construction of the Houston ship channel. Federally funded expansions and improvements of this vitally important world port have continued throughout the twentieth century.

Another significant federal project has been the construction and maintenance of the flood control system in the Houston area. Although citizens who are flooded out of their homes after every heavy rainfall might well deny that such a system exists, the fact remains that federally funded flood control has alleviated the flooding problem.

Houston received another major economic benefit from federal money during World War II. Federal war contracts provided a mighty stimulus to ship channel industries, ranging from shipbuilding to steel production. The petrochemical industry was transformed into a major economic activity, as well. This federal support of a variety of important projects continued after the war. These projects included the federal development of municipal water sources (Lakes Houston and Conroe, among others), intercontinental airports, sewer systems and water lines, wastewater treatment plants, roads, and bridges. Federal support of the Manned Spacecraft Center and the Houston Medical Center has also yielded major economic benefits for the area, not only in terms of more jobs but in terms of a variety of significant high-tech applications and spin-offs.

Local leaders not only accepted federal money, they eagerly sought it. Houston's success in obtaining federal aid can be traced in large part to a highly effective coalition composed of prominent local business leaders and Texas politicians in Washington. It is difficult to imagine the Houston area enjoying its present degree of economic success without a ship channel and port, a flood control system, a petrochemical industry, an extensive public service infrastructure, a space center, and one of the world's great medical complexes. Yet as late as the 1970s local politicians still pointed with pride to the fact that the police department refused federal aid because it would mean a loss of local control.

Houston has not been alone in its heavy reliance on economic aid. Dozens of other urban areas in the state have followed a similar route. The motivation has been above all economic. When the federal government pays for something, local taxes do not have to be raised to do so. The revenue comes from Washington. These federal projects have, as well, been designed primarily to stimulate economic growth: Airports, freeways, bridges, ports, harbors, water and sewer systems are typical examples. They have provided the public services and facilities that are essential to economic development. It is not surprising that federal aid has made a dramatic contribution to the economic growth of the state's urban areas. Most cities in the country have vigorously pursued federal money. What is surprising is that local business and political leaders have long championed a myth of self-reliance and fiscal conservatism. The reality of the situation, however, is that great efforts were made to obtain federal dollars for economic development. The serious criticism of federal funding was reserved for social welfare and police programs.

Federal aid has also contributed to the process of suburbanization. In particular, the federally funded freeway systems have made possible the dispersal of huge numbers of people within metropolitan regions. Federal support of a vast service infrastructure without regard for jurisdictional boundaries has encouraged the proliferation of new governments. It has also helped to create new population and economic centers located at greater and greater distances from the central city. Thus federal aid has worked in conjunction with changing economic circumstances to make decentralization possible.

STATE–CITY RELATIONS

The powerful forces of economic change and development on the one hand, and huge amounts of federal aid on the other, have combined to stimulate the dramatic growth of urban areas in the state. If it were not for the role of the federal government in providing aid for the development of metropolitan-wide services, it is unlikely that the growth of urban areas in the state would have been so dramatic. A region cannot develop economically without freeways, bridges, roads, airports, and water, sewer, drainage, and flood control services and facilities. The federal role has been crucial because state government in Texas essentially ignores its urban areas. Although the county might be an appropriate governmental unit to deal with the problems of urban regions, county officials have neither the power nor the inclination to do so.

One study concluded that Texas was first among the fifty states in terms of the discretion it granted to its cities (Thomas, 1983). That means, on the one hand, that state government leaves its home-rule cities alone. Within broad limits, large cities enjoy great flexibility with respect to taxing, gathering revenue, spending, programs and policies, and annexation. On the other hand, it also means that the state has typically ignored urban problems.

As the state becomes highly urbanized, however, this lack of concern for urban affairs has forced cities to improvise in an effort to manage rapid growth. Since municipalities can expect little help from the state or county, they have turned to the federal government for assistance. Moreover, the special district has been widely employed to deal with area-wide problems. We will discuss both county and special district governments and their roles in solving urban problems in a later chapter.

The continued lack of state government concern for its urban areas might initially be surprising given the level of urban representation in the legislature. In 1981, just three metropolitan areas (Dallas–Fort Worth, Houston, San Antonio) held fifteen of the thirty-one Senate seats and half of the House seats. It should be noted, however, that these urban areas contain wealthy suburbs as well as central cities—and these suburbs tend to be very conservative. Their representatives in the state legislature are likely to have legislative priorities that differ from the agenda of representatives of inner-city districts.

CONCLUSION

Cities in Texas reflect the profound changes that have taken place in the nation's economy. The compact industrial city has given way to the decentralized city. In fact, urban areas in Texas consist of *several* cities and suburbs and sometimes spread across several counties. This decentralization is possible because the major elements of the economy—labor, management, capital, raw materials, markets—no longer have to be in close proximity to one another. Advances in technology and transportation make it possible for these various components to be in separate locations. As a result, the city's population and economic activities no longer have to be clustered around a central business district.

Individuals and businesses have much greater freedom with respect to place of residence and location of economic activities in such a decentralized urban environment.

The political consequences of these trends have been significant. Governmental fragmentation has had a variety of impacts. Its advocates argue that fragmentation has forced governments in metropolitan areas to become more efficient, effective, and responsive. Its critics, on the other hand, charge that fragmented government has produced a disparity between needs and resources and has turned the city into a reservation for the old, the poor, and racial minorities. They also allege that fragmentation of government power prevents cooperative efforts to solve common, metropolitan-wide problems such as crime, transportation, and pollution.

An examination of participation in urban areas reveals that exiting becomes a powerful political option in a decentralized system. If a person is dissatisfied with conditions in his neighborhood or city, he can solve many of his political problems (crime, taxes, inadequate public services) by moving to another jurisdiction in the area. Exiting, however, is a class-biased form of political participation. Because the most desirable neighborhoods tend to be the most expensive in terms of housing, only the wealthy can afford to exit. Therefore, a fragmented political system reinforces segregation of neighborhoods and jurisdictions on the basis of class and income.

Another highly effective form of participation in urban areas is the interest group. Because cities are so eager to keep businesses from relocating to another jurisdiction, interest groups that represent the business community enjoy special access to public officials. Political leaders are well aware that economic considerations play a vital role. Citizens are most concerned with good public services and low taxes. Public officials know that service levels and tax rates depend on the size of the tax base. Economic growth makes the public official's job much easier because it strengthens the tax base. Services can be improved and taxes can be kept low when the economy is strong and expanding.

If a city loses its image as a place that is good for business, however, new industry will not locate in the area and established businesses may decide to leave. A declining economy erodes the tax base. The result may well be higher taxes and poorer services. Consequently the business community is in an excellent position to press its claims upon government in a fragmented, decentralized system.

Central cities in Texas are in a better position than cities in most other states with respect to fighting the effects of suburbanization. Because of their liberal annexation powers, central cities can annex fringe urban areas near their boundaries and combat the erosion of jobs, people, and resources.

Finally, we have noted the role of federal aid in spurring economic growth. Although federal aid is not a major source of revenue for the operating budgets of individual Texas cities, it has played a major role in providing those services necessary to economic development for the metropolitan area as a whole. Federal dollars have financed regional airports, freeway systems, water supplies, medical and space centers, university systems, ports and ship channels, and flood, sewer, and drainage systems. This federally funded service infrastructure has dramatically stimulated economic development and has provided the basis for the spectacular growth of urban areas in the state.

REFERENCES

Alford, Robert R., and Lee, Eugene C. 1968. "Voting Turnout in American Cities." *American Political Science Review* 62 (September): 796–813.

Hamilton, Howard D. 1971. "The Municipal Voter: Voting and Nonvoting in City Elections." *American Political Science Review* 65 (December): 1135–1140.

Mladenka, Kenneth R. 1977. "Citizen Demand and Bureaucratic Response." *Urban Affairs Quarterly* 12 (March): 273–290.

Thomas, Robert D. 1983. "State-Urban Relations in Texas." Paper delivered at the annual meeting of the Southwestern Political Science Association.

Vedlitz, Arnold, and Dyer, James. 1983. "Bureaucratic Response to Citizen Contacts: Neighborhood Demands and Administrative Reaction in Dallas." Unpublished manuscript.

Verba, Sidney, and Nie, Norman H. 1972. *Participation in America*. New York: Harper & Row.

THE POLITICS OF MUNICIPAL SERVICES

U
rban public services are essential to the safety, health, and well-being of citizens. Life could not proceed in any civilized way without them. These services are so routine that the typical citizen seldom considers how vital they really are: police and fire protection, education, transportation, water, sewerage, refuse collection, recreation, flood control, sanitation, and health. One of the myths about these services is that they have little to do with politics. What is political about picking up the garbage, patrolling the streets, educating students, providing an adequate water supply, or maintaining a fire protection system?

In fact, the delivery of routine public services is fraught with opportunities for political conflict, and the political issues inherent in service delivery decisions are significant. Which services should be provided? How much of a particular service should be delivered? Which services should be assigned priority? Who should pay for the service? How should burdens and benefits be distributed among the population? Who will win and who will lose? One observer notes that:

> *Modern urban man is born in a publicly financed hospital, receives his education in a publicly supported school and university, spends a good part of his time traveling on publicly built transportation facilities, communicates through the post office or the quasi-public telephone system, drinks his public drinking water, disposes of his garbage through the public removal system, reads his public library books, picnics in his public parks, is protected by public police, fire, and health systems; eventually he dies, again in a hospital, and may even be buried in a public cemetery. Ideological conservatives notwithstanding, his everyday life is inextricably bound up with government decisions on these and numerous other local services. [Tietz, 1967:10]*

Although media coverage and personal discussions about politics typically center on national issues—war and peace, elections, interest rates, employment, energy, inflation—it is local services that are the heart and soul of government. Imagine what life would be like if the fire department did not come when your house or apartment caught fire, if the police did not control speeders or respond to calls, if the public schools were shut down, if the garbage was not collected, if traffic lights did not work, if rabid animals were not captured, if the streets were impassable, if there were no parks, libraries, water, sewer, flood control, drainage, utility, or public health systems.

Every citizen can recount negative experiences with local government—cops who stop minor traffic offenders while rapists, robbers, and muggers run amok; streets full of huge potholes; garbage collectors who cannot pick up the trash without making a mess; public schools that are a zoo; and parks that are filthy, inadequately lighted, poorly maintained, and dangerous. Everyone has heard about bureaucrats who are underworked and overpaid, arrogant, condescending, and devoted to shuffling endless papers in a soft job from which they can never be fired. At the same time, local government services usually do get delivered. Yet the provision of those services encounters many difficulties. In this chapter we will examine the conditions that make it difficult for city governments to provide services in an effective and responsive way. We will also investigate the extent to which services are equitably distributed across different groups and neighborhoods in Texas cities.

SERVICES: A STUDY IN CONFLICT

Service delivery is made difficult by the considerable variation in people's needs and preferences for services. Poor people, for example, may prefer more parks and fewer libraries. Preference varies with respect to the same service as well. Wealthy parents are likely to expect the public schools to serve as a college preparatory institution. Minority parents may well prefer that more vocational training programs be offered and that the neighborhood be given more control over the way its schools are run—control that extends to the hiring, firing, and promotion of teachers and staff. Similarly, some neighborhoods expect the police to enforce criminal law and apprehend criminal suspects and others expect the police to perform a variety of services.

These conflicting expectations are difficult to satisfy. As a result, it is frequently impossible for local government to please all, or even most, of its constituents. The police cannot be all things to all people. Many citizens expect them to spend most of their time enforcing the law and catching criminals. One study found, however, that 90 percent of the police effort was devoted to functions other than traditional law enforcement (Wilson, 1968). Even the same citizen may expect a particular service to pursue a variety of goals and achieve a number of different and even conflicting objectives. The public wants the police to regulate traffic, engage in community relations, apprehend suspects, investigate crimes, come when called (even though the call may have little to do with a criminal act), and provide information. These conflicting expectations immensely complicate effective delivery because the same service is supposed to perform too wide a variety of functions and achieve contradictory goals. Since the service delivery system is incapable of satisfying these conflicting expectations, the public official makes decisions in an atmosphere of confusion and uncertainty.

Conflict between elected officials and bureaucrats adds another layer of complexity to the delivery process. Bureaucrats are a powerful force in local government. In many departments, they enjoy a virtual monopoly over information, experience, and expertise. Elected officials come and go. Bureaucrats are career administrators. They develop expertise in a narrow area of government operations. Often, elected officials are simply unequipped by virtue of training, information, and inclination to challenge bureaucratic choices. There are too many services to provide and too many decisions to make to allow elected officials to exercise control over dozens of separate agencies.

This observation is particularly accurate when the issues under consideration involve complex technical matters. How should street construction and repair projects be scheduled? Which police patrol strategy should be employed? Decisions that appear to involve only routine choices may actually have significant political implications. Because of bureaucratic power, elected officials are often forced to rely upon the bureaucrats themselves for an evaluation of whether policy should be changed. If they do order that a new policy be implemented, public officials must trust the bureaucrats to put the change into effect. Their powers to force compliance are severely limited.

Delivery is further complicated by the fact that lower-level bureaucrats are often immune from control by top-level administrators. How can the police chief know whether the officer on the street is enforcing all laws rigorously and fairly? How can the department head determine whether the building inspector is performing his duty in compliance with the provisions of the building code? Maintaining control over the "street-level" bureaucrat is immensely difficult and probably impossible.

There are never enough supervisors to monitor performance. The problem is particularly acute for vital services such as police protection and education since the police officer on the beat and the teacher in the classroom *are* the service. Directives from agency and bureau chiefs may be carefully followed by some street-level bureaucrats, partially implemented by others, and completely ignored by still others. If elected officials often cannot get the bureaucracy to do what they would like, it is also frequently the case that the heads of city agencies find it exceedingly difficult to control workers at the level where services are actually delivered to clients (Nivola, 1978; Lipsky, 1976).

Control of the street-level bureaucrat is made even more difficult by the fact that the organizational goals of public bureaucracies are frequently unclear. They are generally implicit rather than explicit, conflicting rather than compatible. In the absence of clearly defined goals, the street-level bureaucrats are *forced* to exercise personal discretion and pursue their own vision of the appropriate organizational mission. Upper-echelon control of employees implies a common set of expectations with respect to performance. Objectives must be clearly stated. In fact, however, these goals are frequently vague or unexpressed. Is the street cop to enforce all the laws? If not, which violations should be ignored? How rigorously should laws be enforced? Should different standards be employed in some neighborhoods and for some groups? Should the law be uniformly applied even if consistent application appears to violate widely shared values in some neighborhoods? Should police officers concentrate on the most serious crimes or should they devote their effort to those offenses most likely to be solved? Should they respond to all citizen requests for service even if many of them are nuisance calls and have nothing to do with violations of the criminal law?

Police departments often provide next to no guidance to the street officer with respect to these and other major issues. Consequently, the cops on the beat are required to make their own determination and apply their own interpretations with respect to departmental priorities and organizational goals. As a result, street-level discretion is encouraged rather than controlled.

Some public services are easier to deliver effectively than others. Park and library services, for example, involve the delivery of tangible facilities at fixed locations. The use of the service is discretionary. While the public employees who staff these facilities are not irrelevant, they are certainly far less crucial than those involved in police work, education, and building inspection. Effective delivery is much easier to accomplish when the service does not require control of the street-level bureaucrat (Mladenka, 1980).

Still another factor that complicates effective delivery of basic public services revolves around the multidimensional nature of service delivery systems. We can think of the service process in terms of at least three distinct stages: resources, activities, and results. In police work, personnel and equipment are examples of *resources*. Patrolling, responding to calls for service, and investigating crimes are all examples of police *activities*. *Results* include crime rates, number of crimes solved, citizen satisfaction with police services, and public fear of crime.

Public confusion with respect to the uniqueness of these different stages makes service delivery more difficult. Demands for better police protection, for example, generally center on additional staff and equipment. Yet significantly greater numbers of police may have only a marginal impact on activities and no discernible effect at all on results. In fact, the relationship between resources and results is very poorly understood. Certainly a variety of factors other than service resources exert a significant impact on results. More police, for example, may have no effect upon crime rates. Instead, crime levels will go up or down depending on such things as unemployment rates.

The public, however, frequently misunderstands the relationship among the various stages. For example, citizens expect that more police officers will translate into better police protection and lower crime rates. The public's failure to recognize the highly tenuous link between resources and outcomes accounts in large part for the public's frustration with government services. When more police officers (particularly when they are accompanied by a tax increase) do not automatically translate into quicker response times, more visible neighborhood patrols, lower crime rates, and more crimes solved, the result is apt to be public disenchantment. The public's expectations for dramatic improvements in service are easily heightened by higher levels of service resources. They are just as easily dashed when these results do not materialize overnight.

EQUITY AND SERVICE DELIVERY

Equity involves justice and fairness. The problem from a service delivery perspective is that which constitutes fairness is open to a variety of differing interpretations. What appears to be fair to the public official and a majority of citizens may strike a substantial minority of the population as eminently unjust. Every service delivery decision involves a standard of equity whether or not it is expressed. Equity is particularly relevant when it comes to distribution. How should service benefits be distributed to various neighborhoods and groups? Should some receive more than others? Under what conditions? There are five basic concepts of equity: equality, need, demand, preference, and willingness and ability to pay. Each concept produces a distinctly different distribution pattern.

Equality in distribution implies only an approximation of strict equality. What is really meant is that differences in the distribution of benefits are limited to some acceptable range of variation. The differences that are tolerated are unrelated to the characteristics of the population and the conditions of neighborhoods. Dissimilar citizens and environments are treated similarly. Moreover, equality in distribution is relevant at each stage of the process: resources, activities, and results. For police services, equality in distribution would mean an equal number of patrol officers per 1,000 population (resources), equality of response times to citizen calls originating in different parts of the city (activities), and equality of crime rates across neighborhoods (results). Of course, equality of results would imply a highly unequal distribution of resources because many more police officers would be required in high-crime areas.

Need as equity assumes that some citizens have a greater need for services than others and that their needs are entitled to preferential consideration. One of the difficulties associated with treating need as equity is the likelihood of generating intense political controversy. Distribution based on need obviously implies a highly unequal distribution of resources and benefits. Some citizens will receive much more service than others.

Demand as equity indicates that public services should be distributed according to variations in citizens' demands. Demand can be expressed in a variety of ways: use of services and facilities or complaints about services. The communication of demand to political authorities may differ widely from neighborhood to neighborhood. Therefore, distribution of resources and benefits on the basis of demand will produce a highly unequal distributional pattern.

Another equity concept is *preference*. Services could be distributed according to the variation in citizen preferences for public programs and facilities. Differences in service preferences are closely associated with differences in personal incomes. Poor people are likely to have a greater preference than wealthier citizens for public recreational facilities because their access to private facilities is limited. The rich are apt to have a greater preference for library services and other publicly supported cultural activities. Responding to the variation in consumer preference therefore results in a highly uneven pattern of public benefits.

A final standard of equity is *willingness and ability to pay.* Many local services are currently provided on that basis: garbage collection, water, sewerage, recreational facilities. All services could be so provided. No citizen would be allowed to use a service unless he or she was willing and able to pay for it at the time of consumption. The personal assessment of specific costs, rather than reliance upon tax and grant revenue, would finance services. The intent, of course, would be to duplicate the operation of the private sector as closely as possible.

Implications of Equity Standards

The requirement that public officials resolve the equity issue complicates delivery because it increases the number of choices. Each equity concept produces a distinct set of winners and losers. *Equality* as equity enjoys the virtue of simplicity because it ignores the variation in need. Under some conditions, however, equality in distribution is absurd. For example, neighborhoods with extraordinarily high crime rates and fire hazards would not be allocated more resources than areas that seldom experience a crime or fire.

Need as equity implies several problems with respect to service delivery. For example, measurement of need is more complicated than it appears at first glance. How should need for public recreation services be determined? Differences in income levels may be too rough an indicator of differences in need. More appropriate measures might include age, crime and delinquency rates, differences in access to private recreational facilities, and unemployment, welfare, and poverty levels.

Demand as equity has several advantages for the administrator. One advantage is that it appears to emphasize rationality in the allocation of public resources. The administrator can easily defend demand by pointing out to critics that the most efficient and effective use of available resources is to distribute them to areas of high consumption. It is unreasonable to provide services to citizens who have not used them or asked for them. It is wasteful to distribute resources on the basis of equality or need since demand alone allows the administrator to determine whether the service will actually be used. Some citizens, however, are more likely to express demand than others. Therefore, demand as equity is likely to produce a differential pattern of distribution.

Preference as equity presents a variety of problems with respect to service delivery. It certainly appears rational to consult consumer preferences about public services. Service facilities and programs that go unused because citizens are not interested in them represent a highly inefficient use of resources. Preferences are exceedingly difficult to measure and respond to, however. First, preferences vary widely from group to group on the basis of income, education, race, and age. Second, the intensity of preference is sometimes difficult to measure. Some citizens feel very strongly about a particular service while others are merely lukewarm. Attempting to assign weights to differing intensities of preference would enormously complicate the delivery process. Third, public preferences are subject to change. Since many public services frequently involve the heavy investment of resources at fixed sites, it is no simple matter to adapt to population movements or changing consumer taste. Consequently, preference as equity is apt to violate notions of efficiency.

Ability to pay is a final standard of equity. According to this notion of equity, no citizen would be required to pay for a service that he or she did not want. People would pay only for the services they use. Government officials would not have to measure the variation in public demand and preference. Willingness to pay represents a precise measure of preference. Specific costs are assessed at the time of consumption. Use is voluntary. The service needs, demands, and preferences of some are not imposed upon others.

Every urban public service incorporates a certain conception of equity. Each standard of equity imposes a different set of distributional consequences. The choice of equity standards represents a significant decision because it determines the winners and losers of service benefits. These equity choices are, however, frequently implicit rather than explicit. There are good reasons for this. Providing public services is, after all, the major task of city government. Distributing these services to citizens implies political controversy and conflict. When city budgets total hundreds of millions of dollars, decisions about which neighborhoods and groups will receive these services and at what levels assume vital significance. Will police, fire, education, sanitation, recreation, and other services be delivered on the basis of equality, need, or demand? To avoid political conflict, urban administrators keep their equity choices implicit rather than explicit. If citizens do not know why they are receiving a particular level of service, they are less likely to complain about it.

Equity and Coproduction

The concept of *coproduction* is also relevant to service delivery. Citizens share in the production of services by contributing to—or detracting from—efficiency and effectiveness in delivery. Some citizens, for example, carefully package their garbage and place it in the appropriate site for collection. Others simply toss it out at the curb. Some citizens take pains to keep their neighborhood parks clean. Others misuse the equipment, discard their trash, and even commit acts of vandalism. Some neighborhood parents play an energetic role in their public schools by contributing time, money, and effort. Other parents do nothing. Some students are well-disciplined and well-prepared and others are delinquent and lazy. The quality of services is determined, in large part, by the citizen's own contribution to these services.

In previous sections we have examined the factors that complicate service delivery, the different standards of equity, and the implications of using one standard rather than another. The next section explains how urban public services are actually distributed in Texas cities.

DISTRIBUTION IN AMERICAN CITIES

Studies of large American cities provide little evidence to support the argument that urban governments intentionally discriminate against the poor and racial minorities with respect to the distribution of a variety of urban services. Instead, studies of Detroit, Oakland, and Chicago reveal that the distributional process is controlled by the municipal bureaucracy and that bureaucrats use standard operating procedures to make decisions about service distribution. Moreover, the distributional pattern is influenced by past decisions, population shifts, and technological changes (Jones and others, 1977, 1978; Levy, Meltsner, and Wildavsky, 1974). Examination of the distribution for parks and recreation, libraries, street maintenance, and schools reveals that demand is frequently used to allocate resources. Repair priorities for neighborhood streets, for example, were made on the basis of traffic volume and citizen complaints. The distribution of resources to branch libraries was made on the basis of circulation rates.

DISTRIBUTION IN TEXAS CITIES

How are services distributed in Texas cities? Do the rich get more than the poor? Do whites receive more than blacks? Are services allocated on the basis of equality, need, or demand? At least a handful of studies have investigated the distribution of services in certain Texas cities and can provide some answers to these questions.

In 1978 the authors studied the distribution of police services in Houston (Mladenka and Hill, 1978). Our analysis of response times to citizen calls for service revealed that it required an average of thirty-eight minutes from the initiation of a call for police assistance until the arrival of the first patrol unit. The results for each type of call are presented in table 12–1.

We then examined whether the Houston police responded more quickly to calls from white and wealthier neighborhoods than to requests originating in black and poor areas. Surprisingly, we found that the police actually responded more quickly to calls from black and low-income neighborhoods. Yet there was no evidence of discrimination in service delivery on the basis of race and wealth. We concluded that:

> *The only independent source of variation in response to calls for police assistance appears to be the nature of the reported criminal activity. Incoming calls for service are not accorded equal consideration. Instead, the police dispatch system apparently evaluates each request for assistance in terms of the seriousness of the reported offense and the probability of an apprehension at the scene. These, rather than demographic considerations, determine the assignment of a response priority. This conclusion is supported by personal observation of dispatch operations as well as by interviews with dispatch personnel. [Mladenka and Hill, 1978:126]*

We also studied the distribution of police personnel in Houston and concluded that patrol officers were *unequally* distributed across neighborhoods.

TABLE 12-1   Average Response Time
by Type of Call

Type of Call	Number of Minutes
Robbery	36
Burglary	52
Theft	55
Juvenile disturbance	38
Family disturbance	30
Other disturbance	23
Discharge of firearms	39
See complainant	48
Shoplifting	37
Suspicious subject	28
Malicious mischief	47
Prowler	20
Serious disturbance	21
Breaking and entering	29

Source: Mladenka and Hill (1978:122).

Some areas of the city were assigned more police patrols than others. Nevertheless, we again found no evidence to suggest discrimination on the basis of race or wealth. Instead the distribution of personnel was determined by crime rates and calls for service. Since black and poor neighborhoods typically had higher crime rates and made more calls for service, they were assigned more police patrols.

Police services in Houston were distributed according to *need* and *demand* as equity. The seriousness of a reported offense determined response priorities to citizen calls for service, while crime rates (need) and calls for service (demand) were instrumental in the assignment of patrol staff. We therefore concluded that:

> *Distributional decisions are left to the discretion of police bureaucrats. . . . Elected officials are uninformed as to the nature of the distributional configurations. . . . [They] do not appear to have the information or motivation necessary to monitor the process whereby police services are distributed in the community. Distributional issues in regard to police resources lack salience. There is no evidence to indicate that questions of resource allocation are resolved through political conflict. Rather, the distributional process appears to be devoid of political content. [Mladenka and Hill, 1978:131–132]*

Antunes and Plumlee (1977) studied one of the most visible of public services: city streets. Using a device known as a Mays ride meter, they examined the roughness of 265 neighborhood streets in both black and white areas in Houston. Moreover, they collected information on the absence or presence of covered storm drains, curbs, sidewalks, and litter. Surprisingly, their data revealed that there were no significant differences in street roughness between black and white neighborhoods. Further, no appreciable differences were found between low- and high-income neighborhoods.

The authors did find, however, that black areas "have a greater number of open ditches and were less clean, overall, than white neighborhoods." The results of their analysis are presented in table 12–2. Antunes and Plumlee then investigated the procedures used by the city to guide street construction. They discovered that in new subdivisions the developer is responsible for providing streets, sidewalks, and storm sewers that meet city specifications. Since the cost of these facilities is included in the price of the home, the new home buyer pays for streets. Thus new neighborhoods in Houston have very good streets. In developed neighborhoods, deteriorated streets will be rebuilt by the city if 75 percent of those owning property along the street sign a petition. In that case, each property owner is assessed a fee to partially offset the construction costs. As a result of these procedures, Antunes and Plumlee (1977:61) conclude that the Department of Public Works

> is not concerned about building or rebuilding local streets; that is the responsibility of developers and property owners. If a local street needs rebuilding, the property owners may have it rebuilt; if they do not choose to do so, then that is their decision and not any concern of the Department of Public Works.

Antunes and Plumlee also found that street repair (as opposed to construction) procedures were decentralized. Specifically, the "squeaky wheel gets the grease." Citizens who complained the loudest about streets in their neighborhoods were the most likely to get something done. In general, the authors discovered no evidence of discrimination on the basis of race and income with respect to street condition, construction, or repair. Although street quality differed greatly among neighborhoods, these differences were not a matter of racial bias. Thus *ability to pay* and *demand* were the equity criteria discovered in this study.

TABLE 12–2   Percentage Differences in Drainage and Litter by Race of Neighborhood

Street Condition	Black[a]	White[b]
Drainage		
Open ditch	43.5%	17.2%
Storm sewer	56.5%	82.8%
Litter		
Heavily littered	1.9%	0.0%
Moderately littered	33.3%	2.8%
Moderately clean	43.5%	17.2%
Clean	21.3%	80.0%

[a]$N = 108$
[b]$N = 145$
Source: Antunes and Plumlee (1977:57).

Robert Lineberry (1977) studied a variety of public services in San Antonio. For parks, he found no evidence of discrimination on the basis of race. Although some neighborhoods received better parks than others, there was no indication that these differences in quality were a function of racial composition. A similar pattern was discovered for libraries. Lineberry gathered data on library books per capita, professional staff per 1,000 population, library expenditures per capita, and new books per 1,000 population. He then analyzed the relationship between these indicators of library quality and the characteristics of neighborhoods and concluded that:

> The quality of library services is very weakly related to attributes of neighborhoods in San Antonio. There is nothing particularly equal about the distribution of library services, but our capacity to relate these inequalities to neighborhood attributes is strained indeed. The best description would be to call it a system of unpatterned inequalities. [Lineberry, 1977:129]

For police responsiveness to calls for service, Lineberry found a pattern identical to the one reported in Houston. The San Antonio police assign response priorities to citizen calls and respond most quickly to the most serious offenses. For personnel allocations, Lineberry discovered an essentially equal distribution of patrol resources across neighborhoods. Again no evidence was found to suggest discrimination on the basis of race or income. The equity standards employed in San Antonio depended on the service. For libraries, demand was the criterion—branches with high circulation rates received more resources. For police response time, need as measured by the seriousness of the reported offense was the criterion. For police manpower, equality as equity was used.

The authors (Mladenka and Hill, 1977) studied parks and libraries in Houston, as well. For parks, we examined the relationship between the characteristics of neighborhoods in the city and indicators of park facilities such as number of playgrounds, athletic fields, and swimming pools. On the basis of our analysis we concluded that "parks located in upper-income neighborhoods do not have more facilities available to users. In addition, there is no evidence to indicate that residents of these areas receive more park acreage per capita" (Mladenka and Hill, 1977:78). Thus equality appeared to be the criterion of equity chosen by the Houston parks bureaucracy.

For libraries, we analyzed the relationship between neighborhood characteristics and measures of library service such as number of books and periodicals, number of professional staff, and budget expenditures. We found that the distribution of library resources heavily favored library branches located in upper-income neighborhoods. These branches were allocated more books, received larger budgets, and were assigned more and better qualified staff (as measured by degrees in library science). Wealthy areas get better libraries because branches in these neighborhoods are used more heavily. Middle- and upper-income citizens are much more likely than poor people to check out library books. In turn, the library bureaucracy distributes money, books, and staff personnel on the basis of circulation rates. Thus the library bureaucracy itself determined that *demands* for service would be the principal criterion for determining the level of service. The impact of this decision, of course, is to ensure that poorer areas of the city are less well served by libraries.

We also found that:

> Elected officials have little knowledge of and, consequently, exercise little control over the manner by which park and library resources are allocated. As a result, the largely invisible process by which the direct benefits of government are distributed within the city is dominated by the bureaucrats. For example, intervention in the distributional affairs of the parks bureaucracy is limited to an occasional inquiry from a city councilman in regard to a needed repair at a particular facility. No effort is made to systematically monitor those bureaucratic decisions whereby the division of available resources among neighborhoods is accomplished. [Mladenka and Hill, 1977:89]

CONCLUSION

Each standard of equity—equality, need, demand, preference, ability to pay—produces a different distributional pattern. Depending upon the standard, different groups and neighborhoods will win and different ones will lose. Bureaucrats determine how urban public services will be distributed. That is, it is the bureaucrats who determine which standard of equity will operate in each service area. It is the bureaucrats' monopoly over information, experience, and expertise that allows this to be so. Since elected officials are generally uninformed about the way in which services are distributed, bureaucrats are relatively free to distribute them as they choose.

The preceding review of service distribution in Texas cities reveals that municipal bureaucrats make decisions about who gets what according to technical and rational criteria. That is, they assign police personnel on the basis of crime rates and calls for service. Responsiveness to citizen requests for police assistance is determined by the seriousness of the reported incident. Street repair efforts depend on the level of citizen complaints (the squeaky wheel gets the grease), while library services are distributed on the basis of circulation rates. Each of these "decision rules" has different consequences for who gets what. The rules used to distribute street repair resources and library services benefit wealthier neighborhoods, for example, while the rule employed to assign police personnel ensures that more patrol officers will be allocated to poor neighborhoods.

Although local public services are vital to public health, safety, and well-being, the public typically has little idea how essential service resources are divided up in the community. Examination of the evidence about service distribution for Texas cities reveals that who gets what in the way of streets, parks, libraries, and police services is a complex issue that is strongly influenced by municipal bureaucrats.

Several factors determine *how much* in the way of public services citizens will receive. First, does the city even provide the service? Public officials must decide which services to deliver. Another factor is the *level* at which the service is funded. As we saw in an earlier chapter, some Texas cities spend much more per citizen and provide higher staffing levels than other cities. A third factor affecting how much service citizens receive is their choice as to whether they will *use* the service. The use of many services is completely discretionary—a person cannot be forced to use parks and libraries, for example. Still another factor influencing the level of service available is the element of *coproduction*. Citizens who carefully maintain their neighborhood parks and participate in programs to improve the public schools will enhance the recreational and educational services they receive. A final factor that has great significance for the service levels citizens receive is the vital issue of *distribution*. Each of the equity standards produces a different distributional pattern and thus ensures that some citizens will receive better service than others.

REFERENCES

Aberbach, J. D., and Walker, J. L. 1970. "The Attitudes of Blacks and Whites Toward City Services: Implications for Public Policy." In J. P. Crecine (ed.), *Financing the Metropolis*. Beverly Hills: Sage.

Allison, G. T. 1971. *Essence of Decision*. Boston: Little, Brown.

Antunes, G., and Plumlee, P. 1977. "The Distribution of an Urban Public Service." In R. L. Lineberry (ed.), *The Politics and Economics of Urban Services*. Beverly Hills: Sage.

Cyert, R. M., and March, J. G. 1963. *A Behavioral Theory of the Firm*. Englewood Cliffs, N.J.: Prentice-Hall.

Eisinger, P. K. 1972. "The Pattern of Citizen Contacts with Urban Officials." In H. Hahn (ed.), *People and Politics in Urban Society*. Beverly Hills: Sage.

Jones, B. D., and others. 1977. "Bureaucratic Response to Citizen Initiated Contacts: Environmental Enforcement in Detroit." *American Political Science Review* 7 (March): 148–165.

Jones, B. D., and others. 1978. "Service Delivery Rules and the Distribution of Local Government Services: Three Detroit Bureaucracies." *Journal of Politics* 40 (May): 332–368.

Levy, F. S., Meltsner, A. J., and Wildavsky, A. 1974. *Urban Outcomes*. Berkeley: University of California Press.

Lineberry, R. L. 1977. *Equality and Urban Policy*. Beverly Hills: Sage.

Lipsky, M. 1976. "Toward a Theory of Street Level Bureaucracy." In W. D. Hawley and M. Lipsky (eds.), *Theoretical Perspectives on Urban Politics*. Englewood Cliffs, N.J.: Prentice-Hall.

Mladenka, K. R. 1978. "Organizational Rules, Service Equality, and Distributional Decisions in Urban Politics." *Social Science Quarterly* 59 (June): 192–201.

Mladenka, K. R. 1980. "The Urban Bureaucracy and the Chicago Political Machine: Who Gets What and the Limits to Political Control." *American Political Science Review* 74 (December): 991–998.

Mladenka, K. R., and Hill, K. Q. 1977. "The Distribution of Benefits in an Urban Environment: Parks and Libraries in Houston." *Urban Affairs Quarterly* 13 (September): 73–94.

Mladenka, K. R., and Hill, K. Q. 1978. "The Distribution of Urban Police Services." *Journal of Politics* 40 (July): 112–133.

Nivola, P. S. 1978. "Distributing a Municipal Service: A Case Study of Housing Inspection." *Journal of Politics* 40 (February): 59–81.

Perrow, C. 1972. *Complex Organizations.* Glenview, Ill.: Scott, Foresman.

Simon, H.A. 1961. *Administrative Behavior.* New York: Macmillan.

Tietz, Michael B. 1967. "Toward a Theory of Urban Public Facility Location." *Papers of the Regional Science Association* 11 (Fall): 1–42.

Verba, S., and Nie, N. H. 1972. *Participation in America: Political Democracy and Social Equality.* New York: Harper & Row.

Wilson, J. Q. 1968. *Varieties of Police Behavior.* Cambridge, Mass.: Harvard University Press.

13

COUNTIES AND
SPECIAL DISTRICTS

The county form of government is hundreds of years old. It was trans-
ported from England by the colonists and has endured as an important
unit of government. Although it is strongest in rural areas, the county
is assuming major responsibilities in urban areas as well. Nevertheless, it has
significant limitations. Few observers have ever accused county government of
being responsive, efficient, or effective. Because counties cannot or will not
deal with many of the major issues and problems within their jurisdictions,
special districts have been created to fill the void. This chapter discusses both
types of government.

COUNTY GOVERNMENT: LEGAL RESPONSIBILITIES

In principle, the county is simply an administrative arm of the state that exists
to collect taxes and carry out state laws and policies. Counties also exercise
broad discretion, however. Although tax rate ceilings are set by the state,
counties enjoy considerable flexibility within these limits. They can impose
the maximum property tax rate or one that is substantially below the legal
ceiling. Moreover, they can spend a great deal of money or very little. They
can emphasize some programs and services and ignore others. Counties, therefore, are much more than simple administrative appendages of state
government.

In fact, the state does not pay much attention to its counties. It does not
insist upon uniform and standardized personnel or financial procedures. It
does not require a minimum level of services. It does not provide any financial
assistance. In short, the county in Texas is essentially an autonomous unit of
government. It is free to chart its own course within the broad limits established by the constitution and state laws.

CONSTITUTIONAL PROVISIONS

The state constitution does not provide the county with many significant powers. It does, however, carefully prescribe the structure and functions of the various governmental offices. Few departures from the system of offices as specified in the constitution are allowed. Counties, unlike cities in the state, do not have the option of home rule. The least heavily populated county has the same form of government as the largest county. This lack of flexibility with respect to structure reflects a governmental form that was adopted to serve the needs of a rural state. There has been no modification in response to rapid urbanization, and the constitution makes no provision for adaptation in response to changing conditions.

An amendment added to the state constitution in 1933 did provide for home rule. Because of its ambiguity, however, it could not provide a workable solution to the home-rule problem. The amendment was deleted from the constitution in 1969. Only three counties ever reached the stage of actually writing charters for home rule under the amendment, and only one proposed charter (in El Paso County) was presented to the voters for approval. It was defeated.

Nevertheless, home rule is not a dead issue. The growing complexity of government in urban areas increases the possibility that residents of urban counties will eventually demand that county governments be given the power to deal with metropolitan-wide problems. A single urban county in Texas may encompass millions of people and hundreds of separate units of government. Only the county has jurisdiction over the entire area. It is the logical choice, then, to assume responsibility for problems that do not respect municipal boundaries. Yet significant changes are required in both law and custom before county governments can play a larger role. Although the growing complexity of local government increases the possibility that such an expanded role may eventually come about, it certainly does not guarantee it.

One major barrier to change in the structure and powers of county government is a lack of flexibility. Counties require a specific grant of authority as provided in the constitution or state statute before they can undertake various programs. Although urban counties in Texas have significantly increased their responsibilities in recent years, this growth can be attributed to factors other than expanded powers. For example, county governments spend much more money on the criminal justice system than previously because of revenue-sharing funds and specific federal grants (such as the Law Enforcement Assistance Administration). Moreover, the federal courts have forced change. The new jail complex in Harris County (Houston) was built under a federal court order. It remains to be seen whether the cutback in federal funds will be compensated for by an increase in locally generated revenues. Most of the innovations in county government in recent years in areas such as law enforcement, the courts, corrections, and prosecution can be directly traced to federal funds and court orders.

OFFICES OF COUNTY GOVERNMENT

The Commissioners' Court

The commissioners' court is the closest thing county government has to a central policy-making body. The court consists of four commissioners (each elected from precincts of approximately equal population) and a county judge who serves as the presiding officer. Each commissioner has responsibility for the county road and bridge construction and maintenance program in his or her precinct. The commissioners' court performs the following functions and duties:

1. Sets the property tax rate within the limits established by the state
2. Sets service charges and fees
3. Approves the county budget
4. Appoints various officers
5. Fills vacancies in office
6. Lets contracts for supplies and equipment
7. Draws the boundaries for justice of the peace precincts
8. Decides which of the optional programs provided by the state will be adopted and funded
9. Submits to the voters proposals to levy certain special taxes as provided by law

The powers of the commissioners' court are significant but limited. One of its most significant powers is exerted through its control over the budget. It has a great deal to say about which services will be provided and at what level. Through its control over the property tax rate (within the limits established by the state constitution) and its power to set service charges and fees, it strongly influences the amount of revenues available to county government. Through its control over how much money will be spent for each service it also influences the level and quality of services.

The commissioners' court also exercises significant power when it decides upon various optional programs and facilities. It may, for example, choose to build an airport, county hospital, or network of park and recreational sites.

The court's powers are also limited, however. One major limitation concerns revenue generation. The only tax the county can levy is the property tax. Further, the rate at which the property tax can be assessed is fixed by the state. And while the court controls how much money is spent for various programs and purposes, it exerts much less control over how that money is spent. Elected officials decide how county funds will be spent in various areas. Since the court does not appoint department heads and direct their performance, its ability to influence *how* county dollars are actually spent is very limited.

Another limitation upon the power of the commissioners' court is that it has very few powers beyond those expressly granted by the state. An active county government would find it difficult to assume responsibilities beyond those specifically authorized by state government.

The power of the commissioners' court is also limited by a factor that has nothing to do with legal and constitutional restrictions. Instead, this limitation is self-imposed. Traditionally, county government has been concerned with providing as few services as possible. Limited responsibility, low taxes, low spending, and minimal service levels have long been the norm for county governments. Commissioners are more concerned with the road and bridge program in their precinct than with setting policy for the county as a whole. County officials have generally found little to complain about in a political system where responsibility is limited and power is fragmented. Such a system insulates public officials from the public's demands and significantly reduces the level of pressure under which most politicians must operate. For example, citizen demands for more and better government services can be dismissed with the response that the state constitution or laws do not allow them.

The County Judge

The county judge is elected by all the voters in the county and presides over the commissioners' court. The county judge's functions include the following:

1. Prepares the county budget

2. Has certain duties with respect to elections (posts notices and forwards election results to the state)

3. Serves as judge of the county court, where judicial responsibilities include probate jurisdiction

4. Issues licenses for the sale of wine and beer in counties that permit such sales

The county judge can, however, be either more or less influential than these specified powers would imply. For example, the county judge has few or no judicial responsibilities in counties where county courts-at-law have been provided to assume these judicial functions. This loss of judicial power has not diminished the county judge's work load, however. Instead, the judge's informal responsibilities have increased—particularly in counties that have experienced dramatic population growth. He or she is frequently the dominant political leader in the county, for example. Given the county judges' prominence in both the government and the politics of the county, they are often called upon to resolve disputes and respond to complaints about services and programs.

Although the county judges are the closest thing county government has to a chief executive, it should be emphasized that they are chief executives in name only. They cannot appoint the major department heads and they cannot remove them. They cannot control how county funds are spent in such major areas as law enforcement and roads. They certainly are not the chief executive of county government in the sense that a city manager in a reformed city and a mayor in an unreformed one are chief executives. The county judge coordinates rather than controls.

Other Elected Officials

The *sheriff* is the chief law enforcement officer in the county. He also operates the jails. In counties of fewer than 10,000 people, he also serves as tax assessor and collector.

A *justice of the peace* (JP) is elected from each precinct. (In Texas the county is divided into four to eight precincts.) The JP presides over a court that has jurisdiction over misdemeanors involving no confinement and over some civil issues. The JP also functions as county coroner except in large counties where the coroner is appointed by the commissioners' court.

A *constable* is elected from each JP precinct. The constable is a process server and serves writs and warrants, as well.

The *county clerk* provides clerical services for both the county court and the commissioners' court. The clerk maintains records pertaining to contracts, voting, deeds, marriages, and mortgages. In counties without an auditor, the clerk also maintains certain financial records.

An *assessor and collector of taxes* is elected in counties of 10,000 population and more. The chief function of this office is to assess and collect the county property tax. Other duties include the registration of voters and the sale of automobile license plates and certificates of title.

The *treasurer* has control over the receipt and payment of county funds as authorized by the commissioners' court. He or she also periodically examines the financial records of county offices.

The *county attorney* has different duties and functions, depending upon the county in which he or she is elected. In counties where there is no *district attorney*, the county attorney serves as a legal adviser and prosecutes criminal and civil cases in both the county and district courts. In counties where there is also a district attorney, the county attorney is simply prosecutor for the county and justice of the peace courts. The district attorney prosecutes cases in the district (state) courts.

Appointed Officials

There are also other county offices provided for by state law. A *county auditor* is required in counties of over 35,000 population or with taxable property valued at more than $15 million. Appointed by the district judge or judges in the county, the auditor inspects financial records and evaluates claims against the county.

A *health officer* is appointed by the commissioners' court to provide medical care to prisoners, to supervise general health services and facilities, and to undertake programs of disease prevention and control and sanitation.

Other appointed county officials include agricultural and home demonstration agents, a county engineer, and a county juvenile officer.

THE PROBLEMS WITH COUNTY GOVERNMENT

Unless otherwise noted, all the county officials noted above are elected by the voters. Consequently, executive authority is fragmented. Department heads are elected rather than appointed. There is essentially no centralized supervision of either personnel or finances. Individual offices and officials are free to chart their own course. Because of the large number of elected officials, all but the best-informed voters are probably ignorant of the various candidates' positions on the issues. The county does not have a chief executive with sufficient powers to implement policies and enforce compliance. He cannot supervise the various departmental programs. Instead county government is fragmented into several separate fiefdoms. Even individual programs reveal divided responsibility. The authority for the county road and bridge program, for example, is parceled out to four different commissioners. Although the county is the logical jurisdiction to assume responsibility for metropolitan-wide problems, it is unlikely that such a development will soon take place. Certainly such an expansion of authority would require changes in the constitution and state law. Because of tradition, apathy, and the power of entrenched interests, it will be exceedingly difficult to bring about such change.

COUNTY GROWTH PATTERNS

Table 13–1 lists the twenty fastest-growing counties in the country between 1980 and 1984 with at least 100,000 population. The table reveals that eight of the twenty were Texas counties. Fort Bend and Montgomery counties, both adjacent to Harris County (Houston), ranked first and second in terms of growth. Fort Bend led the nation with a population increase of 45.8 percent while Montgomery was second with 45.5 percent. In fact, Texas had four of the five fastest-growing counties in the country. Denton (Dallas–Fort Worth) and Collin (Dallas–Fort Worth) counties were fourth and fifth with growth rates of 35.9 percent and 32.3 percent respectively. Ector County (Odessa) was eleventh while Travis (Austin) was fifteenth. Harris (Houston) was seventeenth, and Nueces (Corpus Christi) was ranked eighteenth. No other state had as many counties as Texas ranked in the top twenty.

Twenty-one of the twenty-five counties with the greatest rates of growth are in the Sunbelt. The declining counties, on the other hand, are disproportionately clustered in the Northeast and Midwest. Ten of the twenty-five counties with the greatest population losses were located in Michigan, four were in Illinois, and three were in Pennsylvania. Twenty-four of the twenty-five counties with the greatest drops in population were in the so-called Frostbelt.

These growth patterns for counties in Texas support the argument that county government in the state will eventually be forced to assume greater responsibility. As the urban population spills from the central cities into the previously rural areas of surrounding counties, it will make demands upon the county for a variety of complex and expensive services. County government will have no choice but to respond eventually to these demands. Given what is

TABLE 13-1 Twenty Fastest-Growing
Counties in the Nation: 1980–1984

County	Growth Rate (%)
1. Fort Bend, Texas	45.8
2. Montgomery, Texas	45.5
3. Gwinnett, Georgia	36.7
4. Denton, Texas	35.9
5. Collin, Texas	32.3
6. Anchorage, Alaska	30.8
7. Arapahoe, Colorado	28.4
8. St. Tammany, Louisiana	26.9
9. Marion, Florida	25.2
10. Lee, Florida	23.3
11. Ector, Texas	22.5
12. Cleveland, Oklahoma	21.4
13. Palm Beach, Florida	20.8
14. Brevard, Florida	20.7
15. Travis, Texas	20.4
16. Pasco, Florida	19.7
17. Harris, Texas	19.7
18. Hidalgo, Texas	19.6
19. Seminole, Florida	19.5
20. Harry, South Carolina	19.4

Note: Only counties with at least 100,000 population are ranked here.

Source: Eagle, "Sun Belt Dominates List of 25 Fastest Growing Counties in U.S.," May 6, 1985.

known about government in the county, however, it can be expected that change will be resisted. Increases in the functions and expenditures of county government will occur gradually and grudgingly.

Not all national news about Texas counties has been good news. For example, counties in the state received some unfavorable publicity in January 1986, when a study conducted by Harvard University School of Public Health and the Physicians Task Force on Hunger in America found that the state has the largest number of "hungry" counties in the country with twenty-nine. Brazos County, the home of Texas A&M University, was rated as the hungriest county in Texas and the forty-sixth most hungry in the nation. "Hunger" counties were defined as those where more than one out of five residents live below the poverty line—defined as $10,609 for a family of four—and where less than one-third of those qualified to receive food stamps actually do so.

COUNTY REVENUES

To illustrate where urban counties in the state get their money, table 13–2 presents information on revenue sources for selected counties. The table reveals that property taxes are the single largest source of revenue. In only two counties (Tarrant and Lubbock) do property taxes account for *less* than half of total

TABLE 13–2   Sources of Revenue in Selected Urban Counties:
General Fund for Latest Year Available

County	Taxes (%)	Licenses and Fees (%)	Inter-govern-mental Revenue (%)	Fines (%)	Other (%)
Randall (Amarillo)	55.3	21.6	4.4	11.2	7.4
El Paso (El Paso)	67.9	14.8	3.5	2.4	11.3
Tarrant (Fort Worth)	45.3	22.0	14.6	2.7	15.0
Bexar (San Antonio)	50.4	15.6	10.8	8.4	14.9
Potter (Amarillo)	68.7	15.2	8.6	3.4	4.2
Nueces (Corpus Christi)	61.0	11.0	15.0	2.0	11.0
Travis (Austin)	66.4	19.3	5.5	3.0	5.9
Harris (Houston)	67.2	20.6	4.4	4.4	3.4
Lubbock (Lubbock)	42.7	7.9	17.5	7.7	24.2
Jones (Abilene)	50.0	0	7.6	0	42.3

Source: Data obtained by authors from county budgets.

revenues. In several counties (El Paso, Potter, Travis, Harris) the property tax generates two out of every three revenue dollars. The next single largest revenue source is the license and fees category. Aid from the federal and state governments is not very significant. In no county does this revenue source account for as much as 20 percent of total revenues, and in only three counties does it provide as much as 15 percent.

Urban counties, in particular, in Texas are heavily dependent upon the property tax to finance the operations of county government. They receive relatively little help from the federal or state governments.

COUNTY EXPENDITURES

What do metropolitan counties spend their money for? Table 13–3 presents information on the pattern of expenditures in several urban counties. Before we discuss the results, however, a word of caution is in order. It is very difficult to determine how budget dollars are allocated in Texas counties. A major part of the problem can be traced to the bewildering array of different budgets. Instead of a single budget that provides information on how much money is spent for various services and functions, some counties have a dozen different budgets.

For example, Nueces County (Corpus Christi) has the following budgets: General Fund, Farm-to-Market Roads and Flood Control Fund, Law Library Fund, Airport Fund, Park Operating Fund, Revenue-Sharing Fund, Park Revenue Bond Fund, Courthouse and Jail Debt Service Fund, Road Bonds Debt Service Fund, Navigation District Debt Service Fund, and Road District Debt Service Fund. When there are so many separate budgets for the same government, it becomes exceedingly difficult for the interested citizen to find out how much money is spent for different services and functions. If one wants

TABLE 13–3 Expenditures of Selected Urban Counties: Latest Year Available

County	Total Expenditure	General Administration (%)	Court System (%)	Sheriff and Jail (%)	Roads and Bridges (%)	Health and Welfare (%)	Education, Libraries, Recreation (%)	Debt Service (%)	Other (%)
Harris	$375,011,540	18.8	18.2	12.5	18.4	7.2	10.3	11.3	3.3
Bexar	$ 65,852,273	32.1	15.0	28.7	9.9	5.7	2.4	3.0	1.7
Travis	$ 59,023,183	21.0	15.7	18.9	29.9	9.5	1.3	3.7	0
Potter	$ 12,048,667	23.7	18.0	30.0	6.3	5.8	0	0	15.8
Lubbock	$ 11,242,693	23.3	20.0	27.5	7.6	3.1	5.3	0	13.3
Nueces	$ 33,288,873	34.6	17.9	10.0	21.5	5.7	3.2	4.5	2.4

Source: Data obtained by authors from county budgets.

to find out how much money is spent on road construction and repair, it is necessary to work through several different budgets in order to arrive at a reasonable estimate. Moreover, many counties lump different categories of expenditures together. Frequently the amount of money spent for courts, jails, sheriffs, and prosecution is combined and reported as one category.

Table 13–3 presents the expenditure patterns of selected urban counties. The table reveals that roads and bridges are not the dominant expenditure item. In fact, in only one county (Travis) do expenditures for county roads constitute the single largest expenditure category (30 percent). And in three counties (Bexar, Potter, Lubbock), county roads account for 10 percent or less of total expenditures. Although rural counties continue to spend a significant part of their budget on roads and bridges, other services and functions have come to dominate expenditure priorities in urban counties.

Law enforcement and the judicial processing and jailing of criminals appear to be the major functions of government in the urban counties studied. These governmental activities consume 48 percent of all expenditures in Lubbock and Potter counties, 44 percent in Bexar, and 35 percent in Travis.

Social welfare, educational, and recreational services do not receive much attention in county budgets. Welfare, health, education, recreation and parks, and library expenditures accounted for only 8.9 percent of the budget in Nueces County, 8.4 percent in Lubbock, 5.8 percent in Potter, 10.8 percent in Travis, and 8.1 percent in Bexar. The major expenditure categories for urban counties in Texas are courts, law enforcement, jails, and roads. Social welfare and so-called human services are essentially ignored.

Some of these urban counties also spend much more per citizen than others. Lubbock County spends only $53 per capita while Bexar spends $67. At the other extreme, Harris spends $156 per citizen and Travis spends $141. In what parts of the county is this money spent? These counties include both urban and rural areas. Could it be that county taxes are collected in the urban areas while the resulting revenues are disproportionately spent in the less densely populated part of the county? This may indeed be the case. One study interviewed a variety of local public officials and discovered that a frequent concern of city officials in Texas is the taxing and spending policies of their county governments (Tucker, 1983). Specifically, city officials felt that county governments raise most of their revenues from the cities within their boundaries but spend most of it in the rural parts of the county. The feeling exists that rural residents receive most of the benefits of the county road, bridge, and law enforcement programs, but city residents wind up paying a disproportionate share of the costs.

COUNTY VERSUS CITY EXPENDITURES

As expected, cities spend more per citizen than counties. Table 13–4 presents per capita expenditures for selected counties and for the major city in each county. In every instance, city expenditures are at least twice as high as county expenditures, and in some cases they are much higher. Both Lubbock (Lub-

TABLE 13–4 Per Capita Expenditures for Counties and Cities: 1982 and 1983

County	Expenditures	City	Expenditures
Harris	$156	Houston	$352
Bexar	$ 67	San Antonio	$290
Travis	$141	Austin	$376
Lubbock	$ 53	Lubbock	$219
Potter	$122	Amarillo	$246
Nueces	$124	Corpus Christi	$265

Source: Data obtained by authors from city and county budgets.

bock) and Bexar (San Antonio), for example, spend only 25 percent of the amount spent by their major cities per capita. Lubbock County spends $53 per citizen while the city of Lubbock spends $219. Bexar County spends only $67 while San Antonio spends $290.

At the same time neither level of government spends very much on health and welfare services. Cities emphasize police, fire, and streets in their budget priorities while counties emphasize law enforcement, jails, the courts, and prosecution of criminal suspects. No county spends as much as 10 percent of its budget on health and welfare (Travis allocates 9.5 percent of its budget for this purpose), while Lubbock County spends only 3 percent. Cities, too, spend very little for welfare services.

A CASE STUDY: LUBBOCK COUNTY

Counties in Texas have significantly increased their responsibilities during the past ten years. For example, Lubbock County spent $3,516,273 in 1971. In 1981, it spent $11,242,693, an increase of 320 percent. This amounts to an average annual budget increase of more than 30 percent. Note, too, how expenditure priorities have changed during the decade. In 1971, Lubbock County allocated 10 percent of its budget for the court system, 12 percent for law enforcement, 3.5 percent for jails, 9 percent for health and welfare, and 6 percent for libraries and parks. By 1981, these budget priorities had substantially changed. Although the courts continued to receive a constant percentage of budget resources (12 percent), law enforcement's share had increased from 12 percent to 21 percent and the jails' share grew from 3.5 percent to 20 percent. Some services did not fare as well. The health and welfare category declined from 9 percent of the budget in 1971 to only 3 percent in 1981, while parks and libraries dropped from 6 percent to 5 percent.

Law enforcement and the jails achieved the greatest growth during the decade. In 1971, they accounted for less than 16 percent of the total county budget. By 1981, they accounted for over 40 percent of general county expenditures. During the period 1971–1974, some $867,490 was spent on corrections. From 1978 to 1981, some $9,584,367 was spent for this function.

In terms of revenue sources, taxes were less important in 1981 than they were in 1972 in Lubbock County. In 1972, taxes generated 48 percent of revenues. By 1981 this share had declined to 43 percent. This drop in tax revenues was made up for by an increase in intergovernmental revenues (primarily revenue sharing). This category of revenues grew from 14 percent to 17.5 percent in 1981.

A CASE STUDY: HARRIS COUNTY

The significant growth in county responsibilities can also be illustrated by looking at changes in employee levels and work loads. In 1948, for example, Harris County had only one criminal court-at-law. By 1978 this number had increased to nine. These courts have jurisdiction over all misdemeanors involving confinement and fines of over $200 and appellate criminal jurisdiction over all cases from the justice of the peace and municipal courts. The county criminal courts had 5,831 cases on the docket in 1952. By 1970 there were more than 30,000 cases, and in 1978 there were 50,500 cases pending.

This tremendous growth in the court caseload was also reflected in related areas of county government operations. For example, in 1956 the district attorney's office employed 26 assistant district attorneys and had a total of 49 full-time employees. By 1978 there were 128 assistant district attorneys and a total of 222 full-time employees. The county jail employed 26 people in 1952. This number had grown to 130 by 1978.

SPECIAL DISTRICTS

Amazingly, there were at least 4,193 separate governments in Texas in 1982. This number included one state government, 254 counties, more than 1,100 cities, 1,125 school districts, and almost 1,700 special districts. The number of special districts more than doubled between 1962 and 1982—from 733 to 1,691.

Special districts are the "little" and "hidden" governments of the state. The most numerous type is the water district. Of the 1,691 special districts in the state in 1982, more than one-half (933) were water districts. There are several different categories of water districts. They include 427 municipal utility districts (MUDs), 282 water control and improvement districts (WCIDs), 62 drainage districts, 26 navigation districts, and 19 river authorities.

Water districts enjoy significant powers. The state constitution gives MUDs the authority to provide water and hydroelectric power, to conserve natural resources, to combat water pollution, to provide park and recreational facilities, to dispose of sewage, and to collect solid waste. Water control and improvement districts have similar powers. If created according to one article of the constitution, WCIDs have all the powers of MUDs with the exception of the authority to provide park and recreation facilities. If established under still another article, WCIDs can undertake flood control, irrigation, navigation, and drainage programs.

Water districts perform several governmental functions. Other types of special districts tend to limit their activities to a single function. These additional categories of special districts include housing and redevelopment authorities (398), soil conservation districts (209), and hospital districts (123).

Reasons for the Growth of Special Districts

The proliferation of special districts in Texas did not occur by chance. The rapid spread of these governments can be traced to several factors. First is the inability of existing governments to deal with problems. As indicated in earlier chapters, municipal and county governments do not have sufficient powers to deal with many problems. Frequently these problems do not stop at jurisdictional boundaries. Flooding and an inadequate supply of fresh water, for example, are major problems that generally extend across several jurisdictions within a county or metropolitan area. Yet no single government has either the authority or the resources to deal with the problem. Special districts provide a way whereby the fragmented power that characterizes local government in Texas can be overcome. They permit government to try and deal with issues that are area-wide in nature and extend across several jurisdictions.

Another reason for the spread of special districts is the unwillingness of existing governments to deal with problems. Traditionally, local government in Texas has been very limited government. Local public officials emphasize minimum service levels and low taxes. They seldom champion an aggressive expansion of government spending and programs. Generally, local government does as little as possible. This attitude toward the appropriate scope of government is deeply rooted in the political culture of the state. This emphasis upon a narrow role for government collides head-on, however, with another fact of political life: Texas is no longer a rural state where very limited government will suffice. The demands of dramatic population growth and rapid urbanization require that government undertake certain programs and activities. Drainage, flood control, water, and health care have to be provided. The special district provides a mechanism whereby government services can be delivered without existing governments assuming responsibility for them. Thus the myth of limited government can be preserved. Moreover, public officials are insulated from citizen complaints about inadequate performance. The most effective way for a local government official to deal with outraged citizens is simply to maintain that the problem is the responsibility of another jurisdiction.

The unwillingness of existing governments to cooperate with respect to area-wide problems is yet another reason for the proliferation of special districts. Although cooperation alone would not solve common problems, it would provide a partial solution. Much could be done to address jointly the problems that are now frequently handled by special districts. Instead, individual municipalities and counties show little interest in cooperation. They jealously guard their separateness and appear to be little concerned with working together to solve common problems. In the absence of cooperation, the special district is necessary if action is to be taken with respect to solutions.

Taxing and debt ceilings favor the spread of special districts, as well. Cities and counties are restricted in terms of how much revenue they can generate. State law limits the rate at which the property tax can be assessed. When tax and debt constraints prohibit an existing government from undertaking a new service, the special district provides a convenient alternative. One simply creates a new unit of government to deliver the service. The new government generates the necessary revenue through the assessment of taxes or the sale of bonds.

Certainly there are few barriers to the creation of special districts. Special district governments are relatively easy to establish. As a result, they are more likely to be created to deal with service problems than if the creation process were intricate and scrutinized carefully by various agencies and groups.

Moreover, special districts offer certain advantages to builders and developers. Thus municipal utility districts (MUDs) have been exploited by some residential builders. Since new developments require a variety of services, the MUD has been used to provide them and shift the cost burden to those who eventually buy homes in the subdivision. The MUD has the power to tax and raise revenue. The developers use these revenues to construct essential service facilities. The new homeowners are generally unaware that their purchase of a home in the MUD makes them responsible for retiring the debt incurred. Hundreds of these MUDs have been created in the Houston area alone to finance the service infrastructure in new housing developments. Many more would be in operation if it were not for the fact that they have been annexed by various cities. When a city annexes a MUD, it assumes responsibility for all debt incurred as well as for provision of services.

And, finally, special districts are sometimes used to obtain federal aid. For example, soil conservation districts and public housing authorities cannot levy taxes. (Housing authorities can, however, sell revenue bonds.) Thus they rely heavily upon federal dollars to fund their operations. By the creation of such districts an area can take advantage of federal aid without involving an existing government in a controversial program.

Problems with Special Districts

The criticisms of special district government are numerous. They include the following arguments.

First, special districts are subject to little or no supervision by the state. Consequently, administrative, personnel, and financial practices are inefficient if not primitive.

Second, special district government is neither responsive nor accountable. Public knowledge of these governments is essentially nonexistent. They are shielded from public scrutiny. There are so many of them and their functions are so narrow and technical that they are effectively removed from citizen control. They are antidemocratic.

Third, they compound local problems rather than solve them. Special district government is a stopgap effort. Special districts will never be able to deal adequately with the issues of water supply, flooding, and housing. Instead they simply delay cooperative action by city and county governments. Special districts prevent effective, long-term solutions such as city–county consolidation or a significant expansion of the powers and functions of county government. There is little incentive for local government to change its approach to area-wide problems so long as the special district remains a stopgap option.

Fourth, special districts impose yet another layer of government on local areas that already may have dozens and even hundreds of governments. This increased complexity not only contributes to confusion in government but is actually inefficient. Special district government is small government. It cannot take advantage of economies of scale. It also duplicates certain functions already being performed.

For all the criticisms of special districts, it is unlikely that these governments will diminish in number or significance in the near future. They are symptomatic of an unfulfilled need in local government. That need is for a unit of government with sufficient powers to deal with the problems that counties or cities cannot or will not confront. That the special district has been less than effective in filling that void suggests that fundamental change is required.

School Districts

One very important type of special district in Texas is the school district. There are more than 1,100 school districts in the state. The governing body of the district is the school board or board of trustees whose members are elected by the voters of the district on nonpartisan ballots to three-year terms. The school board performs a variety of important duties. It appoints a superintendent, controls the hiring of teachers, selects textbooks from approved state lists, sets the property tax rate in the district, approves the budget, controls the construction of buildings, and establishes broad policy for the conduct, operation, and administration of the school system.

However, school districts share responsibility for public education with the state government. The State Board of Education sets general educational policy and the Texas Education Agency (TEA) implements that policy in the state's elementary and secondary schools. Financing of public education is provided by the Permanent School Fund, which derives its revenues from the sale and leasing of state lands. Other revenues come from taxes on the production of natural resources. These funds are used to buy textbooks, finance the state's share of salaries for public school teachers, and pay for maintenance and transportation.

CONCLUSION

It is easy to be critical of county government. Executive authority is fragmented among several elected officials and there is little centralized supervision of personnel or financial administration. No executive official has sufficient powers to control the various departments and offices of county government or to ensure program accountability. County government is fragmented into several separate fiefdoms. As a result, responsibility is divided. The large number of elected officials makes it exceedingly difficult for most voters to stay informed about the programs and policies of the various county offices or to be knowledgeable about the various political candidates' positions on the issues.

Traditionally, county government in the state has been limited. Moreover, it is opposed to assuming new and expanded responsibilities. In part, this conservatism with respect to the role of government can be attributed to the state constitution and state law. Although counties enjoy some discretion (with respect to tax rates and which programs they will adopt), a broad expansion of power and responsibility would require a specific grant of authority from the state.

It is likely, however, that the role of county government in urban areas of the state will continue to grow. A greatly expanded county population will inevitably demand more streets, more parks and recreational facilities, and better law enforcement. Given the natural conservatism of county government, these changes will come slowly.

REFERENCES

Katz, Harvey. 1972. *Shadow on the Alamo*. Garden City, N.Y.: Doubleday.

Norwood, Robert E. 1970. *Texas County Government*. Austin: Texas Research League.

Pettus, Beryl P. 1974. "Metropolitan Area Multi-Purpose District Government in Texas." *Municipal Matrix* 6 (December).

Texas Observer. 1972a. "See MUD Run: A Primer." September 22, pp. 7–8.

Texas Observer. 1972b. "More on MUD." October 6, pp. 10–11.

Tucker, Harvey. 1983. *An Assessment of Needs and Legislative Priorities of Texas Metropolitan Governments*. College Station: Texas A&M University.

TAXATION AND SPENDING

T his is the first of two chapters in which we will examine the products of the governmental system of Texas—in other words, the public policies adopted by the state government and its local subdivisions. Such matters have been discussed at several earlier points; yet these two chapters present a more comprehensive treatment and draw together a number of themes and conclusions from prior discussions in the book.

This chapter begins with a description of the structure of taxation and public spending in Texas—that is, the *kinds* of tax instruments and the *kinds* of spending priorities. Next, the *level* of taxation and the *distribution* of public spending across different policy priorities will be considered. Thus you will learn where the state puts its emphasis in allocating both the burdens and benefits of its policies. An important component, as well, will be comparisons with other states in the United States. It will then be possible to offer some conclusions about the policy goals implicit in the state's taxing and spending systems *and* about the social effects of those systems based on who bears the burdens and benefits.

In earlier chapters we examined city and county government spending separately, but in the present chapter we will analyze combined state and local taxation and spending information. This approach is necessary to summarize the overall character of the state's governmental priorities. It is also necessary if we wish our comparisons with other states to be fair—since the states differ to some degree in the ways they divide responsibilities between the central state government and their local governmental units.

THE LEVEL OF STATE AND LOCAL TAXES

The first question that probably occurs to the average citizen when the broad topic of taxes is raised is: Just how high are my taxes? In average terms at least, one can simply divide the total amount of tax revenues raised in a given year by the population of the state in the same year. While each citizen did not literally pay this average amount of taxes, the method provides a general indication of the tax level and is fair for making state-by-state comparisons.

An unusual feature of the tax system of Texas and a few other states, however, means that we might actually prefer for some purposes a second comparison figure rather than the one based on the total amount of tax revenues. Texas receives a notable portion of its tax revenues from *severance* taxes on the value of crude oil and other natural resources when they are initially extracted from the ground. Since severance taxes are ultimately passed on to consumers of such derivative products as gasoline and natural gas, Texans themselves do not bear the whole burden of such taxes. A large portion of these taxes is passed on to the residents of other states who purchase these derivative products.

To account for severance taxes, one can calculate a second per capita tax level that simply excludes this revenue source. This second figure will be called, somewhat crudely, the level of "pocketbook" taxes because it reflects more accurately the state and local taxes that fall on the individual citizens of the state. While Texans do pay a portion of severance taxes when they purchase petroleum and natural gas products, it is impossible to say exactly what that portion is. In 1985 total state and local government taxes in Texas were $1,267 per capita compared to the fifty-state average of $1,465. Our per capita pocketbook tax load, however, was only $1,131 compared to a national average of $1,435.

The conclusion from these figures should be obvious: Texas is surely a low-tax state.[1] Other research has indicated that relatively low taxes have been a traditional feature of twentieth-century Texas government (Anderson and McMillan, 1953:63–70; Penniman, 1965:313–315). Every Texan has reason to be pleased by this circumstance. Who, one might ask, would wish to pay more taxes than he or she already does?

SOURCES OF TAX REVENUES

Just as it is important to examine the level of taxes, it is essential to consider from what sources they are derived. There are several tax instruments the states may use to distribute the total tax load, and these different instruments do not themselves fall equally on all citizens. Thus the selection of tax instruments can have a substantial impact on which individuals or groups bear relatively high or low tax burdens.

The Major Tax Instruments

The most important tax instruments are the property tax, general sales tax, selective sales tax, income tax, corporation income tax, licensing fees, and severance tax.

Property Tax   The ad valorem property tax—assessed as a percentage of the assessed market value of certain property—has been the traditional mainstay of state and local government revenues. Typically it is collected on the value of land, residences, and commercial and industrial plants and equipment. Perhaps the greatest advantage of this tax is that such items are both highly visible and not easily movable. The administration of the tax is facilitated in some respects by these attributes, just as tax avoidance is made less of a problem.

The property tax does, however, suffer from some major problems—principally that of maintaining equitable tax rates for all the items of property in the taxing jurisdiction. The fair market value of some items of property may be quite difficult to assess, the value of others may be subject to considerable disagreement, and the values of all the items on the tax rolls may be changing at differing rates and even in different directions. In consequence, fair and equitable assessment is a difficult and often controversial task. Some of these same difficulties in Texas led to the creation in 1982 of single, countywide tax appraisal districts whose job is to maintain the property tax roll for the entire county. The property valuations on the roll are then to be used by all the separate taxing entities in the county. While this system has made the valuation process more efficient and uniform, it has also made it more conspicuous and politically controversial in many counties.

In Texas the property tax is employed principally by cities, counties, and school districts. Each jurisdiction sets its own rate and then applies it to the values of items of taxable property that have been determined by the countywide appraisal district.

General Sales Tax   General or retail sales taxes are employed in forty-six of the fifty states to tax consumption spending. These taxes are relatively inexpensive to administer, since private commercial establishments do the initial collecting of the tax at the point of sale. The sales tax is widely criticized, however, because it is particularly *regressive* with respect to income. That is, it typically extracts a higher percentage of total income from low- rather than high-income earners. Thus it runs counter to the ability-to-pay philosophy of *progressive* taxation (where high-income earners pay the higher percentage of income in taxes) that underlies much of American taxation. Retail sales taxes can be made less regressive by the exclusion of mass consumption items such as food, but even then the tax remains regressive.

The state government levies a 5.65 percent sales tax on retail sales and some services with the exclusion of food, prescription medicine, and farm equipment and supplies. Many cities and local governments can add an additional 1 percent tax to this base rate. The total tax is collected by retail sales establishments and remitted to the state. The state then returns to each local entity (which has the 1 percent additional tax) its proportionate share of the total revenue raised within its borders.

Selective Sales Taxes   These taxes are imposed on the sale of certain goods— for example, Texas, like most states, has selective sales taxes on liquor and cigarettes. Some have referred to these as "sin" taxes on the consumption of harmful goods; yet the tax level on such products is typically set for its revenue-generating potential and not as a significant barrier to reduce the consumption of such items. All the states impose a sales tax on gasoline but with a different rationale. The proceeds of the gasoline tax are often dedicated to highway construction and maintenance with the rationale that it is the users of highway services who are paying the tax.

Individual Income Tax   Most states have a progressive individual income tax with rates in the range of 2 to 10 percent applied to an adjusted income figure taken from the individual's federal income tax calculations. These taxes are typically quite progressive with respect to income—meaning, once again, that high-income earners pay a higher percentage of their income to this tax. Progressive income taxes are held in high technical repute by most scholarly students of taxation for this feature and several others. As Musgrave and Musgrave (1980:392) observe:

> The income tax has the great advantage of relating tax liability to a comprehensive measure of ability to pay and of permitting adaptation to the personal circumstances of the taxpayer [by means of exclusions, exemptions, and similar devices]. Among existing taxes, it is the personal tax par excellence, and, at its best, it is superior to all other taxes . . . in implementing horizontal and vertical equity.

Texas is one of only seven states that do not have the individual income tax.

Corporation Income Tax   Most states also impose a tax on the net income of corporations to generate at least a modest amount of revenue. Once again, the rates are typically set at low levels. Moreover, states exercise considerable caution so that their corporate tax rate will not be far higher than that of most other states (and thus drive businesses to lower-tax states). Texas is one of only four states that have no corporation income tax.

Licensing Fees   This is a catchall category including licensing fees required of various businesses as a condition of doing business in the state, similar fees required of some professionals as a condition of practicing in the state, automobile licensing fees, fees for taking state professional licensing examinations, hunting and fishing license fees, and so on. Texas, like all states, employs a variety of these fees in an effort to tax directly certain activities or the beneficiaries of certain privileges or users of state services or resources.

Severance Tax   Severance taxes are duties imposed on the value of certain natural resources when they are extracted from the ground. Such taxes are motivated by the idea that these resources are exhaustible physical assets of the state. Thus those who extract those resources for business purposes should recompense the state to some degree for the loss of such assets. There are only a few states in the nation that draw a notable portion of their tax revenues from this source. Texas imposes severance taxes on petroleum, natural gas, and sulfur. The bulk of severance revenues comes from the first two of these products.

The Texas Tax System Compared

To indicate the overall character of the Texas tax system, table 14–1 presents a breakdown of the proportion of total state and local taxes derived from each of these sources in Texas and in the average state. Several comparisons based on that table are striking. First, there is the heavy dependence in Texas on sales taxes. Texas draws 43 percent of its total indigenous revenues from such taxes (the general and selective sales taxes combined), while the average across all the states is only 36 percent. This fact alone means that the Texas system depends unusually heavily on regressive tax instruments.

Second, and equally important for its effect on who pays the bulk of taxes, is the absence of income taxes in the Texas system. This means that the Texas tax system does not have any revenue source that is clearly progressive in its impact and that, hence, is based on the ability-to-pay criterion that stands behind progressive taxation. Thus where the average state draws a quarter of its total income from this kind of taxation, Texas takes none.

The final noteworthy point is the high reliance of this state on severance taxes. Many states derive no income at all from this source—simply because they do not have the appropriate natural resources. Yet Texas has abundant supplies of such resources. The availability of the severance tax income is certainly one reason why the overall level of taxes paid directly by the average Texan has been low. Texans are fortunate that they have been able to pass along to the residents of other states a relatively high proportion of their tax bill.

Yet, as the state legislature learned rather painfully beginning in 1983, there is an unfortunate side to this situation. Revenue from this source is itself highly dependent on the health of the petroleum and natural gas industries. When the market prices of these commodities fall—as they did over the period 1981–1985—then the tax revenues fall, too. And more than just the severance tax declines when the petroleum industry is in recession. If one combines all

**TABLE 14–1   Sources of State and Local Tax
Revenues: 1981–1982**

Source of Revenue	Texas (%)	Average Among All States (%)★
Property tax	37	30
General sales tax	25	24
Selective sales taxes	18	12
Individual income tax	—	20
Corporation income tax	—	5
Licensing fees	8	4
Severance taxes	10	2
Other	2	3

Note: Federal aid is excluded.   ★Rounded figures.

Source: Governmental Finances in 1984–85 (1986).

the state and local tax revenues that arise from the activities of the oil and gas industries—the severance taxes, sales taxes on the purchases made by these industries, property taxes on their holdings, and various business taxes they pay—these items would constitute a considerable portion of total tax revenues. For the state government alone, it was estimated by the State Comptroller's Office in 1985 that 28 percent of state tax revenues come from the oil and gas industries (Fletcher, 1985).

When the oil industry is booming and oil and gas prices are rising, the state government reaps a significant share of the benefits. Yet in periods of relative bust, state revenues drop precipitously and the government is forced to consider drastic spending cuts and new taxes. Since the state comptroller, along with most petroleum industry analysts, originally forecast oil prices through the 1980s that were far higher than have been realized—as figure 14–1 indicates—we are currently in one of those periods of bust. (Recall that oil prices fell as low as $10–$12 a barrel in 1986 and have not risen above $20 a barrel since.) Thus Texas appears to be in for a long period of fiscal retrenchment. While better long-range planning and a diversification of the tax structure have often been suggested to alleviate this roller-coaster tie to the oil and gas industries, the state legislature has so far been unwilling to contemplate such ideas seriously.

THE LEVEL OF STATE AND LOCAL SPENDING

If Texas is a relatively low-tax state, it inevitably must be a low-spending state. The state government itself is restricted by the constitution to a balanced

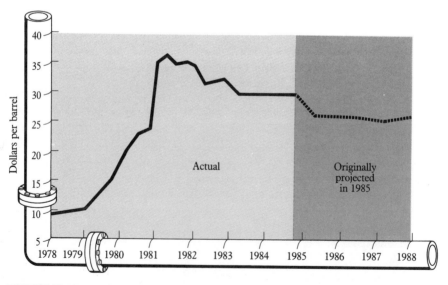

FIGURE 14–1   The Market Price of Texas Oil: 1978–1988.

Source: Comptroller of Public Accounts (1985:4)

budget policy, and local government units are similarly restricted by the state (except for money they are allowed to raise through the sale of bonds as described in chapter 10).

More interesting than the overall level of spending, however, are the distribution of spending across policy areas and the level of spending within each area. Relevant to the first point, table 14–2 presents the percentage distribution of state and local spending across major functional categories—once again comparing Texas to the average state. In these figures Texas does not appear extraordinarily different from the average state. Education and transportation take somewhat larger shares of the total Texas budget, while public welfare gets a notably smaller share. For none of the other categories, however, is there a remarkable difference between Texas and the average for all the states.

The preceding figures only describe how the whole budget pie, so to speak, is divided up. They do not take account of the size of the pie at the same time. To do so, we can compare the actual level of spending or service provided Texans in different policy areas. Such comparisons also indicate some of the relative priorities of Texas government. They begin to address, as well, a second question that a sophisticated citizen might have in mind after the first one of how high his or her taxes are. The second question, of course, would be: What do I get in return for the taxes I pay?

Again we must emphasize that one cannot infer the quality of public service simply from the dollar amount of state spending in a certain category. At the same time, the level of spending is obviously quite closely related to the *possible* level of actual service. Low spending puts significant constraints on the potential quality of public services, while high spending makes high-quality service at least possible. Keeping that caveat in mind, there are several different kinds of spending comparisons that might help us assess relative state priorities and services. For some policy areas we can fairly compare the level of spending by government relative to the size of the state's population. Such per capita

TABLE 14–2 **Distribution of State and Local Expenditures by Function: 1984–1985**

Service	Texas (%)	Average Among All States (%)
Higher education	13	9
Elementary and secondary education	30	25
Public welfare and social services	8	15
Hospitals and health	10	8
Transportation[a]	9	9
Public safety[b]	9	9
Environment and recreation	7	7
Government administration	4	5
Interest on debt	7	6
Other	3	6

[a]Principally highways.   [b]Principally police, fire, and corrections.
Source: Governmental Finances in 1984–85 (1986).

spending data are appropriate when the entire population is at least the theoretical "client" group that might use the public services under consideration. Police protection, for example, is extended in principle to all citizens equally. Hence per capita spending on police service—when compared across the states—is a fair estimate of the relative levels of service provided by the different states.

Table 14–3 presents per capita spending figures for several services for which the entire population might be thought of as the client population. There is a consistent pattern across all these areas: Texas state and local governments spend less or even far less than the average state. You should keep in mind, as well, that this comparison is with the *average* state, not with the most generous and high-spending ones. Public spending levels in Texas would, of course, fall considerably farther below those of the most generous states in these terms. Thus we can conclude that, for the policy areas in table 14–3, it is very unlikely that Texans get public services any better than those provided by the average state—and they might well get services of considerably below-average quality. In other words, Texans get what they pay for. Their taxes are low, but in return they are provided with low levels of public service.

There are also policy areas in which the clients can more appropriately be defined as only a portion of the entire population. In education, for example, the client population consists of students in public schools; in public welfare it is the poor of the state served by government welfare programs. In policy areas like these, strictly per capita comparisons do not make as much sense as they do for the areas considered previously. Instead, we should compare spending per actual student or welfare recipient.

Table 14–4 presents comparative public expenditure data for some specific client populations. The first two comparisons are for what we might call "high-status" clients: students in public schools and colleges. Education, in other words, has traditionally been considered a high-priority service in all states, and many Texans would surely share that concern for the importance of public education and its clients. Evidence for that concern might be inferred from the fact that Texas state and local governments together spend over 40 percent of their budgets on education—as table 14–2 indicated. The latter figure is con-

TABLE 14–3   Per Capita State and Local Government Spending on Selected Services: 1985–1986

Service	Texas $	Average Among All States $
Libraries	$ 9	$ 12
Hospitals	153	158
Police protection	76	94
Fire protection	34	40
Parks and recreation	35	42
Government administration	104	132

Source: Governmental Finances in 1985–86 (1987: 100–101).

TABLE 14–4   **State and Local Government Spending Per Client on Selected Services**

Service	Texas	Average Spending Among All 50 States
Elementary and Secondary Education		
Direct public spending per pupil: 1984–85[a]	$3,158	$3,360
Higher Education		
Current-fund expenditures of public institutions per full-time-equivalent student: 1980–81[b]	6,290	6,500
Public Welfare		
Average monthly payment per qualifying recipient under the Aid to Families with Dependent Children program: April–June 1985[c]	52	119
Corrections		
State and local government general expenditures on corrections per adult under correctional supervision: 1984[d]	2,050	4,817

Sources: [a]*Finances of Public School Systems* (1984–85: ix).
[b]*Book of the States, 1984–85* (1984:363) and Grant and Snyder (1983:146).
[c]*Quarterly Public Assistance Statistics, April–June 1985* (1986).
[d]*Governmental Finances in 1984–85* (1986:29) and *Statistical Abstract of the United States, 1987* (1986).

siderably larger than that spent by the average state. Yet when we consider how much is spent *per education client*, as shown in table 14–4, Texas falls below the average spending level among the states. (Education in Texas merely gets a larger slice of a much smaller pie.)

Many college students in Texas surely recall the controversy in 1985 over whether tuition fees would be raised substantially—which they were—and might find the figures in table 14–4 puzzling at first glance. Was not part of the controversy, a student might ask, over whether the state was spending *too much* instead of too little in supporting college students? Yet that controversy was actually over the *portion* of the cost of their education borne by college students directly by their tuition fees. The fees were raised so that students would bear a larger proportion of the total cost, but that total cost was itself below the average among all the states. The astute student may recall, as well, that college and university budgets were cut at the same time. After those cuts, state spending per student fell farther below the average among the states. Thus, some might conclude, college students were "paying more but getting less" after the 1985 tuition and budget changes.

Table 14–4 also presents information on services provided to what one could call "low-status clients": the poor and those incarcerated in the state's prisons. The welfare program included under "public welfare" is one initiated by the federal government but implemented by the states. The states are allowed to determine their monthly support payments to qualified recipients. Not only was the monthly payment in Texas strikingly below the average in 1985, it was the fourth lowest in the nation.[2]

The comparison figure for corrections spending indicates, as well, that Texas fell well below the national average. While most Texans would probably say they did not want the state to be generous with convicted felons, table 14–4 might help them understand why in 1981 the federal courts found that Texas prisons were outdated, overcrowded, and often allowed abusive or inhumane treatment of prisoners because of these conditions and the limited staff. The outcome of the trial that led to these findings was a federal mandate that the state significantly upgrade its prison facilities. In other words, the state was required by the federal government to spend more to improve the quality of its prison system.

FEDERAL AID IN TEXAS

To this point we have only considered the money raised in Texas by indigenous taxes—that is, taxes of the state and local governments alone. Yet Texas governments, like those of all states, derive a notable portion of their total revenues from federal aid. Previous chapters on local governments in Texas have pointed out how important that aid has been to urban development in the state. Most federal aid is restricted in the sense that it must be spent on certain programs and under specific federal guidelines. What is most important about such aid for the present chapter, however, is that it raises public services above the levels the states themselves can afford. Thus a low-spending state like Texas could, theoretically, provide public services far better than its indigenous tax levels might suggest by the use of supplementary federal funds.[3] Moreover, Texans would presumably desire that their state and local governments get their fair share of federal aid, since individual Texans pay for such aid through their federal tax payments. One might then wish to know how Texas fares in getting its share of such aid.

Table 14–5 provides informative data on this question. It shows that, first, Texas governments derive a low percentage of their total revenues from federal aid. The right-hand side of the table provides information on an even better

TABLE 14–5   Federal Aid for State and Local Governments in Texas: 1985

	Federal Aid as Percentage of State and Local Government Revenues	Federal Aid to State and Local Governments Per State Resident
Texas	12.1%	$330
Average for all states	14.4%	$469

Source: Governmental Finances in 1985–86 (1987).

way of looking at the level of federal aid—the amount received by each state on a per capita basis. And Texas ranked 48th among the states in per capita federal aid received.

Federal aid is not intended to be distributed among the states on a strict per capita basis, of course; different federal programs have different eligibility criteria and distribution formulas. The variety and complexity of these formulas make it difficult to predict what each state "should" receive or what might be its "fair share" of such aid. Yet many federal support programs are intended to alleviate the problems of urban areas—and in chapter 2 we pointed out how highly urbanized Texas has become in recent times. A number of other federal programs are intended to improve the social and economic circumstances of the poor—and we have noted that there are many poor Texans. Some programs also use the total population as one factor in determining the aid a state or local government agency will receive—and we have seen that Texas is one of the largest states by population today. With these attributes apparently in Texas's favor, one might be especially puzzled by the low level of federal assistance enjoyed by this state.

Research on the distribution of federal aid among the states cannot offer a single explanation to this puzzle, precisely because the allocation formulas for the myriad of different federal programs differ so much among themselves. Yet the research clearly indicates three explanations, all of which are important to some degree. First, some state and local government officials are simply not as sophisticated as others in securing federal aid (Stein, 1981). The "grantsmanship" process is highly complex and requires an investment of time, resources, and intellect that many public officials do not have or are not willing to commit. Earlier we discussed the relatively low professionalism of many public officials in Texas. Thus one must suspect that lack of expertise is an important reason for the meager aid received by this state.

Second, research has also indicated that some state and local officials do not *want* to participate in all the available aid programs. Some do not want to accept the federal strings attached to their use of such aid. Some do not judge the aid provided by some federal programs to be worth either the effort of getting it or the costs of submitting to at least some federal controls in the process. One might suspect that the traditionalistic and individualistic political cultures still influence the way in which these officials judge the relative costs and benefits of such aid. Since these two political cultures were argued to be of considerable influence in Texas today (see chapter 3), this factor should also be an important one in explaining the state's low federal assistance level.

Two recent examples illustrate some of the ways low professionalism and disinterest in federal funds have hurt Texas. In 1986 the city of Houston lost almost $3 million in federal community development aid it had previously been granted because the city was not spending the money fast enough. The city even received a warning from the U.S. Department of Housing and Urban Development in 1987 that it was, once again, behind in its spending and could lose more of these funds. In light of the fact that most citizens associate bureaucratic inefficiency with spending money too rapidly and foolishly, this appears a remarkable and distinctive case of low professionalism.

An instance of disinterest in federal aid comes from the city of Bryan. The City Council there chose not even to apply for federal housing renovation aid when it initially became available in the 1960s. As late as 1987 Bryan was still turning down federal housing aid it could have had simply by asking (Skove, 1987). Yet a housing survey by the city administration that same year indicated that the bulk of the houses in one-third of the city's area were substandard or dilapidated and, hence, appropriate targets for federal housing aid.

Finally, some federal aid programs, especially the revenue-sharing program, employ a distribution formula that takes account of the indigenous tax level already used by the state and local government. In other words, the formula assumes that states which have already imposed high tax burdens on their citizens need more federal assistance. Such states, it would be argued further, are already using their own tax resources to a relatively great degree. Obviously since Texas was shown to be a low-tax state earlier in this chapter, it is disadvantaged under such aid distribution formulas.

Taken together, these three explanations suggest why the state of Texas does not fare well in competing for federal aid. It is the relatively parochial and insufficiently professional character of much of Texas government, its political culture which values independence over outside aid, and its low indigenous tax level that explain why Texans benefit from relatively little return of their federal tax dollars.

Finally, it is worth noting some recent trends in federal aid to the states and their implications for Texas. Beginning in 1978 such aid began to level off, and sharp reductions were enacted under the Reagan administration because of its efforts to reduce the federal deficit. Of particular note for Texas, however, is the fact that considerable portions of these aid cuts were for social service programs and those meant to address the special problems of big cities: social service programs, welfare programs, and health and education programs to name but a few examples (Fossett, 1984:156). Earlier in this chapter we suggested that many of these policy areas have traditionally been ones where state and local spending and services in Texas were especially low. Thus recent reductions in federal aid have come in areas where service levels were already low in this state and to which, one must assume, state political leaders have not assigned very high priority. If the priorities accorded such policy areas by local political leaders do not rise in the near future, then—because of the reductions in federal aid—Texans can anticipate even lower levels of such services in comparison to those provided in other states.

DISTRIBUTION OF BENEFITS AND BURDENS

To this point we have examined public spending and taxing separately. Our survey has dealt only generally with the distribution of benefits and burdens arising from the Texas system. Yet several pieces of evidence have already suggested some conclusions about that issue. The relatively high reliance on regressive taxation, the virtual absence of progressive tax instruments, and the low levels of public assistance to the poor in Texas all point to a common pattern of benefits and burdens.

It is possible, however, to assess the distribution of public sector benefits and burdens more precisely. One part of such an assessment should be based on the incidence of tax burdens across income levels—addressing the degree of progressivity or regressivity in the entire state tax system. A number of research studies have produced comparative rankings of the American states in terms of the progressivity or regressivity of their state and local tax systems. The consistent finding of these studies has been that Texas has one of the most regressive tax systems in the United States.

To illustrate this characteristic of the state's tax system, table 14–6 presents comparative data on state and local tax burdens for residents of a number of American cities, one of which is Houston. Because the general pattern of taxation is so similar *within* each state, it is reasonable to use the Houston figures as representative of tax burdens in other major Texas cities.

It is clear, first, that the state and local tax burdens borne by Houstonians are quite regressive. High-income Houstonians, in other words, may pay a larger tax bill in *dollars* than that paid by their lower-income fellow residents, but they pay a smaller *proportion* of their total income in taxes. Second, while Houston and Texas are not alone in having a regressive system, many other major American states have tax systems that are uniformly progressive or are at least progressive through most of the income scale. In the latter states there exists some version of an ability-to-pay tax system. Thus it is not simply one

TABLE 14–6   Estimated State and Local Taxes Paid by a Family of Four in Selected Large Cities: 1981

| City | Total Taxes Paid for Family Income of | | | |
	$10,000	$25,000	$50,000	$75,000
Atlanta	$779 (7.8%)*	$2,343 (9.4%)	$4,702 (9.4%)	$7,093 (9.5%)
Boston	$1,557 (15.6%)	$3,978 (15.9%)	$7,456 (14.9%)	$10,913 (14.6%)
Chicago	$919 (9.2%)	$2,568 (9.9%)	$4,824 (9.6%)	$6,934 (9.2%)
Detroit	$959 (9.6%)	$2,623 (10.5%)	$5,005 (10.1%)	$7,456 (9.9%)
Honolulu	$545 (5.4%)	$2,321 (9.3%)	$4,921 (9.8%)	$7,662 (10.2%)
Houston	$827 (8.3%)	$1,873 (7.5%)	$3,273 (6.6%)	$4,627 (6.2%)
Los Angeles	$615 (6.2%)	$1,841 (7.4%)	$4,157 (8.3%)	$7,315 (9.8%)
New York	$1,036 (10.4%)	$3,213 (12.8%)	$7,482 (15.0%)	$11,085 (14.8%)
Philadelphia	$1,206 (12.1%)	$2,753 (11.0%)	$4,916 (9.8%)	$7,026 (9.4%)
Washington, D.C.	$808 (8.1%)	$2,573 (10.3%)	$5,619 (11.2%)	$8,648 (11.5%)

*Numbers in parentheses represent taxes as percentage of total income.

Source: Statistical Abstract of the United States (1983: 302).

or another single tax in Texas that is regressive; the overall tax system has this character. Such regressivity, while it does characterize certain other states' tax systems as well, is certainly not typical of them all.

Finally, we should note other tax-load comparisons in the table. Low-income Houstonians pay a tax bill that might be called "low-average" in comparison to the other cities in the table—higher than that paid by low-income families in Atlanta, Honolulu, Los Angeles, and Washington and just below that paid in Chicago and Detroit. High-income Houstonians, on the other hand, pay far and away the lowest tax bill of the wealthier residents of all ten cities. And the figures in the table actually *underestimate* the degree of regressivity in our tax system today. Our state's major tax increases in 1984, 1985, and 1987 were mostly in regressive taxes and user fees (the general sales tax; selective sales taxes on gasoline, tobacco, and alcoholic beverages; and auto inspection and licensing fees). Thus current estimates would indicate an even higher relative tax burden for low-income Texans and, hence, an even more regressive system. These comparisons suggest that Texas is, indeed, a low-tax state. Yet it is far more a low-tax state for the wealthy than it is for the poor.

A second way in which we might wish to evaluate relative tax burdens is in comparison to the benefits citizens get in return for the taxes they pay. Several patterns—and justifications for those patterns—are possible here. For example, some states with progressive tax systems might also provide more public services to their high-income rather than their low-income citizens. In such instances we might conclude that the overall system is *proportional*: Those who bear relatively higher tax burdens get relatively more services and vice versa. Alternatively, some progressive-tax states might actually provide more services and programs for their relatively poor citizens than their better-off ones. In this case the net results would be even more progressive than the tax burden alone would suggest. The poor would be paying relatively lower taxes *and* getting relatively more public services.

Turning explicitly to Texas, one could also imagine several theoretical possibilities for the total benefit/burden ratio in this state. If Texas provided relatively high services for its low-income citizens, then the high tax load of such people might be justified on the basis of benefits received. Alternatively, public services proportional to income would simply leave unaffected the regressivity produced by the tax system, and services that favored high-income people would make the overall system even more regressive.

A good deal of the evidence already provided in this chapter hints at the distribution of benefits and burdens in Texas. The tax system itself is highly regressive. Several of the public expenditure comparisons in earlier tables indicated that Texas provides especially limited public welfare services in comparison to the other American states. The combination of the regressive taxes and very limited assistance to low-income citizens indicates that the overall Texas system is even more regressive than the tax burden information alone suggests. Low-income Texans pay more taxes as a percentage of their income than do their higher-income neighbors. Yet they get no more, and probably less, back from the state in services than do those better-off individuals.

Apart from the conclusions we can draw about relative benefits and burdens from the preceding information, there is supportive evidence from a comprehensive study of the extent to which state government programs redistribute income and services to their poorer citizens. In examining the extent to which state and local government expenditures and services either benefited or burdened the lowest-income groups in each state, Booms and Halldorson (1973) found that Texas had the second most regressive system of those in the continental forty-eight states.

CONCLUSION

The first major conclusion of this chapter was that Texas is a low-tax state. Surely the majority of Texans, if not all of them, would be delighted by that fact. Rare indeed is the person who would volunteer to pay *more* taxes than he or she already does or who would not gloat over paying lower taxes than do the citizens of most other states.

The second major finding was that Texas is, as well, a low-service state. One must suspect that many Texans would also applaud this fact. The strong strain of *individualism* in the state's political culture—described at length in chapter 3—helps explain why many Texans would be happy to forgo many state services or programs, or better services than they now get, for the sake of independence. Yet one might suspect that not all Texans would take this position. Some might criticize the quality of certain public services provided by the state or their local city government. One must suspect, of course, that some of this criticism comes from citizens who desire better services but at no more cost than they now pay. The sophisticated citizen, however, surely knows that there is some truth in the adage "you get what you pay for." Thus some citizens might well criticize the current benefits they receive from government *and* be willing to pay higher taxes to secure better services.

This low-service approach also has important social consequences. Texans with sufficient personal income can buy at their private expense additional goods and services—educational, health, police, recreational, library, and so on—to supplement what the state provides. Thus some people send their children to private schools because they believe the education provided there is better than that of the public schools. Many wealthy and even middle-class neighborhoods in Texas cities hire supplementary constables or security services to augment that provided by the municipal police. One could offer a long list of additional examples of this sort; yet, even without a longer list, the implications are obvious.

Those who must rely on public services—because they cannot afford the cost of private supplements—must depend upon relatively low service and benefit levels. And it is not simply the poor who are typically relegated to this position. Most middle-income Texans send their children to public schools and colleges. Most middle-income Texans do not have private security services in their neighborhoods, nor do they belong to private country clubs or other private recreational facilities. Across the range of public services provided by state and local governments, in other words, the majority of Texans must rely on services of below-average quality when compared to those provided nationally.

The third major finding of this chapter was that—because of its governmental system and its tax system—Texas fares poorly in attracting federal assistance. This, too, may be an instance of getting what one pays for. It is probably a circumstance about which the majority of Texans would *not* be happy to learn. Most Texans presumably would agree that, because they pay what they believe to be their share of federal *taxes*, their state should reap its fair share of federal *benefits*. Yet such does not appear to be the case in Texas. And the reasons for this poor success in attracting federal funds are linked to the independent, low-service, "cheaper is better" character of Texas government.

Finally, this chapter has explained how the overall public taxation and expenditure policies of the state of Texas are quite regressive with respect to the benefits enjoyed and burdens borne by citizens of different income classes. In fact, these circumstances constitute a part of the "low tax myth" of Texas government (Hill, 1986). As table 14–6 indicates, low-income Texans pay a state-local tax bill close to the national average for their income level. It is only wealthy Texans who enjoy a light tax burden. And the relatively modest public efforts to aid the poor of this state make the overall effects of the tax *and* spending systems even more regressive. This last circumstance, one must suspect, is not one even a majority of Texans would applaud. This characteristic of Texas public policies virtually means that income is transferred from the relatively poorer citizens of the state to the wealthy. Thus the state does not have simply a "free-choice" system where citizens may supplement state services with private expenditures if they wish *and* can afford to do so. Instead it is a system that penalizes the poor to benefit the wealthy—and does so to a degree greater than almost any other state. Once again, one must suspect that the majority of Texans, if they were aware of this circumstance, would not approve of it. Even those who did not favor a progressive system that benefited the poor more than the wealthy would presumably opt for a proportionate system where benefits and burdens were borne in some sense on an equal basis.

NOTES

1. There is one other perspective that illustrates the low level of state and local taxes in Texas. The U.S. Advisory Commission on Intergovernmental Relations (ACIR) calculates an estimate of the "tax effort" implied by each state's existing tax system. Tax effort is defined by the ACIR as the ratio of actual tax collections in a given year to the amount of taxes that could have been raised if the state had based its collections on the average tax rate among the states (applied to the various taxable aggregates such as income, retail sales, property values, and so on in the state). According to these calculations, Texas had the lowest tax effort

of all fifty states throughout the late 1960s and the 1970s (*Fiscal Capacity as a Method of Allocating Federal Grant Funds,* 1983:7).

2. Public welfare receives particularly little state and local government support in Texas. Take, for example, the Supplemental Security Income program, a federal program that provides monthly cash allotments to poor adults who are over the age of sixty-five, blind, or disabled. The federal government provides the bulk of the funds for the program including a base monthly allotment for qualified recipients. The state governments implement the program and dispense the monthly benefits. The states are also allowed to supplement the monthly allotments provided by the federal government if they believe the support levels are too low. Texas is the only state that does not supplement those benefit levels.

   Moreover, many states have developed "general assistance" welfare programs of their own that help poor people who are not eligible for assistance under the various federal programs. However, until the Texas legislature enacted such a program in its 1985 special session, Texas was one of only nine states that had no substantial program of this kind.

   These examples are not meant to imply that Texas should have such programs or that it should provide more generous public welfare. Such matters ought to be settled in a democratic system by the will of the majority. What is of importance about these examples, however, is the information they provide about the true priorities of Texas government (instead of what they should be).

3. The state and local *expenditure* figures cited earlier in this chapter, it should be noted, included those based on revenues from all sources. Thus federal support for service levels in different policy areas is already reflected in those figures.

REFERENCES

Anderson, Lynn F., and McMillan, T. E., Jr. 1953. *Financing State Government in Texas.* Austin: Institute of Public Affairs, University of Texas.

Book of the States, 1984–85. 1984. Lexington, Ky.: Council of State Governments.

Booms, Bernard H., and Halldorson, James R. 1973. "The Politics of Redistribution: A Reformulation." *American Political Science Review* 67 (September): 924–933.

Bureau of the Census. 1983. *Statistical Abstract of the United States, 1982.* Washington, D.C.

Compendium of Government Finances: 1982 Census of Governments. 1984. Washington, D.C.: Bureau of the Census, U.S. Department of Commerce.

Comptroller of Public Accounts. 1985. *Summary of the Biennial Revenue Estimate, 1986–87.* Austin.

Finances of Public School Systems: 1982 Census of Governments. 1984. Washington, D.C.: Bureau of the Census, U.S. Department of Commerce.

Finances of Public School Systems in 1984–85. Washington, D.C.: Bureau of the Census, U.S. Department of Commerce.

Fiscal Capacity as a Method of Allocating Federal Grant Funds. 1983. Austin: Texas Advisory Commission on Intergovernmental Relations.

Fletcher, Sam. 1985. "Official Paints Gloomy Picture Based on Declining Oil Prices." *Houston Post,* April 5, p. H3.

Fossett, James W. 1984. "The Politics of Dependence: Federal Aid to Big Cities." In Lawrence D. Brown, James W. Fossett, and Kenneth T. Palmer (eds.), *The Changing Politics of Federal Grants*. Washington, D.C.: Brookings Institution.

Governmental Finances in 1984–85. 1986. Washington, D.C.: Bureau of the Census, U.S. Department of Commerce.

Governmental Finances in 1985–86. 1987. Washington, D.C.: Bureau of the Census, U.S. Department of Commerce.

Grant, W. Vance, and Snyder, Thomas D. 1983. *Digest of Education Statistics, 1983–84*. Washington, D.C.: National Center for Education Statistics, U.S. Department of Education.

Hill, Kim Quaile. 1986. "The Low-Tax Myth." *The Texas Observer* (June 27): 6–7.

Musgrave, Richard A., and Musgrave, Peggy B. 1980. *Public Finance in Theory and Practice*. 3rd ed. New York: McGraw-Hill.

Penniman, Clara. 1965. "The Politics of Taxation." In Herbert Jacob and Kenneth N. Vines (eds.), *Politics in the American States*. Boston: Little, Brown.

Quarterly Public Assistance Statistics, April–June 1985. Washington, D.C.: Social Security Administration, U.S. Department of Health and Human Services.

Skove, Cindy. 1987. "Housing Rehab Programs Finally Take Hold in Bryan." *Bryan-College Station Eagle* (September 29): 1B.

State Government Finances in 1982. 1983. Washington, D.C.: Bureau of the Census, U.S. Department of Commerce.

Statistical Abstract of the United States, 1983. Washington, D.C.: Bureau of the Census, U.S. Department of Commerce.

Stein, Robert M. 1981. "The Allocation of Federal Aid Monies: The Synthesis of Demand-Side and Supply-Side Explanations." *American Political Science Review* 75 (June): 334–343.

PUBLIC POLICY

Public policy in Texas is already beginning to reflect the fundamental changes that have taken place in the state during the past twenty-five years. These changes have profoundly altered the economic and social fabric of Texas. The Texas economy is no longer dominated by ranching and oil. Its primary economic symbols now include the computer as well as the cow. Although agriculture and ranching continue to play an important economic role, Texas is one of the most industrialized states in the country. The rural heritage of Texas persists in occupying a prominent role in the state's image of itself although the urbanization of the state has been massive.

It is customary for observers to note that Texas is a land of great contrasts and diversity in terms of its geography, ethnicity, culture, economics, and politics. It is also a land of profound contradictions. In this chapter we will discuss both the changes and the contradictions of public policy in Texas.

HISTORY, POLITICS, AND POLICY

For the overwhelming part of its history, Texas has been dominated by the land—by farming and ranching and oil. Societies that are tied to the land are inevitably conservative. Their natural rhythms are attuned to the harvest, the seasons and the weather, and great calamities such as droughts and epidemics. The emphasis in agrarian societies is upon the individual and the family rather than the group and the mass. The sacred values are self-reliance, hard work, inventiveness. Government is not to be trusted. Public service levels are minimal. Government's role is limited to absolute essentials: fight Indians or criminals, build and repair roads, educate children.

In societies that are tied to the land, individual freedom is of paramount importance. But it is primarily the freedom to be left alone. Government has no obligation to intervene when some have more freedom than others or when one group denies opportunity to another. The winners are the strong, the lucky, the stubborn, the ambitious. The unfortunate, the meek, the disadvantaged, and the less determined are shunted aside.

One great contradiction in attitude and policy that results in landed societies such as Texas is the one that emerges from the conflict between freedom and conformity. For the vaunted freedom of the individual can exist only within certain well-defined limits. Agrarian societies exert great pressures to ensure conformity within the larger community of individuals. The group is highly intolerant of most forms of unorthodox behavior. Freedom has the greatest meaning for the individual acting alone. The group carefully proscribes behavior and punishes deviants who challenge established norms.

But Texas was more than just a landed society. It was also a frontier. To the natural conservatism and insulation of an agricultural state was added the powerful element of the frontier. Agricultural communities are stable, established, and settled. Their patterns and rhythms are set, predictable, and resistant to change. Texas had the farm but for most of the nineteenth century it also had the newness, danger, and unmitigated harshness of completely unsettled territory. To the myth of the self-reliant small farmer was added the myth of the rugged and isolated individualist—the cowboy, the Indian fighter, the Texas Ranger.

And the frontier *was* dangerous. Violence was an integral part of Texas history from the beginning. There was the war with the Mexicans for independence. Before that, and long after it, and for most of the rest of the nineteenth century, there was the Indian. Comanche—the name struck terror in the heart of the settler. The Comanche Moon was a full moon on the frontier, when raiding parties hunted horses, hostages, and Texan scalps.

The Comanche followed the great buffalo herds down from Kansas and Oklahoma into Texas and he fought the Texan essentially to a standstill. The Texas frontier did not close until the 1890s, and that fact can be largely attributed to the ferocity of the Comanche. Widely recognized as the finest light cavalry the continent has ever seen, the Comanche resisted settlement of the state west of Austin and San Antonio for decades.

And there was other violence. The Civil War imposed a compelling and pervasive defeat on Texas and Reconstruction made the bitterness last. The violence of whites against blacks, cattlemen against farmers, cowboys against rustlers, Rangers against outlaws would come later.

Certainly history and traditions have had an impact upon present behavior. While public policy in the state is not directly attributable to the frontier and agrarian heritage, that heritage has exerted an influence. It can be seen in several ways. For example, the dominant conservative ideology has little sympathy for the weak, the unfortunate, and the disadvantaged. Consequently, social welfare programs and other policies designed to assist the deprived receive little support.

Another way in which the history of the state has influenced contemporary politics revolves around the issue of the individual versus the group. The frontier, the farm, and the ranch emphasized the individual rather than the group. Although a sense of community certainly existed, it was a very narrow conception of community that prevailed. The individual relied upon family and neighbors for help in time of need. The notion that the community was relevant to the individual and his needs was an alien one. As a result, there is still a sense in Texas today that the crucial social and political unit is the family and the immediate neighborhood. There is little group action to solve common political and social problems. Therefore, political action tends to be fragmented, piecemeal, and short-lived.

Another effect of the frontier and agrarian heritage can be seen in public attitudes toward government. Texans tend to be suspicious of government. The government that governs best governs least. Government's role should be limited to the performance of absolutely essential functions. As will be seen later in this chapter, however, the business community has increasingly turned to government to provide those services that will enhance the business image of the state. Consequently, it can be expected that government will continue to grow.

UNDERSTANDING PUBLIC POLICY IN TEXAS

Public policy in the state is beginning to reflect the profound changes brought about by industrialization and urbanization.

Rural Influences

Rural, nonindustrial states provide low levels of service. Citizens in these states live on farms or in small towns and frequently do without services that residents of large cities take for granted. The farmer and his family do not expect much, if anything, from government in the way of police and fire protection, public health and welfare, sewage disposal, garbage collection, wastewater treatment, parks and recreation, and libraries. The public services that are provided are absolutely essential and are delivered at a minimal level: education and farm-to-market roads. Citizens do not expect much and they do not get much. Demands are low, services are low, government revenues and expenditures are low, and taxes are low.

Agricultural, nonindustrial states have conservative political systems. Government is very limited with respect to the number and level of services it provides. It does not spend much or tax much. Rural states have less crime and fewer criminals. Therefore they need fewer police, courts, prosecutors, and prisons. They are less concerned with "quality" education and fund their school systems at low levels. Moreover, the citizens have little tolerance for such things as the personal freedoms of prisoners and the need to rehabilitate criminals.

Rural states are also much less involved in the regulation of business activity and the affairs of the private citizen. Government is viewed as a necessary evil rather than as a positive force that should actively seek to improve the lot of its constituents.

Citizens in rural, nonindustrial states believe very strongly in the conservative ideology. The virtues of hard work, self-reliance, and rugged individualism are accorded special status. Personal responsibility is an esteemed value. The private sector is relied upon to provide many of the services that government is expected to deliver in other states. There is little sympathy for the poor and disadvantaged. Economic rewards are bestowed on the deserving. Success is seen as a recognition of hard work and merit. Losers in the competitive struggle are not entitled to special treatment by government. Social welfare programs are nonexistent because they are too expensive and because they would stifle initiative and individual responsibility.

In Texas, these attitudes about the role and function of government were nurtured throughout most of the state's history. As a result, the rapid industrialization and urbanization of the state are destined to create political conflicts that will endure for decades. Industrialization produces great concentrations of people. These huge urban populations place demands upon government that are unheard of in a less economically developed state. Rural states do not need much, nor can they afford much, in the way of police and fire protection, water and disposal systems, mass transit, prisons, and parks and recreation.

Urban Influences

It is the great city and its suburbs, the center of a complex array of economic activities, that creates a huge demand for government services. Urban areas have much higher crime rates than rural ones. Consequently, there is a much greater demand for police protection. More crime and criminals require not only more police officers but more judges, courts, prisons, guards, rehabilitation programs, and parole and probation officers as well. Urban areas also suffer more fires and more damage from fires. Density, overcrowding, and dilapidated housing all contribute to the greater incidence of fire and the greater likelihood of its rapid spread. Consequently, the need for a sophisticated and expensive array of firefighting equipment is increased.

Cities also create a huge demand for a variety of other services. Residential and arterial streets need to be built and maintained, garbage has to be collected, sewer and water systems have to be constructed and operated, fresh water supplies have to be provided, and public health programs have to be implemented. Moreover, government has to respond to the demand for clean and well-equipped parks and libraries.

Conservative Influences

It is ironic that in rapidly industrializing and urbanizing states such as Texas the political conservatives are as supportive of high service levels as the liberals are. In fact, the conservatives frequently take the lead in developing new public programs, projects, and services. The important point on which conservatives and liberals disagree is not big government versus limited government. Instead, the major issue of contention is *which* programs government will spend money on. When public policy in Texas is viewed in these terms, it becomes more understandable.

Conservatives do not oppose all government programs and services in principle. They are not even necessarily opposed to higher taxes. What they are opposed to are government services that are not perceived to benefit and stimulate economic growth. To a business person, wasteful and inexcusable government programs include social welfare services of all types. Efforts to expand and fund such programs inspire attacks that center around "big government," "handouts," and higher taxes. The same person, however, will support other government expenditures as absolutely essential to the economic health of the state.

Conservatives are among the most forceful advocates of "quality" education in the state, for example. Yet their reasons for supporting education differ from the arguments advanced by liberals. A liberal might say that a superior education is crucial to the full development of the human potential. As such, it should not be evaluated in dollars and cents. Instead, it should be supported because it contributes to the eradication of discrimination and injustice, because it breaks down barriers to equality of opportunity, and because it enhances the dignity and worth of the individual citizen. In short, a civilized society requires that the education of the citizen be accorded first priority.

The business person, on the other hand, would justify support of education in economic terms. High-quality education is seen as crucial to the economic future of the state. Many business people support higher levels of funding for both the public schools and higher education because they fear that Texas will begin to lose the battle for industry if the quality of its education declines. It is frequently noted that Texas is ill-equipped to compete in the long run for high-tech industry because its university system cannot compare with the universities found in California and Massachusetts. Business and industry require highly skilled technicians and professionals as well as an institutionalized research capacity. Consequently, a superior university system is needed to secure the state's position in the highly competitive struggle for high-tech firms. The business community supports a variety of other government-funded services and projects. An adequate transportation system, for example, is seen as essential to continued economic growth and development. Thus there is widespread support for airports and freeways. An adequate supply of water is similarly viewed as vital to a robust economy. Thus government programs to provide sufficient water for the state's needs enjoy strong support.

Conservatives do not support high levels of funding for all government services, however. Unless a direct relationship is apparent between the service and a benefit to business and industry, they are likely to oppose it. A careful distinction is drawn between government programs that will stimulate economic growth and create jobs and those that are perceived as handouts to the lazy and undeserving. This distinction can be seen with respect to the current major policy issues in the state. There is widespread support for greater governmental expenditures for education, water, and highways. Program expenditures to improve the prison system, however, have aroused widespread opposition. In fact, prison reform was forced upon the state by the federal courts. The differences in the levels of support for these various programs can be attributed to the idea that highways, education, and water are essential to continued economic growth.

One should not infer, however, that conservatives and liberals have reached a consensus with respect to these policy areas. They continue to disagree over the content, funding, and control of programs designed to address various problems. The important point, however, is that the powerful conservative ideology of Texas politics exalts the virtues of limited government, self-reliance, and rugged individualism. Already this ideology has begun to clash with the demands for expanded public services imposed by industrialization and urbanization. Government not only begins to spend more, but it assumes a much more active role in the regulation of economic and social activities as well. Land use and zoning ordinances have to be developed, tax assessments have to be revised, and civil and criminal codes require expansion. Further, various occupational groups demand regulation of their professions and insurance, housing, public utilities, and other industries have to be regulated.

The Future of Public Policy

The great irony is that public policy in Texas will continue to reflect growth in government even as the conservative ideology emphasizes limited government. Government expenditures will increase, public programs will expand, and government's regulatory role will grow. The great driving force in shaping public policy in Texas during the next few decades will be economics. All major policy proposals will be evaluated in terms of their contribution to furthering economic development and creating jobs. The current fascination with high tech is likely to continue. If high-tech and service industries do come to dominate the American and Texas economies, then it is probable that the role of government in the state will expand even faster than anticipated. It will be recalled from earlier chapters that high-tech firms employ few blue-collar workers. Instead they are top-heavy with highly trained and well-educated professionals. The same situation is true for the various support service occupations. Service industries employ large numbers of lawyers, accountants, bankers, medical doctors, economists, and researchers. The significance of all of these engineers, computer analysts, scientists, lawyers, and accountants for public policy in Texas is that they will demand a wide array of services. A superior public school and university system will be a major priority. Other major service demands will be for parks and recreation and police protection.

Thus several developments in the economy have exerted, and will continue to exert, major impacts upon public policy in Texas. The recent and rapid industrialization and urbanization of the state have placed heavy demands upon government for education, water, transportation, and police and fire services. The conservative business community has strongly supported these expanded services as essential to the continued economic growth and development of the state. That support has not included all government programs, however. Public services that are perceived as handouts to the poor and otherwise undeserving are vigorously resisted. Consequently, welfare services and efforts to improve the prison system are greeted with strong opposition. The state government's role in the regulation of land use, occupations, housing, insurance, and utilities has also expanded.

This trend toward bigger government and greater expenditures for programs favorable to economic growth began in the 1960s and should be expected to continue. In fact, it is probable that major policy proposals in the future will be even more carefully evaluated in terms of their contribution to economic development. The competition nationally among the states for business and industry is much stronger today than it was several years ago. Today, state and local governments offer a variety of tax inducements and economic incentives to attract industry. This intense competition will cause policy proposals to be assessed according to their relevance to economic growth.

We can already see this influence at work in the state budgetary process. The revenue shortfall Texas recently experienced as a result of the decline in oil prices has resulted in budget cuts for a variety of services and programs. Frequently, public officials mention the relevance or irrelevance of a particular program to economic growth as the prime reason for supporting or cutting its funding. This point is illustrated by the fact that in 1987 a federal district judge found the state in contempt of court with respect to grossly inadequate conditions and care of patients at state schools for the mentally retarded. The judge characterized these conditions as "barbaric." Texas ranks fifty-first (behind the District of Columbia) in support of mental retardation services. The Association for Retarded Citizens has reported that Texas has the worst record in the nation with respect to the provision of services to the mentally retarded. Specifically, it discovered that nearly 2,000 mentally retarded citizens are currently on waiting lists for services such as care in group homes. Another 20,000 are awaiting admittance to programs that include participation in supervised activities.

The relationship between public policy and a favorable business image has been heightened by the concerted effort to attract high-tech firms. High-tech industries require a strong university system and a modern transportation network. Moreover, high-tech employees are typically concerned with the quality of the public school system, parks and recreation, and police protection. The perception is widespread that if Texas is to compete effectively for high-tech jobs in the long term, it must upgrade the quality of public services in these areas.

The conservative ideology emphasizes limited government, self-reliance, private-sector solutions to problems, and no government handouts. There is a great irony, then, in the concerted efforts of the business community to lure high-tech firms to the state by attempting to improve the education system and transportation network with government dollars. What is arising is a three-way partnership among government, the business community, and prospective business firms. This relationship involves a fundamental change in Texas politics. Previously the relationship between state government and the dominant sectors of the economy—oil and gas and agriculture—was more passive. The oil and agriculture industries were not indifferent to government, and they surely had enormous political influence. But these groups sought to limit government's role. They used their political clout to restrict government regulation of their economic activities and interests. They also worked effectively to keep services, expenditures, and taxes low.

Significantly, however, no partnership existed among oil, agriculture, and government in a positive sense. That is, industry leaders and public officials did not actively seek to fashion a set of policies that would attract new business and jobs to the state. Oil and agriculture were already here. They worked to maintain the status quo. The partnership, then, was essentially limited and negative. Industry did not need high service levels. Neither did their workers. Roughnecks and sharecroppers are little concerned with the urban service amenities expected by high-tech yuppies. What they wanted was for government to leave them alone so they could explore and drill for oil and raise their cattle and crops. They sought to avoid extensive regulation and high taxes. Beyond that, they did not contemplate a positive vision for the state.

The emerging partnership in Texas between government and business today is active and forceful. It seeks to develop a service infrastructure that will lure business and industry to the state and stimulate economic development. As a result, government will continue to grow. This active partnership between business and political leaders in the state represents one of the most significant developments in Texas during the past several decades.

POLICY CHANGES IN TEXAS

Those who maintain that Texas has not changed much in the past twenty or thirty years do not know the reality of the state. Earlier chapters have already discussed one such change. The industrialization and urbanization of the state have been massive. One effect of this transformation from a rural, agricultural state to a highly urbanized and industrial one has been the great growth in public services and government.

Another major change has to do with public policies affecting racial minorities. One student of Texas politics observes that the Texas of thirty years ago

> *was still a segregated society in which blacks were forbidden to drink from the same water fountain, swim in the same pools, use the same restrooms, eat in the same area, or attend the same public schools as whites. . . . The situation for Mexican-Americans was not a great deal better. . . . Both groups, of course, suffered additionally from widespread discrimination in such matters as employment and housing, and both were discouraged in a variety of ways from full political participation.* [McCleskey, 1974:57]

Today the situation for blacks and Mexican-Americans is greatly improved. Legal barriers with respect to public education, accommodations, employment, and housing have been essentially eliminated. Moreover, minorities now have many more opportunities to participate in the political system. Many hold public office at all levels of government in the state. Although equal opportunity for racial minorities may not exist in fact as well as in law, substantial progress has been made in the state during the past thirty years. However, much remains to be done. For example, in December 1987, Hispanic groups filed a lawsuit challenging the constitutionality of higher education funding in the state. The suit alleges that although 70 percent of the population in South Texas is Hispanic, state per capita expenditures for higher education are only $70 in that region compared to $160 statewide and $390 per capita in Central Texas. Also, South Texas has no state supported professional schools and only one doctoral degree program.

Another important change has been the decline in the political influence of the rural, agrarian interests of the state. The political philosophy and movement known as populism is no longer a major force to be reckoned with. As earlier chapters have indicated, populism was a loosely knit movement dominated by farmers and groups associated with agriculture. It had an essentially conservative ideology centering on the family farm, crops, prices, and markets. The populists tried to gain a greater measure of control over their sources of credit, markets, and prices, and they sought to enlist government in the struggle on their behalf. The populists saw the railroads, the great financial institutions, and the proverbial middleman as responsible for most of their economic woes. They used state government to regulate the railroads and financial institutions.

The decline of the small farm in Texas has dealt a fatal blow to the political influence of agrarian interests. Power has shifted to the great cities and suburban areas of the state. Government is now much more responsive to the service demands of cities than previously.

Another policy change concerns the role of the federal courts. Federal court decisions have exerted a major influence on public policy in the state. Past decisions have desegregated the public schools and reapportioned the state House and Senate according to the "one man, one vote" principle. Now, as a result, urban areas in Texas enjoy much greater representation in the state legislature. Recent court rulings have ordered that local school districts are required to educate the children of illegal aliens and have to provide bilingual education. Moreover, a federal court has decreed that the Texas penal system is wholly inadequate with respect to the housing, treatment, and medical care of inmates. In a later section we will analyze the policy changes that have taken place in response to this decision.

Another major policy transformation has already been discussed. The emerging partnership between government and business to attract industry to the state represents a bold use of public power to achieve economic growth. As such, it signifies a broad expansion of governmental power and functions.

This new breed of political, business, and educational leaders is sophisticated, well-educated, and urbane. They include among their number H. Ross Perot, Dallas-based electronics and computer magnate and spiritual advisor to a host of Texas politicians; Bill Hobby, Lieutenant Governor, heir to the *Houston Post* fortune, and supporter, par excellence, of higher education; Henry Cisneros, Mayor of San Antonio, perennial favorite on various "Best Dressed" and "Sexiest Men" lists, and the most charismatic politician in the state; George Mitchell, Houston oilman and developer and keen supporter of such emerging high-tech fields as biotechnology; and Robert McDermott, head of

USAA Insurance Corporation and a leader in San Antonio's efforts to become a health-care, high-tech, and biosciences center.

That the distribution of power has fundamentally changed in the state is reflected in the fact that less than 20 years ago the power structure was dominated by reactionary oilmen and bankers. No longer. Instead, a young Hispanic is a prominent and forceful spokesman for the new economic and political reality. In a different era these leaders might have been called "progressives" or, in some instances, even liberals. But their message is decidedly not a liberal one. The coalition within which they work could not long endure if it were. Instead, their call is for hard work, private initiative, and the entrepreneurial spirit. The primary assumption upon which they operate is that everyone will benefit from the creation of more jobs, and that government policy can be employed to promote that economic growth. There is nothing liberal in the message. They oppose major spending programs for the poor. Although higher taxes are tolerated in order to maintain a service infrastructure thought to be a precondition of economic development, no effort is made to use the power of government to attack the problems of hunger, lost opportunities, and discrimination. These new leaders are highly ambitious men who have accepted the limits of the Texas political system and have decided to work within that system.

In Texas, for example, it is not particularly profitable for a public figure to support education for education's sake. Instead, in Texas, education is a means to a less noble end. This purely instrumental approach has been accepted by the new leadership. They support higher levels of government funding for education because it provides a well-trained workforce, it generates research, it attracts scientific and engineering talent, it garners federal research dollars, it attracts high-tech managers and professionals, and it creates new jobs. The ultimate purpose of education is economic growth and more wealth.

The educational establishment in the state has bought into this new partnership with unbridled enthusiasm. The faculty at the state's universities find that their expertise is eagerly sought as the business and political leaders scramble to diversify the state's economy. More spending for higher education has been hit upon as the winning formula as the state seeks to escape from the economic doldrums. In 1986, when the revenue crisis (as a result of the plunge in oil prices) first hit, some legislators singled out higher education as a prime target for substantial budget cuts. As it turned out, however, higher education fared better than anyone expected. The university system is now looked to as the panacea for the state's economic ills. It is anticipated that Texas will ride all of that scientific and engineering talent into a glowing high-tech future. But how reasonable is this scenario? We have already seen in chapter 1 that high tech may not be able to deliver on the promise. And if it does not, will the educational system be held responsible for economic failure? In particular, the higher education system is expected to lead the way as the state's government and corporate elites seek to strengthen and diversify the economy. Governor Clements talks about the need to bring the "higher education system into the realm of free enterprise." By way of illustration, $1.8 million in state funding was provided for the initial operation of Texas A&M University's Center for

Technology Development and Transfer, and a Technology Business Development Division. This initiative allows public universities to get involved in the development and marketing of products that result from research successes.

In the following sections we will discuss how the power of government is used to promote policies designed to stimulate economic growth. We will concentrate on public education, water, and prison reform.

THE PUBLIC SCHOOLS

State policy with respect to the public school system has undergone significant changes recently. In 1983, the state legislature failed to enact legislation providing for a pay raise for teachers. In response, the governor appointed a committee chaired by H. Ross Perot to examine a variety of educational issues and problems. The Governor's Select Committee on Public Education (SCOPE) presented a series of major recommendations for the reform of the public school system. In a special session, the legislature accepted most of these proposed changes.

Perhaps the most significant reform had to do with the changes in the system of state aid to local school districts. The old system was not sensitive to differences in the ability of school districts to raise tax revenues. Therefore, districts with large amounts of taxable property were able to generate high revenues while poor school districts were unable to do so. As a result, much more money was spent per student in rich districts than in poor ones.

The differences in the amount of money spent by rich and poor districts were dramatic. In 1983–1984, for example, school districts in the wealthiest group spent an average of $4,227 per student while those in the poorest group spent $2,256 per student. The differences for the districts at either extreme were even greater. Fifty-five of the state's school districts averaged less than $2,000 per student while four districts spent more than $10,000 per student (State Comptroller, 1984a).

The new policies will alter the amount of state aid going to poor districts. Under the new system, the level of state aid is linked to the value of taxable property in a school district. The state will assume 70 percent of the cost, on the average, of educating students with the district paying 30 percent. The actual percentage of costs borne by the state and individual districts will differ, however, depending on the level of taxable property in the district.

Table 15–1 indicates the anticipated changes in state aid per pupil. The table reveals a substantial reallocation of resources to poor districts. In school districts with property wealth valued at less than $83,000 per student, for example, state aid will increase by $727 per student (49.8 percent). Districts with property wealth per student in the $83,000–$107,999 range will receive $608 more per student in state aid (an increase of 41.7 percent), while districts in the $108,000–$134,999 range will receive $550 more per student, an increase of 38.8 percent (State Comptroller, 1984a).

These substantial increases in state aid to poor school districts in the state are not matched by similar increases for wealthy districts. Instead, the 193

TABLE 15-1   Change in Distribution of State Aid Per Pupil by Property Wealth Per Student: 1985

Property Wealth	Number of Districts	State Aid Under Old System	State Aid Under New System	Change	% Change
Under $83,000	72	$1,461	$2,188	$727	49.8
$83,000–$107,999	129	$1,458	$2,066	$608	41.7
$108,000–$134,999	144	$1,417	$1,967	$550	38.8
$135,000–$176,999	174	$1,355	$1,690	$335	24.7
$177,000–$241,999	180	$1,260	$1,463	$203	16.1
$242,000–$430,999	193	$1,125	$1,136	$11	1.0
$431,000 or over	177	$941	$756	−$185	−19.7

Sources: Texas Education Agency and Office of the Comptroller of Public Accounts.

districts with property wealth per student in the $242,000–$430,999 range will receive only $11 more per student per year (an increase of 1.0 percent), while the 177 wealthiest districts (property wealth of more than $431,000) will actually experience a decline in state aid of 19.7 percent (from $941 per student to only $756).

This reallocation of state aid from wealthy to poorer districts is also reflected in the aggregate state aid totals. Of the $846 million provided in *new* state aid, it is estimated that $220–$255 million or up to 30 percent will be allocated to the seventy-two poorest districts in the state. On the other hand, the 177 wealthiest districts will sustain a decline in state aid of from $18 million to $22 million. In order to minimize the impact of a loss in state aid, however, the legislature provided that the state reimbursed districts for up to 60 percent of their funding loss in the first year under the new formula. This proportion declined to 40 percent the next year, 20 percent the next, and now zero.

It should be emphasized, however, that a huge disparity still exists between rich and poor school districts in the state. In fact, in April 1987, a state district judge ruled that the system of public school finance in Texas discriminates against poor districts. The Court ruled that it was wrong that the 200 wealthiest districts can augment state funding to such an extent that they can afford to spend twice as much per student as the 200 poorest school districts. The judge further observed that the poorest districts also have the responsibility for educating children with the greatest needs.

Teacher Pay Raises

The educational reform package enacted by the legislature also provided for a series of pay increases for teachers. The entry-level salary was set at a minimum of $1,520 a month with a maximum guaranteed by the state of $2,660 per month after ten years. This represents a pay raise of 37 percent for beginning teachers over the minimum guaranteed by the state for the 1983–1984 school year. It should be noted, however, that most teachers in the state were already paid more by their districts than these guaranteed state minimum salaries. It is estimated that 96.5 percent of the 170,000 public school teachers in Texas were paid more than the minimum.

It should be pointed out, however, that public school teachers in the state have actually lost ground with respect to salary. In 1984–1985, Texas ranked twenty-first nationally in teacher salaries. In 1987, that rank had slipped to twenty-sixth. The average teacher salary in Texas is $24,927. The national average is $26,704.

Another provision of the revised salary structure was the addition of career ladder steps. This program provides for salary supplements of $2,000, $4,000, or $6,000 per year for teachers who fulfill certain requirements. Moreover, teachers will have to pass a literacy test and demonstrate competence in the subjects they teach. This mandatory examination, officially known as the Texas Examination of Current Administrators and Teachers (TECAT), was first administered in March 1986. Almost 97 percent of those taking the exam passed it.

Requirements were also toughened for students. In 1979, the legislature passed a "core curriculum" law under which students have to take more English, math, and science courses. The new educational reform legislation strengthened these earlier provisions by prohibiting the practice of passing students to the next grade even though they had not successfully completed required coursework. Further, the law now requires that students must pass a competency exam before they can graduate.

Another important provision of the educational legislation establishes a new overall pupil/teacher ratio of twenty students per teacher. Particular attention was given to pupil/teacher ratios in kindergarten through the fourth grade. Beginning in 1985–1986, the ratio could be no more than twenty-two students in kindergarten and the first and second grades. This ratio requirement also applied to the third and fourth grades in 1988–1989.

A final provision of the law establishes a limit of five unexcused absences per class. Any student with more than five such absences will fail the course.

WATER

The projected water shortage in Texas is currently one of the major policy problems in the state and is likely to remain so for the next few decades. Texans use 6 trillion gallons of water annually—enough to cover an area the size of West Virginia with a foot of water. Of the 18 million acre-feet of water used each year, 13 million come from underground supplies (aquifers) while 5 million come from surface supplies (rivers and lakes). Texas has more than 6,000 square miles of surface water, more than any other state. Because of its large land area, however, Texas ranks only twenty-sixth in terms of percentage of water surface to land surface.

Humans require a great deal of water—7 gallons are needed to flush a toilet, 25 gallons are used to take a shower, and watering the typical front lawn for an hour might consume 300 gallons. The grain needed to produce a single slice of bread requires 37 gallons, and one pound of beef takes 3,750 gallons (*Houston Post*, 1985). Currently Texas has enough water. It uses 18 million acre-feet annually, while the available supply is 21 million acre-feet. Many observers predict that demand will eventually exceed supply, however, and that the water shortage will be so severe that the economy of the state will be crippled.

Regional Variations

The water problem is a complex one that varies according to both economic sector and geographic region. Industry, for example, requires much less water than agriculture. The eight major water-consuming industries such as petrochemicals, steel, and paper use less than 2 million acre-feet annually. Agricultural irrigation consumes 13 million acre-feet.

Moreover, not all regions of the state have the same water needs and problems. In fact, some do not anticipate a water shortage at all. The Plains region in West Texas may encounter water shortages as early as the 1990s. The

Plains contains a great deal of water. Of the 430 million acre-feet of underground water in the state, 89 percent or 385 million acre-feet are in the Ogallala Aquifer in West Texas. The problem is that the Plains also uses a great deal of water for agriculture. Some 6 million acres are irrigated annually.

The Border region, too, is faced with an anticipated water shortage. The Border does not have much water to begin with, and agricultural demands and recurring droughts ensure that the region will continue to be beset with increasingly severe water problems. The Gulf Coast, on the other hand, faces problems of a different type. Land subsidence and saltwater contamination are important concerns as a result of the pumping of underground water brought about by industrial and residential development. Moreover, *too much* water is also a problem in some parts of the region. Heavy rains cause major flooding on a regular basis. As a result, flood control is a greater priority than an adequate water supply for many people in the Gulf Coast region.

The Central Corridor has an adequate water supply for present needs. The rapid growth in the region is depleting the Edwards Aquifer, however, and it is anticipated that more surface sources will have to be developed to meet future water demands. The Metroplex (Dallas–Fort Worth) is expected to have an adequate water supply into the twenty-first century. Ironically, the region was forced to confront its water problems as a result of the severe drought it experienced in the 1950s. That water shortage brought about efforts to develop the Upper Trinity river basin. The outcome of this planning effort has been an adequate supply of water for present and future needs.

East Texas is among the most fortunate parts of the state in terms of water supply. It is anticipated that the region has sufficient amounts to meet its needs in the long run. East Texas has the highest annual rainfall in the state as well as numerous rivers and lakes (State Comptroller, 1983).

Water Policies

The fear of a water shortage has prompted public officials to take action—one of the few times that state officials have acted to solve a major policy problem on their own initiative. Generally, change is forced upon the state by the courts or the federal government. In the case of water, the Texas Legislature authorized a policy package that the voters approved in November 1985. The program authorizes the state to issue $980 million in bonds to fund programs to provide flood control and improve water quality and supplies. The money will be borrowed by local governments who will undertake these programs. The legislative water package will also authorize $250 million in bonds to guarantee various water projects at the local level. Finally, the program will issue still another $200 million in bonds to assist farmers and ranchers in buying more efficient irrigation equipment.

The legislative water proposal was not passed without opposition. Legislators from East Texas feared that their water surplus would be used to benefit the rest of the state. Legislators from the Gulf Coast expressed opposition because they felt the proposed water program does not provide adequate safeguards for coastal bays and estuaries.

Texans had rejected three other water plans since 1967. One such plan would have cost the taxpayers $3.5 billion. It proposed to transport water from Mississippi to Texas. Another water plan would have dug a series of canals from Arkansas, Missouri, and East Texas to West Texas. The effort involved to build the canal system would have exceeded that required to construct the Panama Canal. It would have cost $50 billion to build and $5 billion a year to operate and maintain (*Houston Post*, 1985).

THE PRISONS

In 1972, an inmate in the Texas prison system named David Ruiz brought a suit in federal court against the Texas Department of Corrections. The substance of the charges was that Texas prisons violated the constitutional rights of inmates as a result of brutality, overcrowded conditions, and inadequate medical care. In 1981, Federal Judge William Wayne Justice handed down a decision in which he ordered sweeping changes in the operation of the prison system with respect to staffing, overcrowding, health care, and brutality.

As a result of Justice's decision, the legislature was forced to take action. Before discussing the various prison reforms that have been adopted, however, it should prove helpful to describe the prison situation in the state. Many of the problems with the prison system in Texas can be attributed to the huge increase in the state's population. The number of inmates in Texas prisons increased by 120 percent from 1973 to 1983. In table 15–2 we can see that Texas has the second largest prison population in the nation. There were 38,000 prisoners in April 1983. As might be expected, most inmates are male (95.6 percent as opposed to 4.4 percent females). There were more blacks (43.7 percent) than any other racial group. Anglos comprised 37.5 percent of the prison population and Hispanics accounted for 19 percent. The average age was 29.9 and the largest single age group (16.9 percent) was between the ages of 23 and 25.

TABLE 15–2   Prison Population by State

State	Prisoners on December 31, 1983	Prisoners on June 30, 1984	Growth Rate (%)
California	39,373	41,866	6.3
Texas	35,259	35,324	0.2
New York	30,541	32,276	5.7
Florida	26,334	26,686	1.3
Ohio	18,007	18,801	4.4
Illinois	15,595	16,828	7.9
North Carolina	15,395	16,485	7.1
Georgia	15,358	15,535	1.2
Michigan	14,382	14,426	0.3
Louisiana	12,812	13,243	3.4

Source: Office of the Comptroller of Public Accounts.

Inmates who had been convicted of burglary or robbery accounted for 48 percent of all prisoners. One inmate is admitted every twenty-nine minutes to a Texas prison. The prison population comes predominately from urban areas. Inmates from Houston (10,076), Dallas–Fort Worth (9,531), and San Antonio (2,028) alone account for well over half of the total prison population. The urban areas with the highest rates of imprisonment based on number of convictions per 100,000 population are Beaumont (323.9), followed closely by Houston (323.2) and Midland (312).

On the basis of this statistical profile, one can see that the prison population is heavily black and Hispanic. These two racial minorities comprise 62.6 percent of the prison population. The largest age grouping is from twenty-three to twenty-five, and the typical inmate is from the city. These facts alone provide some significant clues why prisons and prison reform are major policy problems. First, prisoners are always the rejects and the deviants in society. Moreover, they are also likely to be members of racial minorities. Thus the typical white Texan is unlikely to have much sympathy for inmate complaints about overcrowding, inferior medical care, and brutality.

In fact, surveys of public opinion in the state reveal that many Texans (38 percent) believe that prisoners have it "too easy," and only 10 percent believe that prison conditions are too harsh (Hill, 1985). Some 48 percent of the citizens also believe that penalties for crimes are too easy, and 75 percent support the death penalty. When Texans are asked to rate their spending priorities, they are most likely to rank prisons at the bottom of the list.

Given this set of attitudes, it should not be surprising that prison conditions and problems are less than foremost in the mind of the average Texan. Similarly, the low level of state spending on the prison system described in the preceding chapter is well explained in terms of such attitudes.

Another clue to understanding the problems besetting the state's prison system can be seen in the large number of inmates from urban areas. Many of the system's current problems stem from overcrowding, and that overcrowding can be attributed in large part to the great growth of Texas cities. Urban areas have much higher crime rates than those found in small towns and rural parts of the state. The explosive urbanization of the state has produced much higher rates of crime and overwhelmed the capacity of the penal system to process and accommodate a much larger inmate population.

Finally, the huge increase in the number of prisoners can be traced to the changing demography of the state. The largest number of prisoners are young. Criminologists have found that individuals between the ages of seventeen and twenty-five are much more likely to commit a crime than older citizens. Significantly, the size of this age group increased drastically during the 1960s and 1970s. Therefore, much of the huge increase in crime and criminals can be attributed to the increase in the size of this crime-prone group. Texas, and other states as well, was simply unprepared for the impacts of this demographic change.

As pointed out earlier in this chapter, changes in public policy in Texas result from either economic factors or decisions forced upon the state by the federal government. In the case of the prison system, policy change was a function of both. Many of the problems can be directly attributed to over-crowded conditions, and that overcrowding can be linked to the population explosion, rapid urbanization, and the expansion of the crime-prone age category.

These population changes alone, however, did not bring about the crisis in the prison system. State government could have responded to increases in the prison population by building more prisons, hiring more staff personnel, and making provisions for adequate medical care. As indicated above, however, the several thousand Texans who are residents of the state's prisons are not a powerful interest group. They enjoy little support and even less sympathy. Moreover, the political leaders in the state are most likely to support policy initiatives that are designed to maintain and enhance the state's favorable business image. Consequently, expenditures to provide water and improve education and transportation services are much more likely to enjoy support from leaders in both government and the business community than programs designed to reform the prison system.

For unpopular policies such as penal reform, it takes a powerful outside entity such as the federal courts to force change. The *Ruiz* case in 1981 was such a catalyst. One result of Judge William Justice's ruling in the *Ruiz* decision was the creation of an early release program; another was the stipulation that the prison population not exceed 95 percent of capacity. As a result, we see in table 15–2 that the state's prisons held 35,324 inmates in June 1984, a decline from a high of 38,000 prisoners in April 1983. The early release program has taken various forms, including good time credit, halfway houses, and earlier eligibility for parole. One early release program freed 9,145 prisoners between September 1982 and April 1984 (State Comptroller, 1984b).

Another impact of the *Ruiz* case has been an increase in expenditures. The increase in the budget for the Texas Department of Corrections was from $189.2 million in 1978–1979 to $621.1 million in 1984–1985—a rise of 228.3 percent. Even so, the department's $6,951 in expenditures per prisoner in 1983 still ranked the state last nationally. This low ranking can be attributed in part to the fact that the state employs fewer guards per prisoner than other states (State Comptroller, 1984b).

It is important to note that the other agencies of the state correctional system actually experienced greater budget growth than the Department of Corrections. Table 15–3 shows that the Adult Probation Commission's budget increased by 111.0 percent, the expenditures of the Board of Pardons and Parole grew by 65 percent, and the budget of the Juvenile Probation Commission increased by 236.5 percent. Although the total budget for the entire correctional system rose from $792 million in 1982–1983 to $935 million in 1984–1985, the Department of Corrections' share of each budget dollar declined from 76½ cents to 66½ cents. Therefore the *Ruiz* decision not only caused greater expenditures but it also brought about a considerable shift in budget priorities.

In a recent out-of-court settlement, the state agreed to a variety of additional changes in the prison system. One major change will be a reduction in the prison population from current levels to 32,500 by September 1989. Other reforms include programs to correct health and safety problems, minimum

TABLE 15–3 State Budget Increases for Corrections

Function	Budget for 1982–1983	Budget for 1984–1985	% Increase
Adult Probation Commission	$54,329,787	$114,635,013	111.0
Board of Pardons and Parole	$44,660,309	$73,715,108	65.1
Texas Youth Commission	$79,110,626	$100,826,319	27.4
Juvenile Probation Commission	$7,226,364	$24,314,345	236.5
Policy Council on Criminal Justice	—	$350,000	—
Department of Corrections	$606,750,695	$621,126,114	2.4
Total	$792,077,781	$934,966,899	18.0

Source: Office of the Comptroller of Public Accounts.

space limits for cells in new prison units, and programs to provide work, education, and vocational training to inmates.

After years of litigation in the federal courts, the state finally appears to be making at least some progress with respect to improving conditions in its prisons. In fact, in April 1987, Judge Justice actually congratulated public officials for having made "remarkable progress toward complete compliance" with his various court orders. As a result, he dismissed fines that could have amounted to as much as $800,000 per day. In addition, the Texas Department of Mental Health and Mental Retardation agreed to a federal court settlement in late 1987 that will increase the staff/client ratio in state mental institutions by 15 percent. The $83 million plan will improve the state's ranking on per capita expenditures for the mentally retarded to thirty-ninth in the country. It is significant, however, that Texas makes substantial progress in its treatment of the needy and disadvantaged only when it is literally forced to do so by others.

CONCLUSION

Public policy in Texas has undergone profound change in the past thirty years. The rapid industrialization and urbanization of the state have placed huge demands upon government to provide a wide array of expensive services. As a result, the role of government has greatly expanded. Government in Texas performs many more functions and spends much more money today than it did several years ago.

Another major policy change is the emerging partnership between government and business to stimulate economic growth and attract industry to the state. This relationship represents an active use and expansion of public power in Texas. It is a particularly noteworthy development because it is the conservative business community that is most forcefully advocating the use of government power to promote economic growth.

It should be pointed out, however, that not all government services and programs will expand at the same rate. The business community is most likely to support programs designed to promote economic activity. It remains strongly opposed to programs that benefit the poor, the elderly, and the disadvantaged. Therefore transportation, education, and water services and programs can anticipate the highest levels of funding. Social welfare services will continue to be financed at low levels.

REFERENCES

Hill, David. 1985. *The Texas Poll: April.* College Station: Public Policy Resources Laboratory, Texas A&M University.

Houston Post. 1985. "State Has Plenty of Water—for Now." February 3.

McCleskey, Clifton. 1974. "Some Changes for the Better." *Texas Observer* (December): 57–59.

State Comptroller. 1983. "Texas at a Glance: Water Needs." *Fiscal Notes* (October). Austin: Office of the State Comptroller.

State Comptroller. 1984a. "School Doors Open to Major Changes." *Fiscal Notes* (September). Austin: Office of the State Comptroller.

State Comptroller. 1984b. "Prison System Faces Change." *Fiscal Notes* (November). Austin: Office of the State Comptroller.

INDEX

315

CREDITS

TEXT

Chapter 2. 27 and 33, Figures 2–1 and 2–2 from "The Imprint of the Upper and Lower South on Mid-Nineteenth Century Texas," by T. G. Jordan, *Annals of the Association of American Geographers*, 1967, 57(December): 668. Reprinted by permission. **Chapter 3. 46,** quote from *Imperial Texas: an Interpretative Essay in Cultural Geography,* by D. W. Meinig. Copyright © 1969 by D. W. Meinig. Reprinted by permission of the University of Texas Press. **47–48,** quotes from *American Civics,* by W. H. Hartley and W. S. Vincent. Copyright © 1970 by Harcourt Brace Jovanovich, Inc. Reprinted by permission of the publisher. **54–55,** Figure 3–1 from *American Federalism: A View from the States,* 3rd Edition, by D. J. Elazar. Copyright © 1984 by Harper & Row, Publishers, Inc. Reprinted by permission of the publisher. **Chapter 6. 122–123,** newspaper article copyright 1986, *The Houston Post.* Reprinted by permission. **124,** quote from *There Also Shall Be a Lieutenant Governor,* by J. Davis, pp. 18–19. Copyright © 1967 by the University of Texas Institute for Public Affairs. Reprinted by permission. **Chapter 7. 144–145,** Table 7–1 from *Politics in the American States: A Comparative Analysis,* 4th Edition, by V. Gray, H. Jacob, and K. N. Vines (Eds.), pp. 458–459. Copyright © 1983 by Virginia Gray, Herbert Jacob, and Kenneth N. Vines. Reprinted by permission of Little, Brown and Co.

PHOTOGRAPHS

Texas People 44 *Top:* Hugh Garnett; *Bottom:* Barker Texas History Center, University of Texas, Austin. **45** *Top:* Allan Pogue; *Middle:* Lone Star Productions; *Bottom:* Alicia Daniel.

Texas Economy 80 *Top:* Texas Tourist Council; *Middle: Texas Observer,* Austin; *Bottom left;* Tony Lama, Admar, Inc.; *Bottom right:* John Spragens, Jr.. **81** *Top:* The Stockhouse, Houston; *Middle:* Bob Lukeman; *Bottom:* NASA, Johnson Space Center.

Texas Politics. 158 *Top:* Allan Pogue; *Middle:* Allan Pogue; *Bottom left:* George C. McLemore; *Bottom right:* Allan Pogue. **159** *Top:* Allan Pogue; *Bottom Left: Texas Observer,* Austin; *Bottom right:* Frederick Baldwin, Woodfin Camp.

Texas History 224 *Top:* Panhandle-Plains Historical Museum, Canyon; *Middle:* Texas State Library, Austin; *Bottom:* Barker Texas History Center, University of Texas, Austin. **225** *Top:* Barker Texas History Center, University of Texas, Austin; *Bottom:* Panhandle-Plains Historical Museum, Canyon.